minor china

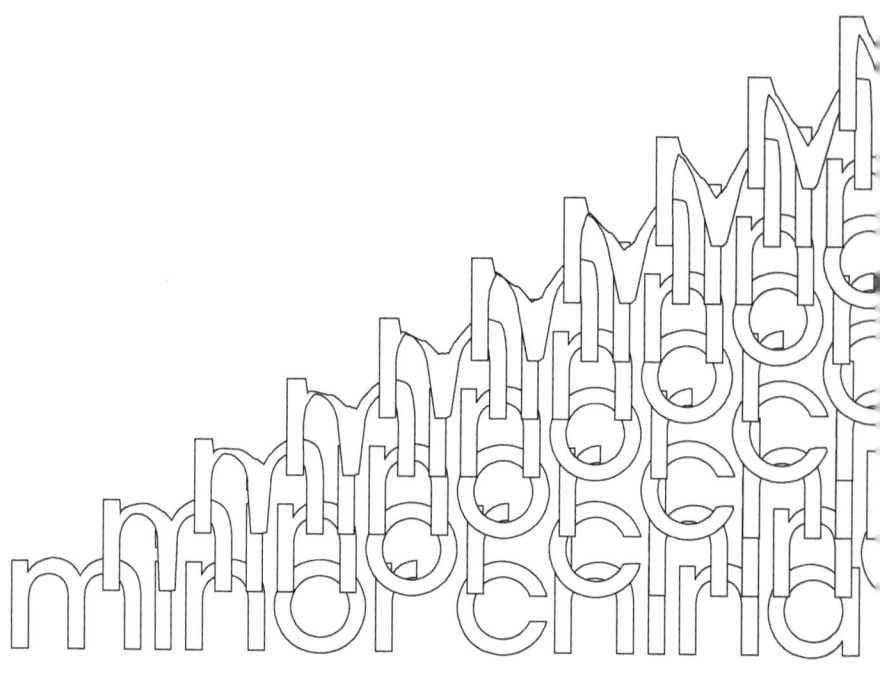

 ANIMA

A Series Edited by Mel Y. Chen and Jasbir K. Puar

Minor China

METHOD, MATERIALISMS, AND THE AESTHETIC

Hentyle Yapp

Duke University Press   Durham and London   2021

Designed by Drew Sisk
Typeset in Minion Pro and ITC Avant Garde Gothic by
Westchester Publishing Services

Library of Congress Cataloging-in-Publication Data
Names: Yapp, Hentyle, [date] author.
Title: Minor China : method, materialisms, and the aesthetic / Hentyle
Yapp.
Other titles: ANIMA (Duke University Press)
Description: Durham : Duke University Press, 2021. | Series: Anima:
critical race studies otherwise | Includes bibliographical references and
index.
Identifiers: LCCN 2020022510 (print) | LCCN 2020022511 (ebook)
ISBN 9781478010470 (hardcover)
ISBN 9781478011552 (paperback)
ISBN 9781478013068 (ebook)
Subjects: LCSH: Art, Chinese—Appreciation—Western countries. | Art,
Chinese—Aesthetics. | Art, Chinese—20th century. | Art, Chinese—
21st century. | Art and globalization. | Art and society. | Art—History.
Classification: LCC N 7345 .Y377 2021 (print) | LCC N 7345 (ebook) | DDC
709.51/—dc23
LC recordavailableathttps:// lccn.loc.gov/2020022510
LC ebookrec ordavailableathttps:// lccn.loc.gov/2020022511

Cover art: Yan Xing, *Kill (the) tv-Set*, 2012. Two-channel video
(black and white, silent), 2:30 min. and 3:06 min. © Yan Xing. Courtesy
of the artist.

Duke University Press gratefully acknowledges the support of the NYU
Center for the Humanities, the Dean's Office at New York University's
Tisch School of the Arts, and the Department of Art
and Public Policy at New York University, which provided funds toward
the production of this book.

CONTENTS

ILLUSTRATIONS

ACKNOWLEDGMENTS

The unexpected pleasure that has arisen from writing about the minor is becoming even more attuned to small details, especially the many forms of hidden and mundane labor, care, and time that go into creating an object. I am truly grateful for those many direct and indirect gestures, chats, and exchanges that allowed me to produce this book. For many mentioned in these acknowledgments, they might be surprised to see their names listed here since their acts might seem unimportant to them or just what one should do. I think this attests to the generosity and kindness of these individuals—something I have refreshingly learned while writing and seek to further embody. The minor, after all, comes from an unstated feminist ethics of attention, of being present with others.

This book first started at UC Berkeley, where the guidance of Shannon Jackson, Mel Chen, Andrew Jones, and SanSan Kwan shaped my initial ideas. I am grateful for their patience, generosity, rigor, and care. Each provides distinct models of being in the academy that have informed my own path in this profession. I am forever grateful for their collective labor and time in reading drafts and offering substantive critique. Leti Volpp and Paul Rabinow graciously contributed their expertise during key moments in my training, and they have left their respective imprints on my scholarship and ideas. The continued support and friendship of Juana María Rodríguez, Brandi Wilkins Catanese, and Gail De Kosnik sustain my life in the academy. Additional conversations and support came from Aihwa Ong, Winnie Wong, Catherine Cole, Lisa Wymore, Joe Goode, Philip Kan Gotanda, Shannon Steen, and Jenefer Johnson. In addition, the time spent at the University of California Institute for Research in the Arts during a Disability Studies Residency connected me with ongoing support, notably from Susan Schweik, Georgina Kleege, Vic Marks, Jürg Koch, Sara Hendren, Catherine Kudlick, and Patrick Anderson. I am also grateful to Mary Ajideh and Robin Davidson for their administrative prowess and kindness.

I would not be able to survive in the academy without my friendship with Iván Ramos, who tirelessly read and critiqued countless versions and early drafts of this book. I feel lucky and fortunate to have encountered an intellectual force and aesthetic sensibility that only Iván possesses; I learn from him every day. Others from my graduate school cohort—Karin Shankar, Heather Rastovac Akbarzadeh, and Omar Ricks—continue to shape my ideas and I am truly grateful for their presence. In addition, my interactions with brilliant thinkers during my time in graduate school continue to nourish me. My gratitude goes to Ragini Srinivasan, Paige Johnson, Corey Byrnes, Jerry Zee, Ianna Owens, Caitlin Marshall, Ashley Ferro-Murray, Sima Belmar, Takeo Rivera, Chiayi Seetoo, Megan Hoetger, Scott Wallin, Nilgun Bayraktar, Catherine Duffly, Thea Gold, Khai Tu Nguyen, Natalia Duong, William Ma, Janelle Lamoreaux, and Laurence Coderre. I am grateful to the Center for Chinese Studies for research support. The University of California Dissertation-Year Fellowship also allowed me to finish in a timely manner.

I must express my sincere appreciation to the artists who made time to converse during early stages of research. Thank you to Cao Fei and Yan Xing for meeting right before the lunar new year to discuss their respective works. In addition, my gratitude goes to Carol Yinghua Lu, Liu Ding, and Su Wei who spent countless hours chatting about their ideas and approaches, which greatly shaped this project. Samson Young is someone I've known for a number of years, and I thank him for his sustained friendship and support. I also would like to thank the above for providing image permissions. The other artists who generously provided images are Ai Weiwei, Isaac Julien, Cai Guo-Qiang, Zhang Huan, Li Liao, Gu Dexin, and Huang Yong Ping. Thank you for contributing to this project in immeasurable ways.

During my time at Pomona College, I came across a host of intellectual interlocutors and passionate colleagues. I am grateful for the support from the Mellon-Chau Fellowship, along with the resources at Pomona while I was there as an assistant professor. Thank you to those in Gender and Women's Studies who informed my work: Zayn Kassam, Pardis Mahdavi, Erin Runions, Anthony Shay, Val Thomas, Kyla Wazana Tompkins, and Peggy Waller. The administrative support from Amy Crown was crucial to thrive at Pomona, and I miss seeing her regularly. Janice Hudgings, Jill Grigsby, and Betsy Crighton provided ample space and resources to develop many of my ideas. The friendships with Kevin Dettmar, Joseph Jeon, Joyce Lu, Lynne Miyake, Todd Honma, and Jih-Fei Cheng are ones I hope to continue for some time. The conversations, laughs, and ideas shared with Mark Andrejevic and Jordan Kirk are truly missed. I cherish my friendship with Sasha-Mae Eccleston; I so value the meals and texts we're able to share together.

This book gained invaluable and additional support at New York University. I would first like to thank Dean Allyson Green for providing the time and resources for me to grow as a scholar and artist. She provides a model of poise and intellect that I greatly admire. In addition, I would not be where I am today without the support of Karen Shimakawa, who has become a source of welcome knowledge that expands theory and the everyday. She has tirelessly supported my work and I have been in awe of her ethics, shimmering ideas, and care. I am also grateful for ongoing support from Ulrich Baer. In addition, the fellowship time spent at the Center for Humanities was a welcome respite, particularly under the leadership of Gabriela Basterra and the administrative brilliance of Gwynneth Malin. I would also like to thank the group of attentive and vibrant colleagues who provided space to take risks and do the hard work of thinking together. The NYU Center for Humanities and Dean's Office both offered generous book subventions, which made publication possible. In addition, support from the provost through the Goddard Fellowship and the Dean's Office enabled leave at a critical moment for this book.

I have been lucky to find an intellectual home that is both challenging and nourishing. Thank you to Kathy Engel for her labor and encouragement as department chair. My appreciation must be expressed for the administrative support from Emily Brown and Kristin Killacky who make the tasks of research, service, and teaching occur with flawless ease and ample sweets. Pato Hebert has served as an endless source of support and I am in awe of his art and ideas. The collegiality and conviviality of Ella Shohat, Karen Finley, Laura Harris, Sheril Antonio, and Ellyn Toscano allow me to take risks with my ideas in research and teaching. I admire your respective ways of being in the world. Beyond my department, I have found an amazing intellectual home in the Center for Disability Studies. Both Faye Ginsburg and Mara Mills have become close interlocutors and friends. In addition, many colleagues from across the campus have provided crucial support and entertainment. I would like to thank those in Performance Studies for engaged conversations: Alex Vazquez, Malik Gaines, André Lepecki, Fred Moten, Deb Kapchan, Noel Rodriguez, Michelle Castañeda, and Ann Pellegrini. Many in Media, Culture, and Communication offer a vibrant space to exchange ideas: Finn Brunton, Paula Chakravartty, Lily Chumley, Charlton McIlwain, Nicole Starosielski, and Helga Tawil-Souri. Further, those in Social and Cultural Analysis have provided an additional welcoming place for exchange: Gayatri Gopinath, Julie Livingston, Lisa Duggan, Awam Ampka, Cristina Beltrán, Carolyn Dinshaw, Jennifer Morgan, Crystal Parikh, and Thuy Linh Tu. Those in other departments and spaces further nourish my intellectual life: Emily Apter, Deb Willis, Licia Fiol-Matta, Jay Wegman, Sonya Posmentier, Edward Berenson, Arang Keshavarzian, Rebecca Karl, Toby Lee, Sebastián Calderón Bentin, Jay Garcia, Una Chaudhuri, and Zeb Tortorici.

I have been fortunate enough to engage with a brilliant writing group, consisting of Kelli Moore, Matthew Morrison, and Isolde Brielmaier. These three have offered true generosity and keen insight, and this book would not be where it is today without their early interventions. I am also enormously grateful for the writing exchange with a group of vibrant scholars, who helped me restructure my introduction: Sharon Heijin Lee, Pacharee Sudhinaraset, and Feng-Mei Heberer. In addition, the friendship of colleagues across campus has been reinvigorating; much gratitude to Cecilia Marquez, Natasha Strassfeld, Sebastian Cherng, and Jacob Faber. Beyond my immediate colleagues, my graduate students, colleagues in their own right, have pushed me to think in new ways. Thank you to Rachel Kuo, in particular, who provided research assistance with edits and image permissions. And many thanks to my graduate students whose ideas make me a better scholar; I am truly honored to be part of each of their intellectual paths.

This project greatly benefitted from interactions that occurred beyond the university contexts in which I circulate. I was lucky enough to encounter the formidable Tina Chen when I participated in the *Verge* Summer Institute at Penn State. Her mentorship has greatly shaped my writing, and I am grateful for her time given to help me become a better scholar. In addition, my fellow aesthetic migrants are an unexpected and amazing source of support. Thank you to Sunny Xiang, Andrew Leong, Chris Eng, Michelle Huang, Cheryl Naruse, Crystal Baik, Vinh Nguyen, Chris Fan, Leland Tabares, and Eric Hayot. Particular thanks to Chris E., Sunny, Cheryl, Andrew, and Crystal for reading earlier versions of my introduction.

The editorial team at Duke University Press is like no other. Many thanks to Courtney Berger for guiding this process with true aplomb and finesse. I am so grateful for her support and encouragement. My sincere appreciation to Jasbir Puar and Mel Chen, who graciously invited me to include this book in the ANIMA series. These two scholars have greatly nourished me and helped me grow in indescribable ways. In addition, Ken Wissoker has continued to be a thoughtful interlocutor. Sandra Korn, Susan Albury, and the editorial and production teams at Duke were a true pleasure to work with, and I thank them for their time, labor, and care. I would also like to express my gratitude to the two anonymous reviewers who took this book seriously and provided intensely critical and generous feedback. Chris Lura additionally provided editorial support for which I am truly grateful. Further, this book would also not have come together without the engagements of various audiences. In addition to those at conferences, those at a variety of institutions helped make this book much stronger: UCLA, University of Pennsylvania, Juilliard, Barnard, University of Michigan, Boston University, Northwestern, Stanford, and San Francisco State University. While visiting UCLA, I have come to encounter a wonderful set of colleagues: Sean Metzger, Suk-Young Kim, and Michelle Liu Carriger. Thank you to the three of you for intense and brilliant engagement. And thank you to Sean for the labor and time that allowed for these conversations that I'm sure will continue.

I would never have finished this book without the professional and social support of Marcia Chatelain. She exhibits an ethical commitment and care that remind me to be better than I am; and her scholarship models all that I hope to become. We will always have our Fridays and big snows. In addition, Neetu Khanna, Megan Asaka, Jesús Hernández, and Briana Masterson continue to be sources of support and laughs after all these years. Tadashi Dozono, Candice Lin, Xandra Ibarra, Shawn Kravich, and Nina Farnia make my intellectual and social lives glimmer in ways that exceed merely sustaining. Thank you for offering continued forms of support amid and well beyond this writing process.

I am also extremely grateful to Marci Kwon who read and edited my introduction in its last stages. Her friendship and intellectual generosity are as rare and singular as her aesthetic sensibilities. C. Riley Snorton has been a true friend and model interlocutor; I find myself in awe of his brilliance and warmth. In addition, Julietta Hua, Evren Savci, Greta LaFleur, Justin Leroy, Viêt Lê, and Ricardo Montez have become intellectual interlocutors and vibrant friends. And although I haven't spent as much time as I'd like in dance studies, I am also quite grateful for the continued support from Rebecca Schneider, Susan Manning, and Janice Ross, particularly through the Mellon Dance Studies Initiative. The connections made with Noémie Solomon, Adrienne Edwards, Dasha Chapman, and Virginia Preston have been nourishing. I am extremely grateful to Jasmine Johnson and Clare Croft; our moments of interaction provide ample giggles and brilliant insights. And although my life in dance feels far away from my academic one, I am forever grateful for those who at an earlier time attuned me to minor forms and gestures whereby training becomes the everyday: Yang Ming-Lung, Abby Yager, Ishmael Houston-Jones, Dennis Cooper, Chris Cochrane, Anouk van Dijk, Bill T. Jones, Donna Faye Burchfield, Lizz Roman, Cory Vangelder, and Tommy Noonan.

In addition, the professional guidance and advice of many have helped me navigate the academy. Many thanks to David Eng, Jasbir Puar, Heather Love, Dorinne Kondo, Hoang Nguyen, Homay King, and Aimee Bahng for invaluable conversations and interactions. The professional interactions with Pete Coviello, Elizabeth Freeman, Jennifer DeVere Brody, and Lucas Hildebrandt have been formative. The intellectual engagements with Summer Kim Lee, Amber Musser, Leon Hilton, Christina León, Roy Pérez, Josh Guzmán, Kadji Amin, Uri McMillan, Vivian Huang, Kelly Chung, Eng-Beng Lim, Joshua Chambers-Letson, and Patty Ahn have provided intellectual inspiration. I have also been fortunate to join the *Social Text* editorial collective, where the collegiality and intellectual community have made New York more of a home. Many thanks to the collective, particularly Tavia Nyong'o, David Sartorius, María Josefina Saldaña-Portillo, Macarena Gómez-Barris, Alex Pittman, Jayna Brown, Anna McCarthy, Vanessa Agard-Jones, John Andrews, Nicholas Mirzoeff, Michael Mandiberg, Nicole Fleetwood, Neferti Tadiar, and Jonathan Beller. This book in many ways emerged even before graduate school. While in Los Angeles for law school, I encountered Robert Diaz, Susan Leigh Foster, and Lucy Burns who helped guide me into academia; thank you for your support and insight during this time. And even those in law school helped me figure out my own path as they related to questions regarding the state, particularly Cheryl Harris, Devon Carbado, Jerry Kang, Cathy Mayorkas, and Kimberlé Crenshaw. Lastly, I would not have begun to think theoretically without the guidance of Gretchen Schultz during college and Richard Hartzell during high school.

Although I began these acknowledgments outlining the institutions in which this book started, it ultimately arose from my families, given and chosen. In the final stages of writing this book, my father died. This has only brought me closer to my mother, Chun Luan, alongside my siblings, Kentyle, Esther, Carlie, and Sharon. It also has made me appreciate in new ways the complicated relationship I had with my father. My attempt to rethink China and the nation-state works against and within his deep relationship to the Taiwan independence movement. Ma and Pa, thank you for providing the base for me to become who I am. One of the many difficulties of immigration is that your children often exceed the dreams you imagined for them. The gift of opportunity (which emerged from your sacrifices) is precisely and ironically what has led to conflict. I know I haven't made much sense to you. Amid this illegibility, please know how much I appreciate that we just keep trying to be together, even when we fail. I would also like to thank my cousins and extended family for reminding me to never take life or myself too seriously. To my chosen family, I am grateful for the friendships that continue to nourish me. Thank you to Marcia, Iván, Chantal, Xandra, Shawn, Marci, David R., Huy, Haines, Hongmai, Riley, Kien, Rebekah, Sabah, John W., Jude, Izetta, Crystal, Yuka, Megan O., Adrienne, Brian, Randy, Leo, and Dan for being present in ways that have sustained me to write, think, and not write and think. Thank you to Anne, Gaylord, and Laura for becoming a welcome addition to my life. And thank you, Alec, for helping create a true home for Ume, Mantou, and us. This book, like me, has been imprinted with your minor forms of care: quiet compassion, subtle cynicism, and gentle reminders to be present.

INTRODUCTION

In 2001, China's Ministry of Culture banned art deemed "bloody, violent, or erotic." Although most nations typically base censorship around public offense, China turned toward defining the aesthetic. The Chinese state's noteworthy and curious emphasis in this ordinance on the quality of art over its social effects demonstrated a shifting mode of governance from regulation to the adjudication of aesthetic categories or traits. This response arose due to the insurgence of performance art at the end of the twentieth century, with the state closing many prominent art shows in Beijing and other areas. In particular, the 2000 *Fuck Off* exhibit located at the Eastlink Gallery was one of the main reasons for the ordinance.[1] Curated by Ai Weiwei and Feng Boyi, the show was an unsanctioned event outside of official activities for the Third Shanghai Biennial. The ordinance was in reaction to the presence of blood, violence, and eroticism, as typified in Zhu Yu's *Eating People*. The photographs from his performance depict the artist biting into a fetus that was procured from a medical school. Forty-eight additional artists presented work, including Xu Tan and Ai Weiwei. The former displayed sexually explicit photos, while the latter exhibited *Dropping a Han Dynasty Urn*, a photo triptych of Ai dropping an antique urn onto concrete. Collectively, these photographed performances inspired state intervention to morph away from the predominant rationale of protecting public morale. The documentation of performance art became the principal means for the state's turn toward regulating aesthetics, as these photos circulated as evidence for such "bloody, violent, or erotic" ephemeral performances. In this way, the medium of photography became the primary means to not only memorialize performance, but also provide evidence to the state. Mediation and memory intertwine with aesthetics and governance.

The Chinese state's censorship throughout the 1980s and into the 2000s has helped place contemporary Chinese art on the global market. However, the notable nuances around the Chinese state's turn toward aesthetics in the ordinance often go unnoticed. Instead, an immediately legible narrative involving that of the authoritarian state and the herculean, resistant artist predominates, which facilitates the rapid circulation of contemporary Chinese art. Through these major and predictable narratives of the state and the resistant artist that play into liberal ideals, contemporary Chinese art amasses hefty price tags and Chinese artists regularly appear in blue-chip galleries and festivals across the globe. The sensational examples discussed above—both the performances and the state censorship—are notable for the way they have come to inform liberal understandings of China; what I describe as a major and proper China. In 1994, early in the development of contemporary Chinese art, noted curator Hou Hanru identified how such accounts of contemporary Chinese art were "full of descriptions of how the artists are enduring official censorship" without "any detailed information or interpretation of the work itself."[2] This book follows Hou's astute call and develops a method I call *minor China* to attend to not only these aesthetic details, but also nuances within the state that are occluded by this condition. Indeed, today, more than twenty-five years later, the accounts of contemporary Chinese art remain largely the same. We tend to emphasize major narratives around resistance and romanticized notions of liberal free speech, while setting aside both seemingly minor details about aesthetics as well as complex action by the state.

China studies scholar Lydia Liu astutely locates how this repeated discourse shapes Chinese subjects as often understood within a "single possibility: resistance."[3] And this understanding is far from complete. Within this repeated discourse, there is an entangled relation between state and culture, one that involves a balance between banning and permitting art. Art market interest in—and therefore the circulation of—Chinese art arises from a toggle between hard and soft powers. On one hand, the Chinese state regulates artwork; on the other, artists gain notoriety precisely through such regulation.[4] Most critics and curators have continually understood the art, however, through a narrative of artist as resistant against the state. After all, most promotional materials, curatorial statements, and reviews of Chinese and most non-Western artists garner public interest by relying on this legible equation. Art and the aesthetic therefore are heralded as the liberal antidotes and primary vehicles for transcendence, possibility, and change, rendering the state as inherently illiberal, behind, and needing to catch up to the West. *Fuck Off* and the subsequent reaction to the show by the Chinese Communist Party (CCP) emblematize a dominant mode of remembering and constructing what has become the proper historical narrative. Through this lens, the history surrounding contemporary Chinese art comes to rely upon a one-to-one correspondence or mediation between aesthetics and politics, whereby artists directly resist presumed backward-state practices.

This book, *Minor China*, looks closely at this constellation of media, history, the state, and aesthetics to rethink the predictable ways the category of art known as global or non-Western—a category which, as I discuss, is also racialized and minoritarian—is curated, theorized, displayed, and remembered.[5] Most critics, journalists, and scholars regularly use China's 2001 ban on specific aesthetic categories in ways that reify China as authoritarian, having repercussions for how Chinese and non-Western art are understood. In particular, non-Western art gains legibility through the logic of the major, limiting which objects circulate, which methods are appropriate, which political and materialist frames dominate, and which mechanisms mediate the circulation of objects. The major privileges immediately legible discourse, analysis, and art, reaffirming liberal and recognizable understandings of the non-West. This book thus uses the minor to rethink this dominant condition for transnational analysis.

Fuck Off is emblematic of how contemporary Chinese art gains notoriety on the art market through the major. Most studies on contemporary Chinese art reference this show for launching the careers of many of its artists, notably Ai Weiwei and Zhu Yu.[6] And according to Ai, the show and curatorial projects enabled him "to advance his artistic career" and "to foster the growth of Chinese experimental art."[7] The show itself is representative of not only how state censorship looms over understandings of contemporary Chinese art—which is often the proper narrative supplied by most critics—but also how the idea of contemporary Chinese art becomes memorialized. The consolidation of these narratives has arisen in tandem with China's economic boom and entrance into global capitalist modernity—key factors that help us understand both China's exceptionality and exemplarity for the enfoldment of other non-Western nations into an understanding of the world.

Ai Weiwei is additionally representative of the ways the non-Western artist and nation have become tethered to expected, major narratives circumscribed by a set of key terms: *history, the state, subject,* and *agency.* For example, when considering Ai's piece that appeared in the 2000 *Fuck Off* show, *Dropping a Han Dynasty Urn* (which was initially created in 1995), critics often first emphasize Ai's allusion to China's long history through his destruction of a Han Dynasty urn (figures I.1–I.3). They then focus on his relation to the state and critiques of China's premodern ways, emphasizing a legible mode of agentic resistance. Following the 2014 scandal that erupted when fellow artist Maximo Caminero smashed one of the urns that Ai

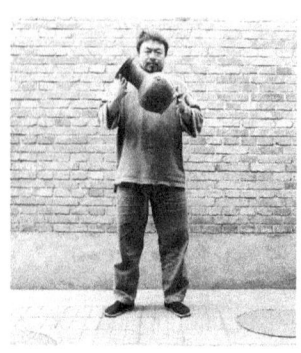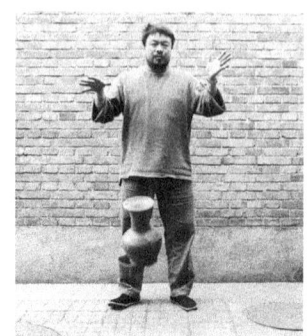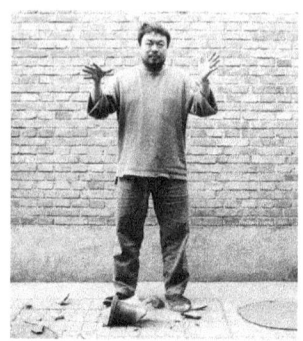

Figures I.1–I.3. Ai Weiwei, *Dropping a Han Dynasty Urn*, 1995. Courtesy of Ai Weiwei Studio.

painted for Miami's Perez Museum, many journalists foreseeably discussed these urns as representing "the modern world's alienation" and situated the work in relation to the Cultural Revolution.[8] The urn, in other words, becomes not only a symbol for the dominant presence of China's ancient history and the contemporary state, but also the Duchampian readymade indicative of capitalist alienation. In the critical and theoretical responses that followed both of these works, Ai's art is discussed in ways that illustrate how China has been predominantly imagined within Western discourse and political theory—where the artist is resistant against an oppressive state. It is through this narrative that China's history and state, alongside Chinese subjects and their agency, are rendered fully legible to Western audiences.

Further, since Ai spent time in New York during the 1980s and 1990s, many critics have attributed what they perceive as his critique of the Chinese state to Ai having tasted the possibilities of Western liberal democracy. In accounts from the *New York Times* to the *Guardian*, authors repeatedly stress Ai's exposure to the West as seminal to his approach. However, beyond such narratives that exceptionalize Western liberalism as the paradigm for political action, there are other ways of reading Ai's work that exceed these normative liberal theorizations. If one focuses less on the sensationalized destruction of the urn and more on the affect of boredom in Ai's face, it is possible to begin to unpack a different relation to history and agency. In particular, Ai does not signal an intense anger or an astonished surprise at the dropping of the urn, an expression which might be more expected when performing a liberal ideal of resistance against the state. Instead, Ai's face remains calm and bored throughout the triptych. This minor detail helps us hesitate from the normative ways Ai is understood. Ai's boredom, in other words, operates as a mechanism to engage other readings: instead of resistance, Ai performs fatigue with the proper narrative prescribed to his work.[9]

Ai additionally plays with the *form* of the triptych and the medium of photography to amplify this exhaustion with routinized approaches to his art. Although the triptych captures the temporal development from Ai holding the urn to its final destruction, it also depicts Ai's sustained boredom alongside his intention to destroy the object. He purposefully drops the urn, as the triptych captures his hands that remain at the same level above his shoulders. His corporeal position illustrates how he remains frozen in time, while the photos capture a developmental sequence. In other words, Ai plays with the temporality associated with the triptych form, pointing to the way non-Western subjects remain stuck in time while ideas of progress move along. These notions of progress are not only about civilizational development but also the avant-garde. The readymade is often understood as progressive experimentation for whiteness and regressive, derivative reperformance for minoritarian subjects. Ai thus engages not only ideas about China's history, but also the differing notions of time (development for the West and static or behind for the rest) embedded in the triptych and the readymade of the urn.

The method of minor China that I develop in this book furthers the approach briefly demonstrated above. The minor, however, does not refer to its usual definition surrounding small or unimportant objects or even minority subjects and spaces. I do not ask us to merely include or consider more minor things (or to humanize minor objects into proper subjects). Instead, the minor as a method highlights the epistemological assumptions and ontological conditions that uphold the order of things, the major. More specifically, this book's method tracks tensions across universalization and cultural particularity, since minor subjects and objects are often either enfolded into universal discourses or rendered singular for purposes of liberal consumption. I direct the term *minor* toward minoritarian ends, as my aim is not to flatten the category to include any body or object that has not been enfolded into recognition. Rather, a commitment to minoritarian ends requires that we track analyses toward the larger goal of reenvisioning our habits and protocols in ways that resonate with historical remediation and a Marxist notion of social structuration. In particular, this book focuses on Marxism to not only provide an attunement of minor methods to political economy, but also name an explicit project that moves us beyond critiques of liberalism. For example, in chapter 2, I return to Ai Weiwei and trace how his aesthetics offer a way to track understandings of the subject that do not default into the liberal strongholds of individual representation and inclusion. Instead, I explore how his uses of repetition with aesthetic objects *and* racialized subjects (for those perceived as "all looking the same") help produce what Petrus Liu calls for as "a theory that is capable of understanding the human as the subject of political action as well as an effect of social structuration."[10]

Throughout this book, I highlight social structuration to bring to the fore the imbalanced historical conditions and theoretical assumptions that predetermine established terms like *history, the state, subject, agency,* and even *the aesthetic.* These terms are presumed knowable across not only Eurocentric but also minoritarian discourses and fields, especially when they demonstrate the merits of including non-Western spaces, racialized others, and cultural production as the means to expand human knowledge. Put more explicitly, the entrenched argument that non-Western art is worthy of inclusion and valuable for demonstrating resistant agency against the strong state repeats static formulations of subjects, culture, and the state and reinforces the logics of liberalism, modern humanism, and capitalism.[11] The minor as method thus hesitates from furthering these logics and attends to the nuanced and vibrant intricacies of minor aesthetics, subjects, spaces, and histories as methods to restructure.

And even so, why engage minorly? The political stakes of this minor method circulate around materialist concerns that grapple with Cold War legacies, global racialization, the idea of a global Left, relational and solidarity politics, and late liberalism. Rather than reify how we conceptualize these structural issues, I turn to the grain of sense.[12] I draw from an admittedly unwieldly archive of the minor—from senses, affects, objects, and things, to those minor subjects who have existed as senses, affects, objects, and things. I do so to examine what insights they provide for a hesitant, minor method. Focusing on the level of sense responds to the exhaustion many minoritarian thinkers experience with most approaches to the social and political. For those theorizing and often enduring forms of major structural violence, there are limits surrounding disciplinary formations, liberal approaches, and dominant Marxist accounts of revolution. A rethinking is needed, one that comes less from major political concerns and, counterintuitively, more from the fact that the minor begs to be sensed differently in order to help us imagine other analytic modes for materialist concerns. And rather than rely on a developmental logic to label these concerns as new(er) materialisms, the focus on sense and minor things expands our methodological approaches to contend with ongoing, old Marxist issues.

This book therefore privileges without glorifying affect and the aesthetic to renegotiate our ideas around the state and its subjects—to read and sense major forms affectively. Affect, a key analytic for this book, refers to not only emotion but also the relations across objects, subjects, and environment. The payoff of these approaches is that they move us away from ethnographic and static notions of difference and liberalist politics surrounding inclusion. Subjects, the state, and objects are in turn reimagined through the minor. Minor China as method thus refuses to replicate the major assumptions behind the key terms that situate the non-West, produce better readings of art for China, or privilege new terms over established ones.

The remainder of this introduction unpacks the minor as it reevaluates the nation-state and the global (Hesitating on the Nation, Liberalism, and Capital), alongside the notion of method (Beyond Minor Subjects toward the Minor as Method). After, I examine how these minor approaches grapple with the place of China within critical theory so as to engage the nation-state affectively (China *in* Theory/China *in* *Theory*). I then highlight the aesthetic and its entwinement with mediation as a key method for this book, arguing for a renewed theory of the aesthetic that reconsiders its relation to the political in ways that are not dictated by liberal representationalism (Aesthetics and Politics beyond Liberalism and Translation). The introduction lastly illuminates the book's contributions to interdisciplinarity (Hesitant Method and Marxist Materialisms).

Hesitating on the Nation, Liberalism, and Capital

Minor China examines what happens when we render non-Western sites minor, particularly China which is currently understood as the prototypical authoritarian strong state. The method I produce considers what maintains the global and historical presumptions that transfix the non-West within a condition of the major. Although we must be critical of how Eurocentrism, racism, and colonization shape this conditioning, we should also hesitate or refrain from solely demanding humanization and from constantly making bids for relevance to the moment. These prescribed responses reinforce liberal humanist logics, instead of reconfiguring who and what the subject is, where and when the geographic and racial collide, and how such notions of racial and human worth are differentially valued to buttress the operations of capital. Minor China thus is a method that *in form* focuses on relational modes that have typically gone undernoticed and undertheorized, and *in function* reconfigures the dominant structures and terms that dictate our discourse. Moreover, this method arises from a close attention to the artists' works. Their aesthetics render China minor in ways that do not dissipate the political but rather redefine the political's bounds and understandings.

The broad task of this method imagines China in its minor form—not as a direct counter to modern liberal humanism but rather as a hesitant method that highlights how modern liberal humanism endures.[13] As Lisa Lowe has encouraged, it can be useful to resist the lure "to recover what has been lost." Hesitation can help serve this goal—to halt, as Lowe puts it, "the desire for recognition by the present social order and stav[e] off the compulsion to make visible within current epistemological orthodoxy."[14] Following Lowe, I produce a method that is less heuristic in scope and asks instead to take pause. I take pause from the immediate demands and seeming urgencies of our moment to refrain from prescribed political debates over how important China is or how relevant the site is to the contemporary. By doing so, we better understand what maintains China and the non-West as major—an approach that is separate from the dominant, and that will not seek to become part of it. The minor as method asks us to pause and hesitate instead of answer and challenge. An interrogatory approach to China privileges a process of asking questions about the nation-state over defining it through knowable and immediately available narratives that argue for its value, centrality, and recognition into a modern world order. As such, hesitation broadens analyses of social structure, as understandings of the economic, state, and transnational are expanded, not stabilized. Through hesitation, the minor as method highlights the assumptions of global logics that uphold the West, the rest, and the world.

Hesitation is critical, since we are in a moment when subjects and institutions are well versed in rendering otherness coherent for purposes of capital gain and accumulation. Indeed, asserting one's identity in proper, intelligible ways pays off. And in fact, challenging institutions through legible critiques against mis- and underrepresentation can similarly reap benefits. Although these liberal multicultural dynamics are typically imagined in relation to the United States, they similarly translate into the transnational, whereby diversity is additionally defined as the mere inclusion of a different site or group of people. Within the US and Western Europe, the inclusion of the transnational exists similarly to how minoritized populations are enfolded into discourse. Both global and minor national subjects have entered institutions through the major, a condition that many have recognized as ethnographic entrapment.[15] The logics and legacies of anthropology inflect how not only non-Western, but also racialized, queer, feminist, transgender, disabled, classed, and a variety of nonnormative subjects are made to become legible, proper, and thus known for consumption and surveillance. These approaches merely demand the inclusion of otherness by upholding and appealing to the logic of the major. Instead of trying to make ourselves intelligible as subjects worthy of entering a modern liberal humanist order or relevant to the realm of politics, we might instead hesitate from doing so.

Since it has become increasingly profitable, institutions like the global art market now regularly engage China, other nations, and social difference (even if only through niche events or when it coincides with the appropriate ethnic or identity-based history month). Institutions deploy and include these populations to stave off public critique and to perform solidarity. In order to quell liberal guilt and fulfill capitalist demands, the minor subject and peripheral nation are encouraged to be included as they help increase ticket and book sales and further normalize the operations of private and public institutions. These minor populations are often seen as "less serious" and a regrettable but necessary inclusion in today's global world. As such, these institutions nonetheless have an objective ideal even amid further inclusion.

Moreover, although there has been a marked increase in cultural production about the non-West and minority populations, institutions continue to enlist these bodies in predictable and proper ways. These minor subjects become recognizable through their major forms and are rarely seen as helping us reconsider larger orders, logics, and structures. The inclusion of those historically denied access has come to index progressive politics, as institutions use inclusion to absolve past exclusionary practices, evade substantive restructuring, and increase revenue. However, even amid the uptick in the representation of otherness, institutions continue to operate in the same ways, whereby profits benefit the same people, the leadership remains in similar hands, and the norms of institutional life endure.[16] Put differently, we exist in a condition C. Riley Snorton and I identify as "representation without Marxism."[17] Within this late liberal condition, China, the non-West, and modes of social difference enter institutions when they are immediately recognizable through the major and further these smooth operations.

This book thus reconsiders China and the non-West beyond this condition through a focus on Marxist formulations of structural change and redistribution, alongside a critique of liberal and modern humanist approaches. Throughout this book, I emphasize several key elements within Chinese art that help us understand how the minor assists in this examination and uncovers the larger logics of the major—particularly the role of form, affect, nonvisual senses, nonanthropocentric objects, and speculation. In the chapters that follow, I focus on a number of artworks to bring the minor into relief, particularly those by Ai Weiwei, Yan Xing, Cai Guo-Qiang, Samson Young, Zhang Huan, He Chengyao, and Cao Fei. Outside of China, I also look at the work of Isaac Julien for the ways his aesthetics reveal important dimensions of the minor that are pertinent to larger global art discourse and the rendering of the non-West. Additionally, curation and the exhibition of non-Western art directly intersect with the discourses and narratives of the major. For example, the Centre Pompidou's 1989 exhibit *Magiciens de la Terre*, which was one of the first shows that centrally featured non-Western artists, helped produce interest in the global art market for not only Chinese art, but also non-Western art more generally. But the show's curatorial lens also demonstrated how what has come to be known as non-Western or global art was being produced within a specific discourse, one that drew on late liberal logics of inclusion. These logics of inclusion continue to underpin the global art market's approaches to curation, and, in the process, these approaches reinforce the construct of major China and perpetuate the norms surrounding liberal recognition and representation. However, by analyzing aesthetics through the lens of the minor, we are able to bring these logics into view. For example, the practices of Liu Ding, Carol Yinghua Lu, and Su Wei provide crucial alternative means for curating non-Western art outside of the lens of liberalism through the minorness of affect, something that I discuss further in chapter 3.

This book's emphases on Marxism and on hesitating from the norms of diversity, equity, and inclusion require that we fully contend with the limits of liberalism, particularly when China is evoked. As Daniel Vukovich has emphasized, liberalism limits our ability to imagine and understand China in more complex and minor ways: "Part of 'our' problem in coming to terms with the rise of China is the prison house of liberalism: it is hard to read contemporary China politically without falling back into familiar histories and conceptual shibboleths about what freedom, individuality, human rights, and so on are."[18] This dominant political paradigm immediately dismisses frameworks outside of a liberal order as simply illiberal.[19] Thus, under liberalism, increasing minority representation in institutions becomes the predominant and most logical answer, whereby demands to radically reorder institutions and a comprehensive redistribution of resources to those historically disenfranchised are dismissed as asking for too much, unrealistic, impossible, and illiberal. Under this formulation, the minority subject is thus seen as equal as any other (common in form), deserving of a space at a proverbial table; however, what is ignored under such a formulation is how the entire apparatus or structure has been built, funded, and premised upon a long history surrounding the minority's subjugation. When all people are rendered common and just like any other, we ignore the interrelated yet singular histories of dehumanization, subjugation, and subjection that have differentially shaped particular populations.

Further, liberalism and capital do not allow space to imagine minor subjects as the very means to rethink how inclusion and the world operate. Liberalism presumes inclusion or increased representation as the logical and universal end game and as indicative of social progress. By extension, the transnational has come to mean that we simply include and consider a foreign space. Through this logic that emphasizes nations as common and equal to one another ("all nations matter"), the transnational appears to not possess a politics: state rationalizations for colonization could be equated with transnational feminist critiques of such colonial forms of violence, due to the fact that both merely discuss the non-West. However, if we shift outside of this liberal and ahistorical logic, transnational analysis comes to possess a politics, a way to help us amend how the dominant, major, and proper sustain themselves. But it requires moving beyond liberalism to consider them. By rethinking this through Marxism, we highlight how domestic and global minor subjects are not simply on the periphery and seeking to be centered, needing to be ethnographically studied for insight, or requiring inclusion into and representation within dominant structures. Rather, minor subjects offer a lens for reformulating our approaches to and understandings of the social structuration of the world. However, such subjects cannot be understood in their proper and major forms; their minor and indeterminate forms are what provide ways to refrain from repeating the normative operations of everyday life and established sense.

Even though China has varied in form throughout history—from the sick man of Asia to a central force in late capital[20]—it has nonetheless maintained a legible type. To be presumed knowable is not primarily an issue with the positive or negative valence associated with one's knowability; rather, the issue with the major is that one remains a solid form for purposes of Western politics, theory, and knowledge. Amid the growing inclusion of non-Western spaces, the very major terms that inform how we understand universal forms like the subject or history remain intact; they are not rethought through the further inclusion of the non-West. China thus operates within what Rebecca Karl calls a "new inclusionary impulse promising a more superficially culturally diverse, albeit economically monotone, global space."[21] Karl's formulation, which bemoans the simplistic additive logic that celebrates the inclusion of proper China rather than questioning how it is rendered legible, highlights how China has been placed within the production of world history. It further points to the need for pausing the impulse to simply celebrate the entrance of China, and by extension arguing for the continued inclusion of other previously ignored nations into recognition and world historical discourse. As Karl underscores, older models of history conceptualize non-Western nation-states as "aggregated fragments," whereby "the global sits there waiting for areas to demonstrate their worthiness for inclusion by virtue of their previous or contemporary enthusiasm and aptitude for 'development.'"[22] And as this book will show, I build upon Karl's insights to reveal how when non-Western nations demonstrate an aptitude for aesthetics, they come to enter into the proper and into a liberal humanist order. Rather than reinforcing this formula, this book actively hesitates from doing so.

To this point, I examine how the nation has existed in another site beyond world history: the global art market. This market has received less attention within transnational discourse in comparison to economics, international relations, and the law. And within discussions on global art, many primarily focus on financialization and circulation and less so on their entwinement with global logics of race and capitalist modernity, which I analyze in chapter 1. But focusing on this market provides an opportunity to contend with how the condition of China as a major form paves the way for other non-Western spaces to be enfolded into a sense of the world, particularly through the operations of the aesthetic alongside capital. As such, the aesthetic is not simply a site for possibility but also a problem itself. We must similarly hesitate on the aesthetic and the minor.

Beyond Minor Subjects toward the Minor as Method

This book uses the complexities of art and aesthetics as lenses and methods to revise the minor outside of its typical mobilization in political, legal, cultural, geographic, and economic terms. In particular, the minor has primarily been understood as a subject to be included so as to increase whom we value or consider. Within liberal frames, non-Western and minor populations are imagined as knowable subjects who require saving from illiberal nations, rationalizing imperial warfare and privileging entrance into a league of civilized modernity. Under this logic, the inclusion of more minor subjects is heralded for increasing those who can enter a liberated liberal order. And as demonstrated by discourses around precarity and the multitude that unify the interests of minoritized subjects and spaces, leftist and Marxist turns to the relational similarly rely on delimited understandings of the non-Western other. Calls to form a unified leftist sensibility out of the multitudes that are affected by late capital often require that these transnational subjects, who are debilitated by Western warfare and extraction, cast to the side histories of racialization and subjugation in order to join a larger movement. In other words, the minor, when framed primarily as subject or geography, becomes simply about increasing *whom* we value, study, or bring into consideration for one's respective cause. Through such a formulation, the minor comes to be flattened under the demands of liberal multiculturalism *and* the dominant Marxist privileging of class. Inclusion, even if it happens to be primarily composed of minorities and the so-called precariat, appears to be the answer for both liberalism and orthodox Marxism. And beyond political theory, the minor as subject has played a critical role for producing and claiming identity, which has been a crucial project for many (myself included). By extension, though, some then argue that more minor subjects and non-Western spaces need to be enfolded into liberal recognition and its attendant forums, such as the art market and academic curricula.

However, this book interrogates if this is the larger point of the minor—to be recognized and to play a role as subjects of history. The task at hand is not to gain legibility as minority subjects through the very means of the major and proper. Instead, the task of the minor is to rethink the terms, conditions, and operations that define not only whom or what we value but also *how we value*. After all, although one can push for inclusion and increase whom we value or place into consideration, the very mechanisms of exclusion will remain for an other. As such, I formulate the minor beyond the subject toward method so as to revise these dominant approaches and to *decipher* the apparatus and logics that uphold our world and how we produce value.[23] The minor, in particular, offers a way to perform structural analysis that does not solely rely on a focus on institutions or political economy. Oftentimes, the minor is dismissed as primarily about feeling or the individual subject. This book, however, deploys the minor as the very means to engage the *structural*.

Notably, my turn to global and non-Western art, with China as one of the earliest spaces included into the market, hesitates from presuming substantive social change through subject inclusion. The reason I focus on China in this book is due to the fact that it would be easy to recapitulate the established and popular consensus of the nation and its subjects as major and relevant to the world. However, I engage China differently and hesitantly in order to illustrate the crucial need to produce another project for the minor beyond liberalism. I thus attend to the formal, minor, and affective dynamics within non-Western art to better analyze the rules and regulations around how we value. For example, in this book, I move away from thinking of art as an ethnographic index of proper China. By moving away from art being an aperture into a single space like China, the minorness of aesthetics opens up understandings of the total world at large. To further illustrate this, as I discuss in chapter 4, most critics view the performances of Zhang Huan as a prime example of endurance art that exemplifies liberal ideals of resistance. But what happens when we turn instead to contemplate his work through the haptic, affect, and notions of time that move beyond the space of endurance, the duration of start to finish? Similarly, works by He Chengyao are typically interpreted within a discourse surrounding trauma and Chinese women, something that positions the feminized non-West as in need of saving. But what happens if we instead contemplate the work's sensory elements related to meditation? By hesitating in this way in the minor and the aesthetic, we are able to track the logics of the major and larger value systems that dictate our established understandings of the state, resistance, and political critique.

I thus develop the minor from emphases on aspects that are often discounted due to an overreliance on language or text over relations or emotions (affective turn); visual economies over other senses (sonic, aural, haptic, and olfactory); anthropocentric accounts over objects and things (new materialisms and object-oriented ontology); and demands for realistic, practical solutions over less determined meanings (speculative realism). Each of these "turns" have their respective genealogies and critiques, yet I place these multiple theoretical registers under the rubric of the minor to capture the essence of their critiques that direct us to imagine, feel, theorize, and politicize otherwise.[24] However, even amid this project of the "otherwise," I hope not to remain in the minor. After all, the affective turn and other related movements have become quite popular and the minorness of play and affect has been well integrated into neoliberal art markets.

This book, in other words, does not focus on the minor for minor's sake. Instead, a focus on the minor ultimately benefits historically minoritized communities by contending with racialization and by redistributing intellectual capital toward those who have often been denied full access. As such, I pair the minor with China and Marxist notions of structuration to produce a method that not only gestures toward an otherwise, but also refuses to linger solely in possibility. I propose projects surrounding redistribution, reordering, revolution, and structural analysis by targeting our intellectual efforts toward renegotiating the terms that shape existence, like the human subject, rather than including more individuals into the category. And although I ask us to hesitate, hesitation is a momentary action, not a permanent state. Hesitation involves a pause but does not stop, as one nonetheless continues an action or speech, albeit changed. Put differently, hesitation is not nihilism.

This pairing of minor with China, nonetheless, might still seem counterintuitive, since the country is quite central to theorizations of the global as an imperial and colonial force. China's treatment of its own minority populations requires concern and action. Racial logics undergird the CCP's privileging of Han bodies and the violent policing of ethnic and religious populations like the Uighurs. Beyond its immediate borders, China plays a central role in the management of international debt with its active trading with many partners on the African continent. In my afterword, I examine these questions as they relate to subjects (like the Uighurs) who are minor in, and spaces (like Hong Kong, Tibet, and Taiwan) that are minor to, the Chinese state.

My use of the minor does not discount these realities. Even amid China's contemporary dominance within global empire,[25] the minor is nonetheless the means to hesitate from established approaches that presume intelligible the state and its subjects and that delimit any critique of China as solely informed by liberalism (about speech and rights). Although it is important to contend with China's current political significance and its imperial and authoritarian tendencies, a perpetual focus on relevance and contemporary concerns eclipses other ways of knowing and theorizing a space. China should not simply be further included into discourse nor be deployed as an example that paves the way for other nations to become central to empire and capitalist modernity. As such, the method of the minor approaches China and Chineseness as concepts in order to examine the political and theoretical possibilities of differently engaging the subject, state, and social structures as affective entities, rather than solid facts. Through the molecular and relational, affect offers an important mechanism to track the production of sites, the state, and other objects presumed to be transparent, absolute, and fully knowable.

Minor China therefore responds to the force that prescribes how and why proper context predominates in overdetermined ways that presume the Chinese state and its subjects as clear and solidified truths, what Jacques Derrida calls the *force of law*.[26] Derrida defines the concept as "the urgency that obstructs the horizon of knowledge."[27] Due to political crisis and its attendant feelings of urgency, we are often compelled by this force to privilege legible answers. However, by reacting in immediate and direct ways, the force of law limits more open and hesitant responses that may seem initially illegible, unreasonable, and illiberal. Yet, they are intensely needed. For example, in moments of crisis, activists often retort that they need practical solutions to a problem and that there is no space for the luxury of overthinking things. This compulsion and force limit minor theorizations due to the immediacy of the moment. Yet, the minor as a method helps us envision movements beyond a single-issue politic and refrain from replicating the power dynamics that often plague activist work, like respectability politics, ableism, or masculinist dismissal.

For China studies, the force of law translates into theorists critiquing China under the auspices of liberalism or showing the true realities of the non-West to question the long history of Eurocentric and racist configurations of the non-West and its subjects—something that is seen in the way Chinese artists are categorized and discussed for their value as herculean resistors to an authoritarian state. Ai Weiwei has become emblematic of this, although he is by no means the only one. Rey Chow locates this predicament more broadly at the level of subjective experience: "Often, in an attempt to show 'the way things really are' our discourses produce a non-West that is deprived of fantasy, desires, and contradictory emotions."[28] Extending Chow's astute analysis, I study the work of artists like Yan Xing, Zhang Huan, He Chengyao, and Cao Fei, among others, to delve deeply into fantasy, affect, and feelings—seemingly minor forms particularly under the force of law which demands legibility and direct critique. For example, in chapter 4, by looking at Cao Fei's photo series on cosplay through the lens of fabulation, we come to understand the major presumptions around political action that are informed by Marxist discourses on demystification, alienation, and performativity. Cao Fei's use of affect rethinks the premise that the performance of agency must always translate into direct action in order to be considered properly political. Nonetheless, to argue for the import of looking at affect, fantasy, or contradictory emotions in this way is not to simply assert their inclusion into academic analysis ("we need more feeling in theory").

The minor as method, as such, does not seek to produce new theories or redefine the major terms that respond within the norms of the force of law. Instead, minor China pauses before the moment of prescription and counterargument. This book's method hesitates by turning to the basic building blocks that structure universal notions, specifically those minor details that are often eschewed by the force of law. In other words, I critique the universal without dismissing it, following an established tradition within postcolonial studies and China studies. As Dipesh Chakrabarty astutely observes in relation to Frantz Fanon's simultaneous critique of and belief in the Enlightenment notion of the human, "there is no easy way of dispensing with these universals in the condition of political modernity."[29] Similarly, as Wang Hui argues, "as we correct the errors in the idea of Asia, we must also reexamine the idea of Europe."[30] Although writing from different contexts, they emphasize the need to critique yet work within the limits of these dominant concepts and ideas.

To ground this methodological approach for the minor, let us consider the affective *relation* between the major and minor within bodily registers. Major and minor muscle groups support one another, while the former tends to be the most physically dominant or noticeable in form. When one removes the minor, however, one notices the relation between the two once the major fails and cannot function as usual. One could focus solely on the discrete operations of minor muscle groups. However, when one attends to the physiological functions of the minor as they relate to major muscle groups, we glean more about the reliance on major muscles in their relation to minor ones. This particular relationship of the minor redirects our focus from the subject itself to (affective) relations *and*, most importantly, how the major operates. This example thus illustrates how an affective reading is necessary to not only reorder major formulations like the state, but also avoid simply privileging the minor. To be explicit, the minor cannot exist without or merely replace the major or universal.

Another corporeal dimension of the minor corresponds to sound. The minor's relation to the major is akin to the aesthetic structure of major and minor scales, where the latter has a different affective tone in comparison to the former yet both interrelate in terms of content or structure. Every major scale has a relative minor which shares the same key signature; the minor key, however, has a more "serious or melancholic" affect.[31] This affective distinction of the minor from the major enables one to track the resonance of the major. Further, tone constructs these major and minor sonic qualities. Within a tonal music system, the relationship between major and minor tones creates either consonance or dissonance. Although music systems are culturally defined as to what is perceived as consonant and dissonant, the metastructure of how major and minor tones interrelate informs my analytic model for the minor. From the standpoint of musicology, the major and minor system is one rooted in Western-defined ideals, with Enlightenment investments in placing classical music as part of the higher order within natural(ized) law.[32] With civilizational sensibilities being closely aligned with the high construction of the major key against the naturalized, low order of the minor, a system came into place to produce our sonic norms. The very notion and logic of major and minor tones rely on the creation of a heptatonic system, involving seven notes. However, the vast majority of the minoritarian world deploys a sonic scheme involving five notes, a pentatonic scale. For a listener primarily conditioned within a heptatonic system, the auditory difference of the pentatonic evokes the exotic. In fact, the invocation of Oriental sonic tropes that opens up Carl Douglas's "Kung Fu Fighting" and the Vapors' "Turning Japanese" demonstrates the use of the pentatonic in a globalized cultural imaginary. Thus, our musical system reproduces colonial logics that transfix the racialized as below civilizational ideals into an ostensibly natural sonic order. Through an unequivocal focus on the seemingly less important or minor system, we come to better understand the very terms and logics that undergird the major's operations, its force.

China *in* Theory / China *in Theory*

A core goal of this book is thus to reimagine the methods for transnational analysis through the minor. An attention to not only major political concerns but also minor details helps us understand what upholds the major and politics, while the major amplifies the ethical commitments of the minor. This dialectical method arises from the differences between how China has functioned *in* theory and what it means to situate China *in theory*. In particular, we must attend to how China has operated across area and ethnic studies, particularly with regard to the ways each conceptualizes the state. Both question the ways China with*in* the tradition of critical theory has become arrested as unmodern and behind. However, both fields, albeit differently, have limited how we might think of the state affectively, or China *in theory*. These rubrics, in other words, highlight field overlaps, alongside the need to develop an apparatus for approaching the state speculatively and affectively, as a *becoming*. This method through the minor thus helps us not dissipate the state into pure affect nor overdetermine its contours.

China *in* critical theory has been rendered major and proper in several identifiable ways. German idealist Georg Wilhelm Friedrich Hegel set the stage for disciplinary approaches with his philosophy of world history, whereby Asia occupies the beginning of time while Europe represents "the end of History."[33] Most importantly, Hegel's philosophy of world history casts China within theory as peripheral and supplementary to the center. The minor other is understood as outside of the major—the minor must simply be enfolded into this order so as to presumably fix Hegel's errors. His construction of China within theory thus prescribes two predominant responses: humanize the minor outsider to be central to history and learn more about the other so as to be represented. This book, however, reconsiders these responses as the proper ones.

In light of China's "rise," a number of fields have directly countered these proper and major renderings. For example, as scholars from ethnic and area studies have come to grapple with China in the global, some have responded in ways that are immediately legible under the force of law. China has historically been—and continues to be—presumed as fully knowable, whether this be understood as "the sick man of Asia," a burgeoning locus for global Marxism, or even a space to produce a diasporic sentiment for solidarity. Area studies has long sought to decode and make knowable Chinese ways, customs, and languages. Further, ethnic studies has rendered stable the nation of China and the region of Asia to produce a diasporic ethnic identity, known as Chinese American or Asian American. Even as these fields work in different ways against limited and racialized understandings of China *in theory*, they similarly arrest the nation-state's form in economized ways in order to counteract Eurocentrism and racism.

Asian American studies was originally inspired by activist movements from the 1960s. Mobilization eventually led to the field's institutionalization. With such an orientation, China, or more broadly Asia, was imagined as a stable geographic locale. China and Asia became the diasporic centers which immigrants, and those whose families had been in the US for decades, could identify with to form solidarity that challenged the racialized aggression from within the United States. Of course, some Asian American activists were part of larger Third World movements that critiqued and challenged US empire. However, what interests me is how Asia comes to be produced or solidified. Although Asian American studies is typically imagined as distinct from Asian studies, the region of Asia has been understood in entangled ways. To enable solidarity across diverse groups that have substantive differences and tensions, the category of Asian American renders race and Asia stable and knowable. Asian American studies rejects essentialized understandings of Asia yet imagines a stabilized locale of "Asia" for its racialized migrants on US soil so as to unite distinct groups. Both area and ethnic studies have historically approached China through knowable, particular, and major forms of representation surrounding geography and history (for area studies) and race and diaspora (for ethnic studies), thus allowing them to attend to what are typically viewed as "classical" political concerns.

Even though a rapid change in understanding China occurred during the twentieth century—from sick and unimportant to a space that produces diaspora, a global Marxism, or a critical presence in late capital—the nation nonetheless is an economized object presumed to be geographically bound, tidy, and clear. China operates within a logic of economism and abstraction that mediates the West's anxieties and political desires. In other words, China with*in* theory may shift in form yet maintains its status as knowable. This condition arises across political ideologies and from within China itself. In a study from the 1960s, Donald Lowe notably examined the political function of "China" for Marx, Lenin, and even Mao.[34] Lowe tracked how the figure of China was operationalized with*in* theory for the Left and for China itself. Vukovich has gone on to describe the use of China as always existing as an abstraction to fit arguments within continental philosophy. China, from this perspective, provides a "labor-saving operation" whereby an "econo-mism" around theoretical arguments deploys China as the West's imagined other.[35]

In the wake of global shifts during the 1960s, China *in* theory took a turn. Following mass decolonization movements across the Global South, Maoism in China buttressed global Left yearnings for political and cultural change. French intellectuals and activists from the student movements of the 1960s drew inspiration from economized understandings of China and Maoism.[36] Regardless of the political purpose, China existed in a knowable and codified form. Further, with shifts in late capital and the opening of China's markets at the end of the twentieth century, the nation took on a different narrative form, although it remained within the condition of China *in* theory. This larger condition produces China into its economized, knowable form as major China. Major China provides the basis for multiple fields, theoretical approaches, and political leanings to place their anxieties and hopes into proper notions of the state and its attendant citizen-subjects. Since China currently plays a critical role for contemporary political economic questions around power and late capital, most discussions around China and its subjects respond through proper and legible means as dictated by the force of law. To work against earlier dismissals of China as inhuman and sick, our impulses economize China in order to be applicable to today's political world and to be recognizable in form.

This move to make China legible in today's world—the primary responses of which include the impulse to humanize the Chinese, to argue for China's relevance to global affairs, or to critique yet simultaneously reinforce the notion of the authoritarian state—has led to a radical shift in how major

China is understood in Western theory. As noted by Vukovich: "Whereas in the recent past one would not have had to reference China without a specific, direct interest in the revolution or culture, today it is difficult to avoid it. It simply *must* be referred to by the critic at large. As if the West must now respond to China—a remarkable reversal of the classic model of Sinology whereby China must respond to 'us.'"[37] Such a reversal operates under the norms of the force of law, whereby this revised condition often necessitates the masculinist, major force of inclusion and "righting" or rewriting the historical record. Since the nation has always been conditioned to be legible to the West, the counterresponse is to make others contend with the truths and realities of China. A number of thinkers—including Wang Hui, Gao Minglu, Dai Jinhua, and others—have complicated past narratives and uses of China by offering counterfactual histories and theorizations that reassess China's economism for theory. These figures, in addition to Vukovich and Donald Lowe, ultimately force us to contend with the condition of being abstracted in this way for leftist agendas. Rather than merely arguing for truths about China to be unearthed or for us to have a deeper area studies orientation, we might hesitate and pause to consider this repeated conditioning of China with*in* theory.

———

A number of scholars and theorists provide useful formulations for approaching the non-West beyond the major and beyond how the non-West has circulated with*in* theory. The provocations discussed earlier by Chakrabarty, Fanon, and Wang to render the non-West minor or in speculative ways—whereby a place like China can be understood in theory but not overly universalized so as to dissipate history—are a generative starting point. To render an object *in theory* means to speculate and not presume its borders defined. For the arguments in this book, this means moving away from understanding China in its prototypical form as an economized object. It does not, however, simply mean arguing for the dissolution of borders, a post–nation-state discourse, or the end of history. Rather, to render China *in theory* is to provide space to sense the changes and shifts within the established nation-state form, while retaining a sense of its materiality and history. And in fact, this call to rework overdetermined understandings of the subject and nation has been echoed throughout American studies,[38] women of color and transnational feminisms,[39] China studies,[40] Black feminism, disability studies, queer of color critique,[41] and Asian/American studies.[42]

In addition, to imagine the state *in theory*, Deleuzo-Guattarian concepts provide critical insights. Many of the artists I engaged often theorized and produced in ways that resonated with Gilles Deleuze and Félix Guattari. In particular, their notion of becoming came to inform my understanding of many of the practices in this book, as becoming provides the mechanism by which to situate China as minor and *in theory*, the state through affect. The nation-state form is both real and not fully predefined. This model of molecularization tracks minor contours within the nation-state—at the level of its becoming. To engage the past, Deleuze distinguishes becoming from history: "one being to follow the course of the event, gathering how it comes about historically, how it's prepared and then decomposes in history, while the other way is to go back into the event, to take one's place in it as in a becoming, to grow both young and old in it at once, going through all its components and singularities. Becoming isn't a part of history; history amounts to only the set of preconditions, however recent, that one leaves behind in order to 'become,' that is to create something new."[43] Becoming differs from historical contextualization in that the former does not presume the knowability of time, space, or an event. As a method, becoming provides additional modes to formulate and imagine time and space. In turn, becoming approaches objects and events in "unassimilated" and "not yet established" ways—where they can be understood speculatively or *in theory*.

Deleuze and Guattari not only help us produce China *in theory* and as a becoming, but also illustrate the disciplinary tendencies and formations that often preclude the thinking of China and the transnational speculatively. In particular, they are often less cited to engage the state. In a general sense, Deleuze and Guattari are more central for queer studies than area and ethnic studies.[44] Deleuze and Guattari have a relatively stable position in relation to certain branches of queer theory, particularly for discussions around affect. This schematic delineation demonstrates how these theorists, as citational figures for affect, becoming, and other minor approaches, are thus questioned for their lack of "classical ideas of normativity and political critique," an ongoing concern across the humanities.[45] When compared to Michel Foucault or Jacques Derrida, Deleuze and Guattari possess less of a citational pull for area and ethnic studies.[46] In other words, Deleuze and Guattari play a secondary role for theories about subjects and representation, while they operate as primary influences on theorizations around what I have been calling the minor turn. In addition, Deleuzo-Guattarian ideas possess a genealogy in China. Henri Bergson is known to be a central figure for Deleuze and Guattari's theories. Bergson heavily influenced one of the first curators and central theorizers of contemporary Chinese art, Fei Dawei. He trained in philosophy and focused his studies on Bergson, translating many of his works from French to Chinese. This relationship offers a moment to reexamine the theoretical bases of how discourse around contemporary Chinese art was inflected by a key figure central to Deleuze and Guattari.[47]

And yet, as I argue throughout this book and particularly in chapter 3, the excesses of minoritarian subjects cannot be fully enfolded into major discourses surrounding history and context. Such subjects cannot be completely known. Thus, to render China *in theory* is to decipher this limitation, and to embrace it—the minor as method offers a means to do so. Following Deleuze and Guattari, I privilege a stance of *becoming China* which means to imagine China *in theory*. Importantly, becoming enables incomplete and affective engagements with China without delving into a purely universalist discourse or dissipating borders. China is not necessarily different but has differently become. Becoming balances an acknowledgment of difference without reifying and ascribing such difference to all Chinese people. This sense of becoming thus teeters across the fine line separating essentialism from antiessentialism, a key issue that has often kept area and ethnic studies apart. The aim in tracking the becoming of China is not merely to argue that we all happen to come into being—becoming might happen universally but the process is far from equivalent. Put differently, we all might become, but how it feels and how power inflects becoming is a different story.[48]

Aesthetics and Politics beyond Liberalism and Translation

A minor method relies upon the formal and more seemingly minor details of artworks to illustrate how context and history for understanding the transnational have been privileged over an examination of its becoming. The aesthetic, however, is not simply heralded as pure possibility or rendered major; instead, this book theorizes the aesthetic in ways that implicate it within and through the structural. To illustrate the method of minor China, I look at the production of a number of artists, primarily ones working after the Cultural Revolution. Although some have complicated this history of how avant-garde aesthetics and practices came to enter and develop in China well before 1979, I rely on this particular historicization for contemporary Chinese art less as historical fact and more as a way to identify the dominant narrative surrounding the genre. I thus consider, in chapter 1, how and why the Cultural Revolution and 1989 become the primary means that make the idea of contemporary China proper and legible to larger audiences (China *in* theory). My chapters engage some canonical artists in this field, along with many identified as feminist and queer. I analyze artists like Cao Fei, He Chengyao, and Yan Xing, since their identities as women or gay often invoke overdetermined narratives around the perils of tradition and their fight for a representative voice. Although I do not discount the abuses of the Chinese state against minoritarian communities, I ask what these narratives surrounding feminist and queer artists reproduce. I also consider canonical artists like Ai Weiwei and Zhang Huan, as both of them are often taken to represent masculinist and herculean responses against the state. The ways both sets of artists are discussed on the global art market ultimately reproduce the dominant liberal narratives around the Chinese state, with canonical artists representing the masculinist and resistant challenges against the state and the minoritarian ones illuminating the strong hand of the state and tradition. The context of contemporary China provides the opportunity to rethink how we imagine the transnational and aesthetics outside of these major, prescribed ways.

To do so, I renegotiate the established discourse on aesthetics and politics through the method of minor China. The relationship between aesthetics and politics is often presumed to involve a direct, linear mediation, whereby the aesthetic responds to and shapes the political. The discourse on aesthetics and politics, as influenced by Jacques Rancière, and which I discuss in more detail in chapter 1, emerged around the same time as the concept of global art (around 1989). Anna Kornbluh astutely summarizes this Rancièrean approach: "far from being an epiphenomenon dispelling politics, aesthetics amount to the core of politics."[49] For Rancière, the proliferation of the aesthetic operates similarly to liberal logics surrounding representation, whereby an increase of art by those historically excluded will presumably expand *whom* society values and what it deems sensible.

This book develops a theory of the aesthetic in its relation to the political that does not exist within this liberal model, privileging instead social structuration and an analysis of *how we value*. To this point, during the interviews I conducted with many of the artists discussed in this book, the conversations would eventually touch upon how or if they considered themselves political. Many artists acknowledged that this label enables modes of circulation for their art. Others would respond in ways that resonate with "no, but people think I am." These moments underscore how dominant discourses surrounding aesthetics and politics are limited in their capacity to address more complex understandings of both terms. As such, this book is less interested in entering established debates over the agency or significance of the aesthetic and focuses more upon rethinking how we conceptualize and structure the mediation across aesthetics and politics. I thus use the framework of mediation to highlight how dominant models assume art's capacity to linearly respond to the political akin to liberal representationalism—an increase of art from those previously excluded supposedly translates into a broadening of our communal sensibilities. Another mode of *indirect mediation* expands and revises this presumed direct mediation of aesthetics being at the core of the political.[50]

These different models of mediation, from linear to indirect, help us grapple with 1) the limits of linear mediation to conceptualize culture and politics, and 2) the dominance of translation to understand aesthetics and politics in the global. First, in order to rethink this presumed equation across culture and politics, I turn to aesthetic objects and analytic readings that do not always mediate a direct relationship to the political. I focus on works that cannot be properly understood as "political" because they allow us to hesitate from defaulting into discourses that mediate a singular relation across aesthetics and politics. Such a direct mediation is often registered under the framework of resistance. In addition, even if a work might initially be framed as properly political, I offer analytic readings that engage such a work minorly. This reading against the grain expands how we perform aesthetic analysis beyond a linear mediation. Direct mediation fuels the major and proper. Through indirect mediation, we delve into the problems and possibilities of the aesthetic on its own terms, rather than debating its direct value for the political. In other words, this book privileges developing a fuller discourse for the aesthetic (one that embeds the aesthetic further with and through the structural) over arguing for its relevance or role in shaping politics. The aesthetic is not used to illustrate possibility (as in resistance) or problem (as in emblematic of capitalist logics); it is simultaneously both.

This book thus lingers with the minorness of the aesthetic, rather than rendering it as a major or significant mediating force like politics. I thus approach the aesthetic similar to how I theorize minor subjects through the question of method. I do so because the aesthetic produces the very means to operate indirectly and to pause before the force of law takes hold. The aesthetic does not always make immediate sense in relation to the force of law, which demands that the aesthetic reacts with parity to material "urgency." If we continue to analyze art for the ways it increases our political sensibilities (à la liberal representation) or changes the social as equal to law or activism (through resistance), we miss other critical tactics that operate in a different plane and rhythm. It is precisely within such limited capacities that I track minor methodological impulses so as to query our established terms and to hesitate from responding in fully legible ways. Although cultural objects can certainly attempt to respond with immediacy, I privilege objects and readings that veer away from such a direct correlation between aesthetic response and discursive urgency. Some may claim that "confusing" works and minor analytic readings are not as political as those that respond with parity against the demands of political life. However, I argue that such responses are often predicated on a desire to render aesthetics into a social possibility that is equivalent to politics and on a reinstantiation of politics as that which can directly respond through the proper terms at hand—the terms that are immediately legible.

For example, how might we contend with works that are more formalist in nature and less overtly political or sensational than Zhu Yu's *Eating People*? Yan Xing, whom I discuss in chapter 3, is one artist whose queer identity renders him as a proper subject who questions homophobia within the state and across society. However, his video installation *Kill (the) TV-Set* speaks to many formalist concerns and abstract aesthetic experimentations with mediation and reperformance (figure I.4). This piece reenacts a performance by Charlotte Moorman and Nam June Paik, which originally reperformed a sound score by John Cage. In other words, Yan Xing reperforms a reperformance of a sound performance directly engaged with minimalism and modernism. On one hand, if one solely focuses on purely formalist approaches, we run the risk of decontextualizing and dehistoricizing Yan's work away from rich insights around formalist and modernist trends in China or the history of new media and film. On the other, the reliance on deep contextualization limits what the aesthetic can offer for a structural, political critique, often defaulting into overdetermined accounts of how queer artists resist the state or how their growing inclusion expands our communal sensibilities. I engage and take the aesthetics of objects like *Kill (the) TV-Set* as providing the methods for reexamining these limited approaches to Chinese art and for reconfiguring the terms at hand for discussing the political.

Second, in addition to bringing to the fore the need for an indirect relation between aesthetics and politics, mediation refigures the role of translation for understanding non-Western art. The minor as method offers a way to situate China *in theory*, as a mediating and mediated form, whereby China becomes material in construct yet porous in its details and operations. I frame China through mediation so as to further the notion of China *in theory*, thereby expanding the dominant way the non-West is often discussed: translation. I develop mediation as a way to grapple with the ever-increasing

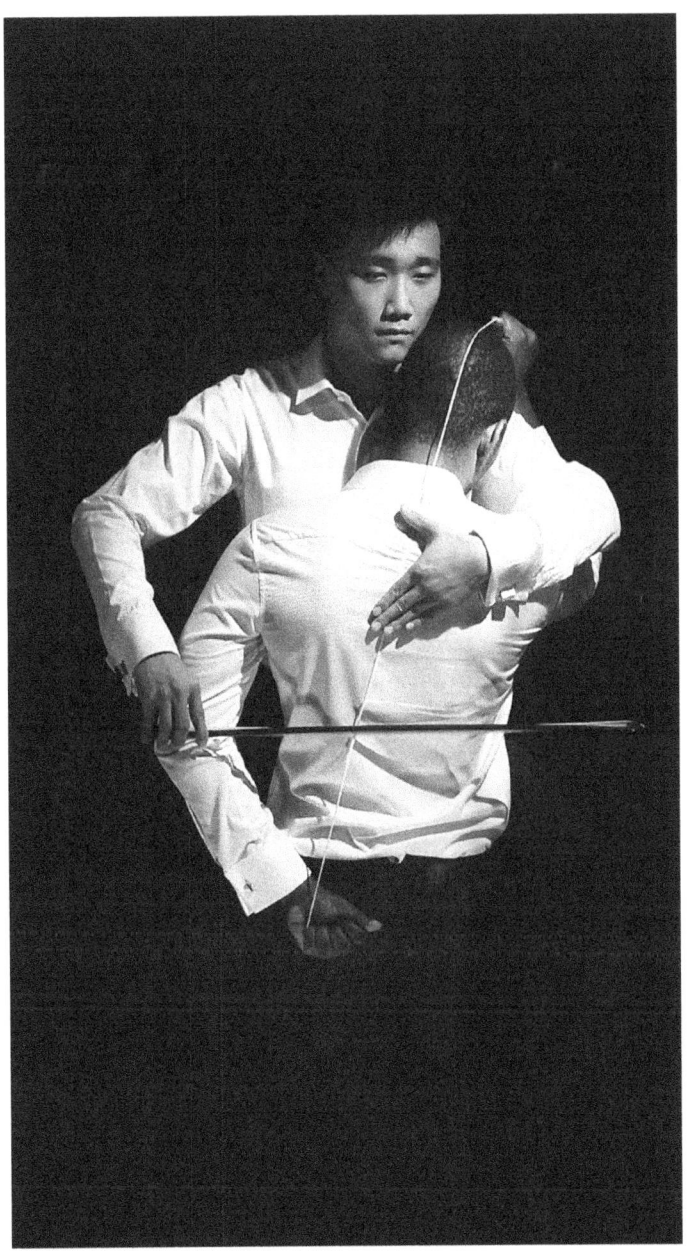

Figure I.4. Yan Xing, *Kill (the) TV-Set*, 2012. 2-channel video installation, 1st channel, single HD digital video (b/w, silent, loop), 2'30". Dimensions variable. © Yan Xing. Courtesy of the artist.

circulation of visual, mediated, performance-based, and sonic objects that are not predominantly language-based nor purely representational. Since translation is and continues to be a critical method and approach,[51] mediation is deployed as a supplement to this frame. Performance theorist Sean Metzger highlights the predominance of translation to provocatively ask which nonlinguistic notions help us produce a sense of China.[52] With China's linguistic system, many have turned toward translation with a focus on the ideogram. I thus deploy mediation to explore other ways of contending with China and globality.

The medium of performance in China exemplifies the need to account further for a model of mediation. Performance art, what was often called "apartment art" by early practitioners, emerged during the 1980s and early 1990s. Due to increased regulation, many artists in China began to present work in smaller venues, primarily involving a network of private apartments. This era of "apartment art" often relied on performance for a variety of reasons. Economically, the use of the body for artistic exploration was cheaper than purchasing materials, which was of concern for most as they regained financial grounding after the Cultural Revolution. Logistically, performance initially did not involve documentation, which was appealing for some trying to avoid regulation. Quite central to the development of contemporary Chinese art, performance, however, takes on different inflections depending on the term deployed. *Xingwei yishu*, which means "behavior art," is the Chinese term oft-used to refer to performance art.[53] Although *biaoyan* is more closely analogous to the English meaning of performance, *biaoyan* possesses a closer relation to theatrical and dance genealogies. Thus, why choose behavior to describe performance, when other translations might be more literal or direct? Archival research shows debates occurring between Gao Minglu and other figures in the 1990s art scene over the use of this term. The choice of behavior (*xingwei*) arose from an antitheatrical stance, where the Chinese version of "performance art" (*xingwei yishu*) came to be differentiated from spectacle and the virtuosic associations of theater and dance. Meiling Cheng highlights Yang Zhichao's choice of *xingwei* over *biaoyan* in order to establish how Chinese performance artists desired to translate or Sinicize Western concepts, such as performance art.[54] Although Cheng helpfully directs us toward the translation-based and culturally engaged use of the term, the different meanings for performance in China require grappling with mediation and medial relations. Performance, as internal behavior *or* external theatricality, offers two different means by which to mediate the aesthetic with the social or political.

Although one could delineate the distinction between *xingwei* and *biaoyan* as one solely about translation (in that we must choose the "best" or most local term), their meanings also direct us to mediation. *Xingwei* translates as "action," "behavior," or "conduct." The first character *xing* has a variety of meanings that primarily circulate within the realm of pedestrian acts, such as walking, behaving, and doing. The second character, *wei*, is a preposition, which means to be in the interest of and toward the goal of such pedestrian acts. Unlike the pedestrian frame embedded in *xingwei*, *biaoyan* circulates within acting, dancing, and playing. The first character, *biao*, indicates expressive action oriented toward outside reception. Opposed to the internal focus of *xing* on behavior, *biao* orients itself externally as its meanings encompass how people judge an act. The second character, *yan*, connotes a sense of practice inherent to performance: evolve, practice, and put on. This second character reveals how the external orientation of *biao* must be rehearsed in order to maximize its potential.

This book's exploration of the minor highlights the importance of focusing on the ways these words are understood for not only concerns over translation, but also differing forms of mediation. The internal focus of behavior and the external practice of theater highlight how these terms are not solely about the practice of translation but also multiple modes of mediation, whereby internality and externality differently convey the body to self, self to others, and aesthetics to politics. Further, embedded in the single medium of performance art are multiple media and their respective approaches. Xingwei privileges the everyday; its antitheatrical stance obscures additional analytic tools like those from dance and theater, or biaoyan. These medial relations reveal how dance and theater are often considered minor in relation to a visual and performance art orientation for xingwei yishu. In most accounts of performance art in China, the discourse relies upon understandings of visual art. However, what might happen if we reimagined expanded art practices in ways that could contend with not only these multiple etymologies, but also multiple forms of mediation? If hapticity, corporeality, staging, repetition, and choreography become additional analytics by which to work through the dynamics of contemporary Chinese art practices, we might better attend to multiple levels of mediation that help us rethink theorizations of the subject, aesthetics, and politics. My turn to mediation thus contends with questions of medial specificity; different models of how we grapple with situating the body and culture with the political; and how information is relayed, received, and processed.

Hesitant Method and Marxist Materialisms

Ultimately, this book's development of the minor contributes to discourses on disciplinarity and interdisciplinarity, specifically through its proposal for a model of hesitation. The transnational artists and their aesthetics that I discuss throughout this book consistently demonstrate the need to engage their work from a wide range of fields, directing us to the disciplinary limits that often hinder how we analyze and theorize. Similar to Ai in his work *Dropping*—which brings to the fore concerns related to fields ranging from ethnic to area studies, art history to performance, and socialism to liberalism—the artists whose works I discuss in each of the following chapters consistently highlight these limits.

What if we attended to these calls by transnational artists and thus hesitated in our engagements with citations, methods, and disciplinarity? I hesitate from established citational practices throughout this book in order to grapple with tensions and fractures across disciplines that are often eclipsed by the fervor for interdisciplinarity. In particular, I think through the place of two bodies of theory, along with their intersections,[55] as they complicate a study of the transnational and Asia: *Francophone metaphysical thought* and *Black feminist theory*. Scholars from the former include Henri Bergson, Deleuze, Guattari, and Frantz Fanon, among others; scholars from the latter include Hortense Spillers, Audre Lorde, and Saidiya Hartman, among others. By engaging China through the minor, I develop an analytic from these two locations of thought to produce a different ethical orientation that does not reproduce disciplinary expectations around citation. Further, the interplay across these two entwined approaches brings to the fore questions surrounding materialisms and method.

Although both discourses engage the universal and particular, Black feminism is often situated as too particular while Francophone metaphysics is viewed as overly universal. I nonetheless focus on how both share a focus on minor objects, subjects, and methods to revamp established materialist concerns, while also not losing sight of critical tensions and overlaps between the two. Further, they both animate their critiques at the minor level of sense to ultimately engage the political and structural.

Although Black feminist theory, which has been developing for centuries, draws from across the social sciences and humanities, the main thrust of the project has been to reconsider how minor identities function in relation to institutions. Many of these theorists direct us to the limits of "classical" approaches to being and state power, including Francophone metaphysical discourse itself. A focus on the category of Black woman is deployed not as an insular fixation but rather as the method to revise universalizing frames around power and institutional life. A more recent development from Black feminist theory has been a turn toward affect, the haptic, and other sensorial relations to objects. Thus, key questions for the humanities today are how exactly we methodologically "listen to an image" (per Tina Campt's suggestion), grapple with fungibility as a political, sensory, and aesthetic category (per C. Riley Snorton), contend with sensation and flesh (per Amber Musser and Hortense Spillers), and "sense" or "haptically" relate to visuality (per Rizvana Bradley drawing from the earlier work of Laura Marks).[56] This book offers explicit methodological takes on such questions, since hesitation reorders not only intellectual practices but also our senses.[57] Of course, the minor turns discussed throughout this book have a longer genealogy related to not only Black feminism, but also women of color discourse, queer of color critique, crip theory, and indigenous studies.[58]

Francophone metaphysical thought similarly overlaps through a focus on the grain of sense. The project is also unwieldy with a range of theorists and approaches from figures like Gottfried Wilhelm Leibniz and Baruch Spinoza to Simone Weil, Frantz Fanon, Édouard Glissant, Deleuze, and Guattari. It encompasses questions surrounding ontology, sensation, imagination, and perception, traversing through discourses like affect, phenomenology, psychoanalysis, and existentialism. From this approach, Deleuze proposes a "hesitant method," which involves "the means of that knowledge which regulates the collaboration of all the faculties." He reminds us to reorganize our senses and what makes sense in this world: "There is no more a method for learning than there is a method for finding treasures, but a violent training, a culture or *paideia* which affects the entire individual (an albino in whom emerges the act of sensing in sensibility, an aphasic in whom emerges the act of speech in language, an acephalous being in whom emerges the act of thinking in thought)."[59]

Although both projects have multiple and complex goals, I focus here on the way they offer minor methods that not only restructure sensory faculties, but also suture the minorness of sense to Marxist materialist concerns. They each provide mechanisms to rethink multiple scales throughout our world. Rather than understanding either as enabling newer materialist concerns, I fixate on how they respectively turn to the minor to help us grapple with old questions surrounding social structuration, archives and memory, institutions, state power, globality, and racialization. Each of these projects furthers Marxist materialist questions, although admittedly they both have complex relations to one another and, most critically, to dogmatic Marxism. Schematically, Francophone metaphysical thought, particularly through Deleuze and Guattari, locates the import of desire to help us produce what Nicholas Thoburn calls a "minor Marxism."[60] Their approach generally grapples with materialism through a rethinking of subjects, alongside a reformulation of theories of power that are not only structural or hierarchical but also lateral and rhizomatic. Similar to Francophone metaphysicists, some Black feminists have used and reworked psychoanalysis to reconsider subject formation. Further, Black feminist theory engages Marxist materialism by questioning dominant accounts as to how institutions and subjects function. By doing so, Cathy Cohen revises theorizations of the subject through social structuration, developing "a politics where one's relation to power, and not some homogenized identity, is privileged in determining one's comrades."[61]

Both projects overlap in ways that draw from minor subjects for their "relations to power" (the proletariat and Black women, and their overlapping existences) to produce minor analytics. This conceptual shift ultimately allows us to move beyond identity without forgetting it. To move beyond comes from within. This enables a relational politics that exceeds the bounds of particularity to grapple with social structuration. In addition, they focus on the codes that construct our lives. Rather than understanding difference as naturalized in bodies, they denaturalize difference and provide the sensual and minor approaches to do so. The minor thus becomes not solely about insular, singular, knowable, and representable subjects. As such, Black feminism and Francophone metaphysics further the minor as method as the means to enact and reconfigure the project of relationality.

Beyond these two terrains, additional engagements with method inform my approach. From the works of Chela Sandoval and Linda Tuhiwai Smith to the development of queer method, there has been a growing consideration of method beyond critiques of it as masculinist and scientist.[62] It may, at first, seem counterintuitive to pair minor and method together, considering many have attempted to render the openness of the minor away from the scientism implicit in method.[63] Method is an easy intellectual discourse to fetishize, with its connotations of masculinist and deracialized rigor for the humanities and humanistic social sciences. Despite the racialized and gendered underpinnings of method, however, it has been an ongoing and productive concern for minoritarian fields.[64]

Moreover, China itself stages concerns over materialisms and method. China, as a postsocialist space, indexes changes in Marxist politics. Further, Chen Kuan-Hsing's *Asia as Method* centers method to consider Asia as an "anchoring point" to think beyond its immediate geographic borders.[65] Chen aims to decolonize, deimperialize, and de–Cold War thought by situating his work on minor spaces toward minoritarian ends.[66] A noted difference, however, with the method I produce here is that I analyze the anchor of the West in relation to China. The point of Chen's work is to turn away from an area studies model of single nation-states and from a focus on Asia with the US and Europe, as he emphasizes the relations across Japan, China, and Taiwan, for example. Although my goals are similar to Chen's in that method offers ways to hesitate from dominant understandings of Asia, I primarily refocus on the dialectic perpetuated with the West due to its dominance within the global art market.

Chapter Outline

This book addresses multiple audiences who might best take a moment to re-work the very terms that construct their economic, aesthetic, and intellectual projects. For the humanities, my hope is to theorize the broader minor turns around ontology, materialism, and affect in ways that account more critically for materiality, race, and the transnational. By approaching the state and subjects affectively, I demarcate the larger political projects of social structuration and political economy for our minor turns. In addition, this book engages the ongoing debate around social context and form and situates it in relation to questions surrounding the non-West.[67] Although I do not fully attend to these debates—which are happening primarily in literary theory—I examine what aesthetic minorness provides for this larger concern. And I do so with a deep consideration of the transnational, since it brings to the fore the limits of how we even define context and form in the first place. Although this book highlights the minor in relation to China and the global art market, it ultimately produces a larger methodology for not only non-Western art, but also academic fields whose fractures reproduce the very limits described in this introduction.

For the art world, particularly curators, this book renegotiates how non-Western others are framed and included. Relatedly, for artists and activists, I expand understandings of the political, aesthetic, and critique by analyzing institutional relations beyond direct resistance and frameworks that refrain from responding in terms solely legible to the very institutions that we are theoretically trying to work beyond. The rise of contemporary Chinese art occasions reimagining how otherness has been and can be differently enfolded into academia, the art world, and their publics. I take stock of and question the available methodological and theoretical frameworks for this body of art. Most importantly, this book's minor method reorders the disciplinary orientations and overdetermined assumptions that limit how we understand otherness in this world through key ideas: history, the state, subjects, and their agency. Rather than arguing further for the multicultural inclusion of minority bodies, this book deploys minoritarian life to revise the very terms that structure existence.

Before illustrating these goals and delving into what I identify throughout each chapter as a set of minor modes as they relate to social structuration, I offer background in chapter 1 on contemporary China and its art. I expand this, however, beyond a localized examination of China to contend with larger issues surrounding late liberalism, race, financialization, capitalist modernity, the culture wars, and interdisciplinarity as they shape the art market around 1989. In particular, I analyze Cai Guo-Qiang's *Venice's Rent Collection Courtyard* to illustrate concerns around postsocialism, reperformance, and late capital; the work ultimately helps us produce a theory of the aesthetic for its relation to the political beyond a model of liberalism.

Chapter 2 turns to the ways the art market has included China. I examine the work of Ai Weiwei and read his aesthetics against the dominant ways he is discussed as a resistant artist. I instead turn to his formal use of repetition, which I situate in relation to his critique of the racist trope that all Asians look the same. I argue that the artist does not simply counter this racist trope by humanizing Chinese subjects. Ai moves us beyond modes of multicultural inclusion and intersubjective exchange in order to think through socialist legacies, comrade aesthetics, racialized masses, and the multitude. I offer the structural affect of racial anger, arising from being repeatedly read as "all looking the same," to reformulate how inclusion is conceptualized by not only liberalism, but also leftist and Marxist discourses around the multitude.

Chapter 3 renegotiates history and context, as they relate to recurring debates over the universal and particular. I focus on two projects. First, I discuss how the curatorial practices of Liu Ding, Carol Yinghua Lu, and Su Wei produce alternative formations of the history of contemporary Chinese art. Rather than structuring their exhibits based on historical time, they emphasize how artists related to one another and felt. In other words, they turn to affect as a curatorial method and shift away from depicting the history of Chinese art through a linear or filial model. This seemingly simple shift renegotiates teleological formations of time that structure the non-West within understandings of developing from ancient to modern. Second, I examine the work of Yan Xing. His use of fuzzy, molecular, and formal aesthetics, along with his engagement with parody, renegotiates how bodies, ranging from individual to national, can be read through affective means. The overall goal of this chapter is to situate how minor analytics from Deleuze and Guattari bring to the fore disciplinary fractures across the very fields that engage minor subjects. This pairing of art projects ultimately reconsiders the debate surrounding universality and particularity. These works do not provide an answer per se; rather, they each question how and why this debate recurs, allowing us to scale back (not discard) the idea of the universal.

Following history and context, I then pivot in chapter 4 to overdetermined theorizations around subjects and their agency, questioning the narrative of resistance that structures non-Western artists. I examine two minor modes of imagination—fabulation and meditation—that reconsider strong forms of resistance and cognition. Both meditation and fabulation intervene in the Marxist model of demystification as it enmeshes with performativity. Demystification and performativity structure the normative foundations of political critique as a linear relation across demystified subject, art object, and performed resistance. I first revisit the canonical work of Zhang Huan to reconsider his performances against the grain. Most have situated Zhang through endurance as he is commonly understood as resisting the rapid modernization of China; however, I focus on his use of meditation as a cognitive mode to rethink agency and demystification. In addition, He Chengyao's use of meditation within her artistic practice directs us to less stable forms of critique that do not default into ableist norms surrounding cognition. Her performances undo narratives of trauma that dominate our understandings of Third World women. Lastly, I discuss how Cao Fei's photos document the phenomenon of cosplay and direct us to the imaginary form of fabulation that complicates what counts as political critique.

Chapter 5 situates minor China in relation to the grand notions of totality and social structuration. I examine Black queer British artist Isaac Julien's turn to the history of China in *Ten Thousand Waves*. This immersive video installation depicts divergent moments in Chinese history to reformulate the Marxist tradition around totality, the Deleuzo-Guattarian monad, and the Frankfurt School use of minor forms through the *Denkbilder* (the "thought-image"). By focusing on structural changes across capital and late capital, modernity and postmodernity, and the bodies we use for the labor in these shifts, we obtain a fuller sense of all worlds, what Édouard Glissant calls the *tout-monde*, through the fractures across different forms of racialization. In particular, Julien focuses on China in ways that require different senses to contend with late capital and the tout-monde. In addition, the artist engages the different roles Chinese women play across theater and film to reconsider racialized and gendered objecthood. As both theatrical surrogate and cinematic icon, the Chinese woman offers an ethics for renegotiating object repetition and relationality in the *tout-monde*.

Moreover, chapter 5 highlights a central objective for this book: to consider what minor China as a method offers for the relational turn occurring across the humanities. Affect, becoming, and other minor approaches have provided mechanisms that blur our understandings of individual subjects and spaces in order to consider them in relation, beyond their singular bounds and identities. In this way, subjects come to be in relation to one another to produce forms of solidarity and to imagine other modes of political engagement. Amid this relational turn, afforded through minor methods, a number of questions arise surrounding how we presume relationality as stable or finite and what we do with histories around different forms of racialization (particularly anti-Blackness and indigenous genocide) that are often obscured in bids for connection. I bring to the fore questions around relationality, particularly in chapters 2, 3, and 5.

In the afterword, I close the book with a discussion of the idea that, in fact, China is quite major, especially for those who are minorities within China and minor to China (Taiwan, Hong Kong, Southeast Asia, and other spaces). When we consider China's own colonial relations throughout the region, alongside the hegemony of Han Chinese, it initially appears difficult to respond to the minor as proposed in this book. I contend with this question through the work of Hong Kong sound and media artist Samson Young. His *Songs for Disaster Relief* at the Fifty-Seventh Venice Biennale provides a critical example of how to engage the immediacy of China's presence through the minor.

1

We're Going to Party Like It's 1989

PROPER CHINA, INTERDISCIPLINARITY, AND THE GLOBAL ART MARKET

China refers to either a proper or common noun. As a proper noun that names a specific location, China becomes capitalized. As a common noun that names a general or nonspecific set of porcelain things, china is lowercase. This difference between China and china has been captured quite well by modernist writer Gertrude Stein: "In China there is no need of China, because in China china is china."[1] Although the common noun china ordinarily refers to fine objects like bowls, teacups, and other collectible items, Stein considers another connotation for the common form. Proper China becomes common china, when the nation is not sensationalized in its prototypical mode as the West's major dialectical other. This delineation between the common and proper for China brings to the fore how the nation is predominantly understood in its major form across a variety of areas, from world history and critical theory to the global art market.

Institutions that engage China rely on and reproduce proper understandings of the nation and its culture, since they are immediately recognizable. For example, the photo of a person standing up against a column of tanks at Tiananmen Square on June 5, 1989, exemplifies the economized, proper, and major images that have become shorthand for China as authoritarian and its resistors as proponents of liberal freedom. Through the proper, the non-West's legibility is prescribed through a discourse that appeals to established sense. The proper makes sense of and renders stable the objects we encounter. By contrast, when a nation is imagined as common, then we might begin to ask some clarifying questions: Do you mean an object? What kind of object? When does China become china? How so? And can this only occur within China or can China be china in the global? Rendering China common is impossible; however, it is the common that inspires an interrogative, hesitant mode. To lower-case China in this way does not simply mean to domesticate nor familiarize the nation. When institutions view other sites as equal or just another country, it merely expands the West's purview of the world rather than reordering its logics and terms. Our goal should not be to make a non-Western site common and equal to all nations, thereby rendering it easy to include into discourse. In other words, Stein's playful delineation between forms of China reminds us to hesitate from the immediate allure of arguing to be included and thus recognized as commensurate to other (Western) nations.

This chapter examines how the proper functions as a governing logic for the global art market and beyond. The proper informs the liberal logics of inclusion that propel the rapid circulation of cultural objects (through immediately legible means) and accumulation of capital. In other words, the proper lubricates the relationship across inclusion, circulation, and profit, bringing to the fore the dominant inflections of liberalism and late capital for institutions. This chapter describes and historicizes China's entrance into the global art market in order to highlight how the proper undergirds many arenas well beyond art organizations. Most studies on the art market have focused on shifting forms of financialization, providing historical background on the key players responsible for the rapid rise in financial stakes.[2] Others offer a more intimate view of the art world through insider or ethnographic insights.[3] While some have been critical of the financial benefits and tax havens afforded by contemporary art transactions,[4] and most approaches situate the market in relation to changes in financialization, they generally do not provide a more global historicization in terms of its emergence and overlap with late liberalism, race, and capital.

These approaches often leave in place visions of the non-West and a notion of culture that are predetermined; they do not adequately grapple with the role of this market in relation to capitalist modernity and to the global logics surrounding inclusion. To help bring this into view, I offer a broader contextualization of the market and show how the proper and China play central roles in these dynamics. More specifically, I furnish a general overview of the political, medial, and theoretical discourses that fuel the increased circulation of the proper non-West across a range of fields and practices that occurred at the end of the twentieth century. I do so to illustrate the expansive network that relies on immediately legible narratives of the non-West and its culture. I also offer background on China's contemporary art scene in order to analyze how the proper limits more complex understandings of this history.[5] Overall, this chapter traces the overlap of aesthetics and politics discourse, the global art market, the culture wars, and interdisciplinarity around 1989 as it conditions the emergence of China and approaches to the non-West. To help illustrate how these issues intersect with contemporary art and artists, I end this chapter with a consideration of Cai Guo-Qiang, an artist whose *Venice's Rent Collection Courtyard* (1999)—which won the Golden Lion Award at the Venice Biennale to great controversy—provides a particularly useful lens into these larger structures.

Although one cannot per se produce a causal relationship across China, aesthetic politics discourse, multiculturalism, and racialization as it relates to the transnational, interdisciplinarity, the culture wars, and the global market, these elements nevertheless coagulate and enable a condition of late liberalist logics to predominate. By looking across these contexts and institutions—but without trying to offer a definitive correlation across them—it is possible to trace the larger conditions by which proper China and liberal inclusion dictate our understandings of culture and the global. This chapter ultimately tracks a large range of discourses and illuminates the institutions and logics that uphold the proper. These are offered so as to rethink and highlight the limits surrounding the constant inclusion of minor subjects and minor geographic spaces in today's world. In the literature on the global art market, little has been written on these multiple threads that construct the post–Cold War and postdecolonization movements that occurred globally to inform a specific and "proper" understanding of culture from the non-West for the art market.[6] But the logics of the art market, critical theory, academic field formations, and political institutions overlap in significant ways. To grasp the way China is rendered proper, it is essential to look closely at these connections, particularly by affectively approaching ideas of culture, the political, and history.[7]

To do this, I focus on the year 1989, specifically as a lens for historicizing the above-mentioned coinciding contexts. Across this range of fields and institutions, 1989 is a notable year. Some use 1989 to mark the beginning of what have come to be known as contemporary art and world art.[8] Alongside the rise of the global art market, 1989 also marks a moment when the academic discourse on aesthetics and politics gained significant traction. How and why does 1989 become the year when both the global art market and the discourse on aesthetics and politics develop considerable momentum, although they each existed well before? Furthermore, at the same time as the art market and these discourses both increased in use, the global Left was also waning, as 1989 is often declared a wistful year for Marxist politics. Rather than provide a full historical account, I use this period to index how China is perceived, along with China's own complicated relationship to the Cultural Revolution and late capital; 1989 helps trace a critical transitional moment in terms of modes of governance, with shifts from Maoism to Chinese capitalism. Of course, well before this key year, China existed in proper ways within the West's imagination, from early trade routes established during the Qing empire to the Opium Wars and various immigration acts. Immediately preceding 1989, the Cold War, for example, shaped Orientalist visions of China as both foreign and threatening, with President Nixon's visit to China in 1972 and the academic industry surrounding area studies fueling the production of China as proper and translatable (after intensive study). Even when China has been seen as mysterious and its subjects inscrutable, the task for area studies and state intervention has been to methodically render the nation legible through accounts of its history, languages, and people taken as solidified truths and "ontological absolutes."[9]

Events in 1989 buttress this historical rendering of China as knowable and proper, even as the nation changes in status within the global imaginary. China's position in the world radically shifts during the end of the twentieth century. The excesses of the Cultural Revolution come to be mediated through a different form of autocratic rule and relation to capitalism. As such, the widespread distribution of the mediatized events at Tiananmen Square in 1989 illustrate this change, particularly as it coincides with the global curiosity and interest in not only what are perceived as illiberal and autocratic forms of governance, but also culture through contemporary art. The events at Tiananmen directly preceded the inclusion of Chinese artists in one of the first shows that centrally featured non-Western artists, the Centre Pompidou's 1989 exhibit *Magiciens de la Terre*. The Paris show helped produce interest in not only Chinese art, but also non-Western art more generally, as the exhibit featured over a hundred artists with 50 percent of them from the non-West. Moreover, the afterlife of the show illuminates the accelerated global art market interest in China. There was an explosion of shows explicitly focused on contemporary Chinese art following *Magiciens* at the Venice Biennale and other global art centers. Further, *Magiciens* catapulted the careers of the three Chinese artists and many of the other non-Western artists included in the show.

As a result, there came a swift rise in the market share for Chinese art. And in 2016, Chinese art became the first to demand higher prices than American art in international auctions: China garnered 38 percent (for the US, it was 28 percent) of the $12.45 billion in public fine arts sales.[10] During the end of the twentieth century, shifts in financialization with global entities, like the International Monetary Fund and the World Bank, facilitated faster trade that extended well beyond agriculture and consumer goods. And although other regions are currently gaining a larger share of the market, China nonetheless is the first non-Western space to eclipse Western nations to this degree. Further, for contemporary art auctions, the vast majority of the highest sellers are from the US and Europe; the non-Western artists included within the top sales are Chinese (Cui Ruzhuo and Zeng Fanzhi), with one Japanese artist (Yayoi Kusama). Additionally, Huang Yong Ping became the first Chinese-born artist to represent France at the 1999 Venice Biennale. Huang, who was featured in the 1989 *Magiciens* show, exemplifies the expansion of contemporary Chinese art beyond the confines of a single nation. Also, during the 1999 Venice Biennale, nineteen additional Chinese artists, including Cai Guo-Qiang, participated, which outnumbered the combined total of American and Italian artists that year. It is for these reasons that China offers a critical aperture into the larger logics of the market, particularly its turn toward inclusion.

This chapter illuminates these logics that inform and drive the swift rise in the market for contemporary Chinese art in order to resist the lure of and fervor for the further inclusion of other non-Western sites and minor subjects. This history points to how China indexes the operations of this market, alongside the limited ways in which culture comes to be understood. In particular, how China is included indicates the larger production of what has come to be known as non-Western or global art, particularly through racial logics. Immediately following China's inclusion into the global art market, there was an uptick in contemporary art coming from regions outside of the US and Western Europe. Thus, rather than simply include more nations and bemoan the lack of attention paid to other countries that have yet to be considered in the purview of or recognition under canonical discourses, we should instead understand the structures and logics that maintain these uneven systems in the first place. China becomes the starting point by which to track what upholds such limited, proper notions of culture and the non-West. Thus, before illustrating throughout this chapter the particular institutions and discourses that maintain the proper from within China around 1989 and globally, I briefly sketch out these mechanisms and structures

41

within the art market, film industry, culture wars, and academic discourse on aesthetics and politics.

Approaching China in this way helps us unravel the entwinement of racial logics, global capital, and practices of inclusion. Such an analytic and approach that historicize 1989 are necessary since this market interest has been shifting to South Asia, the Middle East, Central America, West Africa, and Southeast Asia. Even as the list keeps on growing, the same disagreements and underlying assumptions remain. For China *and* other spaces, debates develop in predictable ways: primarily foreign scholars engage a site; arguments ensue around contextualization; locals demand specificity; universal-particular debates erupt; and then the market moves onto the next site, with certain collectors accruing returns from their art investments. This discursive pattern structures how non-Western art continues to be received and emerges from disciplinary fractures following Cold War policies and area studies. But to see how these discursive structures have imposed limits on our understandings of China, rather than enter debates over particularity, universality, or contextualization, it is important to analyze such disciplinary divides *and* the presumptions and terms (like culture, art, and the political) that construct these ongoing and predictable debates. The economy of the global art market relies on reproducing the proper forms of the non-West in order to enable a quick circulation of culture that translates into profits for art-owning classes.

The art market, of course, is not simply produced through the West. The São Paulo Biennial was founded in 1951 and is the second-oldest after Venice; and the Havana Biennial began in 1984 with a specific focus on artists from the Global South. Although China is not the first non-Western country to enter this global network, China comes to enter it with a different intensity. Further, Asia has become quite central to the production of the market, with biennials and contemporary art museums emerging across the region at a rapid pace. Within mainland China itself, thirteen biennials currently exist, along with over 5,100 museums (a massive increase from the 349 that existed in 1978). Although many of these museums are not for contemporary art and are minimally used or resourced, the sheer number of museums exemplifies state and private investments in the notion of culture. Beyond China, biennials and museums have similarly arisen in quantity across Hong Kong, Singapore, South Korea, Japan, Taiwan, and Vietnam, among other countries. The art market is global in scope, and Asia has come to play an important role in its entrenchment.

Beyond the art market, the development and distribution of international art house cinema comes to similarly fuel the rise of proper understandings of China. Changes in media practices and distribution enable novel ways of circulating and consuming the non-West. The end of the Cultural Revolution and the expansion of art education in China sync with the growth of the film industry and art world. Although world cinema has existed since film's inception at the end of the nineteenth century, it developed during the 1960s and gained momentum at the end of the twentieth century, alongside the growth of the art market. Further, although Chinese cinema has an established history well before the end of the Cultural Revolution, it is during the 1980s and onward that Chinese film comes to be enfolded with greater intensity into a larger transnational market. One can track these overlaps through the growth in recognition in both China's film directors and artists: those known as the Fifth and Sixth Generations of directors arise at the same moment as art-world stars. In addition, at the end of the twentieth century, photojournalism intensified the circulation of images due to technological advances through the 1970s, such as increasingly portable cameras and improvements in lighting technology. This momentum in the circulation of images helped reproduce the rendering of China proper, notably the images of the Tiananmen Square protests of 1989. The increased rates of circulation from journalism and cinematography, as well as visual art and performance through images and film, all buttressed this rendering of China proper. The proper thus facilitates this circulation through digestible and legible narratives about major China.[11] Even though many of these artists and artworks provide more formally and politically complex ideas, proper discourses obscure these presumed minor details.

Additionally, 1989 marks an important moment for changes in the logics of inclusion that were operating in both national and transnational contexts and across these medial spaces. In particular, 1989 heralds the culture wars inside and outside of the US academy and the subsequent rise and dominance of inclusionary logics. While curricula expanded to include gender and ethnic studies across a variety of disciplines, analyses of the non-West also gained traction. The assumptions and approaches around race and difference during this time inform how the non-West is understood and engaged: as minor, peripheral subjects to be enfolded into discourse. The end of the twentieth century indicated a broader inclusion of other sites that were historically excluded from the idea of the global. However, this extension did not simply render China into china. Instead, the larger reach of the global established and continues to maintain the non-West in its proper, racialized form: China remains China. Additional inclusion has not led to rendering China into a common entity but has rather further exacerbated its difference from the West.

More importantly, although inclusion expands our purview of certain areas across the world, it only does so with respect to areas that buttress the growth of late capital, what Rebecca Karl identifies as an "economically monotone, global space."[12] Indeed, 1989 also depicts a moment when the global Left was waning, and, for many, the year has come to represent the production of a world dominated by late capitalist logics, or what Francis Fukuyama problematically called "the end of history." This pivotal moment and its lingering aftermath have been heralded as a new liberalism, in the words of Roderick Ferguson, or a late liberalism, according to Elizabeth Povinelli.[13] As Ferguson establishes, new or late liberalism operates by "using difference to foster capitalist distribution while curtailing social redistribution for underrepresented folks."[14] As both of these theorists emphasize, and as I historicize further below, inclusion occurs through legible and proper understandings of the non-West and does not fundamentally change how institutions function. Late liberalism, in other words, deploys inclusion and increased representation so as to facilitate the normative operations and growth of late capital.

Lastly, the time period around 1989 marks the publication of theoretical projects that establish aesthetics and politics as a discourse. Within art history, many grappled with the field's relations to postmodernism and postcolonialism during the end of the twentieth century, with a push for scholars and curators to reconsider their own practices. Many drew from insights afforded by anthropology's self-reflexive moment, along with the development of standpoint epistemology from feminist studies, to engage in these disciplinary shifts. Rasheed Araeen's inauguration of the journal *Third Text* in 1987 demonstrates the push for such concerns around the non-West, theory, postcolonial critique, and the condition of the proper for the non-West. Further, Jacques Rancière's initial musings on the framework of aesthetics and politics, arguably one of the most established approaches, was first published in 1990 in his book *Courts voyages au pays du peuple*. Rancière primarily attends to the experience of class in film and literature, further developing his theorizations on aesthetics and politics in texts that followed. Although *Courts voyages* focuses on the short voyages and experiences of class within Western Europe, Rancière begins his book with the specter of proper China and the Cultural Revolution: "The dull gray of a winter sky upon concrete apartment blocks . . . of a shantytown can fulfill the traveler if it represents him with what he has long sought and can immediately recognize, in its very foreignness, as just like what he has already spoken, read, heard, and dreamed: the proletariat in person. Such was the flower, its living reality just waiting to be plucked, that a certain text of Mao Zedong's promised to those who agreed to go out, leaving behind books and cities, and get down off their horses."[15]

China appears in its proper form as represented by Mao, which becomes an animating force for many of Rancière's ideas.[16] And beyond China, the notions of culture, art, and aesthetics are additionally engaged in proper ways. Under late liberalism, culture takes on a limited meaning, understood as apart from yet central to the political. The aesthetic and culture are in turn conceptualized as significant for politics because they are presumed to expand communal sensibilities around *whom we value* by increasing the representation of those minor voices that were previously excluded. The minorness of the aesthetic is not approached on its own terms or in its entanglement with social structures; rather, the aesthetic's value is articulated through an appeal to late liberal logics, equating increased representation with progress through the broadening of communal sensibility. This chapter develops a theory of the aesthetic that is not based within a model of liberal representationalism so as to articulate culture's relationship to the political. Contemporary theorizations surrounding the politics of aesthetics (or, aesthetics and politics) formulate the aesthetic to be as major as the political. As a result, culture comes to be fetishized as the recurrent place for possibility and resistance against the state. Culture is thus imagined as enshrined away from rather than entwined with the problems, limits, and possibilities of the political and social. Rancière's discourse on aesthetics and politics recapitulates and reinforces this late liberal definition of culture, art, and aesthetics by producing agency for these minor terms in ways that separate them from the political so as to render them core to politics.[17] And when situated within the cultures wars of the 1980s and 1990s, this limited understanding of culture comes further to the fore.

The art market, theoretical discourse, proper China, multiculturalism, academic disciplines, the rise of neoliberal economic logics, and the transnational turn overlap in dynamic ways around 1989. This chapter traces through these unwieldy yet uncanny convergences to track how the proper predominates to fuel the circulation of capital and to buttress logics surrounding the global. China, as one of the first countries to be heavily enfolded into the global art market, established some of the rules of inclusion for other non-Western spaces. Before discussing this in more detail, however, it is important to bring into view some of the key discursive developments of contemporary Chinese art.

Before 1989: The Cultural Revolution and Proper China

The Cultural Revolution is one of the main events that informs our understanding of modern China. This is widely evidenced across global, political, aesthetic, art, journalistic, and academic discourse. Consequently, the majority of art historians and curators within the global art market situate contemporary Chinese art with the Cultural Revolution. With the defeat of the nationalist Kuomintang (KMT) Party to the Chinese Communist Party (CCP) in 1949, the larger project of unifying China through communism came to be a critical yet daunting task. What media, political maneuvers, organizing, labor, education, language, infrastructures, agricultural development, and artistic production were needed to facilitate the unification of about 500–600 million people over 3.7 million square miles? Art, along with all other areas of life, was expected to directly mediate the interests of the CCP. Mao Zedong, as its chairman, led the efforts to deploy every form of social and private life for the sole purpose of communism. A series of efforts came under the framework of the Cultural Revolution, which began in 1966. The goal was to reeducate China's urban elites to understand the realities of rural workers. With the support of student activists known as the Red Guard, Mao solidified his leadership of the CCP and inspired a movement for widespread socialism. The Red Guard and enforcement of the Cultural Revolution led to the creation of reeducation and labor camps in rural areas and the persecution, and, at times, execution, of millions of individuals not seen as fully sympathetic to the cause.

The Cultural Revolution, which Mao declared over in 1969 but which did not halt until Mao's death in 1976, has come to shape most every narrative surrounding modern and contemporary China—particularly notable in the discourse of contemporary art. These narratives are focused on the traumatic effects of the Cultural Revolution on artists, intellectuals, citizens, and daily life. However, from an analytical perspective, it would certainly be possible to think of the Revolution as serving many other purposes. For example, looking at the radicalization of youth cultures during the 1960s, the Red Guard and the student movements inform how the world received Maoism during global revolutions of the 1960s and, for French Maoists, May 1968.

Further, the revolution demonstrated profound aesthetic shifts that went beyond mere propaganda. A number of scholars have turned to thinking about the aesthetic qualities of the revolution through notions of kitsch and political change.[18] But even if these other approaches consider the revolution in more nuanced ways through youth cultures and aesthetics, most accounts of contemporary Chinese art and artists tether artists' psyches to their artistic production.

For those artists who immediately experienced the Cultural Revolution as adults, their works are often framed as responding directly to state abuses (usually through realist techniques). For those who were children or born during the revolution, their art objects are understood as contending with witnessing state abuses upon their families and responding with less of a direct critique or sense of urgency (thus, a turn to abstraction). For those born after 1976, their works are often situated as not being as burdened by the aftermath of the revolution and seeking to imagine other pasts, presents, and futures for China (hence, they deploy more open explorations with form and content). This generalized framework dominates how most artists are understood within a formula that links generational relations to a proper historical event, psychoanalytic states, and aesthetic output. Realism corresponds to immediate trauma; abstraction responds to slight distance from the event; and experimentation reveals a less direct mediation with the past. The revolution thus becomes the shorthand by which to particularize China into the proper. This schematic, of course, is not meant to discount the import of such frames; however, it is their predominance and repetition that arrest China into the major and proper.

For example, the 2012 exhibit *On/Off* at Beijing's Ullens Center for Contemporary Art relied on this temporal logic that weds historical context to artistic production. The show focused on artists born after 1975 to illuminate a generation's concerns beyond the anchor of the Cultural Revolution. Curators Bao Dong and Sun Dongdong chose the title to reflect the online proxy networks that younger Chinese use to circumvent the government's firewall. By focusing on those born after the Cultural Revolution and media surveillance, the curators narrow the analytic possibilities of the works in *On/Off*. Their curatorial frame replicates the assumption of a direct relation between generational status and artistic production. This oft-deployed framework presumes an immediate and legible mediation across history, psyche, and creative output. The works presented, however, exceed the logics of historical contextualization. Li Liao's performance *Consumption* (2012) involved documentation of time spent working at Foxconn, one of Apple's manufacturing plants. Upon earning enough to purchase an iPad, the artist left the factory and ended his performance (figure 1.1). Although the piece certainly deals with new media and aesthetic experimentation, Li Liao's performance additionally allows us to consider a deeper history. For example, although the artist experiments with and directs us to the divide between material and immaterial labor in today's digital world, such concerns have ramifications surrounding the state of postsocialism. In particular, a direct return to the Cultural Revolution might help us grapple with changes in labor practices as they demand different approaches for socialist ends. Yet, the curatorial frame limits this piece within generational concerns that are delinked from longer temporal arcs. Earlier exhibitions of contemporary Chinese art have similarly relied upon the Cultural Revolution to serve as the legible historical anchor that explains artistic concerns. *On/Off* illustrates this developmental logic, as Li Liao's and others' works are primarily framed as working beyond the Cultural Revolution through aesthetic experimentation. The overdetermined relation between object and context economizes how China and other non-Western spaces have come to be understood.

This turn to context, with the Cultural Revolution as the organizing moment, was necessary because earlier journalistic and art historical discourses tended to minimally situate the works in relation to China's history. As such, many Chinese authors demanded further historicization and localized accounts of the art's emergence.[19] In other words, the force of law, as discussed in the introduction, shaped the immediate reactions by Chinese theorists and art historians. In these bids to show the vibrant dynamics and realities of Chinese art, however, the discourse came to congeal in immediately legible and proper ways. The predominance of such demands for context limits other possible engagements that might appear minor or decontextualized at first blush. The continual demand for specificity and particularity has culminated into the solidification of the non-West as properly knowable when translated by native informants.

Following these initial preoccupations, the second wave of criticism primarily cataloged key artists and movements, a framing that continues today.[20] The Cultural Revolution nonetheless remains a central anchor, even as a fuller picture of art practices across China has emerged. Scholars with art historical knowledge of Chinese art explore histories that expand the temporal parameters of contemporary Chinese art and broaden the central figures involved in the movement. In particular, academic research began to examine art groups that emerged between 1984 and 1986, specifically those experimenting with form and media, most notably the Stars,

Figure 1.1. Li Liao, *Consumption*, 2012. Performance documentation, readymade materials (iPad mini). © Li Liao. Courtesy of Eli Klein Gallery and the artist.

Northern Art Group, Pond Association, and Xiamen Dada. They were located in divergent geographic locations across China and had different aesthetic agendas.

Following this expansion of the historical parameters and figures involved in contemporary Chinese art, historians and theorists also focused on issues surrounding migration, diaspora, globalization, and modernity.[21] Most edited collections on contemporary Asian or Chinese art follow this arc from contextualization to globalization.[22] Even amid turns to the global, proper forms of China are reproduced, particularly through accounts of exile. These narratives reinforce a discourse about the authoritarian state without engaging "the artists' creative efforts and the cultural-intellectual values of the work."[23] Curator Hou Hanru locates this as a "methodology of the Western official ideological propaganda during the Cold War."[24] Hou notably points us to proper formulations of China that predominate over other understandings of this body of art. This overview of the discourse reveals a reliance on historicization, with the Cultural Revolution and state authoritarianism as its central anchors. Although later trends in criticism have turned toward the global, the organizing logics around the state and generational divides nonetheless predominate as exemplified by the curatorial frame for the *On/Off* exhibit. Proper understandings of China as authoritarian continue to shape more recent accounts of this art in its distribution and circulation. Although the demand for context initially emerged to counter earlier Eurocentric discourses, it has reigned in ways that further condition China through the proper.

After the death of Mao in 1976, struggles around control of the CCP arose. Most leaders sought a shift in politics from that of the Cultural Revolution. Under the guidance of Deng Xiaoping, China liberalized its approach to education and economic development. As part of this process, many art institutions reopened during the 1980s. Film, literature, art books, and theoretical texts were easier to access. Art journals proliferated, specifically *Jiangsu Pictorial (Jiangsu huakan)*, *Fine Arts in China (Zhongguo meishu bao)*, and *The Trend of Art Thought (Meishu sichao)*. Further, works from and accounts of contemporary Japanese and Western art became increasingly available in Chinese; art objects from Europe and the US were exhibited with greater frequency. An exhibition that is often cited by artists and historians is Robert Rauschenberg's 1985 exhibit at the National Art Museum in Beijing. The *Rauschenberg Overseas Culture Interchange* exhibit was the first American show in China in fifty years and included over 125 works. After an apprenticeship at the world's oldest paper mill in Jingxian, Rauschenberg sought to tour his show to Beijing. The exhibit attracted an estimated 300,000 viewers in its twenty-day run. Rauschenberg's show inspired a renewed emphasis among Chinese artists on experimental practices, although many of the practices that gained energy at this time were already occurring before 1985. This moment of avant-garde and conceptual art came to be known as the '85 Art New Wave.

In addition to the Cultural Revolution, Rauschenberg's show became another anchor for theorists and historians of contemporary Chinese art. The show brings to the fore larger issues surrounding how contemporary Chinese art has come to be narrated through debates over the art as derivative of and mimicking Western art. This moment of increased global circulation usually results in disagreements over originality—a common debate for non-Western art at large. Most famously, the political pop movement of the 1980s and cynical realism of the 1990s were both dismissed for being derivative of Western contemporary art. The aesthetics of these two movements shared characteristics with that of Andy Warhol, including his use of everyday commercial objects, and Max Ernst, particularly his hyperbolic and surrealist depictions of the body. However, many viewed Chinese artists as simply replicating these Western "masters" while adding Chinese characteristics.

Holland Carter, the *New York Times* art critic, opened his 1996 review of the Asia Society's exhibit *Traditions/Tensions: Contemporary Art in Asia* by quoting a friend who accompanied him to the exhibit: "Contemporary Art in India? There is no contemporary art in India."[25] This anecdote illustrates how Asian artists are myopically situated within notions of tradition, making any gesture toward formal experimentation seem unimaginable or else merely derivative. Vishakha Desai picks up on this account to note how the early discourses on contemporary Asian art primarily questioned the originality of contemporary Asian works, foreclosing other modes of engaging the art beyond this proper discourse surrounding innovation and derivation.[26]

To counter such critiques, scholars have emphasized the need for deeper contextualization and historicization—a turn to specificity. For example, Gao Minglu in *Total Modernity* encapsulates this demand for the particular: "It becomes unlikely, therefore that either of these [avant-garde] theories (Marx's alienation nor Bürger's institutionalized capitalism and avant-garde) will work for the Chinese model of the avant-garde, because the Chinese institutional system has been constructed in a totally different way."[27] This push toward specificity is meant to complicate discourses on derivation and originality. However, the continued insistence on particularity reinforces the proper, as it is meant to be the most legible way to respond to presumptions of the non-West as derivative. Such concerns were privileged over more minor ones, such as the formal, emotive, relational, and theoretical aspects of these works. As such, the discourse takes shape from the privileging of major notions like history and context in order to respond to Eurocentric and racist dismissals of art from the non-West. But this example further highlights the general trend surrounding how other non-Western spaces have come to be theorized in relation to culture: questions around derivation and the West emerge, critiques of Eurocentrism are launched, and an emphasis on history and context ensues. In this way, to be legible within this situation requires that an artist be discussed within the proper.

Curating 1989 and Beyond

In addition to the Cultural Revolution and debates over originality, the Tiananmen Square student protests of 1989 shape the narration of contemporary Chinese art. Global interest in Chinese art increased following the incident, as the event reinforced and played into discourses surrounding the authoritarian state. The year 1989 indexes changes in China's forms of governance from the decentralization of power given to the Red Guard during the Cultural

Revolution to a more centralized autocratic rule. Amid this shift in global perceptions surrounding the nation-state, publics came to transfix the art through this proper narrative that conflates autocracy with authoritarianism.

Before the June episode at Tiananmen, however—and pointing to the existing discourse on China connecting the authoritarian state to proper China—there was already a global proclivity toward the eventual reaction to the Tiananmen Square student protests. For example, earlier in 1989, one of the largest shows of experimental art practices in China opened in February: the *China/Avant-Garde* exhibition at Beijing's National Art Gallery. Although plans for it first occurred around 1986, the show came together after a series of negotiations with the CCP. The symbol for the exhibit was a "No U-Turn" traffic sign, which represented the inability to turn back. The 1989 showing extended throughout six exhibition halls totaling about twenty-two thousand square meters, with the inclusion of visual art, performance art, installation, and sculpture. The event, however, was temporarily shut down twice. On the opening day, it was first closed due to an unscheduled performance entitled *Dialogue* by Xiao Lu and Tang Song. The original installation involved a mirror with two phone booths, one on each side. In the unplanned performance, Xiao Lu entered the museum and shot a gun at the installation. As a result, the police shut down the show for five days. The second instance involved a fake bomb threat, which closed the gallery for three days. Increased national and international interest followed both of these closures, with narratives surrounding the authoritarian state rapidly circulating.

One exhibition that benefitted from the timing of the *China/Avant-Garde* exhibit and the events at Tiananmen was *Magiciens de la Terre*, which opened in Paris in May a month before the 1989 televised protests. *Magiciens* exhibited over a hundred artists and was the first show to include contemporary Chinese artists within Europe or the United States. The show was envisioned as a critique of the Museum of Modern Art's (MOMA) *"Primitivism" in 20th Century Art: Affinity of the Tribal and the Modern*. The 1984–85 MOMA show was accused of limited representations of non-Western art, when the proper then took the form of primitivism. The head curator of *Magiciens*, Jean-Hubert Martin, sought to showcase a broad array of art from around the world, particularly the non-West.[28] As part of this massive gesture of inclusion, three Chinese artists were part of this show: Gu Dexin, Huang Yong Ping, and Yang Jiechang. Fei Dawei served as Martin's interlocutor, introducing him to artists across China. *Magiciens de la Terre* is important for the way it underlines how curatorial choices render the non-West proper, along with the shifting logics in what makes the proper legible. This show, moreover, highlights how the proper toggles across primitivism to historical context around the unmodern state. Put differently, the racialization of the non-West remains proper by locating backwardness in either its people or the state. For China around 1989, backwardness came to be located in the latter. In the coming years, many other large exhibits would go on to focus on contemporary Chinese artists. For example, in 1993, the Forty-Fifth Venice Biennale included contemporary Chinese artists for the first time.[29] Then, in 1999, ten years after *Magiciens*, China had its own pavilion at Venice. This trend of including Chinese artists in highly visible global art exhibits occurred within a span of about ten years and illustrates how quickly the conversations surrounding inclusion in the global art market took shape. Along with this, a growing need arose to rapidly develop a discourse to contend with art emerging from these diverse contexts. These exhibitions, along with many others that proliferated across the globe at this time and which consistently framed Chinese art and artists through the lens of the proper and relied on liberal approaches to inclusion, were central to the distribution of contemporary Chinese art.[30] In the section below, I turn to tracing the broader global dynamics that catalyzed this movement.

Beyond China, c. 1989

As outlined in the previous sections of this chapter, the conditions that enabled the entrance of China into transnational consideration—specifically the global rise of late liberalist logics that facilitate the very conditions that produce the minor as subject—have rendered China properly understood as a subject/object to be included through contextualization and state discourse. In this section below, I outline the historical and academic conditions that dictate how minorness—a key method for grasping the larger structuration of proper China—becomes primarily ascribed and limited to a subject or geographic position. I additionally locate the roles of culture and the aesthetic as they relate to these concerns.

Roderick Ferguson and Sara Ahmed have offered trenchant accounts of the connections between the operations of the global and understandings of diversity. According to Ferguson, "the U.S. constitutional project would give birth to twins—the modern idea of empire and the modern idea of difference; under that ideological formulation, the management of the international would coextend with the management of diversity."[31] Within this framework, China is situated within the logics of inclusion that similarly conceptualize the enfoldment of racialized nations with the inclusion of minority difference. In both cases, the minor other only becomes a knowable and specific subject to be included, rather than a source to methodologically rethink the operations of established frameworks and terms. However, in order to understand how China is rendered within larger structurations of power, it is critical that we interrogate how minorness became primarily ascribed to a subject or geographic position.

China is indicative of the rise of late liberalism and its logics of inclusion; China offers a blueprint to understand how otherness becomes enfolded into discourse, art markets, and history. The global rise of liberalist logics is not simply evidence of the triumph of liberalism or, as Fukuyama would have it, the "end of world history." Instead, liberalism has come to buttress the proper and to delineate accepted presumptions across a liberal and illiberal divide. Proper logics are informed by liberal forms of recognition: representation and inclusion. China becomes legible within a global order when it is recognized as representing its proper form as authoritarian and the West's dialectical other, with contemporary culture and aesthetic production revealing possibilities and resistance to major China. In other words, China is properly illiberal, with culture envisioned as its proper liberal antidote. This comes to be the oft-deployed formula when discussing the non-West.

Many art historical accounts provide a broad contextualization of global art in relation to post–Cold War sensibilities and the economy.[32] However, it is important to extend the purview of these critical works toward these logics of inclusion as buttressed by not only neoliberal ideologies but also late capital and late liberalism. Povinelli has argued that it is necessary to move beyond liberalism as a historical marker in order to understand ways of contending with difference following global decolonization and other key movements, like Maoism, that occurred around and after the middle of the twentieth century. Unlike neoliberalism, late liberalism responds to questions around liberalism's legitimacy following the production of decolonized, utopic spaces. To contend with this, late liberalism shifted liberalism toward "a crisis of how to allow cultures a space within liberalism without rupturing the core frameworks of liberal justice. In short, in late liberalism to care for difference is to make a space for culture to care for difference without disturbing key ways of figuring experience—ordinary habitual truths."[33] Povinelli emphasizes the need to contend with the aftermath of earlier formations surrounding area, ethnic, gender, and queer studies. She establishes how these previous approaches to inclusion have led to a new demand whereby the minor other only finds value in its proper form. We tend to include at a more rapid rate without disturbing our dominant order and logics; we have arrived at a place where we now presumably care more about (or, perform care for) the other, but we do not invest in changing how we understand and approach the other and world. After all, such changes would involve letting go of established privileges, along with a redistribution and revolution in how property and power have been allocated. In addition, Povinelli directs us to the role of culture in this process, which has come to be understood as separate from yet significant to the political, institutional, and structural.

As the histories outlined above reveal surrounding how scholars came to react against past universalist discourse, the continual exclusion of China informs the force of law. This force demands proper legibility to counter Eurocentric and racist understandings around the minor other. However, in late liberalism, inclusion has become normalized whereby the minor as subject continues to be further included and represented but only in its proper form. In addition, the aesthetic and culture have been reduced to merely tools that assist in this project of increasing representation. In this way, I offer the minor as method to rethink and reformulate these late liberalist logics surrounding not only inclusion but also culture and the aesthetic.

Interdisciplinarity Goes Transnational

This reigning late liberal order arises from the production of the global, and it extends well beyond China and the art market, although the areas to which it extends are often intricately connected. For example, in universities, considered central for the production of knowledge and often interwoven with broader art market and curatorial discourses, the same liberal logics underpin many disciplinary boundaries and approaches—something that feeds back into the aesthetic and politics discourse on contemporary art and proper China. The notion of interdisciplinarity, which is often presumed as the vanguard for intellectual projects, is a useful illustration of this. In the context of the university, interdisciplinarity has emerged due to fractures between existing departments. For instance, area studies arose following the Second World War and was further consolidated during the Cold War to provide intelligence about nations central to US expansionism and economic concerns.[34] Area studies is therefore often separated from ethnic studies (in this case, Asian American studies). And as Karen Shimakawa and Kandice Chuh have pointed out, Asian American studies emerged from a history of student activism informed primarily through race and critiques of imperialism, both of which distinguish themselves from the goals of area studies.[35] More recently, Anjali Arondekar and Geeta Patel have located the interdisciplinary field of queer studies to reconsider the import and problems with both area and ethnic studies.[36] The project of interdisciplinarity, which is meant to smooth these fractures but which engages liberal logics of inclusion, does not resolve these foundational issues. Instead, they are glossed over and even entrenched, particularly when considering the transnational.

Within what has been called the transnational turn, interdisciplinarity is interwoven with late liberalist approaches to inclusion. The project of interdisciplinarity presumes that the increased representation of global otherness is the key goal, rather than reconsiderations of academic protocol and disciplinarity amid engagements with the non-West. Moreover, as Ferguson has noted, the logics of interdisciplinarity extend well beyond the university and art market toward state interests and capital accumulation: "Interdisciplinarity becomes much more than a matter contained within the academy. It becomes the episteme that organizes the regimes of representation for academy, state, and capital. . . . Hence, the institutionalization of difference becomes a question much larger than any single institution but becomes a logic of practice that establishes a network between all institutions in the United States."[37] When situated in relation to turns toward the non-West and the transnational, interdisciplinarity often limits such understandings of structural power that extend well beyond the university. With a dominant focus on increasing the representation of global otherness, interdisciplinarity expands our attention to different geographic locations through what Ella Shohat has called an "additive operation," without fully grappling with uneven foundational theories, frameworks, and the global dynamics surrounding capital accumulation and extraction.[38]

Put differently, we often include and increase representation without re-ordering. The proper conditions academic approaches, as they, at times, view a non-Western space as simply another site to be included without revising intellectual protocols and assumptions and without understanding the non-West as a source of methodological and theoretical import. When considering contemporary Chinese and global art within this turn to the non-West, we must contend with how minor subjects (from national minorities to non-Western sites) are operationalized through the proper. The minor, when rendered solely as a subject, prohibits other conversations beyond context and history. These broader turns within the university, and public and political discourses, inform the way proper China is rendered, while also illuminating how contemporary Chinese art comes to be established within late liberal logics of representation and inclusion. Our academic approaches often minimize other possibilities and models for deploying minoritarian and non-Western thought and production.

The 1989 *Magiciens de la Terre* exhibit illustrates these late liberalist approaches that inform both academic and curatorial modes of inclusion. *Magiciens* sought to place non-Western art tout court at the same "level" as Western art, according to the show's curator. The show exhibited Western and non-Western artists alongside one another, attempting to communicate a sense of equality and commonality across regions. This manifested in the curation of half of these artists coming from the West and the other from the non-West. By doing so, the show did not contend with the material differences and historical structures of colonization and race that have continually placed the non-West as proper (and as debtor nations). In other words, the late liberal logics of inclusion facilitate the forgetting of race and history in ways that equalize countries through the act of inclusion (rendering them theoretically common). The academic analogue to this is to include more non-Western sites and forms of social difference into curricula without considering how these populations afford a revision of the academic project at hand.

Late liberalism glosses over structural and historical issues, particularly when culture and the aesthetic are in play. Culture and the aesthetic are seen as mere indexes of and apertures into the non-West; they are not presumed as embedded in and, hence, as complex as the structural. In this way, acts of inclusion through culture are understood as safe, quaint, and appropriate ways to access the other. And even as contemporary discourses argue for the aesthetic to possess agency and to be significant for the political, the aesthetic and culture are nonetheless rendered separate from yet central to politics, structures, and political economy. As such, the continual reliance on a narrative of art as representing resistance against the state perpetuates limited formulations of the aesthetic; this discourse fulfills the desire to make the aesthetic valuable and worthy of study and momentarily placates those who have been under- or misrepresented. Such inclusion through culture renders the other legible and as an equal to the "West," while delimiting a full engagement with the histories around racialization, imperialism, and capitalist extraction that have afflicted the non-West and have unevenly produced our discourses, frameworks, and political imagination.

Consider Martin's opening remarks in *Magiciens*'s exhibition catalog: "However, from the idea of an investigation on the creation of the world today, one could imagine only presenting artists not from the Occident, knowing that we do not doubt the existence of art from our own centers. This would continue to place these creators in a ghetto, within an ethnographic category that comes from the archaic legacy of colonialism, while it is important to affirm their existence in the present moment."[39] Martin's approach uses inclusion to place non-Western art at the center; however, by framing these art practices as equivalent and common to all, he avoids explicitly contending with the structural and historical racism that has rendered such art proper. In turn, the show's curation deployed a universalizing frame to rationalize the inclusion of these divergent works: "All these objects, from here or elsewhere, have in common the possession of an aura. . . . It is the word 'magic' that captures what we find in common with one another in the lively and inexplicable influence that art exercises upon us."[40] This turn to Benjaminian aura becomes the vehicle by which to sidestep a deeper contention with what these multiple non-Western sites might provide as a method. These sites and the aesthetic could have been used to direct us to the structural barriers that render the non-West and culture putatively proper. Instead, the organizing framework for the show became "magic" as a way to universalize the function of art on the psyche. The mystical, however, perpetuates proper and historically racialized understandings of the non-Western other as the source of mysterious power requiring decoding and knowledge. In this case, the proper shifts from the primitive to the mystical. In other words, the turn to "magic" or aura nonetheless upholds the logics surrounding the non-West as proper even with the good intention of inclusion. As such, good liberal intentions only get us so far.

Such late liberal logics can be traced more specifically in the curation of China and Chinese art within *Magiciens*. Chinese artists are described in terms that make them immediately legible to US and European audiences. Gu Dexin's use of earth-toned plastic resembling organs and other ambiguous matter provides space to conceptualize not only human and social waste, but also affects like disgust and discomfort (figure 1.2). Although his work involves a complex melting of plastic objects resembling organs and uncanny shapes, the catalog places his piece within the discourse of Duchampian readymades. Moreover, for the works of Marina Abramović and Ulay that were presented in the show, China, as represented through the Great Wall, served as a mere backdrop. Both of their contributions drew from their solo time walking across two different ends of the wall. Their performance documents their eventual meeting and encounter in the middle of the Great Wall. The exhibition catalog describes this performance as the culmination

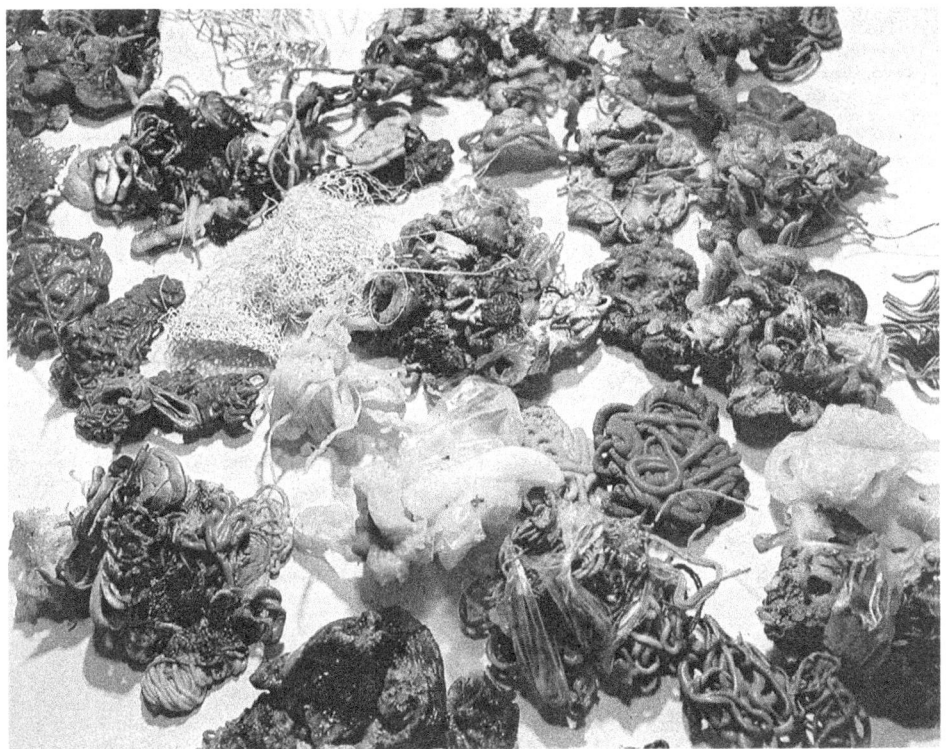

Figure 1.2. Gu Dexin, *Plastic Pieces—287*, 1983–85. 287 parts, overall dimensions vary with installation, CC Foundation. © Gu Dexin. Courtesy of Gu Dexin, Fei Dawei, and Asia Art Archive, Hong Kong.

of their travels, tracing their work with aboriginals in Australia and locals in Thailand to their final meeting in China. China becomes just another global space for these artists to traverse and include, providing an apt metaphor for the operations of late liberalism.

In the case of Gu's work, he is situated within China in its proper form, as the artist's piece is rendered immediately legible through Western discourse, as a Chinese version of Duchamp. For Abramović and Ulay, China remains proper China as well, as it serves as a mere backdrop for their performance. China, when refracted through either a Chinese or non-Chinese artist, cannot become common in ways that broaden theoretical and aesthetic concerns beyond the legibility of context. In other words, China operates in its prototypical proper form regardless of the artist involved. China remains China, never china.

The non-West is taken in its proper and legible forms so as to facilitate an ease in circulation and accumulation. Circulation and accumulation, however, occur at many different levels: private collectors, curators, state-sponsored institutions, private museums, attendees, artists, and the media. Since these levels operate at varied intensities, it is difficult to trace causal relations across them. What might be more helpful then is to understand how the proper lubricates the ease with which the non-West is presumed knowable and objects obtain value. This art market system, however, does not simply occur in the West. As noted earlier, there is an established history of biennials and other contemporary art festivals throughout the non-West, with a particular rise across East Asia. Specifically, Hong Kong has become a central locus for international art fairs. Similar to China entering the "global" stage in terms of governance and control, the rise of East Asian centers for the art market is not simply cause for celebration. Instead, their inclusion should force us to track the logics that permit entrance into this global order. They become another center of accumulation for late capital, broadening its reach. Their growth and inclusion indicate and ensure that this system runs with greater capacity and ease.

How We've Done Things to Culture

This overview of how China arises in the art market and academic discourse brings to the fore the import of grappling with how we conceptualize culture, art, and aesthetics. Although these terms are usually understood as minor in comparison to the major realm of politics, they are often rendered proper and to be as important and effective as the political. These minor notions surrounding the aesthetic, when paired with the non-West, operate in service of late liberal approaches to difference, minor subjects, and the proper. In particular, the rise in the art market of the non-West informed academic fields to what has come to be called global art and world art studies. In 1992, John Onians coined the term *world art studies*, which was also part of the renaming of his own university's department, to produce a universalist approach to art capable of understanding culture's power.[41] Moreover, in order to render culture central for considerations of the global, Onians relies unsurprisingly on interdisciplinary methods, ranging from anthropology to literature and visual art. World art studies approaches culture through a universalist frame, akin to *Magiciens*'s reliance on magic and aura, so as to focus on the individual object or singular artist as the means to communicate to others. Culture's power and its effects are thus imagined as universal in nature and inherently arising from the artist or art itself.

Such an approach, however, obscures the structural and historical aspects at play that predetermine what even counts as universal, art, culture, and subject. Interdisciplinary fields that are invested in the aesthetic and culture are often seeking to evidence their worthiness for study; however, in such bids for legibility through narratives of culture's power, we limit culture from being fully theorized as implicated with larger apparatuses and structures. We hinder theorizations of the aesthetic for both its import *and* limits in our rush to render it as central to the political or as contributing to the universal. We either insularly fixate on culture or else argue for its value to our world at large. However, for this latter goal, we tend to then analyze culture's import for contributing to other material areas of life by obscuring the drawbacks of the aesthetic.

In the overlap between art market and academia, this late liberal notion of culture is consolidated around 1989. This definition of culture comes to the fore when considering the broader context of the culture wars of the late 1980s and 1990s. Although China does not necessarily have a central place in this primarily US-based history, the culture wars illustrate the late liberal logics at play. More specifically, the assumptions around what is considered culture within the culture wars buttress the operations of the global art market and academia. As Povinelli reminds us, culture has a complex relationship to anthropology, along with the production of art: "In the first instance, culture had to become equivalent to artifact—something that could be said to have specific qualities that could then be measured and evaluated."[42] Under late liberalism, since culture is equated to artifact, art and the artist are conceptualized as fully knowable and, most importantly, limited in scope. This definition of culture narrowly specifies its parameters to solely an object and its maker and avoids understanding how we come to understand what counts as object, maker, and culture. In other words, culture comes to be delinked from the structural. Even if culture possesses a universal appeal or effect (as magic, let's say), it nonetheless is delimited to an individual's creation. And when this limited notion of culture is placed within a transnational context, culture is further relegated as artifact and as an aperture into its non-Western site of origin.

The culture wars rely on this precise definition of culture, resulting in debates over *what or whom we value* rather than *how we value*. The culture wars of the late 1980s and 1990s argued over what counts and should be included within the confines of culture, as opposed to how we have come to arrive at our very definitions and what structures and histories have led to them. Multiple texts on the culture wars reproduce this late liberal conceptualization of culture, as they maintain the locus of critique on culture itself rather than upon the failures, presumptions, and operations of liberalism. Texts like James Hunter's *Culture Wars* place blame on moralism and how "people determine whether something is good or bad, right or wrong, acceptable or unacceptable, and so on."[43] This text is emblematic of other works that direct their focus on the question of cultural morality for the culture wars, which presumes that culture is merely about what society deems of value and collectively decides to include (in other words, a community's *sensibilities*).

This view of culture is advanced in contemporary discourses that theorize the relationship between aesthetics and politics. The aesthetic and the realm of culture are seen to remedy the lack of representation surrounding minor subjects and those coming from minor geographic spaces; the logic goes that if only we are able to represent more minor subjects through the aesthetic, we can then expand what our sensibilities, our common sense, consider of worth. The aesthetic becomes the liberal antidote that extends what and whom society values. Put more explicitly, liberal logics and a liberal model of representationalism undergird the dominant theories that attempt to articulate the aesthetic's relation and significance to the political. Might we develop a theory of the aesthetic beyond such a model?

These understandings of culture are perpetuated and furthered across fields. The structures and histories, along with the dominance of the proper, that produce our value systems and the dominant idea of culture are placed aside. In other words, the ongoing focus and theorizing of the aesthetic as expanding and including more into what we value displaces and obscures an analysis of how we value. This late liberal notion of culture permeates not only the culture wars and art market, but also the discourse on aesthetics and politics that is reinvigorated around 1989. Peter Osborne notes the reappearance of these terms at the end of the twentieth century: "Furthermore, in its recent Rancièrean and (on occasion) Deleuzian guises, it has provided a medium for posing, once again, the now-classical modern question of art's relationship to politics, after a period in which both directly intellectual and political issues were progressively excluded from critical discourse."[44] Although this question of art and the political has been a trenchant one from the likes of Aristotle to Lu Xun and Adorno, a sense of urgency for these questions arose around 1989, particularly as academic and aesthetic concerns turned further toward the global.[45] Rancière's work on politics and aesthetics has dominated the discourse, becoming institutionalized in university curriculums and curatorial frameworks.[46] The rise in aesthetics and politics as a curatorial frame can be traced toward the end of the twentieth century, particularly through his ideas.

Rancière's notion situates aesthetics at the center or core of how politics are produced. According to his model, it is possible to change "the distribution of the sensible" by including and bringing in those voices and perspectives that have been historically denied.[47] In this way, the aesthetic represents possibility; the aesthetic becomes the means to expand the political. Rancière's framework relies on the aesthetic to be a direct form of mediation with the political, as the aesthetic is conceptualized to directly respond to, shape, and possess agency with regard to the political through the production of what is considered sensible. When Rancière explains that the politics of aesthetics involves "the sensible delimitation of what is common to the community," his theorization of the aesthetic relies upon its separation from the political in ways that render and sanction the aesthetic as pure possibility.[48]

Through this model, the aesthetic operates akin to the logics of liberalism and democratic representationalism, whereby the inclusion of culture by more minor subjects presumably remedies the historical lack of representation. According to this framework, the aesthetic expands representation and, in turn, our common sense surrounding what and whom we value. The minorness of the aesthetic by minor subjects comes to possess major possibilities for the political. However, the increased representation of minor subjects through the aesthetic has not translated into substantive institutional change, as the notion of late liberalism helps explain. And as outlined in the introduction, the rampant inclusion of underrepresented perspectives has created limits and a larger set of problems for these exact populations. More importantly, however, this dominant model relies on the aesthetic as being theorized apart from the political, as the source of possibility.

Of course, it is understandable that one might argue for the significance of the aesthetic, given the long history of dismissal surrounding the aesthetic along with the glorification of the aesthetic as a universal and sanctioned realm untainted by the political. However, in contemporary bids to argue for the centrality of the aesthetic as it relates to the political, we have merely centered it without considering the underlying assumptions of what the political and major are that render the aesthetic minor. In other words, instead of hesitating on this minor form in ways that help us understand the structures, histories, and systems that maintain its minorness, we have merely entered the minor of the aesthetic into the major and within its underlying liberal assumptions.

As such, the established discourse on aesthetics and politics inherits and perpetuates the late liberal definition of culture. With less of a focus on structuration and on the failures of liberalism, the discourse primarily assumes culture, art, and aesthetics as identifiable objects (artifacts) separate from the political that have an agency and are constitutive of politics. With the aesthetic and culture having agency, they are thus presumed unique from yet central to the political itself. This has resulted in a conceptualization of the aesthetic as the remedy for institutional problems, rather than as entangled with them. In other words, culture tends to be heralded as outside of power and as the answer, hope, and possibility for social ills (in ways, à la Rancière, that increase representation, what we consider to be common sense, and what we value). Culture is not often understood as fully imbricated and implicated (as problem and possibility) with the political and systemic. However, when they are understood within the structural, culture and the aesthetic possess the ability to index how we value, our systems and assumptions.

As a result, the realm of the aesthetic is often used to absolve the failures of liberalism and inclusion, which ultimately displaces blame onto culture and individuals. This proper formulation is set up to fall short. When these efforts to use the aesthetics and culture of the other to remedy societal ills fail (which they most always do), it is blamed not on the structures and assumptions of our institutions but rather on the notion that the art, artists, and culture were just not good enough (particularly those that do not work in the proper ways). And even when such art or artists are deemed worthy, it is often achieved by being immediately legible through the proper. This ultimately limits the parameters surrounding how we analyze art by minor subjects and those coming from minor geographic spaces. As such, the proper is sustained, thus maintaining the systems and logics that determine *what* is deemed legible and of value. We tend to debate the merits of aesthetic objects, rather than focus on the structural frames and terms that dictate these very debates (*how* we value). When art by racialized, queer, trans, non-Western, and other minoritarian subjects is critiqued, it is primarily directed at the artists' identities or at the quality of their art, as opposed to the ways we define culture and otherness through the proper. In other words, these criticisms do not to focus on the value systems in place.

Furthermore, when this larger discourse and conceptualization of culture consolidates around 1989 alongside the rise of the global art market, non-Western artists are further entrenched within this standard. Although there is not a direct causal relationship between global art and Rancière's framework, I highlight the late liberal logics at play so as to better understand how and why the proper predominates for the non-West. These minor subjects from minor geographic spaces only become legible and worthy of circulation when they demonstrate and fit under a rubric of their aesthetic production as being central to and formative of the political. As such, the narrative of the resistant artist against the authoritarian state comes to predominate, since this narrative is proper and immediately legible as it reifies the aesthetic as social possibility. Moreover, it should be of no surprise then that the disagreements over Chinese art as derivate of the West afflicted its emergence and continue today. Those who dismiss non-Western art as derivative presume that the only value in this art is anthropological in that it indexes truths about proper understandings of minor subjects and minor places; there is nothing of formal or aesthetic worth—let alone political. Under this late liberal logic, the worth of minor art is primarily gained through proper understandings of context and history (expanding the inclusion of other sites to our halls of knowledge and what we value), whereby minor art cannot formally innovate like the West nor rethink the value systems that uphold our world. In this vein, to solely argue for the increased inclusion and representation through art and culture of minor subjects from minor places furthers this dominant late liberal logic. And as such, we ultimately ignore the very structures that dictate our understandings and approaches to culture, art, and value.

Revisiting 1979 and 1989 in 1999: Cai Guo-Qiang in Venice

The overlap of theory, art markets, and the university around 1989 illustrates the proper as shaped by late liberalism. The controversial reproduction by Cai Guo-Qiang of Wang Guangyi's 1965 *Rent Collection Courtyard* for the 1999 Venice Biennale helps demonstrate the overlap of these multiple areas, along with the effects of late liberalism that have informed the expansion of the global art market. Among others in this book, Cai is an art-world star. With the liberalization of China's markets, artists began to enter new labor relations with the state. They were able to move away from state-sponsored roles in art practice to become freelance artists within and outside of China. With such a shift, both artists and curators have been able to accumulate capital at much faster rates. These changes in labor practices facilitate the distribution and profits for the art market. The art-world star and curators are of course not absolved from critiques of capital but are rather quite central to its functioning (hence, the aesthetic is not pure possibility but it also cannot be dismissed as merely an expressive causality arising from capital). Many of the artists' careers that I focus on in this book have been built around proper understandings of China and culture, and these renderings enable the art market, academic fields, and theoretical discourse to operate with ease. I highlight this fact so as to avoid exceptionalizing the artist as a figure of potential even for the minor. As I've been arguing, culture, art, and artists are imbricated with the problematics of the social and political; these entities are not merely outside or resistant. In addition, there is an inherent tension in a focus on art-world stars as depicting minoritarian concerns. These figures do not per se represent minoritarian or proletarian interests; however, their access to these worlds and how they are understood highlight the ways minoritarian politics are flattened through the proper. The art star's circulation indexes how minoritarian concerns come to be delimited as global publics learn about the other.

At the 1999 Venice Biennale, Cai won the Golden Lion Award for a reproduction of Wang Guangyi's iconic sculpture. The original 1965 work was lauded by Chinese revolutionaries, since it directly depicted and mediated socialist ideals. The piece involves multiple life-sized clay figures that are arranged doing intensely laborious tasks across twenty-six scenes: pushing goods, tilling the soil, and picking crops. The faces of the workers are not cheerful about their pastoral lives; instead, their pained expressions reveal a critique of previous feudal realities which the Cultural Revolution sought to remedy. During the Cultural Revolution, Mao's wife, Jiang Qing, praised the original 1965 work for embodying socialist ideals. Within this earlier context, the work demonstrated a *direct* mediation across aesthetics and politics, whereby socialist political goals were depicted by the plight of the rural proletariat living under abusive, feudal relations. Although Cai's reproduction was acknowledged by the international art world, the piece caused massive controversy. The Sichuan Fine Arts Institute threatened to sue the Venice Biennale for lack of copyright.

Cai's *Rent Collection* was continually filtered through the proper. For the Sichuan Fine Arts Institute, Cai's goals veered away from the institution's desire to provide laudatory images of China. Controversy over Cai's reproduction ensued through debates over copyright, along with the fact that Cai was not considered properly Chinese. The press release by the Fine Arts Institute frames Cai's rendition as an "appropriation" that is done by "an overseas Chinese artist, domiciled in Japan, and then subsequently reproduced and renamed *Venice's Rent Collection Courtyard for the 48th Venice Biennale,* without copyright permission."[49] The press release is preoccupied with the original proper meaning of the work, along with Cai's status as an overseas Chinese subject. Since the original piece has become quite iconic, the press release insinuates that it can only be re-created by someone who deploys artistic production to reveal Wang Guangyi's original intent, purpose, and politics. In addition, for the global art market, Cai's reproduction was celebrated, especially as the work referenced a legible moment in Chinese history: the Cultural Revolution. For Venice and the art world at large, Cai's version of China is nonetheless understood as proper China, with the artist viewed as reproducing a legible formulation of the aesthetic. In particular, most critics during the opening of the 1999 Biennale described Cai's work as "political" and as an aperture into the realities of China with the work "reminding people that life might be tough under Mao, but it was horribly worse under feudalism."[50] In other words, Cai's art comes to be framed as demonstrating a political statement against illiberal Maoist and feudalist states, thereby making the aesthetic properly legible as critique and resistance. In this vein, Cai's work is continually understood through late liberalism and Rancière's framework, whereby art and the aesthetic not only increase the representation of the non-West, but also perpetuate our sensibilities surrounding what we value and what we deem properly political.

Cai, however, offers less direct forms of mediation surrounding socialism and the Cultural Revolution. For his reproduction, the artist hired some of the sculptors who had previously worked on the original piece; the team re-created the sculptures in real time throughout the festival (figure 1.3). Cai's larger aim was to focus on it as a performance to renegotiate our relationship to sculpture: from one of "looking at" it to "looking at the making of sculpture."[51] The artist sought to consider how performance helps us think differently about this iconic piece—from a true and immediate depiction of politics to a less linear understanding or mediation between art and the political. By allowing audiences to watch the making of sculpture in the Arsenale building at Venice, the artist highlights the labor surrounding aesthetic production, bringing to the fore culture's imbrication with the social and political. Put differently, Cai was not trying to solely demonstrate a resistance against the illiberal state or to critique the state for current and past (feudal and Maoist) ills. Rather, he sought to revisit previous socialist ideals in order to reconsider labor under Mao and within late capital and to understand the idea of the state as shifting in form, in theory, and a becoming.

In particular, Cai uses tensions across media (sculpture and performance) to highlight differing understandings of labor. By deprivileging the

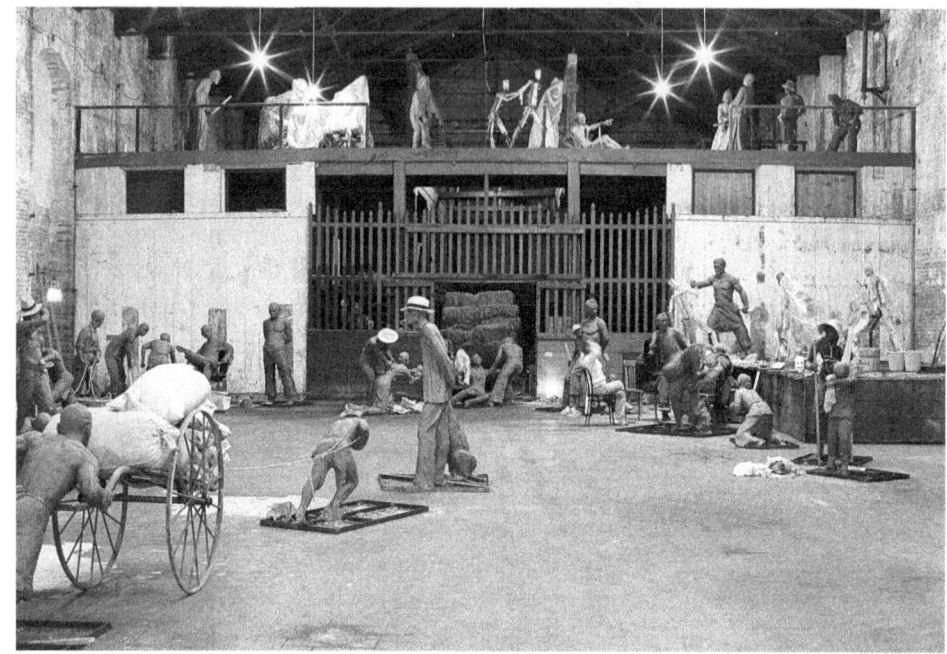

Figure 1.3. Cai Guo-Qiang, *Venice's Rent Collection Courtyard*, 1999. 108 life-sized sculptures created on site by Long Xu Li and nine guest artisan sculptors, 60 tons of clay, wire, and wood armature. Commissioned by the Forty-Eighth Venice Biennale. Installation view at Forty-Eighth Venice Biennale, 1999. Photo by Elio Montanari. Courtesy of Cai Studio.

final product as a sculpture, Cai reminds viewers through the sculptors' labor as performance how living labor and aesthetic production are closely entwined (perhaps one and the same). This condition around labor and the aesthetic is one that ultimately helps us take stock of the place of work, particularly changes in our relations to labor from socialism (before 1979) to late liberalism (1989, 1999, and beyond). Through mediation, Cai also highlights how such a rethinking is important to grapple with the idea of work as it relates to the past, present, and future of socialism and China. As such, the artist nuances the state and attempts to render China common by examining how socialist ideals have shifted since the original work was created, complicating understandings of the state beyond authoritarianism. And by focusing on the production of the work, Cai uses performance to consider how older and newer generations of sculptors could become part of this work beyond state-sanctioned discourse. Cai discusses this piece as one that takes stock of the shifting "relationship between artists and their time and politics," which requires a more capacious articulation across aesthetics and politics due to the role of history and changes in the state and its political ideals (from socialism to liberalized markets).[52] However, the institutional apparatuses of the art market and late liberalism render these concerns opaque, privileging proper formulations of China as articulated through a legible historical moment and a direct relation between aesthetics and politics. Through the proper, Cai's focus on socialism becomes illegible, unimaginable, and illiberal.

As such, a theory of the aesthetic that is not based in liberal ideals or late liberal logics is needed. Cai's *Venice's Rent Collection Courtyard*, along with the artists and art objects in the remainder of this book, offers moments to take note of our dominant tendencies and gestures toward ways to develop less linear engagements across aesthetics and politics. Even though late liberalism reinforces proper China, the proper non-West, and narrow understandings of culture, we must attend to these minor aesthetic and medial details of artworks. They enable a method that highlights the dominant assumptions, epistemological foundations, and ontological conditions that limit how we engage non-Western art and artists. In particular, Cai's aesthetics attend to socialism in ways that bring to the fore how the illiberal and Marxist thought come to be obscured under late liberalism. Although 1989 has been noted as a wistful moment for the global Left, Cai's performance and sculpture remind us of the import of socialism. It offers a deeper consideration and theory of social structuration, as the aesthetic and culture are not heralded as pure possibility but rather understood as elements entangled with the limits of our world.[53] Thus, as Michael Dutton notes about Cai's work, these returns to socialism help us deal "with humanity and the question of the political differently."[54] Cai brings to the fore the illiberal, whereby culture and the aesthetic not only enmesh with the problems of the social, but also revise proper formulations of China and what we consider to be political. The remainder of this book attends to the complexity, illiberality, and indirect mediation of works like Cai's that expand our understandings of the political and aesthetic beyond the proper and toward the common, indirect, minor, and improper.

2

All Look Same

AI WEIWEI'S MULTITUDES, COMRADE
AESTHETICS, AND RACIAL ANGER
IN A TIME OF INCLUSION

My response to racism is anger.

—Audre Lorde, "The Uses of Anger"[1]

The relationship of intellectuals to victims . . . is
above all a question of those contemporary
intellectuals who in general have lost their
Marxist points of reference and shamelessly
surrendered to liberalism.

—François Laruelle, *General Theory of Victims*[2]

The inclusion of those who were historically misrepresented or not represented presumably signals progress. Under democratic theory, change has traditionally been understood as occurring by increasing the inclusion, representation, and interests of minor subjects in the polity so as to mitigate "the tyranny of the majority."[3] However, there are many failings of democracies that exceed opportunities for remedy in the project of liberal inclusion, such as redistribution, reparations, and social restructuration that could substantively (although not fully) ameliorate historical and ongoing injustices, particularly with regards to race. Further, the inability to fully grapple with modernity's reliance on yet disavowal of racialization accretes into negative affects like racial anger, which liberalism additionally fails to register. The art market, however, has predominantly followed a late liberal orientation to race and inclusion, through its rapid curation of social difference and the non-West. I thus turn to how inclusion manifests within this world so as to understand the practice's limits. Ai Weiwei's work and career, in particular, illuminate the logics of liberal inclusion and direct us to other genealogies to reconsider its predominance.

The broad reach of Ai Weiwei's persona and art projects can be attributed to many different factors: media attention and savvy, the increased capital investment in contemporary art, China's economic rise, multicultural inclusion, state involvement, and Ai's own aesthetics. Due to his popularity on the art market and within public culture, Ai is the easy target for both praise and mockery in relation to the merits of his artistic worth.[4] Additionally, he is upheld as the quintessential dissident artist who challenges the state.[5] These narratives illuminate prototypical and major understandings of non-Western artists, where it might initially appear difficult to engage them through the minor. Although Ai's works vary with regard to political critique, they have been made into emblems of artistic resistance due to the harsh state-sanctioned censorship and imprisonment he has endured. This proper formulation fuels his constant inclusion and global circulation. However, Ai's work and career also provide opportunities to look at issues that are not always considered in relation to his art, particularly late liberal relations to race and inclusion. In this chapter, I examine Ai's oeuvre to confront some of the problematics and limits surrounding liberalism, particularly those which are referred to in the two short epigraphs to this chapter: what Audre Lorde identifies as the structural mode or affect of racial anger—something that is incompatible and often not dealt with within liberal and leftist spaces that gloss over negativity—and also the tension that François Laruelle points to across Marxist and liberal commitments with regard to inclusion. As I discuss throughout this chapter, Ai's oeuvre—particularly his work *Fairytale*—produces a method that investigates these restrictions across liberalism and even Marxism. More specifically, I examine how Ai reconsiders the curation and practice of inclusion by reworking how we conceptualize the subject beyond those worthy of being recognized as human toward, what I call, a comrade aesthetics.

In 2007, Ai presented his installation *Fairytale* at *documenta 12* in Kassel, Germany. This piece is especially useful for considering the conditions surrounding increased global inclusion. Ai produced a large-scale project that involved multiple objects: 1,001 chairs sprinkled throughout the festival spaces and an outdoor sculpture made of salvaged doors and discarded building materials from the massive increase of commercial and residential construction across Beijing. Most importantly, the project involved live bodies. Ai raised over $3 million to bring 1,001 Chinese people to *documenta*; they arrived in groups spread out over the full period of the festival and explored the city during the duration of their stay. In addition, Ai created a documentary about the process surrounding the large-scale piece. Through the use of multiple media, Ai generated a network of seemingly indistinguishable bodies and objects at Kassel.

In *Fairytale,* Ai displays the repetition of seemingly similar parts and objects: discarded doors, old chairs, and Chinese people (figures 2.1, 2.2, and 2.3). Although each of these objects is certainly individualized and unique, when seen in mass, they become indistinguishable to an untrained eye. Doors, chairs, and even Chinese people begin to all look the same. It is precisely Ai's reliance on mass repetition that directs us to a sense of racial difference for the 1,001 Chinese. However, Ai does not rely on common tropes like multicultural inclusion, intersubjective encounters, or humanization to work against the racist notion of the Chinese as all looking the same, despotic hordes, and lacking individuality. Through the formal construction of the documentary film, along with other aesthetic modes, Ai deploys repetition and multiplicity in ways that rework liberal humanist frameworks. He highlights their limits and brings to light the presumptions that inform and uphold these dominant approaches to global, racial difference. Although Ai can certainly be understood through modernist discourses around the ready-made and repetition, race provides a valuable way to reconsider repetition in excess of modernist strongholds like mass reproduction, consumption, and play. Ai contends with global forms of racialization in ways that do not default into these established art historical narratives.

From another angle, his work grapples with race as a fracturing force in the world, rather than something to be included, considered, remedied, or made whole. Ai minorly explores what it means to be seen as a faceless mass and horde—those repeated as objects of history. This condition of "all look same" plagues those who are part of the same historically defined racial group. After all, I myself have often been mistaken for another Asian or Asian American person (regardless of gender presentation and physical features) by not only strangers but also those I consider colleagues. Rather than rejecting this repeated and exasperating experience, I ask us to hesitate within it and to resist the urge to demand humanization and recognition as a full liberal subject. To be clear, the problem with "all look same" is not

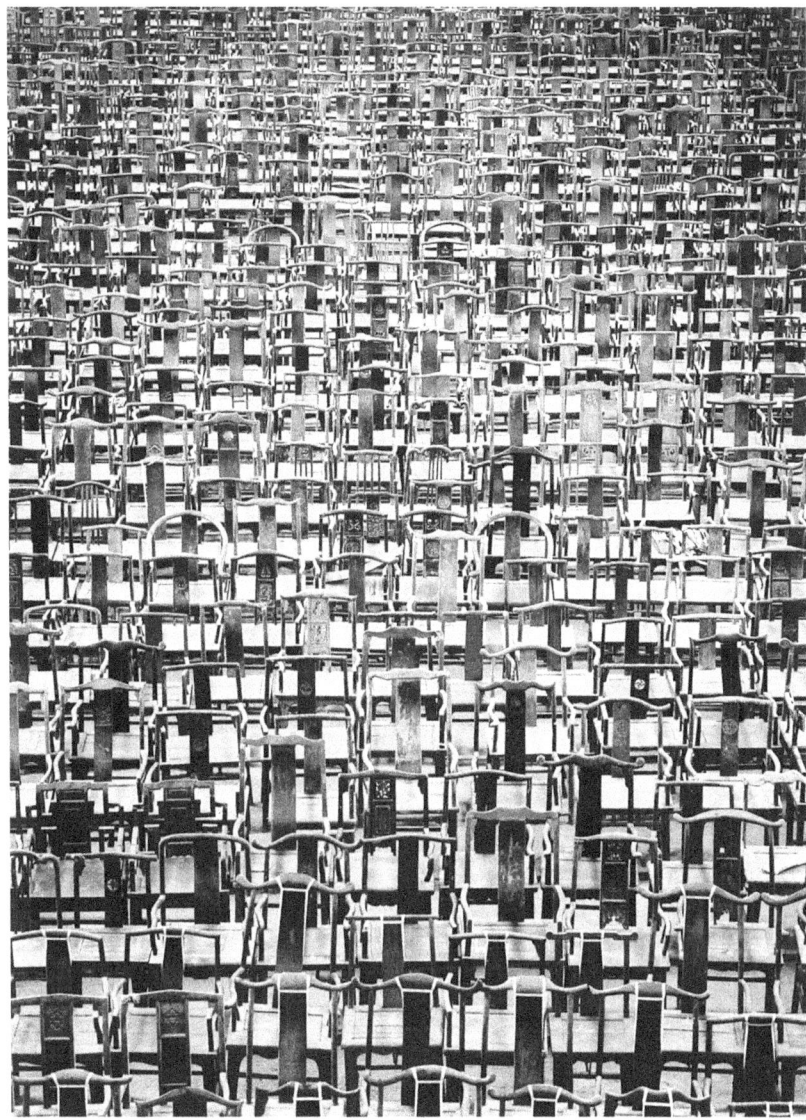

Figure 2.1. Ai Weiwei, Chairs (*Fairytale*), 2007. Courtesy of the artist; Leister Foundation, Switzerland; Erlenmeyer Stiftung, Switzerland; and Galerie Urs Meile, Beijing-Lucerne.

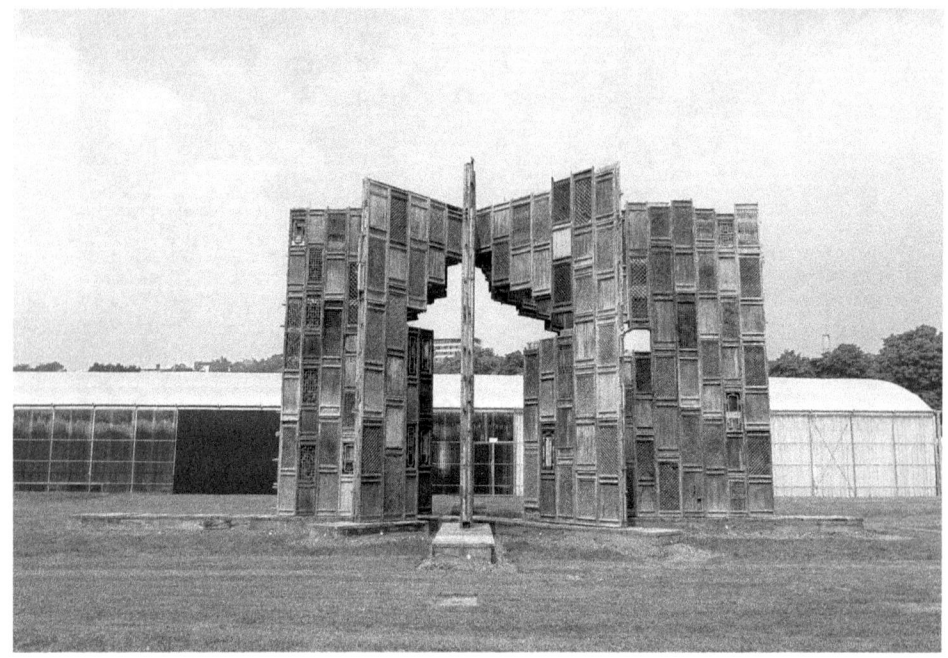

Figure 2.2. Ai Weiwei, Template Tower (*Fairytale*), 2007. Courtesy of the artist; Leister Foundation, Switzerland; Erlenmeyer Stiftung, Switzerland; and Galerie Urs Meile, Beijing-Lucerne.

primarily about how racialized subjects are perceived, which would involve a remedy that appeals to the majority's empathetic capacity. Rather, this condition fuels capitalism, since these subjects must be seen as a horde so that their value comes from their contributions to capital. The techne of dehumanization operates by rendering subjects as less so as to expect and extract more from their labor. We must hesitate from demanding recognition and representation so as to grapple with these connections across race and capitalism. Ai's aesthetics provide the mechanisms by which to hesitate within this condition and direct us to the import of such a move.

The dominant frameworks for understanding global inclusion in the art market stress connection across subjects and cultures, especially since these artists are viewed as exposing art publics to "new" and "different" global spaces. However, Ai's formalism and minor use of aesthetics help us trace the liberal humanist logics embedded in these frames. In the bid to work against the repeated dehumanization of non-Western subjects, most discourses have

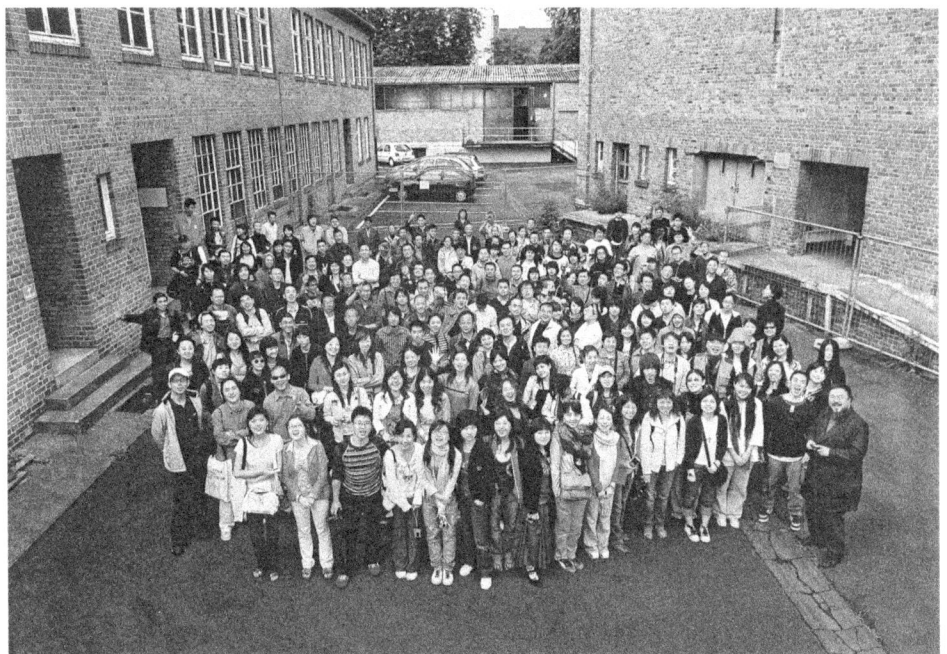

Figure 2.3. Ai Weiwei, Group Photo of Participants (*Fairytale*), 2007. Courtesy of the artist; Leister Foundation, Switzerland; Erlenmeyer Stiftung, Switzerland; and Galerie Urs Meile, Beijing-Lucerne.

centered around three tactics for global art that (1) humanize the non-West, (2) stress an intersubjective encounter across humanity to learn from one another, or (3) produce a relationality across minoritized and dehumanized populations. These three dominant frameworks render the presumed other legible and proper through the singular (humanizing) or the relational (connections across individuals or groups). Ai's use of repetition to illustrate "all look same" directs us to the limits of these three frames.

Since non-Western artists have not historically been central to art beyond serving as a presumably primitive counterpoint to or magical resource for the high culture of modern societies for centuries, why and how did the market suddenly shift to include them at the end of the twentieth century into discourses on art history and aesthetics? Considering that larger publics lack contextual information about such art, does one need to offer contextualization for each non-Western space or does this merely resituate such art back as indexes of otherness and difference? In light of these complex questions, most narratives of non-Western contemporary art have relied on frames that gloss over the difficulties inherent in the practice of inclusion. The difference of the Chinese other is often included through the three above frames, while historical and structural affects like racial anger are occluded in the bid to humanize the Chinese or relate them to others. These modes of multicultural inclusion obscure the ruptures that construct how racialized others not only personally and immediately experience, but also collectively and historically endure, the condition of "all look same." As a result, the accumulative affects of anger and spite that inform racialized subjects offer an important rubric through which to rethink the ways we imagine the inclusion of others in late liberalism.[6] Despite the problematic and uneven ways anger has been gendered and racialized, often deployed against Black women, anger nonetheless offers an additional rubric by which to rethink the ways we image the inclusion of others.

In reassessing the practice of inclusion in late liberalism, exploring other political genealogies is generative. Chinese Marxism, for example, offers a different theoretical basis by which to reimagine the figure of the subject and its inclusion through aesthetic means. Under liberalism, the minor subject is waiting to be included; under Chinese Marxism, the minor subject brings to light the structures that maintain the other as minor. In the case of Ai's work, this differentiation is crucial. In particular, Chinese Marxism understands the impersonal, the notion of the comrade, and structural power in ways that reframe the practice of including subjects differently than how it is predominantly deployed within late liberalism. For example, to some extent, Ai's approach in *Fairytale* used redistribution—the project funneled resources to many of its participants who would have never been able to travel abroad, particularly to Europe. Although this redistributive function is limited within *Fairytale*, Ai's direct engagement with (rather than rejection of) the condition of global raciality deploys minorness beyond subjects to be included as in late liberal logic, and it is achieved through a turn to Marxist thought. However, this turn to Marxist thought does not idealize this specific agenda. In particular, "all look same" might initially resonate with leftist theorizations of the multitude and political relationality. These frames, at first, appear as convenient ways to engage Ai's use of repetition and the way he focuses on political practices over purely identitarian means. Ai, however, interrogates and questions how racialized groups are asked to put aside repeated historical dehumanization (a structural affect I call racial anger) in order to join relational multitudes. This chapter thus distinguishes between the many ways of aestheticizing relational masses that contend with distinct histories of racialization. Indeed, long-standing forms of racial anger prevent the flattening of Ai's political theorizations into the broader rubrics of the multitude and the relational. In other words, I engage a form of relational critique that seeks to avoid defaulting into racial liberalism.

This chapter focuses on several key issues relating to proper China and the minor. In addition to looking at the way the curatorial goals of *documenta* rendered both *Fairytale* and the artist legible within a proper understanding of the political, this chapter also analyzes a critique Ai wrote of a 2012 London exhibit called *Art of Change: New Directions from China*. In his critique, Ai offers a commentary of the show that utilizes a different political register beyond liberalism. He states a revealing assessment of the curatorial goals in *Art of Change* that suggests alternative ways to curate the non-West, particularly through a turn to social structuration and Marxism. This turn to social structuration and Marxism—both of which Ai's installation draws on—works beyond the inclusion of minor subjects. By looking at Ai's oeuvre through this lens, however, it is possible to examine how the minor as method enables a structuralist analysis without an exclusive reliance on institutions or political economy for insights. Furthermore, in looking at *Fairytale* through this lens, I situate Ai's use of "all look same" as an engagement in Chinese Marxist critique. By doing so, I aim to rethink the dominant frames that are used for including non-Western art within its curation, display, and study: intersubjectivity, humanization, and relationality.

The bringing of 1,001 Chinese to Germany could easily be imagined as an intersubjective encounter or humanizing moment and, in fact, has been theorized as such within curatorial and academic discourses. I, instead, examine his use of mass and plurality to explore what happens if we yield to and linger within the racist notion of "all look same." Ai inappropriately grapples with the abject position of being always plural before ever considered singular, to build off of and tweak the work of Jean-Luc Nancy. I thus situate Ai's reworking of the subject toward the impersonal and structural through what I call a *comrade aesthetics* and what Marx identifies as the *lumpenproletariat*. The comrade and lumpen reconfigure not only intersubjectivity and humanization, but also relationality. Rather than situating Ai's aesthetics of repetition and mass in relation to the oft-cited notion of the multitude, I demonstrate the limits of this Marxist frame as it relates to Chinese Marxism. Through an account of negative affects and racial anger, Ai ultimately renegotiates the multitude and relationality that have sought to contend with global difference through bonds that exceed identity.

Curating a Fairytale

As a key institution in the global art market, *documenta* has played a central role in developing the public visibility of contemporary Chinese art. The event, which occurs every five years, has exhibited many Chinese artists. The artists involved are not normally announced until the opening of the show, although they are often given two years in advance to prepare. *Documenta* is located in Kassel, Germany, which is where the Grimm Brothers established themselves as fairytale collectors and linguists. With Kassel as both a contemporary and historic cultural capital, Ai deployed the city as a starting point to think through fables, imagination, art, and our current condition surrounding inclusion. Beyond the art objects of chairs and statues, the centerpiece of *Fairytale* was not technically on display—the 1,001 Chinese citizens. Ai's producers raised funds from foundations, government entities, and individual donors to provide travel and housing for these attendees to experience the festival and the city of Kassel.

Documenta 12's curatorial approach centered around three major concerns: "Is modernity our antiquity?," "What is bare life?," and "What is to be done?"[7] These objectives aim to specify our historical moment in relation to modernity, while implicating cultural production as directly mediating and responding to (what is to be done) our current political condition (bare life). This curatorial framing, spearheaded by Roger Buergel, conceptualizes art as holding the possibility of working within the critical political and material questions of our time, as art, with regard to notions of bare life, "dissolves the radical separation between painful subjection and joyous liberation."[8] In addition, art is imagined as the place for education, since "[art's] mediation sets the stage for a potentially all-inclusive public debate."[9] Both Ai and his objects are understood within this curatorial frame. As imagined by the curators, the minor subject of art, along with the artists themselves, possess major political possibilities for the twenty-first century. Within this curatorial push toward making art applicable and as a direct mediation and intervention into the political (which greatly resonates with Jacques Rancière's framework, as discussed in chapter 1), the non-West plays a crucial role for imbuing art with possibility and change. Non-Western art is often framed to answer and directly mediate political concerns, a result of late liberal logics as discussed earlier. As such, the inclusion of non-Western artists follows the trend of political legibility, whereby the bid to "know" more about others emerges through proper narratives. For example, other non-Western artists at *documenta 12* were framed in similar ways to Ai. Palestinian artist Ahlam Shibli is discussed as responding with explicit political critique. Meanwhile, artists from the US or Western Europe are often lauded for their forms of experimentation. The choreographer Trisha Brown is praised for her medial explorations across dance and visual art, while Ai is framed as answering pressing political questions.

Buergel appears to include Ai because he embodies—and his works represent—some of *documenta 12*'s curatorial ideals that privilege the aesthetic for its direct mediation of politics. The festival frames Ai's work within not only minor notions, such as it being playful or absurd, but also major possibility as it is grapples with the state, civilization, and culture. *Documenta* situates his art as minor objects, which take on an immediate political critique at the interplay of modernity and tradition.

Further, *documenta* relies on discourses of humanization and relationality to frame the 1,001 Chinese visitors to Kassel. On the one hand, *Fairytale* is situated as playful, interactive, and imaginative; one of *documenta*'s press releases discusses *Fairytale* as if it were a moment from summer camp, emphasizing the insignificant but fun and memorable interactions between Chinese and Germans. The press release describes a seemingly multicultural and intersubjective moment where a group of Chinese youth played soccer against Germans at a local park.[10] Photos document the game, along with the crowds of Chinese viewers, evoking a lingering sense of the halcyon days of summer camp. The multicultural and intersubjective are deployed to frame Chinese citizens as connecting with locals and non-Chinese tourists in Kassel. On the other hand, *Fairytale* takes on political potential. Ai screened an eight-hour version (taken from over fifteen hundred hours of footage) of the process of choosing and bringing together the 1,001 Chinese. *Documenta* advertised the film as offering a nativist view into the realities of China. *Documenta* renders Ai as the subject who utilizes minor concepts and subjects, like play, the fairytale, and the aesthetic, to critique and reveal the problems with China, modernity, and bare life. The reliance on the minor within a curatorial framework for an international art event is emblematic of the current market that privileges minor subjects to possess major political possibilities ("This work comments on the bare life conditions in China and the world") or to market the object ("The framework of the fairytale shows the play and agency of the Chinese"). The non-West becomes the means by which to imagine the operations of bare life and dispossession amid aesthetic play.

Art of Change(?): Comrade Aesthetics

According to *documenta*'s curatorial framework, *Fairytale* and Ai Weiwei's oeuvre possess multicultural, intersubjective, and humanizing potential for the Chinese. However, Ai reworks the ways non-Western artists are forced to become legible through a direct mediation of and proper relation to aesthetics and politics. The framing of Ai as a resistant artist is often associated with his time spent in New York City for twelve years before returning to Beijing. The narrative surrounding his time in the US implies that he experienced the extraordinary possibilities of Western liberal democracy. But Ai's aesthetics of repetition and "all look same" do not respond by arguing for inclusion within a liberal humanist project; instead, he centralizes how "all look same" is produced through structures and histories that repeatedly dehumanize racialized populations. In other words, Ai's use of "all look same" evokes the minor as method that directs us to the dominant presumptions undergirding global inclusion and global formations of race.

Inclusion is not a problem per se. However, in its dominance as political panacea, inclusion has come to be presumed as the most logical of approaches. In the show *Art of Change: New Directions for China* (2012) at the Hayward Gallery in London, the limits surrounding inclusion come to the fore. In a review of the show in the *Guardian*, Ai critiqued it for deploying a liberalist approach to the curation of Chinese performance art. Chief curator Stephanie Rosenthal produced *Art of Change* to examine performance and installation art. The notion of "change" was the show's curatorial frame; this "change" was considered in terms of each "artist's development," "as rooted in Eastern philosophy," and as an aesthetics of "transformation."[11] But in the *Guardian*, Ai chastised *Art of Change* for its lack of social engagement and structural critique. He highlights the liberal impulse of inclusion that avoids contending more directly with history, the state, and social structure.

Ai pointedly asks, "How can you have a show of 'contemporary Chinese art' that doesn't address a single one of the country's most pressing contemporary issues?"[12] According to Ai, the curator's idea of change was not being emphasized in its relation to China's own political landscape. Although at first it may seem that Ai is demanding direct and legible political engagement, it is important to remember that Ai's sense of the political is informed by his complex relationship to Western politics *and* Chinese socialism. His critique does not merely replicate dominant liberal understandings of the political. By demanding that art should engage the idea of change in materialist ways, Ai's comments reconfigure liberal understandings of what the political means: "Any show curated without respect for the people's struggle, without concern for an artist's need for honest self-expression, will inevitably lead to the wrong conclusion. Anything that calls itself a cultural exchange is artificial when it lacks any critical content. What's needed is open discussion, a platform for argument. Art needs to stand for something."[13] Considering how he is critical of both China and Western consumerism, Ai's call for "meaning" works beyond a liberal ideology.

More specifically, in his review, Ai also criticizes the CCP for its authoritarian tendencies, along with its use of "soft power" initiatives to promote a brand of China. He cites the Chinese state's use of culture, along with its public relations campaign in the US that features large-scale video billboards of China's actors, athletes, and classical pianists throughout Times Square: "To me, these are an insult to human intelligence and a ridicule of the concept of culture—vehicles of propaganda that showcase skills with no substance, and crafts with no meaning."[14] Ai's critique is not fully informed by a liberal democratic sentiment. In fact, he criticizes the show for including Chinese art as a mere "consumerist offering," articulating an equally biting assessment of Western approaches that similarly deploy an uncritical use of culture. Ai highlights how inclusion, as a liberal practice, only approaches inclusion as an additive process, whereby minor subjects come to be (ac)counted for without a consideration of the social structures that maintain the minor as a knowable and includable subject. Ai's simultaneous critiques of the West and of China are informed by Chinese Marxism. This political genealogy shapes Ai's hopes for China to live up to past socialist ideals espoused during the founding of modern China.

Throughout his career, Ai has refused to serve as a mouthpiece for colonial tropes that privilege the West as the primary source of modernity. Ai's political orientation is not geared toward a simplistic privileging of liberalism; instead, his politics are based on practices in not only democracy but also Maoism. Christian Sorace has argued that Ai's politics are influenced by early socialist ideals: "Ai continues state discourse in a subversively orthodox manner by enacting its own failed promises as the material for his own discursive struggle."[15] Such an orientation does not necessarily mean that all art should take a singular form; rather, Ai renegotiates how we curate contemporary Chinese art in terms of the dominance of liberalism that predetermines understandings of the political. He reexamines the liberalist tendencies in our inclusionary practices that seek to add in subjects without a full consideration of social structures. By looking at Ai's relation to the state beyond both direct critique and the privileging of Western democracy, we disturb the linear narratives surrounding how non-Western art functions within the art market. In this way, one can see that Chinese socialism and Western democracy are not simply the only two options; Ai points to the complex possibility of simultaneously navigating both.

Petrus Liu, whose work is helpful for contending with the legacy of Chinese Marxism today, has emphasized the ways in which Chinese Marxism shifts away from the liberal focus on the individual, privileging the structural that constructs human experience. Liu's comparison of different approaches to queer theory, for example, between US liberally informed theoretical approaches and those constructed by a longer history of Chinese Marxism between Taiwan and China, is particularly illuminating: "By contrast [to US formations of queer theory and queer of color critique], Chinese theory of the geopolitical meditations of queer lives does not begin with the concept of social identity; instead, it emphasizes the *impersonal*, *structural*, and *systemic* workings of power. Whereas US queer theory responds to the failures of neoliberal social management by postulating an incomplete, foreclosed, or irreducibly heterogeneous subject of identity, Chinese queer Marxists develop an arsenal of conceptual tools for reading the complex and overdetermined relations between human sexual freedom and the ideological cartography of the Cold War."[16]

Ai hails this Chinese Marxist legacy that Liu describes. By shifting away from a model of individual inclusion, the notions of the mass and the impersonal emerge. Chinese Marxism complexly navigates individual, mass, and infrastructure. By accounting for the interactions across the three, Chinese Marxism offers an alternative to understanding the political. From this genealogy, the notion of the subject becomes about, as Liu puts it, both "political action as well as an effect of social structuration."[17] Chinese Marxism, in other words, theorizes the subject in terms of both agency and structure.

Comrade Aesthetics and Ethics

From Chinese Marxism, the comrade is a figure that allows us to reconceptualize the liberal subject toward this more expansive theorization. The comrade always exists in relation to a social structure and history. Although comrades certainly possess individualized characteristics, they have a tacit relation to structures of power. Today, the use of *comrade* in Mandarin Chinese vernacular (*tongzhi*) refers to queer subjects. This association illustrates the critical shift from the personal to the impersonal and structural. Although scholars debate the significance of this association across tongzhi and queerness in relation to neoliberalism, this association nonetheless highlights the way an identity comes to be sutured with and through historical and political inflections.[18] In turn, a (queer) comrade aesthetics articulates a temporal knot across socialist pasts and neoliberalized present, whereby a subject is always situated within larger systems and histories. Queer comrade aesthetics involve less of a preoccupation with knowing the individual's story surrounding how one feels or exists as queer; rather, the impersonal predominates. An atmosphere of temporal and structural connections is stressed over the individual (queer) narrative. In this vein, noting the queer inflection of the comrade is important to counter liberalism's rendering of the minor subject as predominantly an insular, decontextualized, and transhistorical identity.

Ai's project produces a comrade aesthetics through the impersonal and atmospheric. Within the town of Kassel, one cannot fully track each individual participant throughout the entire performance, since waves of Chinese citizens circulate in and out during the entire festival. Ai, in other words, reveals the difficulties in solely focusing on humanizing an individual; he aestheticizes the need to slacken (not dismiss) commitments to the subject. Through a comrade aesthetics, Ai highlights a problematic for theorizing the global: how do we contend with the structural without losing a focus on individuals and without reifying the major form of social structures? Moreover, as Lisa Lowe has pointed out, due to the magnitude of globalization, grappling with individuals and structures has to do with *the problem of representation itself* with respect to our late modern present."[19] Metaphor and culture help us contend with this problematic. More specifically, Lowe identifies the disciplinary fractures that delimit the cultural from the social, whereby the social sciences conceive culture "as secondary and epiphenomenal to, rather than constitutive of, the social": "While social scientists commonly declare that culture is an important barometer of globalization, many analyses have tended to treat culture as a passive effect of political economic processes."[20] Culture thus has the ability to revise our understandings of the social and change, particularly when culture is understood as entwined with and not unique from the political and social.

These dilemmas are brought to the fore in *Fairytale*. At the end of the documentary, following interviews with German citizens that depict their racist understandings of the Chinese, Ai interviews Chinese citizens about how they experienced Kassel and *documenta*. One of his interviewees echoes Lowe's insights and emphasizes the limits of representation and the impossibility of capturing the global: "We can grasp our immediate environment. But we can never have a complete understanding of human beings. We can only have a general impression. What is that general impression? It is the movement of many things, which are similar to you." Although the speaker directs us to the difficulties in grasping beyond our immediate environs, he also finds possibilities in relations that "are similar to you." Ai highlights this interview in order to shift away from a focus on an individual's experience without fully dismissing it. Drawing from a Chinese Marxist legacy, Ai sutures the institutional and structural directly to the cultural and subject. He stresses this relation in order to deemphasize an individualist, herculean agency and to privilege a focus on the way the individual is articulated through and with others and institutions. Akin to Lowe, Ai's interviewee emphasizes the impossibility of directly knowing and representing globality; thus, relations and other less linear connections provide the minor yet key ways of understanding how we exist within the global and structural. *Fairytale* emphasizes this unknowability of others, scale, and the transnational.

The aesthetics of Ai's work operate with a fuzziness and mass that do not allow for an individual to fully represent oneself; rather, one must find relations to others and within a structure. In this vein, the process of inclusion promotes a different political end outside of liberalism: a comrade aesthetics and ethics. Rather than privileging a representational reading of the chairs, ceramics, or *Template* installation, Ai produces and emphasizes an affective and relational engagement with objects and space. Each chair could represent a seat for the 1,001 Chinese in Kassel. Beyond being representative of a Chinese past tradition (objects) or of the visiting bodies (performance), *Fairytale* lingers in the affective feeling of what is missing or lacking. This affective notion demands that *documenta* attendees locate themselves in relation to an other and within the structures that surround them. The empty chair is not only a place for a Chinese body to sit, but also the location for a viewer at Kassel to realize someone is missing. This affective relation to the empty chair opens up a space for the audience member to feel and ponder why such chairs exist and who could be occupying them. Ai multiplies this affective effect through the distribution of 1,001 chairs.

Further, Ai constructs 1,001 luggage pieces that he gives to the participants in similarly expansive and affective ways (figure 2.4). He attaches white velcro to the outside of their carry-on luggage in order to attract objects. In his documentary, he includes a vignette of him visiting the fabric store and discussing his intentions for his use of velcro. His choice emphasizes a static and clingy relation to space, as velcro often traps dirt and other debris. In other words, the luggage does not simply represent or symbolize Chinese citizens entering true cosmopolitanism through European tourism. The luggage

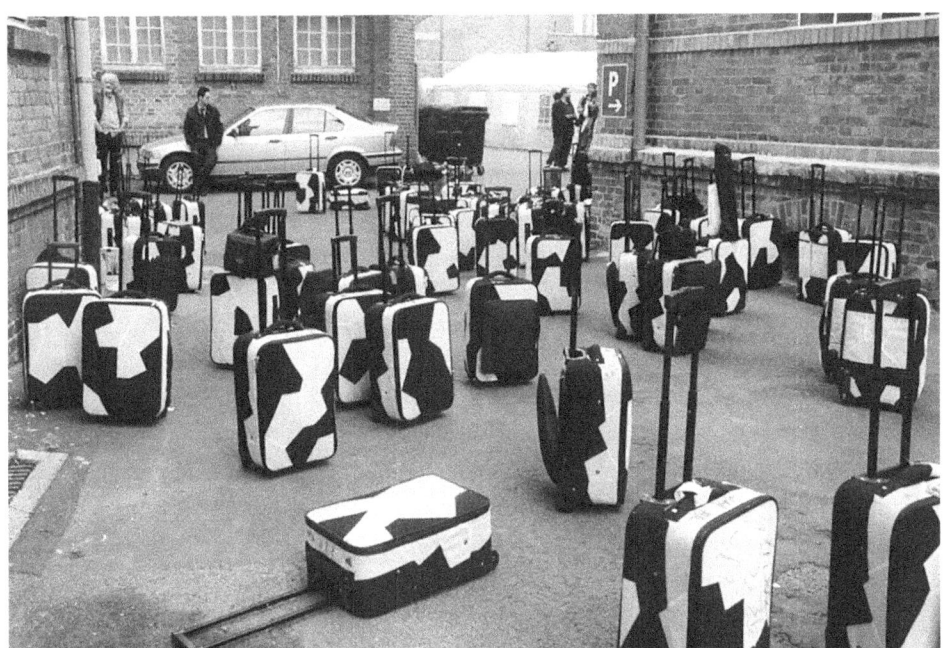

Figure 2.4. Ai Weiwei, Luggage Pieces
(*Fairytale*), 2007. Courtesy of the
artist; Leister Foundation, Switzerland;
Erlenmeyer Stiftung, Switzerland; and
Galerie Urs Meile, Beijing-Lucerne.

pieces produce an affective relation to space and others. The luggage attracts
attention (due to its striking contrast of black against white), along with debris and other matter. These objects force one to extend outside of oneself
and continually place one in a phenomenological relation to others, space,
and structures. Without fully relying on social scientific methods and political economy, Ai illuminates how the minor and comrade aesthetics provide
important methods for structural analysis.

Being Plural before Singular: Humanization and Intersubjectivization

Non-Western artworks are often interpreted as demonstrating intersubjective exchange, humanization, and plurality since such works often circulate
in contexts outside of their immediate geographic locale. Intersubjectivity
involves a focus across subject to subject; humanization surrounds the recognition of each subject as part of the communal; and plurality or multiplicity

engages related modes of dispossession across time and space. These three frames primarily rely on a connection across subjects presumed to be equally human so as to universalize the non-Western other as just another person (and hence, removed from a history of race). However, Ai complicates these dominant frames by revealing the limits surrounding how the subject is conceptualized. When equality assumes that each subject is universally equivalent and common, we sidestep the long histories surrounding racialization and miss grappling with other forms of the subject like the comrade.

The Chinese are often seen as a faceless mass and as putatively less than human. As the largest population (although with diverse ethnic groups across the Chinese, which Ai emphasizes in *Fairytale*), the Chinese appear to be not only a mass within China but also a diasporic horde infiltrating the world. It might be tempting to argue against this racist understanding by humanizing and seeing each Chinese as an individual subject, by multiculturally enfolding these people into the universal notion of humanity, or by articulating an intersubjectivity whereby Chinese and others learn from one another. However, Ai resists these moves and amplifies an aesthetic of mass repetition to bring to the fore the limits surrounding these dominant curatorial and aesthetic approaches to inclusion. Ai traces the shape of the mass, loosening our reliance on the individual subject and directing us toward structure.

Ai's use of repetition animates both formal and theoretical preoccupations. Formally, he has used repetition throughout his work. In *Sunflower Seeds* (2010), Ai hired artisans from Jingdezhen to hand paint over 100 million ceramic replicas of sunflower seeds. His installation filled the Tate Modern's Turbine Hall. In addition, from 2008 to 2012, Ai inaugurated and spearheaded a project to commemorate the lives lost during the 2008 Sichuan earthquake. In response to the many missing children who were attending poorly constructed schools during the quake, the artist sewed together children's backpacks and snaked them along a museum's ceiling. Another part of these works is *Straight*, which involved salvaged rebar from the collapsed construction sites in Sichuan that were meticulously straightened and displayed throughout museums. This aesthetic of mass repetition has preoccupied Ai before and after *Fairytale*. In a 2014 commissioned piece at Alcatraz Island in San Francisco, Ai retooled his use of repetition through the use of multiple Lego pieces. Lego portraits were made in the image of different dissident artists from across the globe and throughout history. And since 2016, Ai has deployed repetition to grapple with the refugee crisis. These works frequently involve the repetition of inflatable rafts and vests used on rescue missions.

Fairytale is a precursor to Ai's now well-established use of repetition and mass. The objects he repeats throughout *documenta* are chairs and discarded doors from construction, along with human bodies. Although every object and body has individualized characteristics, Ai relies on their repeated and coagulated presence to bring to the fore the predicament regarding "all look same." Ai refuses to argue against such a dehumanizing position. Through Ai's repetition of 1,001 subjects and objects, *Fairytale* opens up space to think beyond recognition and the liberal individual subject, particularly for those who have historically been rendered flattened objects of history.

Intersubjectivity and Humanization

Ai's use of "all look same" reveals the limits of the first two dominant frames often used for inclusion: intersubjectivity and humanization. Both intersubjectivity and humanization deploy a similar logic, whereby an imagined exchange from one liberal subject to another produces an empathic connection. Intersubjectivity focuses on the mechanisms and benefits of this exchange; humanization makes a bid for one's subjecthood in order to be recognized within a universal ideal. These frameworks imagine a directly mediated connection from human subject to human subject. *Fairytale* could be and has been situated within these liberalized renderings of intersubjectivity and humanization.

Drawing from Husserlian phenomenology, intersubjectivity describes the means by which subjects construct a sense of self by distinguishing themselves in relation to another. Maurice Merleau-Ponty and others have developed the notion to situate subjects as they relate to the structural and questions surrounding Marxism. However, some scholars have deemphasized the structural aspect of this frame in ways that privilege moments of identification across individual subjects so as to produce the communal. These scholars have relied on intersubjectivity to represent how one becomes a "center" to be compelled "to recognize the co-existence of those who frame [one's] margins."[21] Within this particular model of intersubjectivity, the other may not complete but rather complements the self. Intersubjectivity becomes the expansive glue that produces a community and relations. Meiling Cheng formulates her analysis of contemporary Chinese art in relation to the use of multiple bodies as a mode of multicentricity which "is then intersubjectivity multiplied, extending the interpersonal to the inter societal, the international and the inter glocal and perhaps, one day, when extraterrestrials decide to join us earthlings, to the inter global and the intergalactic."[22] For

Cheng, Ai's use of mass represents a way of integrating multiple perspectives together. I build upon Cheng's work to imagine other possibilities for the mass—specifically the way Ai fractures a sense of humanization and the intersubjective.

In *Fairytale*, Ai works against the tendency to humanize each and every Chinese person that appears in his documentary. Further, he resists providing the payoff of intersubjective exchange. Ai pushes against the overromanticization of community and the intersubjective by emphasizing the disjunctions produced at Kassel and among the 1,001 Chinese subjects. He also renegotiates a sense of *being singular plural* to reassess the intersubjective.

This reassessment of the intersubjective can be seen at the end of the documentary, when Ai interviews German citizens on their interactions with and insights on the Chinese visitors. Among the comments from the German citizens, there are some that appear intersubjective—where Germans learned about "Chinese" perspectives. However, many responses are, put simply, racist. They reveal assumptions about Chinese bodies as lacking a sense of humanity and being uncivilized or not modern. This is the condition of "all look same." Ai begins his interviews with German citizens' experience of the Chinese in a seemingly multicultural way. One interviewee states, "Before I had bad impressions of Chinese, I've had unpleasant experiences with them. They always make loud noises while they're eating. That's what I saw in Australia. They didn't behave very well there. But now, very good! They're nice and very neat." After this moment, however, Ai thwarts the liberal sentimental payoff of intersubjective exchange. For example, one interviewee discusses how the Chinese gathered in Kassel: "Maybe they get together somewhere. Perhaps in the rice fields. [Laughter] I don't know. Maybe they just stand in the fields, and that is presented as a work of art." Upon the interviewee associating the Chinese with the labored position of rice field workers, the interviewer then asks if the interviewee would like to meet any of the Chinese citizens. The German respondent replies, "Not really. You can meet all kinds of interesting people in Kassel. I don't care if they're part of an art project." Afterward, as she walks away, she beckons her child, who follows obediently; the camera follows the child holding her mother's hand.

Beyond revealing European forms of racism, the comments also engage the impossibility of intersubjective exchange, particularly for subjects who have historically been racialized and presumed to all look the same. This interview, among others, reveals the limits of intersubjectivity. Ai emphasizes how racism precludes an equal human subject-to-subject relation. Instead of concluding the film with positive moments of change or progress due to the inclusion of minor subjects, he ends by highlighting that the work done through his art cannot amount to a substantive intersubjectivity. Intersubjectivity and the humanization of each Chinese person becomes radically impossible considering the history of global racialization.

This reworking of the liberal subject and a fractured notion of the communal resonate with Jean-Luc Nancy's oft-cited work on being singular plural. Nancy renegotiates Heideggerian theorizations of being by foregrounding both the individual and the other. The Marxist inflections of being singular plural have been central for reworking liberal subjecthood, and being singular plural resonates with Ai's work. However, Ai extends Nancy's theorizations for those who have never been imagined as being singular in the first place—for those who "all look same" and are pluralized first and foremost as their ontological starting point. He explores what it means for those whose sense of being is always plural before ever being singular. Ai works within the tensions of being singular plural, revealing how racialized others are never afforded a full sense of singularity.

Akin to Ai, Nancy differentiates being singular plural from the intersubjective: "The 'with' is not the sign of a reality, or even of an 'intersubjective dimension.' It really is, 'in truth,' a mark drawn out over the void, which crosses over it and underlines it at the same time, thereby constituting the drawing apart and drawing together of the void. As such, it also constitutes the traction and tension, repulsion/attraction, of the 'between'-us."[23] The difference between Nancy's being singular plural and the intersubjective is that the former is always implicated with a sense of being with. The latter, however, presumes and maintains the notion of singular individuality for the subject. This subject only becomes intersubjective and related to another when they are brought into relation with another individualized liberal subject. Being singular plural reorders the subject to be always implicated with others, destabilizing the dominant ontological understanding of the subject. And from this place, being with does not implicate a simplistic care for an other but becomes "the disturbance of violent relatedness."[24]

Although some have certainly deployed intersubjectivity in critically productive ways, the notion, especially when delinked from the structural, reproduces the subject as fully autonomous and presumes community as integrated.[25] Ai's project, however, operates at a different register that focuses on the impersonal and the ways the communal comes to be romanticized. As he demonstrates in his interviews with German citizens, community is never achieved. *Fairytale* focuses on the affective disconnects between Germans and Chinese. The Chinese in Kassel are often understood as always being plural before any sense of singularity is bestowed upon them. Community is not stable for Nancy nor for Ai's work; instead, community involves dissensus.[26] In addition to the racist understandings of the Chinese as uncivilized rice field workers, the Germans also situate the Chinese within uneven modes of modernity. One interviewee discusses how bringing the Chinese to Germany introduces them to civilization; he opines that this could have a "true" fairytale ending for the Chinese: "If the hosts do a good job, then it might really be a fairytale. It could be a huge step for them, for people who have never known modern civilization, such as electricity, hot water, automobiles, and aircraft, or all the little aspects of technology. This experience could become a fairytale for them." Similarly, another German citizen explicitly lays out the unidirectionality among understandings of modernization: "It's important that they learn about us, but not the other way around. To know how the Europeans are living." Ai disrupts moments of seemingly intersubjective and multicultural exchange, highlighting the impossibility of a global community. He works against the communal by creating a space and process filled with fissures, disconnects, and perpetual negotiations between bodies, languages, and affects. Ai captures the logic of how modes of modernization are unevenly distributed, highlighting how racialized populations are perpetually imagined apart from a global commons.

All Look Same (Sorta): Han-Normative

These fractures exist not only globally, but also within China. In *Fairytale*, Ai additionally explores the limits of intersubjectivity among the 1,001 visitors. In one scene of the documentary, Ai focuses on a dark-skinned farmer, walking alone amid the well-dressed, cosmopolitan, and generally light-skinned crowd of *documenta*.[27] While looking pensively at the fake giraffe in Peter Friedl's *The Zoo Story*, he is asked by a reporter speaking Mandarin Chinese what he thinks about the work. The farmer is unable to communicate in Mandarin, as he speaks another dialect that requires translation from another participant. This moment of linguistic difference within the Chinese-speaking world reveals the limits of "community" within China itself. Throughout the documentary's interviews with the farmer, as he walks through the exhibition halls, the director highlights the farmer's disconnect from not only *documenta* attendees, but also other Chinese participants.

In addition, Ai does not romanticize art for producing community, counter to *documenta*'s curatorial frame. For example, in the background during the interlude with the Chinese farmer, Friedl's work looms within the frame. The work—which includes the fake giraffe the Chinese farmer is looking at—grapples with questions surrounding war, animal domestication, and Israel's occupation of Palestine. Brownie the giraffe was initially from South Africa and shipped to the West Bank's Qalquiliyah Zoo. During construction activity amid Israeli settlement of the Palestinian town in 2002, the giraffe panicked and died from head trauma. Friedl's preservation of Brownie attempts to capture these multiple meanings, as they situate the viewer in relation to these localized politics. When the farmer is asked if he thinks this giraffe is "art," he responds, "if it's realistic or life-like, then it's good." Upon a downpour of rain at *documenta*, he is asked if the rain or the giraffe excites him more. He expounds that "farmers are always thinking of rain." The seeming naiveté embedded in his answers highlights the limits of art. His answers do not reveal the transnational frameworks of war, animality, and sovereignty that Friedl considers. Rather, art takes on a more minor, limited function for the farmer. He is distanced from not only other Chinese, but also the art itself. Ai presents a scene in which art does not necessarily possess the "power" to change politics, radicalize the subject, reorder established sensibilities, nor create connections between people. Instead, Ai focuses on art's limits, its inability to produce intersubjective exchange, global community, or proper political consciousness.

During the documentary, Ai states that his intentions for this work are to explore how Chinese locals "experience the so-called high culture" and "to look at their way of looking." Ai limits the communicative and global potential of art; its reach and effects might perhaps be more minor, as opposed to forming community or radical critique. The farmer is thus neither completely isolated nor fully integrated into the art world and with other Chinese citizens; he exists in limited relation to both communities. Within these scenes, disconnect arises from language, both aesthetic and cultural. Ai explores this sense of being singular plural and the limits of the liberal intersubjective encounter.

Being (Plural) Singular Plural

The linguistic and cultural distinctions that exist in different regions in China are often obscured when we consider race in a global context. This is due to the fact that liberalism conditions our responses to racism by primarily humanizing the Chinese to counter the idea that they all look the same. We thus ignore fractures and dissensus within communities in order to privilege humanizing or singularizing the other. This dynamic points to the fact that the Chinese are always considered first and foremost as *being plural* before ever being considered *being singular* or human. Although I do not deny that racialized subjects can individually connect with others, these limited moments do not substantiate a reworking of the historical and institutionalized conditions that render these figures as racialized masses. Ai emphasizes this condition, whereby one always already exists as *being (plural)* before being singular. Ai thus amends Nancy's ideas by producing an aesthetic of *being (plural) singular plural*: the racialized as "all look same" are first and foremost understood through plurality. Within a global landscape, being for the Chinese does not hold the same ontological condition as being for the West. As a result, the proper and major emerge and aggregate from this ontological difference.

In establishing how being is conditioned toward plurality for the Chinese, Ai then provides an understanding of singularity throughout the documentary and at *documenta*, as discussed above. However, this singularity is not meant to humanize; this being (plural) before becoming singular is not a nihilistic move to simply state that being is just plural ("we are all part of the mass and multitude"). Instead, Ai produces a *being (plural) singular plural* to contend with the complexities and fracturing force of racialization. Throughout the documentary, the director focuses on the experiences of a few of the 1,001 participants. Ai depicts them with a sense of singularity. One such group of people are the elders from Jichang village in Guangxi Province. They are filmed leaving their hometowns to interact with Germans on the plane ride to Kassel. Some of these participants had never traveled before; they were located in rural areas where they not only had never received a passport, but also were never given "official names." They had to produce names before they traveled, literalizing this sense of being (plural) before becoming singular.

In addition, Ai films a long sequence on Liu Yu, a safety inspector at a highway checkpoint in Yingkou City in Liaoning Province. When we first encounter Liu Yu, he is framed within the banality of his daily life, directing trucks at a toll booth. However, Ai juxtaposes his routinized life against his desire to travel abroad and to Kassel. This worker, in many ways, is the ultimate being (plural) for the non-Western other, as he occupies an extremely unromantic position—he is neither a rural peasant nor a glamorous cosmopolitan. His comfortably middle-class status pluralizes him, as he is neither the abject migrant worker nor the capitalist flexible citizen so often discussed in popular culture and academic accounts of China. Yet, the way the director treats the subject is one that singularizes and gives voice to this everyday, middle class worker. Ai directs us toward a sense of this being (plural) singular within the narratives of both the elders and traffic control worker. In addition, one obtains a sense of this being (plural) singular throughout the film as the Chinese visitors perform in conga lines and take pictures of the landscapes and one another. These moments produce a sense of joy that arises when people are provided the opportunity to interact and laugh, from being plural to *being (plural) singular*.

However, in producing this being (plural) singular, Ai does not simply stop his critique and humanize the Chinese. Ai does not amend pluralizing with a sense of individualism nor cosmopolitanism; rather, he conditions singularity to always be in relation to others. Racialization arrests being as always (plural) before singularity can be granted to such subjects, reworking Nancy's being singular plural. Ai, as such, considers the condition of the non-West into *being (plural) singular plural*, by which the racialized condition of being plural is provided a sense of humanity that does not retreat into a multicultural or intersubjective moment. Although we see individual singularity throughout the film, Ai stresses, "I think, even when we talk about individualism, it's not the act of one person."

Ai Weiwei, in other words, redirects the singular back to the plural, the relational. At the end of the film, after he interviews German nationals, Ai chats with Chinese participants. One of them gestures toward the condition of being (plural) singular plural: "As we come to Germany from China and go back to China, what state are we in in the midst of this movement? Maybe I have respect for myself as a part of a whole. As one out of one thousand one." The speaker directs us to the being (plural) of the initial encounter; however, he then emphasizes the movement of also being singular plural through his sense of "respect for myself" (singular) and then becoming "part of a whole" (plural). All of these moments captured by Ai depict the figure of the comrade in its singularity and plurality to others and social structures. As such, Ai lays the groundwork for a relational politics that extends beyond the self.

Why All Look Same?: Relationality In Spite of Being (Always) Plural

Ai Weiwei's aesthetic of repetition reworks not only humanization and intersubjectivity, but also the third approach of relationality. This latter project can be traced in the ways the artist references politics beyond his immediate interests, extending his analytic beyond the self. *Fairytale* confronts the conditions of always being plural and "all look same" to produce a relational politic based on global racialization—such an analytic, in turn, revises our understanding of humanity beyond a universalist notion. Following *Fairytale* and after his house arrest, which occurred between 2010 and 2015, Ai has continued to focus on causes outside of the context of China. Most notably, he turned to depicting political dissidents in China, Russia, the United States, South Africa, and other nations in his massive Lego installations. Ai also used the repetition of objects to engage the refugee crisis in his documentary films and art installations in Florence, New York, and other cities. In essence, Ai reworks relationality through a reconsideration of the multitude, a term that seeks to unify across difference to counter late capitalist forces—forces that create issues like the refugee crisis.[28] This Marxist analytic initially seems helpful for theorizing Ai's use of plurality and his focus on relationality, considering his formal use of repetition and his ongoing relations to political causes outside of China. However, Ai revises the multitude and relational through two entangled notions: racial anger and the types of subjects imagined to produce relationality.

First, although Ai's work can be understood through the multitude, he exceeds its current theorization. The bid for relationality, at times, flattens power dynamics that materially structure racialized lives. Ai thus enables a similar yet unique form of relationality that reconfigures and brings to light how liberalist impulses linger even within the leftist intervention of the multitude. In particular, Ai confronts the accumulated affects of anger and spite that structure how racialized populations have historically navigated and currently experience capital. Racial anger emerges from not only the historical repetition and ontological condition of being plural, but also the structural forms of violence and capitalist extraction that have produced modernity's tragic conditions. Racial anger is therefore a structural affect, not an individual singular feeling. Unlike white hatred's amnesic relationship to history, racial anger is located in history and the production of modernity. When whiteness's privileges are challenged, questioned, or redistributed, white hatred inflames, at the individual level, and forgets the histories by which whiteness has accumulated property value. As such, through the dynamic across anger and the unforgiveable, Ai broadens anger from individual feeling to accounts of state practices. Ai helps shift our focus from individual affect to state and structural power in order to account for the negativity some feel toward liberal frameworks like intersubjective exchange; leftist bids for a deracialized relationality across human populations; and racially liberal ethnic studies accounts that privilege relationality and race in ways that obscure anti-Blackness and indigenous genocide (different *forms* of racial anger that are the foundations for the production of modernity).

Second, Ai's minor aesthetics highlight how the "subject" is imagined in the multitude. For relational projects, the idea of the subject must be revised, since its autonomy, singularity, and sovereignty come into question. In order to unite across different forms of subjugation, the subject thus becomes distributed, extended, generic,[29] impersonal, a third person,[30] a comrade, rhizomatic, or part of the multitude. These *neutralized* subjects allow political relationality to form through bonds that exceed identity. However, the many forms this neutral and expanded subject can take require that we tease out these many possibilities. In particular, the multitude accounts for diverse subject identities through an additive logic. Even within this frame, a racialized subject remains knowable and enfoldable. However, by expanding how the subject is imagined, Ai presents other possibilities for the relational.

In particular, he offers the occasion to theorize this condition of all look same through another figure, in addition to the comrade, that shares a similar condition: the lumpenproletariat. The lumpen is a nonidentity that exists as a faceless mass. The lumpen are those often unable to fit into the model minority of revolutionary action: the proletariat. Marx and Engels refer to this category as a mob (those who "all look same" often become a swarm and horde) and as those working outside of productive modes of labor.[31] As such, the lumpen involves figures difficult to fully enfold into not only dominant liberalism, but also dominant Marxism. When racialization is understood through the lumpen, we revise inclusion as a practice. Inclusion becomes not about the additive, whereby we enumerate and account for every possible identity into consideration. Instead, through the lumpen, we reconceptualize inclusion as a project, practice, and process to always consider who else is missing. Inclusion shifts away from being a finite act toward an ongoing method and approach. Due to the fact that within these frameworks there is no coherent subject to be included, we are forced to always ask who is missing and how we might constantly restructure so as to account for them. In this vein, the lumpen resonates with the comrade in that they both engage structure and rely on neutral, non-identity-based subjects without defaulting into additive logics. Ultimately, the lumpen clarifies how the impersonal, comrade, and condition of "all look same" provide a method that continually seeks to account for those in excess of inclusion.

As discussed above, Ai's *Fairytale* points to a number of ways for contemplating the limitations of the liberal notions of minor difference and inclusion. Racial anger, which Ai's work directly contends with, is another important affect for reconsidering these limits. Within a liberal logic, racial anger is delimited to an individual emotion, rather than a structural affect. But thinking of racial anger as structural and historic helps reveal the limits of inclusion for the relational turn.

Inclusion is considered a tool to remedy exclusion and inequality within not only liberal but also Marxist projects. In these efforts to advance inclusion, however, racialization's many different forms and affects are often obscured. For example, in their work *Multitude: War and Democracy in the Age of Empire*, Michael Hardt and Antonio Negri develop the multitude as an answer to a global network of power they call Empire: "Insofar as the multitude is neither an identity (like the people) nor uniform (like the masses), the internal differences of the multitude must discover *the common* that allows them to communicate and act together."[32] From this perspective, in the production of the multitude, the subject is hailed to let go of one's singularity in order to join others, whereby differences are cast aside in order to find what is in common.[33] The authors attempt to resist the urge to create a multicultural understanding of difference; to do so, they footnote Audre Lorde's essay "The Master's Tools Will Never Dismantle the Master's House" in order to move away from difference as a negative force.[34] Hardt and Negri also call for a radical transformation of the world by "tak[ing] away the limiting, negative, destructive character of differences and mak[ing] differences our strength (gender differences, racial differences, differences of sexuality, and *so forth*)."[35] This approach, however, which mischaracterizes Lorde's ideas, flattens other modes of difference beyond class into the category of the "so forth"—a flattening that represents the dominant ways difference is often theorized within leftist approaches through a logic of finitude. Through such an account, relationality is produced out of spite for difference. Difference here is conceptualized as something that can be enumerated and must be put aside in order to join the common cause. Put differently, inclusion for the multitude exists through an additive logic.

Whereas approaches like Hardt and Negri's locate the problem with difference in how it is deployed as either "the limiting, negative, destructive character of differences" or "strength," Lorde is not preoccupied with how difference is included in ways that are either challenging or empowering.

Rather, she deploys difference as the method and practice that expand how we imagine our relations. Difference is "a fund of necessary polarities between which our creativity can spark like a dialectic."[36] For Lorde, crucially, minor subjects are not to be added to a roster of "so forths" that help us account for all; in the context of her original talk, she warns against simply including more difference into the category of woman. Instead, differences are the source and method for rethinking approaches to inclusion. In this way, Lorde conceptualizes minor subjects beyond individual identities toward method.

Lorde provides the means to rethink the additive logic of inclusion for the multitude. Ai's aesthetics and Chinese Marxism additionally help us grapple with other ways to imagine minor subjects beyond a dominant inclusionary impulse. Like Lorde, in *Fairytale*, Ai contends with difference as method, bringing to the fore the problems with both liberal and leftist approaches to inclusion. Grappling with multiple forms of difference requires that we deal with subjects and objects that are in excess to the multitude.

In particular, repeated and historical forms of racialization lead to feelings and affects that make it difficult for certain groups to simply forgive and forget history and to focus on what they have in common with others. These subjects are not bitterly refusing to make difference a strength. Anger informed by histories of race is a potent structural affect that cannot be glossed over by the lure of relationality. In one section of Ai's documentary, for example, a mother expresses her frustration for her son having been fired from his job and denied a visa to attend *documenta* due to the son blogging about police corruption. Her anger is coupled with a sense of desperation and exhaustion. Ai uncomfortably focuses his camera on the mother's face as a way to emphasize her pain and rage that seem almost uncontainable on the screen. Anger here emerges from conditions within China and outside that produce extreme frustration. On one hand, the mother expresses rage toward corruption in China. On the other, we must trace why and how corruption emerges. Corruption in China responds to not only the extreme global demands of late capital through unregulated production, but also the racialization and gendering of the Chinese as efficient laborers that can "handle" these first world, capitalist demands. After all, the condition of "all look same" is not simply about how one perceives a racialized subject; this racialized condition fuels the global economy by rendering such subjects as a horde so that their value comes from their labor and contributions to capital. Rather than eschewing anger to produce a relational critique of late capital, however, Ai brings to the fore additional issues surrounding global racialization and labor. Ai directs us to the racialized and gendered conditions and affects, specifically *spite*, that undergird the limits around turns to the multitude.

Racially informed anger emerges not solely from immediate injustices, but also from historical and repeated forms of subjugation and colonization that have led to the world's funding and founding ("all look same" and being plural are historical conditions). As a structural affect, racial anger thus produces a commons *in spite of* being plural. To be in spite is to have an affective relation of anger and frustration. And to produce a commons in spite of this frustration requires that one does not simply let go of one's anger. Ai brings to the fore the need to deal with anger and negativity as resources that revise relationality, particularly the concept of the multitude. This anger is important to contend with since there is no easily identifiable target toward which one can direct one's ire.

Racial anger informs the comrades and lumpen who have existed throughout modernity.[37] The anger caused by racialized violence emerges from the production of our modern world; this world, according to David Scott, exists through tragedy.[38] And as Saidiya Hartman has brilliantly noted, in relation to slavery and Black subjection, forgiving and forgetting are impossible: "It is impossible to fully redress this pained condition without the occurrence of an event of epic and revolutionary proportions—the abolition of slavery, the destruction of a racist social order, and the actualization of equality. The incompleteness of redress is therefore related to the magnitude of the breach—the millions lost in the Middle Passage and the 15 million and more captured and enslaved in the Americas—and to the inadequacy of remedy."[39] The magnitude of racial subjugation and Black subjection will not and cannot enable forgetting because of the impossibility of redressive action. In invoking the work of Hartman, I do not aim to collapse social death into every other form of institutional violence. As Jodi Byrd, building off the work of Jodi Melamed, reminds us, racial liberalism equates and collapses all forms of racial subjugation.[40] Instead, I seek to contend with the impossibility of forgetting racial anger due to the fact that such violences (albeit varied) existed and still remain—they are preconditions to our modern world order. And since racial anger manifests differently across distinct racialized communities, we must develop accounts of the various *forms* of anger. Anger that arises from histories of anti-Chineseness is not the same as anger from anti-Blackness, indigenous genocide, or war logics emerging throughout Southeast Asia. The fractures amid communities must always be accounted for as we continue to theorize the relational, as will be discussed further in chapter 5. Crucially, Hartman's work reminds us that we must confront historical state action amid the minor. Racial anger is not simply a floating or individualized affect; it is tied to the state.

The target of racial anger should be state practices, particularly the ongoing institutionalization of racialization that informs our norms and common sense. However, the state not only is an identifiable figure, but also operates in the background of its violences. Thus, historical devastation becomes naturalized, obscuring the purposeful actions and intents of the state and its actors. And furthermore, the target, known as the state toward which to cast one's anger, cannot be effortlessly and immediately identified. Anger therefore becomes scattered rather than directed, considering the historical and contemporary magnitude of what counts as the state alongside our own respective relations to it. In this vein, racial anger cannot fully resolve itself through forgiveness, considering the impossibility of full redress from the state and the fact that these violences produce the conditions and reality of everyday life, sense, and discourse; it is indeed tragic. Moreover, the state itself controls the legibility of the act of forgiveness, as trenchantly established by Lisa Yoneyama and Jacques Derrida.[41] Since the scale of historic ills manifests institutionally, we need to theorize a notion of racial anger that deploys forgiveness beyond state-defined means like liberal rights, memorialization, and citizenship. In sum, racial anger must shift away from an account of the self toward an account of the state, while simultaneously understanding the limits of the state and the impossibility of full redress—the attempt and process become the goal rather than completion and finitude.

Although a near impossible act, forgiveness requires that we turn to the structural rather than the personal. Lorde echoes this call in her focus on anger. In her 1981 speech to the National Women's Studies Association, "The Uses of Anger: Women Responding to Racism," Lorde theorizes the possibilities of anger for political change. Lorde clarifies how racial anger is not a masculinist force, in comparison to the individualized feelings of (white) hatred which "is the fury of those who do not share our goals." Instead, she brings to the fore state enactments of violence as they relate to histories of racialization and the daily realities of modernity. She reveals how a structural focus for racial anger should concentrate on who "profits from all this. . . . For it is not the anger of Black women which is dripping down over this globe like a diseased liquid. It is not my anger that launches rockets, spends over sixty thousand dollars a second on missiles and other agents of war and death, slaughters children in cities, stockpiles nerve gas and chemical bombs, sodomizes our daughters and our earth."[42]

Although Lorde helpfully directs us to the state, it is critical to remind ourselves of the ways we each profit from these actions, especially for those of us working from, what M. Jacqui Alexander calls, "the seat of empire."[43] Racial anger not only involves a tacit account of the state, but also implicates the self and each other for the ways we complexly "profit from all this." One's anger thus becomes not simply a narcissistic inability to forgive and forget or to let go of one's identity or difference. Instead, racial anger is a way to exist in the tragic conditions of our world, accepting the *impossibility* of fully obtaining yet the crucial *necessity* of working toward relationality. In other words, racial anger is an ethic and mode of accountability; this anger cannot be immediately remedied through facile fixes or fast critiques of easily identifiable targets. Instead, we accept that we exist and are implicated within this tragic condition that requires a commitment to the impossible—to continually engage in this project that hails us so as to be in relation, in dissensus.

By identifying the role of the state and its entwinement with capital, racial anger becomes the generating force and method that inspire a continual process to rebuild beyond the bounds of self-interest. And yet, even upon doing so, we must recognize that contending with racial anger in this way will not resolve or fix history. This is another part of this tragic conditioning for existence: the impossibility yet necessity of redress. This condition should not defeat us nor drive us into defaulting into a liberal optimism that flattens discourse in ways that forget history and analyses of structure. We must always produce ways to exist within tragedy. As such, finding relations with others in the present and past who similarly have contended or are contending with racial anger is a necessary and minor act. These relations, in turn, compel us to function through a notion of optimism that resists the lure of liberalism and exists instead within the impossible, illiberal, and tragic.

Comrades and the Lumpen

Racial anger, in the context of Ai's documentary for *Fairytale*, is not used to enforce an additive logic of inclusion. Instead, it directs us to an ethics and continual practice of asking who is missing, producing a relationality in spite of our tragic conditions. This project moves away from understanding the self beyond a liberal, sovereign subject toward a neutral one. Throughout the documentary, Ai focuses on people from very disparate walks of life to help acknowledge difference within China: from the rural farmer to the middle-class highway inspector. The arc of his film is driven by him searching for multiple types of subjects, knowing the incomplete nature and impossibility of such an act. And although finite as a number, the grandeur of 1,001 gestures toward the inability to be complete or whole. The reference to *One Thousand and One Nights* contributes to both Ai's play on Orientalist appeal and the openness of the fairytale that seems to never end.

In this way, Ai's aesthetics shift inclusion from a completable and finite act toward a process of perpetually searching for others. In other words, his work directs us to an understanding of inclusion that moves away from both liberal and leftist sensibilities around addition and finitude. He, instead, reconceptualizes inclusion as a structuralist practice of always considering who might be missing. In turn, through Ai's aesthetics, the subject for inclusion becomes neutralized so as to refigure its bounds. In spite of being always already plural, these comrades do not seek to be made whole and humanized. These neutral subjects linger in their incompleteness, produce modes of illegible connection, and search for those other comrades in the past, present, and future. Racial anger directs us to an ethics, practice, and method that perpetually inquire who might be missing—an unfinishable and infinite yet critical task.

This conceptualization of a relational subject does not fully resonate with theorizations of the multitude. Instead, such a relational subject requires that we render inclusion to become an infinite process rather than a finite task. To search for those who might not be accounted for aligns more closely with theorizations around the lumpenproletariat. The lumpen do not demand inclusion and parity; rather, Marx theorizes the lumpenproletariat as a means to contend with difference within the overuniversalizing operations of the proletariat. The lumpen are those who are in excess of the proletariat, who operate outside of respectability politics, and who are required to relinquish their difference—the lumpenproletariat are the "so forths." Nicholas Thoburn identifies the lumpen as those incapable of being enfolded into narratives about the working class that privilege productive and extracted labor. Thoburn highlights how Marx develops the lumpen as a class to account for "difference and anomaly."[44] However, Thoburn moves beyond an understanding of the lumpen as solely a concrete identity based on social class. For him, the lumpen are "less a group of people than a *mode of practice* that is premised on the minor condition that people are missing."[45] In other words, Thoburn explores the methodological possibilities of focusing on the lumpenproletariat as a condition and practice that inquire about those missing from inclusion.

The lumpen and comrade are important neutralized figures that reconfigure relationality, beyond those already provided by notions like the third person or impersonal. The lumpen and comrade offer space to rethink inclusion beyond additive logics and the representation of the "so forths." Put differently, these figures inspire a minor method and practice that revise inclusion beyond a liberal or deracialized leftist project. In turn, the very understanding of the subject shifts away from notions surrounding respectability, recognition, and being considered or made whole. The lumpen and comrade push beyond singularity, autonomy, and sovereignty so as to ultimately produce relations with others—an idea of humanity that is created not out of spite for difference (to gloss over historical racial anger), but rather *in spite of* difference. If racialized anger becomes the driving affect for inclusion (rather than a flattening and smoothing over of negative affects in order to make everyone else feel good), then how we include becomes more of a practice rather than an end goal. Humanity thus becomes a process, continually made and remade, rather than a notion assumed to be transcendent, universal, or fully inclusive.

The privileged feeling or affect for Marxism has historically been alienation. It fuels the model minority known as the proletariat to come into realization of capital's abuses and thus become an enlightened subject. The proletariat then enacts change against an identifiable wrongdoer, often referred to as the capitalist. These victims of capital are ultimately envisioned as relating to one another to produce a multitude that revolutionizes our world. However, the lumpenproletariat contend with other affective registers for those not included, the so forths, and the "all look same": anger and spite. These affects, however, do not have identifiable targets so as to directly demand and seek retribution and repair; in other words, there is no immediately identifiable capitalist to critique and challenge. And even if one can identify the state as the repeated wrongdoer, the depth of the state's breaches surrounding historical racialized dispossession excludes retribution and repair which are nonetheless predefined by the state. Thus, since racial anger does not always have a direct target for critique unlike alienation, there is no subject that can be made whole or rendered fully human—this is the tragic reality of modernity. Rather than nihilistically giving up, we accept this condition and hold onto racial anger as a way to fuel the lumpenproletariat and refuse the demand to embody a coherent subject identity. To produce relationality in spite of being (always) plural involves expanding the affects available to the masses.

3

Minoring the Universal

AFFECT AND THE MOLECULAR
IN YAN XING'S PERFORMANCES
AND LIU DING, CAROL LU, AND SU WEI'S
CURATION AS ART PRACTICE

As demonstrated in the previous chapters, major China is maintained through predetermined notions of history and context. When properly understood, these terms replicate the dynamic whereby China is considered "universally particular" while Europe remains "particularly universal," as articulated by David Eng, Teemu Ruskola, and Shuang Shen.[1] History and context, as such, track the long-standing debate across the universal and particular. This chapter analyzes the theoretical assumptions that undergird how history and context have been deployed to examine China's particularity amid its overuniversalization. Since others have articulated critical arguments within the universal-particular debate, the primary aim of this chapter is to take stock of the citational figures that maintain its recurrence.[2] The minor as method not only contends with overdetermined notions of history and context, but also considers the disciplinary histories and intellectual references that sustain our preoccupation with the universal and particular.

On the one hand, the particularizing move through context entraps non-Western subjects into a single locality. Even amid calls to relate the particular to broader concerns, the anchor of particularity nonetheless triangulates the self/artist with the nation and transnational, what I discuss as an Oedipal scheme or complex. More specifically, Chinese artists are narrated within a resistance narrative that situates them with the modern West and against the unmodern non-West. Non-Western artists are thus discussed across debates surrounding the universal and particular: how much particularized knowledge about their contexts is needed and how much can they really provide for more "universal" discourses? History and context become the metrics by which we obtain a "true" understanding of Chinese art, while Chinese art presumably becomes a "true" index of the history and context of China.

On the other hand, the turn to universalization has come to be dismissed to a point to which bids to broadly situate a non-Western artist within the universal come with a heavy dose of suspicion. The conceptual limits with the particular and universal debate demand not better discourses, but rather a closer attention to what sustains and maintains its recurrence (i.e., the Oedipal). The artists I analyze in this chapter render supple the particularity provided by history and context by understanding these terms as molecular, affective, and *in theory*. Instead of presuming the knowability of history and context to tell us what Chinese art is really about, the artists in this chapter speculate upon and help us imagine other ways of understanding established, material, and bounded forms like the body and state. In addition, these artists scale back the notion of the universal in ways that question Eurocentrism without fully relying on the particular.

Although it might be tempting to insularly localize discourse and theory to individual sites, a myopic focus on the particular through history and context removes us from a larger project of theory making that contends with theory's Eurocentric legacies. A full retreat to particularity maintains Eurocentrism because the former does not rethink the latter's relation to transnational sites. An uncritical reliance on the particular reaffirms the assumptions of key terms used to shape its discourse. These terms, like *history, the state, subject,* and *agency*, are deployed without a rethinking of their histories as they relate to modern humanism. Thus, I resist arguing against such an extreme or promoting a simplistic mediation of the universal with the particular. As noted in the introduction, both postcolonial and China studies have helped us grapple with the impossibility of being fully universal or particular. These fields have considered how Eurocentric concepts cannot simply be discarded or fully decolonized; they can only be revised to think beyond locality, and we must hesitate by holding Eurocentric thought accountable.[3] I thus turn to the ways fields, and the citational figures they respectively rely on, consider history and context. This task is important because transnational art practices require multiple disciplines, like area, ethnic, and queer and feminist studies, to contend with their complexity. Further, the range in media practices (dance, film, performance art, theater, new media, visual art, and installation) possesses genealogies and intellectual figures that inform each of these discrete and interrelated aesthetic approaches. Although the complexity of art requires multiple fields and expansive medial engagements, disciplinarity nonetheless shapes and limits our academic engagements with artists and their objects. It is through the practices of artists that we begin to grapple with the disciplinary restrictions and fractures that maintain our constant return to history and context, as exemplified through the universal and particular debate.

Two intellectual figures have varied relations to the fields heralded by Chinese artists, along with different uses across medial-specific arenas: Gilles Deleuze and Félix Guattari. As briefly mentioned in the introduction and as will be elaborated upon below, these figures help us minorly analyze the tendencies that inform field formations.[4] Thus, rather than merely apply Deleuzo-Guattarian frames to Chinese art, I track how these theorists' insights provide methods that attend to material forms yet extend beyond them to rethink history and context, the universal and particular. Further, and more importantly, I take stock of Chinese artists' production of frames that resonate with these theorists. These artists enable minor methods that help us do the work of "reexamin[ing] the idea of Europe" and contending with the tendencies of citational figures that maintain the continual return of the universal and particular debate.[5] This chapter shifts the focus from a canonical artist like Ai Weiwei toward practitioners who expand the expectations and discourses established by earlier figures. The two art projects I focus on rework a prescribed economy and discourse surrounding history and context and the universal and particular. Yan Xing's video and performance piece from 2012, *Kill (the) TV-Set*, and Liu Ding, Carol Yinghua Lu, and Su Wei's collective curatorial practices both produce frames that resonate with the work of Deleuze and Guattari. These two projects examine the particularities of history and context in relation to universalism.

Yan Xing is a queer Chinese artist born in 1986 in Chongqing. He was previously based out of Beijing and, as of 2015, began to work out of Beijing and Los Angeles. As one of the youngest Chinese artists circulating on the global market, he has garnered much attention. Yan's *Kill (the) TV-Set* (referred to as *Kill*) was one of the earlier pieces that established his career. The piece is a two-channel black-and-white video which plays for about three minutes (figures 3.1 and 3.2). *Kill* offers a critical reworking of universalized notions of bodies ranging from subjects to nation-states. In the installation, one video is a reperformance of *Charlotte Moorman with Human Cello* (1965),

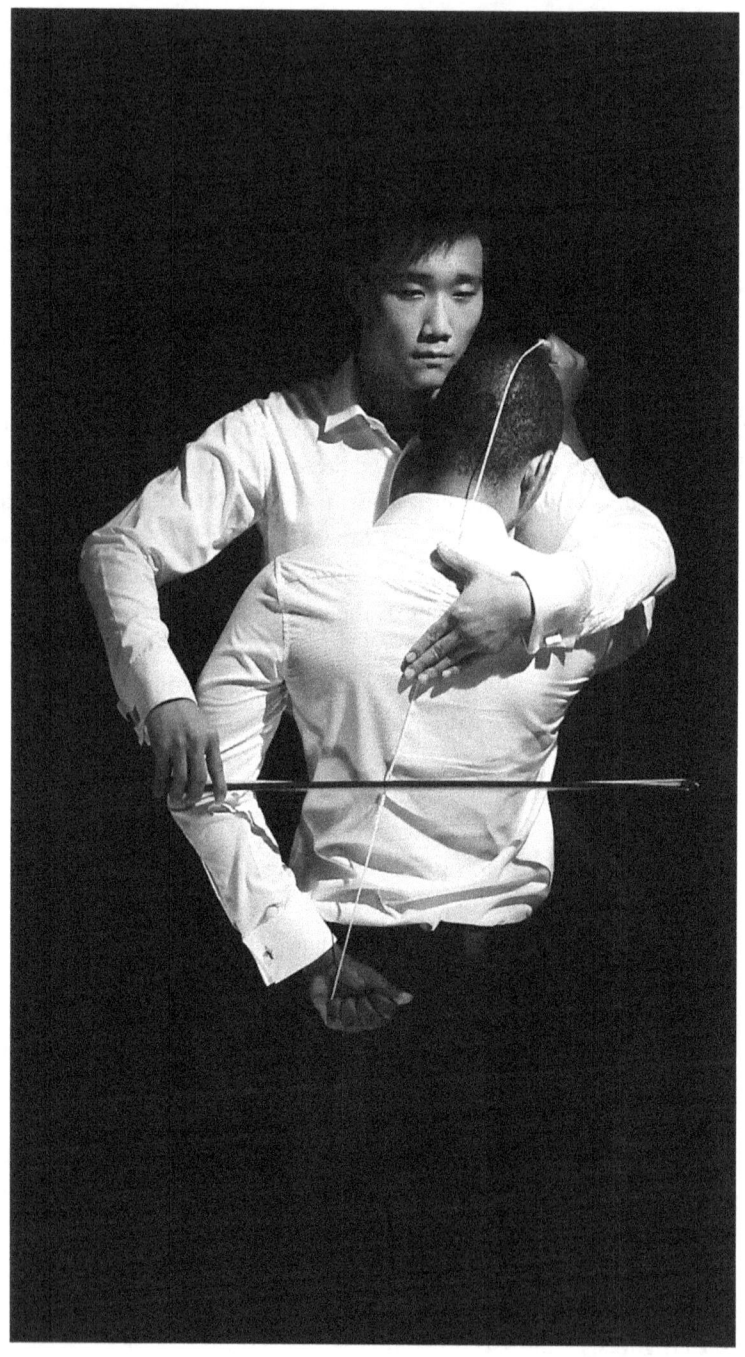

Figure 3.1. Yan Xing, *Kill (the) TV-Set*, 2012. 2-channel video installation, 1st channel, single HD digital video (b/w, silent, loop), 2'30". Dimensions variable. © Yan Xing. Courtesy of the artist.

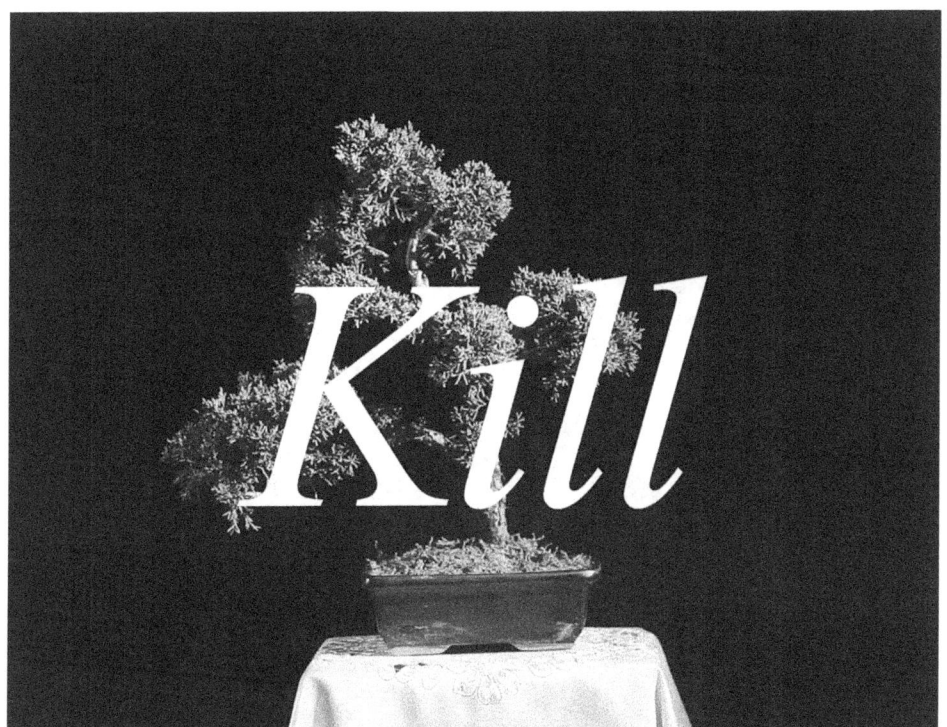

Figue 3.2. Yan Xing, *Kill (the) TV-Set*,
2012. 2-channel video installation,
2nd channel, single channel digital
video (b/w, silent, loop), 3'06".
Dimensions variable. © Yan Xing.
Courtesy of the artist.

where Moorman simulated playing John Cage's *26'1.1499"* (1955) across Nam
June Paik's back (figure 3.3). Paik and Moorman are seminaked and face each
other, while Paik holds a string along his spine. His head rests above Moorman's left breast. Through film, Yan reperforms Paik and Moorman's iconic
work that was documented through photography. Yan's reperformance references two pieces: Paik and Moorman's interpretation of Cage's sound project. In Yan's staging, the artist, dressed in a freshly starched and cuff-linked
white button-down that is tucked into his black trousers, stands in a similar
position to Moorman. Nigerian actor Agu Anumudu performs Paik's role
and stands facing Yan in the same semiformal attire. Yan and Anumudu's
conservative clothing is striking in comparison to Paik and Moorman's exposed flesh. Yan's face peers into the space directly below him, while he lightly

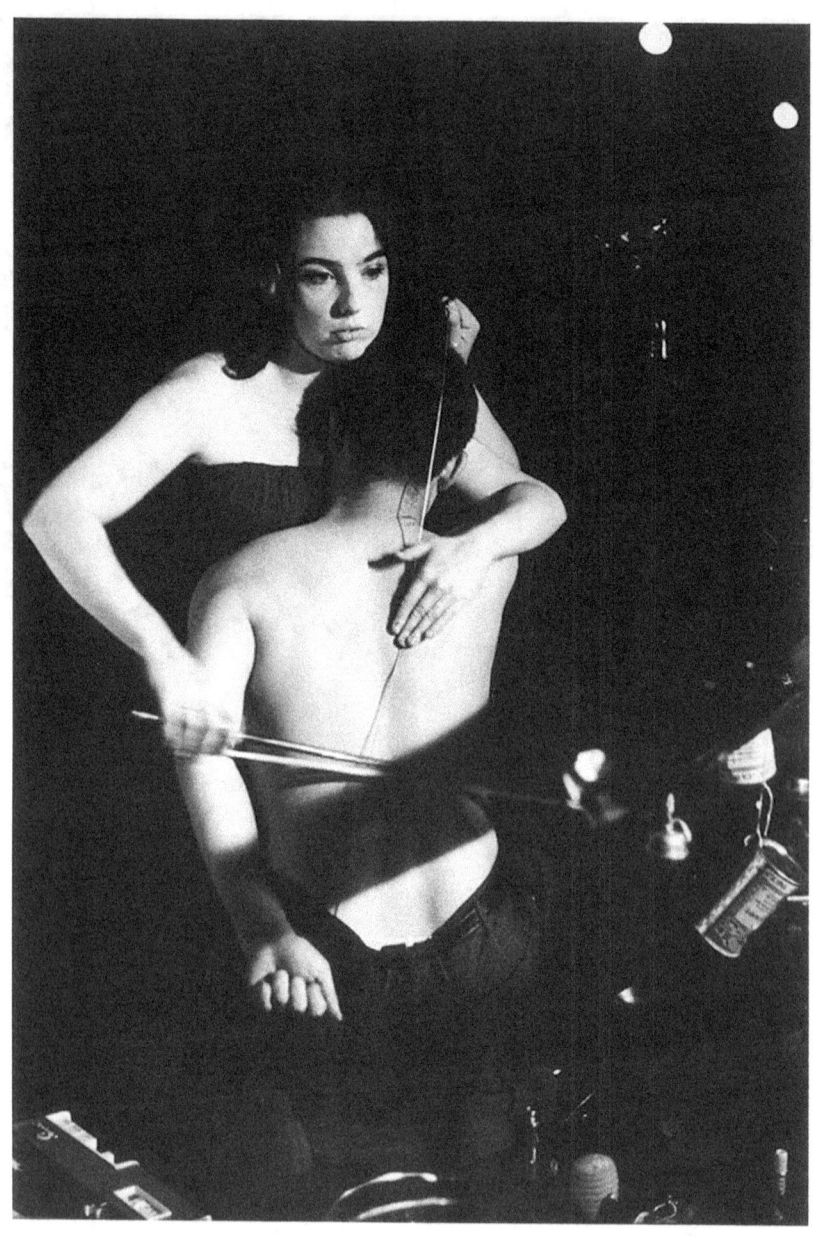

Figure 3.3. Peter Moore, Charlotte
Moorman and Nam June Paik
performing John Cage's *26'1.1499"*
for a String Player (Human Cello
section). Café Au Go Go, New York City,
October 4, 1965.

caresses a bow across the string held by the actor. The other video is a shot of a bonsai tree that Yan groomed. In the foreground, the screen repeatedly flashes, in bold white letters, the sequence: "Kill," "(the)," and "TV-Set." Yan's films run in silence. This piece explores Deleuzo-Guattarian notions like the anti-Oedipal, affect, and becoming to contend with how we contextualize non-Western subjects in relation to the particular. In other words, Yan helps us grapple with the particular by tracking history and context *in theory*, as speculative and molecular entities. By doing so, Yan Xing methodologically approaches the bounded ideas of individual and national bodies. Yan complicates how we might theorize and situate corporeal and state bodies outside of an Oedipal economy centered around the artist/self, Chinese nation, and global/liberal art world. History and context, as the main methods that show us what an artwork is presumably about, are rendered unstable in *Kill*.

Beyond film and performance, in this chapter, I also focus on a different practice—curation—that grapples with disciplinarity, universality, and history. The artist Liu Ding collaborated with Carol Yinghua Lu and Su Wei to curate a series of shows. Born in 1976, Liu Ding is from Jiangsu Province and based out of Beijing. He eschewed a formal art education and has been working within performance, painting, installation, photography, and conceptual art since 2001. In 2009, he represented China at the Fifty-Third Venice Biennale; since then, his work has shifted toward curation as art practice. Although many of his paintings, sculptures, and installations deserve critical attention, I focus on his turn toward curation in collaboration with Carol Lu and Su Wei. Born in 1977, Carol Lu is from Guangdong Province and is an active curator, writer, and art theorist based out of Beijing. She is a central intellectual force in the global art market. Lastly, born in 1982, Su Wei is from Beijing and based in Hong Kong. His curation and art criticism are deeply informed by his doctoral research in continental philosophy and contemporary art. In 2011, the three presented *Little Movements*, which curates different international projects, from China and elsewhere, that relate to one another not in terms of temporal or geographic scope but rather in terms of minor aesthetic and political approaches. Liu Ding, Carol Lu, and Su Wei grouped together the varied artists, producers, and intellectuals in *Little Movements* because they utilize aesthetics beyond the didactic to emphasize minute ways of critiquing life and the social, thereby renegotiating the political (figure 3.4).

The Seventh Shenzhen Biennial, entitled *Accidental Message: Art Is Not a System, Not a World*, builds upon their curatorial goals in *Little Movements* to reflect on the development of Chinese art during the late 1980s through

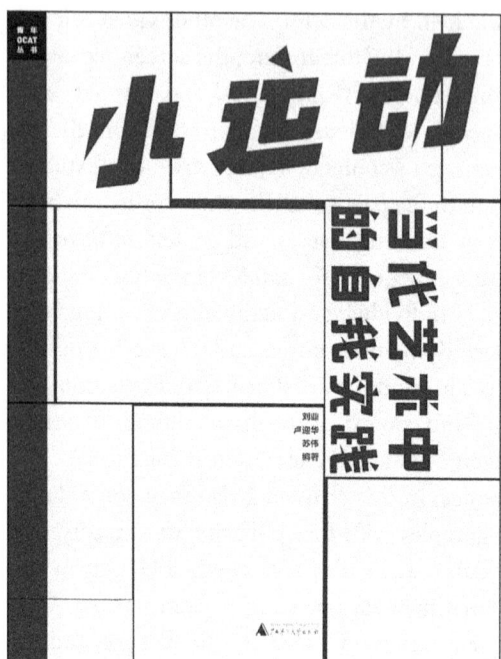

Figure 3.4. Liu Ding, Carol Lu, and Su Wei, *Little Movements*, 2012. Image of book cover. Courtesy of the artists.

the 1990s. In this large-scale project, the artist-curators organize objects not merely to represent key moments in art history, but rather to revisit how creators (artists and producers alike) envisioned their production and ideas. Their overall goal is to reexamine this genre of art at the level of artistic engagement and connections across individuals, instead of fitting the art into a social context; they explore the oft-ignored contours of internal feelings and external relations that exist in these emblematic works. They bring to the fore the minor details embedded in these objects that are typically eschewed as unimportant for or irrelevant to most historical accounts of contemporary Chinese art. As such, they deploy affect as a curatorial method, rather than linear formations of time, to construct a history of contemporary Chinese art. These artists expand the universal in ways that allow Chinese artists to relate to other racialized populations beyond their own site of China.

These art projects do not resolve debates over the universal and particular. Instead, the video work and curation projects deploy the minor as method to hesitate and take stock of what maintains and fuels these debates. In particular, Yan Xing produces the anti-Oedipal, affect, and becoming to grapple with disciplines, subjects, and the state that shape how we particularize context.

Liu Ding, Carol Lu, and Su Wei deploy the minor as a way to confront the notion of universal history amid a modern world based on racialization. The team reexamines the dominant logics that undergird curation as a historiographic project: the proper, import, and possibility. By using affect as a curatorial method, they rethink curation as a practice to produce a minor sense of the universal and history. Before turning to these projects, I first take stock of Deleuze and Guattari as they help us grapple with the continual return of the universal and particular debate. Afterward, I examine these art practices for the ways they rethink the epistemological bases and presumptions of the particular, through Yan Xing, and the universal, through Liu Ding, Carol Lu, and Su Wei.

Deleuze Your Daddy?: The Anti-Oedipal beyond Minor Subjects

At first, Deleuze and Guattari may not seem to be the most obvious interlocutors for contemporary Chinese art. Other theorists initially appear more helpful: Lu Xun, for example, assists in tracking the entwinement of modernism, modernity, and socialism; Michel Foucault offers an articulation of negotiating power or a trenchant theory of sexuality that one might rework in relation to a queer subject like Yan Xing; and Wang Hui grapples with changes in the Chinese state, neoliberalism, and globalization. In fact, many of these theorists have been deployed across fields related to contemporary Chinese art. I, however, turn to Deleuze and Guattari to reexamine our disciplinary tendencies and habits, as they help us track what maintains and sustains the universal and particular debate.

Let us begin with Yan Xing's *Kill*, which plays with many of these tensions. Although his works have circulated throughout China, Ukraine, the United Kingdom, Italy, and the United States and he has exhibited alongside established artists like Vito Acconci and Ai Weiwei, Yan is nonetheless taken not only to represent geopolitical context or antagonistic relations to the state, but also to reference Western "masters," other Asian artists, or tradition. Since he is one of the few Chinese artists identified as queer within the global art market,[6] his work gains currency through narratives of resistance against state and social discrimination. Furthermore, Yan has become known for his use of nudity and for his blog focusing on his family, sex, and Chinese politics. The blog inspired his performance *Daddy Project* (2011), which involved a video recording of him reading a letter to his father and addressing his childhood being raised by a single mother. His art has thus been discussed as emblematic of a globally queer aesthetic as some critics situate him "as [an] openly gay [man who] lives in a country (if not a world) that tends to frown upon (if not actively suppress) displays of sexuality that are deemed outside of the norm."[7] Since he was born in 1986 in Chongqing and graduated from the Sichuan Fine Arts Institute, his success is often attributed to the ways he is framed in relation to being "queer" (representative identity) and born after the Cultural Revolution (referential context). The proper, as produced through the referential and representational, reinscribes this minor subject within an Oedipal complex. The Oedipal, in other words, operates as a universalizing frame that predetermines how Yan is understood, forcing us to rely on contextualization and referentiality to counter this dominant logic. Yan's own multiple allusions to past fathers and forms of media bring to the fore the Oedipal frames embedded in discourses like cross-medial art practice, citationality, and genealogies that become the obvious choices to narrate *Kill*.

However, Yan's aesthetics formulate a methodological understanding of the minor that directs us to the work of Deleuze and Guattari. Rather than providing answers that clarify the status of queerness in China (his most immediate, particular context), Yan creates modes of illegibility that do not reproduce representational accounts of minor experiences in minor, non-Western spaces. Furthermore, Yan devises a minor aesthetic that humorously deploys sensation and other minor means. This piece makes repeated references to the past referential figures that contextualize his work to playfully goad the dominant frameworks of cross-medial art practice and referentiality. Yan finds new relational modes that work outside of the previously established economies of Oedipal triangulation: the Western modern, the Chinese unmodern, and the dissident; the universal and global West, the particularity of the rest, and the avant-garde artist; and daddy, mommy, and self. Yan's work highlights the limited discursive options that are embedded within such triangulations. In other words, he hails the work of Deleuze and Guattari by producing an *anti-Oedipal* relation to such configurations.[8] Yan's aesthetic amplifies the absurdity of this condition. He repeatedly hails references in order for a viewer to take note of such conditions, making transparent the contextualizing frames that overdetermine Yan's art. For example, Yan references not only the works of Nam June Paik, Charlotte Moorman, and John Cage, but also established Chinese artists like Ai Weiwei who become tethered to, dictate, and condition any discourse on a younger Chinese artist. In other words, Yan produces a minor method that reveals the dominance of particularity, referentiality, and representation that frame his works and minor subject position within the proper.

Yan's production of Deleuzo-Guattarian frames also enables a critical attention to the fractures amid multiple fields: area (Asian), ethnic (Asian American), queer, and transnational studies. Yan's aesthetics emphasize the limits across disciplines, with their differential relations to representation and referentiality. In this sense, Yan hails multiple references to forefathers to shift away from an Oedipal discussion of his work. Deleuze and Guattari help us develop the minor as a method by examining the field tensions that Yan cites. Through the invocation of such famous art historical figures from the likes of Cage to Moorman, it might be tempting to narrate *Kill* as embodying a progression of media (from sound to performance) or representing a genealogy of avant-garde fathers. After all, in the repeated invocation of the television, Yan conjures Paik, who is often attributed as one of the founders (or a daddy) of media art since he was the first to use televisions in visual art. Paik, along with other Asian artists, was quite central in the development of Fluxus during the 1960s and 1970s. In addition, Paik holds a similar subject position to Yan, as the former comes from Asia (South Korea) and circulates widely in Western fine art circles. However, Yan complicates these linear models of historical development and artistic referentiality through his formal aesthetics. He reveals the problems surrounding teleological understandings of time and filiation. Rather than replace or assert his Chinese presence into this genealogy of art historical and medium-specific practices, Yan makes this linear (filial) logic transparent. In other words, there is no original referential father in Yan's reperformance of a reperformance. Yan pinpoints the existence of such a model that conditions and creates predetermined narratives for non-Western artists via the figure of the metaphoric daddy. Yan disrupts this dynamic, highlights this narrative trope, and makes comical and transparent the many forefathers that shape the discourse for his work.

Yan brings to the fore his relationship to his pasts, attempting to find configurations that are not solely filial, linear, or Oedipal. Through the use of exposure, absurdity, and the "killing" of the many hailed fathers, along with a demand to not replicate presumed relationships between the artist and his particularized context or past, Yan's work develops an anti-Oedipal aesthetic.[9] Deleuze and Guattari wrote *Anti-Oedipus* during a moment when Freud's Oedipal complex became a dominant framework for scholarship.[10] The anti-Oedipal imagines relations between subjects that are not predefined by a triangulated frame like mom, dad, and self. Their critique of the Oedipal extends to their oft-cited work on minor literature, as it relates to Franz Kafka. By moving away from "unfortunate psychoanalytic [Oedipal] interpretations" of Kafka's "Letter to the Father," they emphasize how his minor literature's "goal is to obtain a blowup of the 'photo,' an exaggeration of it to the point of absurdity." In other words, Yan's hailing of forefathers similarly operationalizes the minor as a method by critiquing the dominance of the Oedipal through an anti-Oedipal stance that "enlarge[s] to the point of absurdity," the complex.[11]

Anti-Oedipus revamps the psychoanalytic narratives that privilege a son's normative development through the desire to kill the *pater*. Rather than rejecting the Oedipal, the authors emphasize the need to find new pathways: "The question of the father isn't how to become free in relation to him (an Oedipal question) but how to find a path there where he didn't find any."[12] This minor approach hesitates from simply discarding older models (and replacing them with new or decolonized ideas) and, instead, takes note of the limits surrounding established frameworks. The minor as method, in other words, is less about replacing the dominant than understanding the limits and assumptions of the dominant. Yan's multiple reperformances offer different pathways that do not perpetuate the Oedipal model of filiation, representation, and referentiality. Yan does not replace or refute the existence of his father figures. He amplifies the absurdity of this problematic condition through his reperformance of a reperformance of a performance. In other words, Yan shifts the emphasis from "*Who's* your daddy?" to "Who *is* your daddy?" The shift from asserting a daddy role (*Who's* your daddy?) to the search for identifying the daddy figure (Who *is* your daddy?) directs us to a predicament—one that changes from asserting clear roles to lacking clarity. Rather than claiming and asserting his sociohistorical context, Yan invites the audience to identify the problem of referentiality, particularity, or contextualization, the condition whereby one must situate artists, and more frequently non-Western ones, within a clear and identifiable lineage. References to Paik demonstrate neither a rejection nor a direct representative relation. Instead, Yan fractures such subjects as not fully knowable.

In engaging Deleuze and Guattari, I do not propose discarding past frames and replacing them with Deleuzo-Guattarian approaches to Chinese art; rather, I work through Yan's invocation of these authors to examine the disciplinary divides discussed above and in the introduction. Through multiple invocations around representative references, Yan emphasizes the racialized condition whereby minor subjects are predominantly framed within filiality and lineage. Yan neither accepts the norms of nor rejects the Oedipal. Instead, he produces a Deleuzo-Guattarian project that engages the minor as a mode that questions and remarks upon the dominance of available frames, alongside the limits of disciplines. Yan teaches us to hesitate.

Before I further engage Yan's *Kill*, let me briefly clarify how Deleuze and Guattari as citational figures contend with disciplinary tendencies that undergird universal and particular debates. Deleuze and Guattari bring to light the differences between minor subjects and methods. These authors engage materiality and power through this differentiation. Their critique of the Oedipal complex emerges out of a denunciation of French colonization. The Oedipal becomes a universalizing discourse that perpetuates predetermined understandings about a particular space and people. These authors develop their approach of the anti-Oedipal from colonialism to reveal how the Oedipal complex has become an overdetermined framework even for sites outside of Europe. By situating their critique of the Oedipal complex within anthropological accounts of Egypt, India, and other non-Western spaces, the authors develop the anti-Oedipal by revealing how the Oedipal is a colonizing model: "An Oedipal framework is outlined for the dispossessed primitives: a shantytown Oedipus . . . the colonized remained a typical example of resistance to Oedipus . . . the colonized resists oedipalization, and oedipalization tends to close around him again. To the degree that there is oedipalization, it is due to colonization."[13] These theorists provide a model by which to rethink the colonizing force of both the universal and particular. The universal glosses over contingency and difference, while the particular eschews relations and broader theoretical insights.

In addition, as citational figures, Deleuze and Guattari exist at the periphery of most fields. And as further noted in the introduction, they have greatly influenced the minor affective turn yet some have questioned their applicability for more "classical" concerns surrounding the political. As such, their approaches are less disciplinarily oriented which provides a model for both theoretical and aesthetic production. Their engagements with the social and particular expand the minor beyond being an index of "other," non-Western worlds and people toward a method that activates and renders minor the universal.

Forming the Particular through Queer Affect in Yan Xing's *Kill (the) TV-Set*

In *Kill*, Yan Xing contends with the forms that help us particularize and, as some conceptualize it, problematize the universal. By focusing on forms ranging from individual bodies to nation-states, Yan questions the particularizing mechanisms that we use to renegotiate the universal. In other words,

Yan shifts away from the dominant move that provides context so as to use the particular against the universal. Moreover, Yan engages other Deleuzo-Guattarian notions to hesitate from contextualizing further; he highlights our tendency to continually rely on contextualization and particularity. Yan Xing produces China *in theory*, whereby context becomes molecular and affective, opening up additional avenues to read *Kill* beyond the Oedipal.

Throughout Yan's performance, he produces a disengaged affect. The juxtaposition between his distant look and the flashing of "Kill" on the opposite screen creates a rhythmic disjuncture, as he does not perform at the same intensity as the repeated words. Although his detachment could be attributed to reperforming Moorman's look, the formal construction of and rhythmic disconnects between the two screens offer a different, queer relation. *Charlotte Moorman with Human Cello* is the structural basis for Yan's piece. Paik and Moorman's collaboration was a reinterpretation of Cage's *26'1.1499"* sound work, which involved a structured solo for either a single player or an ensemble. Cage's composition lasts twenty-six minutes and 1.1499 seconds and deploys chance operations. The soundscape consists primarily of the player's fortissimo stringing, which is punctuated by momentary ruptures of breath, short statements ("Hey"), and staccato taps on the instrument. Moorman and Paik's goal in deploying fine arts and performance is to sexualize classical music, which at that point had not been done. Their exposed flesh comes into contact, as Moorman sits in between Paik's straddling knees. Their use of nudity, corporeal position, and media interrupts music's puritanism, as Paik asserts that "music history needs its D. H. Lawrence, its Sigmund Freud."[14]

Similar to Deleuze and Guattari's explicit critique of Lacan and Freud in *Anti-Oedipus*, Yan's shift from these psychoanalytic figures helps us reconsider Paik's commitment to them. The lack of sex in *Kill* amplifies this pivot. Yan notably desexualizes his reperformance by dressing formally. In comparison to Yan's past works, *Kill* is much less sexually explicit. Many of his earlier pieces deploy nudity. For example, in *The History of Fugue* (2012) and *Sexy* (2011), bare buttocks and penises are displayed in large-scale videos and framed photos. Even after *Kill*, other works, such as *The Sweet Movie* (2013) and *The Sex Comedy* (2013), furthered his exploration of explicit sex by respectively documenting pornographic film and archiving sex toys. As such, this notable desexualized shift in *Kill* complicates how we define and represent queerness: through the representation of sex or perhaps other less explicit possibilities. Through this change in tone, Yan pushes the goals of Paik and Moorman's project to new territory: rather than representing sexuality and queerness via a subject's body, one's identity, or acts, Yan delves into queerness's instability through an exploration of medial form. As a reperformance of Paik and Moorman's performance of Cage's sound work, *Kill* produces multiple citations through divergent medial practices. Yan focuses away from Paik and Moorman's sexualizing of the nude body to another queer possibility: the daddy relation. Yan highlights the many referential figures that structure his reception and aesthetics: Paik, Cage, Moorman, the Chinese state, Western avant-gardism, and other Asian artists. However, rather than simply representing these daddies through their attendant media (sound, video, etc.), he deploys medial forms to develop queerness through affect. His reperformance of two canonical works produces a double layer of referentiality that forces one to consider what the function is of being twice removed from a sourced material. Form, media, and reperformance enable an affective understanding of queerness.

Yan deploys the minor as an affective mechanism, which refrains from reading how symbols in a work represent an outsider queer subject status. For example, instead of discussing Yan's embrace of a male body as a stable representation or commentary on queer life, I privilege an affective engagement that approaches the subject's body as concrete and real yet simultaneously open to additional understandings. Yan methodologically attends to a form with openness. His embrace of the Nigerian actor Anumudu might symbolize not only bodies but also nation-states and relations across minor geographies, since there are geopolitical shifts with Chinese migration and capital into countries throughout Africa.

However, queer affect, as tracked within Yan's formal aesthetics, produces another dimension for the minor that destabilizes understandings of subjects, bodies, and nation-states. Although there is an embrace between men, it appears disconnected. There is no sense of shared passion. Anumudu is not closely held as a fake cello, since even an instrument requires involved handling. Unlike the way cellists passionately press their fingers into a string, Yan's entire palm flatly rests against the string and Anumudu's shirt. Yan hovers his arms across Anumudu, as if half-heartedly following stage directions. The work's queer dimensions arise from indeterminate, formal relations, or what might be called its affective qualities. Affect produced between objects, forms, and bodies enables the viewer to ask questions and imagine multiple relations between Yan and the other. By focusing on form in this work, however, I do not intend to imply that Yan teleologically queers the past media of sound and video through performance; rather, affect through form emerges through a less linear engagement with media. For example, Yan's reperformance runs in silence. Rather than retracing or reproducing the sonic landscape created by Cage, Yan deploys silence and a slow aesthetic to allow space for other narratives to arise.

Further, as a reperformance, Yan builds off of the photo documentation of Paik and Moorman's collaboration. Rebecca Schneider helps us understand how Yan deploys live performance to work through the photographed memory of this piece. She reveals the oversimplification that delegates "live performance as vanishing in time and photography as capturing time" that has distinguished the two media.[15] Yan uses a slow and silent performance to produce an instability between these two media—an affective and medial rupture that cannot be captured by a representational analysis of Yan's queer identity or the use of bodies. At first, the video appears to be a still photograph of Yan's reperformance of Paik and Moorman's piece. However, as the film develops, the subtle use of breath and slow gestures from the moving bow indicate a shift in the medium. This intermixing of performance and photography caught through film fractures the distinctions that separate performance "as vanishing in time" and photography "as capturing time." The movement of bodies through breath and gesture enables a perpetually ruptured sense of stillness that confuses the line between photography and performance. Furthermore, the high level of pixelated definition directs a viewer to the fuzzy details of breath and movement, which might be overlooked by a viewer observing the work as a *tableau vivant*. One witnesses Yan's chest and Anumudu's back slowly rise; twitches in Yan's face sporadically appear.

These moments of affective fuzziness and indeterminacy resonate with Deleuze and Guattari's approach to bodies. Rather than presuming the social to be static or rendering bodies and nations as fully knowable, their method attends to the minute vibrations that are often overlooked to discover connections that span time and space:

> What defines a minority, then, is not the number but the *relations* internal to the number . . . the minority is defined as a non-denumerable set . . . What characterizes a non-denumerable set is neither the set nor its elements; rather, it is the *connection*, the "and" produced between elements, between sets, and which belongs to neither, which eludes them and constitutes a line of flight . . . the minorities constitute "*fuzzy*," nondenumerable, nonaxiomizable sets, in short, "masses," multiplicities of escape and flux. . . . The role of the minority is to bring out the power of the nondenumerable even when it consists in only one member.[16]

Deleuze and Guattari situate the minor in relation to the nondenumerable. This concept connotes numbers that cannot be associated with integers or be positivistically represented by known numbers. In other words, the nondenumerable does not correlate meaning with representability. The minor cannot fully correspond to numerical representation, directing us to rely on an indeterminate fuzziness to track subjects and objects. Deleuze and Guattari offer theoretical insights for the minor as method as it relates to *Kill*. Affect approaches subjects, ranging from the body to "area," as representations with nuance and difference. By focusing on "units" and other affectively fuzzy means, Yan develops the minor for its function, working with the Deleuzo-Guattarian goal of moving away from "the dreary games of what is representative and represented in representation."[17] The fuzzy implicates two meanings: a tactile sensation and a cognitive state of vagueness. These definitions together highlight that an affective approach entails engaging a subject as a solid form while simultaneously sensing its vibrations that are not predetermined by how it is dominantly defined. The fuzzy that arises from affect situates subjects in both material and open means. China is not only a knowable form but also an indeterminate construction, akin to Allen Chun's early reconstruction of China's "boundedness."[18] This approach privileges the affective and fuzzy contours of an object, without solely relying on its dominant form and attendant narratives, to understand it as both real and constructed. A queer, fuzzy affect emerges through the medial relations noted earlier, along with the complex web of reperformances that Yan weaves. By relocating queerness within aesthetic formalism and the affective foundations of the work, Yan allows "the minor, forgotten, overlooked, disavowed, unsung, second, double, and 'lesser' [to] gain a kind of agency in the re-do."[19]

Yan animates a minor and limited agency within his reperformance; he provides a political thrust to the affective and fuzzy. By dislocating queerness away from subjects and bodies toward affect, Yan engages Deleuze and Guattari's attention to a work's surface and affective fuzziness rather than deeply unconscious and representative meanings. Yan enables a minor agency that does not manifest through overt resistance; rather, this agency brings about space to hesitate, ask questions, and destabilize assumptions around identities, subjects, and objects. The minor as method involves a weaker, hesitant, and interrogatory mode of agency that produces questions rather than meaning or critique. Queerness becomes less about Yan's identity and more about his creation of a disconnected affect that emerges when juxtaposing multiple media. Queerness can certainly arise from the representation of bodies; however, it also exists through indirect modes of mediation. I bring to the fore the affective contours in *Kill* to flesh out the minorness of affect that is often occluded by the proper frames of the Oedipal, particularity, representation, and referentiality. An affective approach reworks what some presume queerness is in China and as represented by two men.

Yan fractures and presents subjects ranging from individual to national bodies as vibrating entities—they have solid form yet shift in meaning. Through Yan's fuzzy renegotiation of dominant representational accounts, one can structure different relations within the social. These relations do not presume a grand narrative or way of being. Minor methods do not replace the dominant; they operate in less impactful ways and privilege fractures over completion. The political operation of affect is thus to produce alternative "codes" that may not be subsumed by dominant, major structures.[20] However, these codes require a deep attention to contours and details. One focuses on the affective to notice the minute details that allow us to imagine a subject differently. As such, this minor method also contends with detailed insights from a field like area studies to amplify the possibilities of the relational, which I discuss below. Area studies helpfully directs us to an attention to code.

The politics of minor affects operate beyond the register of direct critique. However, this does not eradicate the import of subjects. Affect and contingencies within the minor rework the political toward the relational. In the words of Deleuze and Guattari, these relations to other subjects are discovered through connections that span time and space: "vibrations . . . express connections, disjunctions, and conjunctions of flows that cross through a society, entering and leaving it, linking it up with other societies, ancient or contemporary, remote or vanished, dead or yet to be born."[21] These relations are not universalized to flatten the racial:

> We have seen several times that minorities are not necessarily defined by the smallness of their numbers but rather by becoming or a line of fluctuation. A minority can be small in number; but it can also be the largest in number. That is the situation when authors, even those supposedly on the Left, repeat the great capitalist warning cry: in twenty years, "whites" will form only 12 percent of the world population. Thus they are not content to say that the majority will change. And the very curious concept of nonwhite does not in fact constitute a denumerable set.[22]

Deleuze and Guattari centralize not only relations to other dispossessed populations but also whiteness to complicate their affective method. The minor as method is not devoid of subject position. Yan develops this critical aspect of the minor by focusing on racialized and sexualized bodies, while simultaneously emphasizing fuzzy and minor moments that offer different understandings for such subjects that are normatively assumed knowable (as solid facts or ethnographic objects). Yan thus aestheticizes this Deleuzian shift away from a subject-based analysis, whereby the minor (subject) does not solely involve full knowability and proper numerical representation. However, although the minor as method is less about a clear and knowable subject position, it nonetheless attends to material experience.

The minor as method that privileges the affective and fuzzy enables one to hold on to a dominant form—to outline its contours—while also sensing its internal structures. Such variations provide avenues to construct and imagine other political dispositions and relations. Looking at Yan's work through this multifaceted method allows one to approach *Kill* without a predetermined reading, allowing the object to breathe beyond the proper. The tension from maintaining an attention to the major form, alongside an examination of new avenues provided by affect, produces such a possibility. Affective fuzziness is not simply about openness and indeterminacy. Contextual details afforded by a field like area studies are what enable the fuzzy and affective to transpire. An attention to form brings to the fore the minor details embedded within an object, ultimately allowing us to read the dominant form in less congealed ways. Form cannot simply be dissipated but must be held onto in order to render it anew.

Becoming China, Fracturing Minor Geographies

The anti-Oedipal and affect are minor methods that put into question the stability of the body and queerness. However, what are the ramifications of this minor approach for the transnational, considering that the non-West is consistently deployed to operate as the particular counterexample to the universal? What arises by extending this affective method toward not only the contours of the individual subject but also other aggregate bodies, such as the nation?[23] Minor methods attend to minor geographies by affectively engaging nation-states beyond stabilized spatial positions. In a similar vein to affect, minor contours provide avenues to take note of the dominant theorizations surrounding the nation and globality.

After interviews with Yan during research trips to China, I struggled with situating the artist's work within a context of localized queer politics in China, other peripheral sites, or a transnational network of diasporic (queer) Asian artists. These models, informed by my training in area and ethnic studies, presumed established modes of theorizing China: the particularity of context, the relationality produced across sites, and a relational queer diaspora. However, I found these approaches could not fully grapple with the complexities of *Kill* and could not substantively contend with how China is neither unique nor universal. I sought to rethink these available models as they relied on either (1) particularity, the Chinese context; or (2) relationality, a generalizability that connected Yan to others based on subject status or geographic position. However, when I shifted from trying to find an alternative and new model to culling minor details within *Kill*, I began to obtain a sense of the instability and becoming of China.[24] Rather than produce an original model, I hesitated and thus relied on minorness to gauge the disciplinary and methodological assumptions surrounding transnational analysis.

Two models predominate for theorizing the transnational. Particularity involves a focus on and stabilization of a specific geographic space. Relationality emerges by tracking commonalities across space and time. The relational undergirds both queer diaspora and minor transnationalism, which searches for connections across peripheral sites.[25] The particular and relational, at times, appear contradictory to one another, as theorists often deploy one to replace the other.[26] However, I hold both together to engage their productive limits. I trace here a minor method from the sense of becoming China within Yan's piece, which emerges from the particular and relational.[27] Rather than presuming what we may understand to be the culture and history of China or the racialization of Chinese populations globally, thinking of China as becoming approaches the nation affectively. This approach offers a different sense of the minor from minor spatial position to question the disciplinary fractures that fix the particular and relational within a binary.

China has differently become, as discussed in the introduction. Becoming balances an acknowledgment of difference without ossifying such difference onto particular spaces and people. For example, Yan fractures a stable sense of Asia. The bonsai tree that serves as the background for the flashing of the phrase "Kill (the) TV-Set," along with his racialized body, are presumed to be stable representations of Asianness. Yan performs slowness through his reperformance of the photograph of Paik and Moorman's original work; the unhurried and lingering gesture of the cello bow produces an aesthetic that some may identify as Chinese or Asian.[28] However, Yan repeatedly punctures the stability of Asia and this slow aesthetic with the constant flashing of words, specifically violent ones like "Kill." Yan's use of English, rather than Chinese, not only indicates how his work circulates in international art circles but also disrupts the wholeness of what may be presumed to be a racialized aesthetics of slowness. Yan refuses a clear legibility around his reperformance. It is neither a cohesive Chinese reappropriation nor a Westernized, derivative, and assimilationist piece.

Yan produces an ambiguous sense of Chineseness to situate the nation-state affectively. China becomes affectively fuzzy through Yan's multiple narratives about the site. Yan does not rely on linear modes of engagement that behold the nation as stable. Rather, his aesthetics offer space to work through dominant form alongside vibrations; objects and form teeter between stability and fuzziness. Yan enables the viewer to peer into the fuzzy and to grasp the dominant modes of imagining China *in theory*. Becoming tracks how different forms and understandings of China have shifted throughout time. Becoming is the transitory space where one particular thing merges into another related space. Within this conceptual frame, China is not only understood as a concrete social body but also seen for its affective, molecular contours. By attending to the minorness of affect, we discover singular differences within the nation. This act of tracing what arises within the in-between provides an account of what it means to become China: through the contextualized and textured form of the nation and its transitional states. It is only through a deep engagement with history and context and a full sense of an area's becoming that one can begin to see a national body beyond its static form. Yan enables this sense of becoming China to grapple with both particularist and relational approaches to the non-West.

Becoming nuances the particular. Although area and ethnic studies have historically been separated, they often rely on similar modes of stabilizing the notion of *area*.[29] Becoming tracks the specter of essentialism that distances fields from one another. *Kill* is dually legible as Asian and Asian American. The appearance of the bonsai tree exemplifies this ambiguous status, bringing to the fore the differences and similarities in how area and ethnic studies engage representation. The tree, as an object, enables fuzzy understandings of Asianness. Yan deploys bonsai to harken multiple genealogies and uses; Chinese, Japanese, and other cultures throughout Asia have furthered the art form. Yan groomed for about one year the tree that he filmed, highlighting the practice of bonsai as a living art. However, the cultivation of these trees on a plate has become a global, kitsch phenomenon. As such, the tree inspires a generic sense of Asianness and globality, as bonsai becomes a stable object signifier with unclear signifieds. The tree is simultaneously real and an artificial construction that becomes legible as a construct of Orientalism. These teetering meanings are further amplified aesthetically; the tree as object remains still while the flashing words interrupt its stable appearance.

The use of changing words negates the possibility of a singular meaning for the tree.

Becoming also revises the relational. This frame privileges connections across minor sites (avoiding a reliance on the center) or through a diasporic network. Building off of insights from chapter 2, becoming allows us to understand subjects as neutral and not predetermined. Rather than replace relational models, becoming nuances diasporic and center–periphery frameworks through more indirect and incomplete understandings of China and its subjects. In other words, becoming helps us understand non-Western subjects and sites beyond being "ontological absolutes."[30] For both diaspora and minor transnationalism, the metaphor of flows and directionality across sites often maintains these relational models. However, Yan's aesthetic of fractures challenges this metaphor of directionality. Fractures arise through the indeterminate narratives on both screens. On one, the phrases "Kill," "the," and "TV-Set" circulate every one and a half seconds, generating a rapid rhythm that does not cohere or culminate in meaning. There is no payoff for a viewer. On the other screen, Yan holds Anumudu's body in a disconnected fashion. Anumudu is neither a cello nor a lover; the embrace is cold and does not offer a legible narrative. In both screens, Yan rejects a sense of narrative flow. The artist highlights the predominance of fluidity, directionality, and narrative meaning or closure that undergird the relational. The metaphors of flow and directionality track connections and relations across sites and bodies. However, Yan's affective and fractured aesthetic renders this dominant metaphor transparent so as to privilege less complete modes of relationality for both aesthetics and the transnational.

Discourses like diaspora and a focus on peripheries have yet to fully contend with how the minor and subject have come to be defined. Alexander Weheliye highlights some of these limits through critiques of diaspora: "national boundaries, or linguistic differences . . . become the ultimate indicators of differentiation. In this process, national borders and/or linguistic differences are in danger of entering the discursive record as *ontological absolutes*, rather than as structures and institutions that have served again and again to relegate black subjects to the status of western modernity's nonhuman other."[31] Within this articulation, the minor as a subject leads to overdetermined, absolutized forms. This skews how the minor subject or geographic position has been deployed in the production of dehumanizing populations. As such, "diasporic populations appear as *real objects* instead of *objects of knowledge*," whereby such subjects remain stable.[32] By not fully grappling with how we define queerness and subjects, we obscure how global difference is central to the formation of a universalized sense of Man and the production of genres of the human.[33]

Yan's fuzzy and indeterminate methods shed light on disciplinary presumptions and renegotiate the dominance of fluid directionality implicit within some of our theoretical models for globality. In addition, the framework of flow that creates relations across space or throughout other minor sites nonetheless relies on a presumed center. Immanuel Wallerstein's world-systems theory is the implicit model that establishes how we enact connections across sites.[34] The center–periphery is the main framework within which these relational models operate. Even when one focuses on the peripheral or across diasporic sites, the center remains the implicit place that both models seek to work against, reaffirming its dominance. The metaphor of flows and directions upholds the center–periphery framework, as clear tracings across minor spaces or minoritized subjects are privileged over fractures, indeterminacy, fuzziness, and affects. Although Wallerstein's work has undergone critique, the center remains a dominant assumption for transnational work. The reliance on the minor subject reaffirms the minor spatial position as always framed within directionality: diaspora is articulated through a center–periphery or periphery–periphery relation. Regardless of the directionality that queer diasporic and other models provide, they continue to operate within the conditioned framework of directionality that enables the center to remain intact.[35] Arif Dirlik emphasizes the problem of such conceptual reversals and inversions.[36] He critiques the move of multiplying the notion of modernity because it "legitimizes the most fundamental assumptions of modernization by rendering them globally valid, forecloses serious consideration of alternatives to modernization, and reintroduces Eurocentrism by the back door."[37] Analytics that multiply or reverse dominant concepts reaffirm the existence of the center. Flows and directionality reassert the center because they do not fundamentally restructure or privilege more fragmented, affective, or molecular possibilities for understanding globality. Dirlik emphasizes the need not simply to ignore the existence of the center or Eurocentrism; instead, only by revealing the dominance of such concepts can one begin to provincialize them, in the words of Dipesh Chakrabarty.[38]

Yan provincializes the center by puncturing the model of directed flows for the transnational, producing leaky understandings of how the global and aesthetics articulate themselves. Yan does not simply reverse this flow; rather, through the tree, rhythmic punctures, and the cold embrace of Anumudu, he refuses to generate a clear direction or meaning to make such a presumed flow more transparent. His work relies on a non-linear narrative, refusing to fulfill an expectation of transparent realism and meaning that is often demanded of minoritized subjects. Even the cyclical nature of the work enacts this specific narrative form, as Yan structures *Kill* to repeat and loop without a sense of finitude. Yan's production of becoming China privileges incomplete analyses, directing relationality beyond not only a proper sense of the subject, but also an absolutized understanding of China. When China is seen as the proper particular or exception, this dynamic situates the transnational to flow from the West to the rest. The center becomes the universal and the source for the transnational. Yan's anti-Oedipal ethics and affective aesthetics disrupt this presumed flow by generating questions rather than answers. Rather than producing new models and enacting a logic of replacement, one might deploy minor methods to hesitate in order to imagine history and context anew and askew.

Scaling Back the Universal: Curation as Art Practice

In addition to affective approaches that reconfigure the minor beyond the particular, contemporary Chinese artists grapple with the universal. Liu Ding, Carol Lu, and Su Wei engage how we produce the history of contemporary Chinese art to render minor and scale back the universal. The team closely examines the norms of curation in order to contend more broadly with historicization, contextualization, and the ethics surrounding the (re)presentation of the non-West. Since the practice typically requires the selection and organization of a collection of objects for purposes of constructing history and context (or a theme), curation provides the opportune grounds to contend with the minor, particular, and universal. In particular, the curators move beyond linear accounts of contemporary Chinese art history in order to rethink history as a condition—the universal ways in which we construct and enact history. Their approach ultimately places contemporary Chinese art within larger global dynamics in ways that toggle across universal concerns and historical detail.

The 2012 Seventh Shenzhen Biennial, *Accidental Message: Art Is Not a System, Not a World*, provided an overview of the formation of contemporary Chinese art practices during the late 1980s through the 2000s. Liu Ding, Carol Lu, and Su Wei curated the biennial to shift how we historicize contemporary Chinese art beyond particularity, social context, and Chinese specificity. Their main goal was to organize and display works in ways that do not simply represent key moments in art history. In other words, they revise the norms and presumptions surrounding curation and historiographic practice. They instead deeply consider how art practitioners related to one another to curate the past. Affect becomes their curatorial method. The biennial was informed by their earlier collaboration *Little Movements*, which similarly curated art objects in ways that emphasized the affective as opposed to the contextual.

One of their main curatorial goals has been to reconfigure proper understandings of contemporary Chinese art. The team does not achieve this by solely including less cited works and artists, although this is one of their tactics. They additionally rethink the proper through the production of physical space. One curatorial strategy reconceptualizes exhibition halls as an affective atmosphere, whereby works and artists can be displayed to be in relation to one another. In particular, they construct the walls of their shows with short ledges, rather than the usual height that separates rooms from one another. This spatial organization enables a viewer to phenomenologically shift from engaging an individual work within a single room, to take in multiple sensations across the entire space. The curators purposefully create lines of flight between works. The team paints the bottom of these walls in royal blue to emphasize and draw our attention to those details often overlooked and to suggest pathways for a viewer to create relations across works. This approach is amplified by the location of the biennial. Shenzhen is not considered a central locus for contemporary Chinese art. Bordering Hong Kong, the city is in Guangdong Province and exists peripherally to the global art center. In addition, Shenzhen similarly plays a minor role in the history of contemporary Chinese art. The location itself enables the curators to help us rethink dominant narratives surrounding how we historicize the movement.

I open with a brief description of the Shenzhen Biennial and *Little Movements* as these curatorial projects highlight some of the problems surrounding historiography as it relates to the universal. Most approaches to non-Western art maintain stable understandings of Chinese culture, history, tradition, and people, in order to produce a historiography that excavates and reveals a particular context for outside, global audiences. Within this formula, art presumably indexes China, its world and people, as absolutes. Liu Ding, Carol Lu, and Su Wei rework the established approaches to curating contemporary Chinese art, as these dominant approaches were outlined in chapter 1. The curators do not produce their shows to be in conversation with those interested in offering a more accurate, vibrant, or "real" account of China. Instead, their larger goal is to question what exactly we understand history to be and how we function within it—an admittedly grand and universal concern. Similar to Yan Xing, these curators focus on the affective and molecular. However, these curators build upon Yan Xing's rethinking of particularity in order to grapple more explicitly with theorizations of the universal as they relate to historiography.

Through a focus on affect, their artistic project and curatorial goals destabilize both our epistemological approaches to (how we know) and ontological accounts of (what is) history. In other words, the team allows us to hesitate and take note of how we curate the idea of history. They trouble what we understand to count as historical proof. Further, by shifting the epistemological registers in the accounts of contemporary Chinese art from narratives and facts to affects and feelings, they ultimately direct us toward the ethics of representing the non-West. When we reexamine how we approach or display otherness and what we define as investment in an other, the ethical arises. I thus investigate these multiple dimensions of epistemology, ontology, and ethics in these curatorial projects. The curators destabilize major accounts of China through an exploration of ontology and affect, where one focuses more on sensations and relations to the past. Through the minorness of affect, we question both the epistemological approaches and the ontological accounts of China, time, and art. In doing so, we open up space to think about the ethics of whom we include in universal, historical accounts. The universal, as such, is scaled back and becomes less of a standard and more of a process.

As discussed in chapter 1, the 1989 show *Magiciens de la Terre* at the Centre Pompidou illustrates the ways in which this movement has come to be remembered through the proper, particularly works by Huang Yong Ping, Gu Dexin, and Yang Jiechang who were included in *Magiciens*. Liu Ding and his team rethink the inclusion of such figures and emphasize affect to reconsider how we understand context and history. Rather than rewrite this historical account, the curators direct us to the shadows, feelings, and relations that normally go overlooked. The team's commitments are to rework proper understandings of China, as solely a particularized, non-Western example; they do not seek to simply include China for global consumption. Instead, the team examines the ethical ramifications of how and why the other enters into such a discourse. They direct us to the ontology of the other.

The curators, however, do not solely amend who is included in the canon. More importantly, they operate at the level of *how* we produce a canon and *what purpose* it serves. At Shenzhen, they incorporate two out of the three artists who were in *Magiciens*: Huang Yong Ping and Gu Dexin. The *Magiciens* show included Huang Yong Ping's iconic piece *The History of Chinese Painting and the History of Modern Western Art Washed in the Washing*

Machine for Two Minutes (1987), which involved a clump of paper from two texts on Eastern and Western art history that were put together in a washing machine. In addition, *Magiciens* included Huang's *Reptile* (1989) installation which built off of his practice of washing books.

The curators do not include these two canonical works in their overview of contemporary Chinese art. Instead, they display Huang's *Bat Project II* (2003), a half-complete replica of the rear of a US spy plane (figure 3.5). In 2001, a standoff between a US spy plane and two Chinese fighter jets led to a fatal collision in Hainan, heightening tensions between the two countries. Huang was originally commissioned to rebuild the plane for an earlier Shenzhen Sculpture Biennial, which was not curated by Liu Ding and the team. However, the project was abandoned, with Huang's name and artwork removed from the exhibition, due to diplomatic tensions between French, American, and Chinese governments. Since the abandonment of the piece, the half-constructed plane has been left on undeveloped land and has become a notable public landmark, often referred to by locals as "that place with the tail of an airplane." Eleven years later, Liu Ding decided to include this abandoned and half-created work in the biennial, as opposed to Huang's more notable pieces that have become almost symbolic of the contemporary scene during the 1980s and 1990s.

The curatorial choice to not include Huang Yong Ping's iconic works is important to note. *Bat Project* helps us rethink the relationship of art to the proper and indexicality. The subtitle of the biennial indicates that art is not a system, not a world. Rather than rendering art to be indicative of truth or an index to a specific space, they explore the minor functions of art. The curators' statement about *Bat Project* explores these themes: "We will officially exhibit and list this artwork as part of the 2012 Shenzhen Sculpture Biennial. As we see it, it provides a new opportunity for projection. What we are projecting onto it is the importance of art having a lasting relevance not based on time, and the importance of establishing connectivity that is internal to the creation. Though the event it touches on is already in the past, as we see it, this massive object's existence as an artwork serves as a reminder that the internality of the artwork is not moved by time."[39]

Art is usually presumed to be an index or portal to a world, whereby contemporary Chinese art is supposed to offer a view into Chinese life. The curators, however, resist replicating this dominant logic and instead direct us to our overinvestment in art to produce this voyeuristic and ethnographic aperture. By focusing on seemingly minor things like affect and internality, they deflate art's potential. In particular, Huang's large-scale work evokes

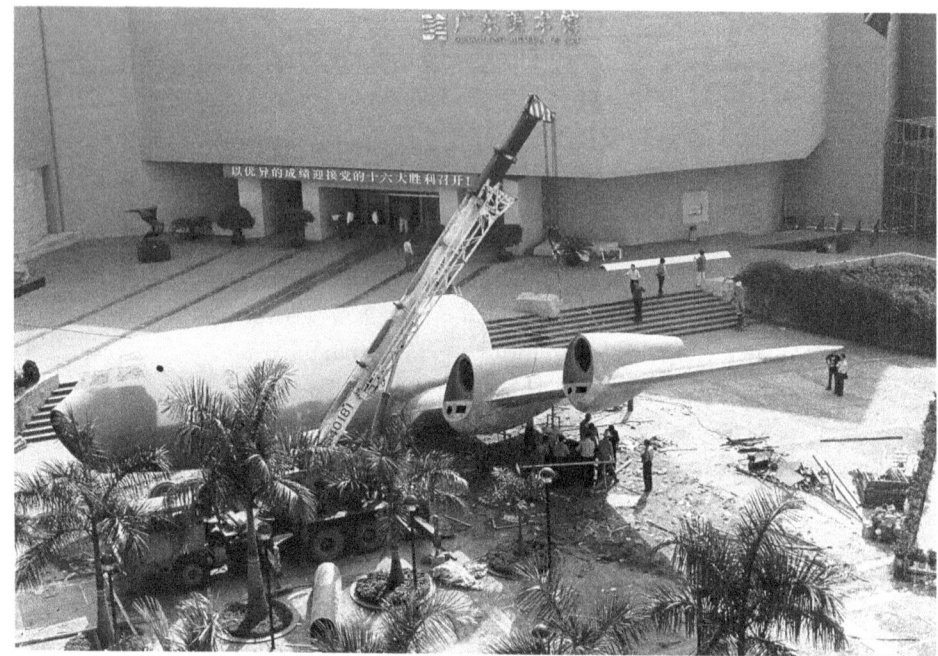

Figure 3.5. Huang Yong Ping, *Bat Project II*, 2002. Metal sheets, 20×15×6 meters. Guangzhou Triennial 2002, Guangdong Museum, China. Courtesy of the artist.

questions around the *how*. Rather than asking *what* the abandoned plane represents and symbolizes (a view of Chinese worlds and life), the curators focus on the sheer size of the half-rendered plane to ask how it got there. Questions of *how* concentrate on the process of the work. Locals in Shenzhen refer to the work as "that place with the tail of an airplane," rather than "the site of Huang Yong Ping's *Bat Project*." Referring to "that place" exemplifies the public's affective relation to an artwork that simply remarks on its existence and presence, as opposed to identifying its meaning or auteur. The artwork operates within a minor affective register that does not index Chinese reality.

The curators' privileging of *Bat Project* over Huang's more established works is not meant to simply expand the canon of contemporary Chinese art. Rather, they use *Bat Project* to reconsider the role of and minimize the potential of art. By directing our focus toward the *how* of art as opposed to *what* art represents, the curators ultimately query how we produce a canon that may not be reliant on ideas like import and potential. Curation typically canonizes what we understand to be a specific movement, as it often relies on displaying works that represent significance. The curators highlight and rethink this dominant logic of import through their focus on *Bat Project*, renegotiating how we produce or practice history and context.

Gu Dexin is another artist who was presented at *Magiciens* and the Shenzhen Biennial. His iconic *Plastic Pieces* (1987) was first included in *Magiciens* and established his notoriety. The installation consists of wads of melted plastic in faded earth-tone colors. The pieces are hanging from walls or placed on the ground and in mounds. The sculptures evoke the grotesque, as the figures resemble intestines and mounds of trash. The exhibition catalog for *Magiciens* places Gu's work within a universalized idea of art: "For him, art is a radical way to liberate sensuality and instinct. It's also a way to approach intellectual truth."[40] In addition, the work was exhibited in *La Grande Halle*, in the fourth section of the exhibit labeled "Does the decor make the wall?"[41] The piece is situated in relation to decorative art and is framed in relation to artistic process, rather than its affective and sensorial qualities.

The curatorial team for the Shenzhen Biennial did not include this earlier iconic work. They instead displayed Gu's equally iconic *1996.8.26*, which refers to the date August 26, 1996 (figure 3.6). The piece involves a close-up of a photo of a hand that is overexposed in red. The work documents the process of a hand rubbing a single piece of meat until it is rendered flat, save for tendon and bits of flesh. For the curators, the piece has "become so cheap and unreliable" since most predictably narrate the work in relation to violence.[42] The curators shift the focus from this major construct toward the minor detail of its title, a date. The date has no prescribed meaning. Instead, the curators hope their focus on the work's title will allow a viewer to simply ask what was happening on that date—what sensations and relations are embedded in a specific date? The curators emphasize the work's "ambiguity and grandiose sensory nature [to] lead us to reconsider the nature of images, of writing, of history, and imagination, if only for a moment."[43] Rather than sensationalizing the piece for violence and using it to index or offer truths about China that were specifically occurring on August 26, 1996, the curators render the art to have a more minor function. Their catalog description therefore emphasizes mundane sensations over the symbolics of flesh: "the oily sense and texture of that meat which has been rubbed in the hand for so long."[44] Unlike the description of Gu's *Plastic Pieces* in *Magiciens*'s catalog, the curators focus on texture, asking viewers to imagine the feelings involved

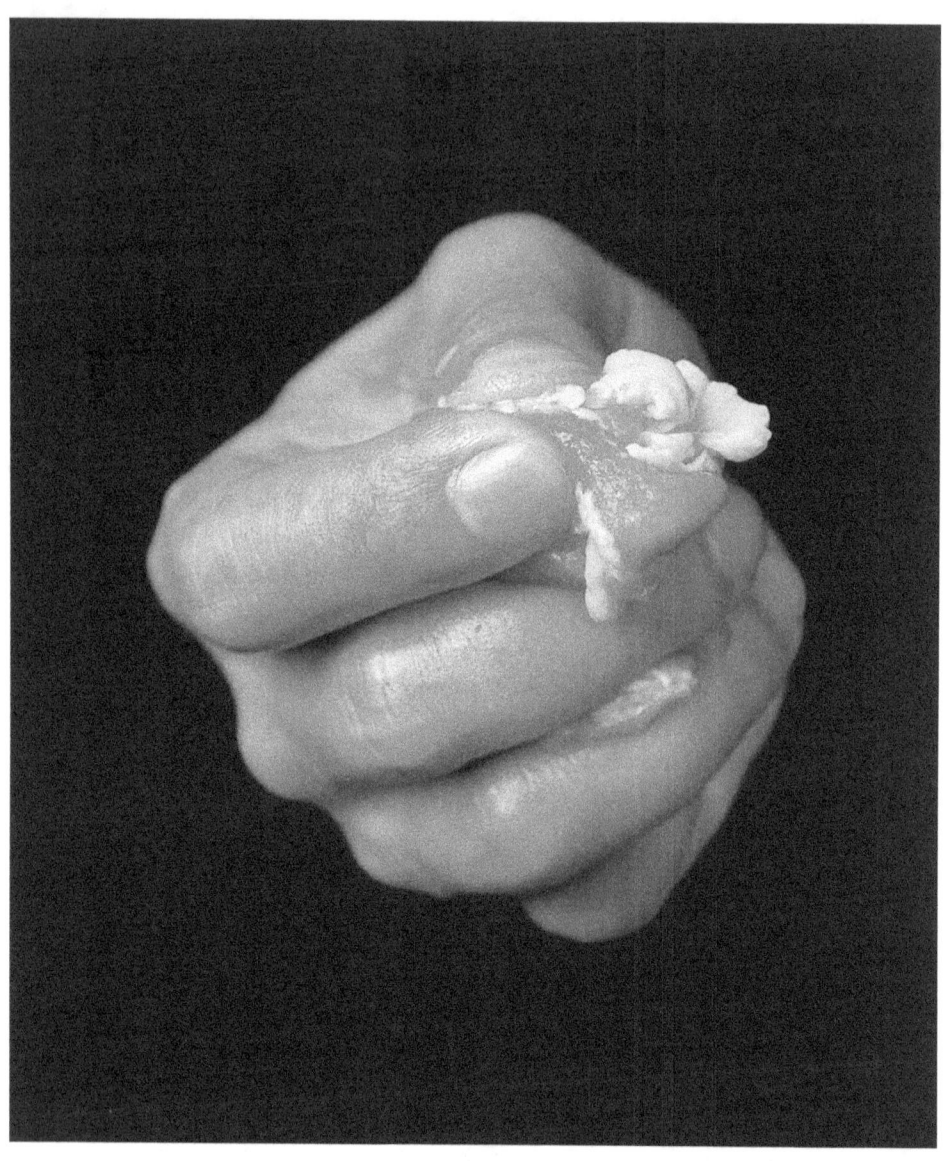

Figure 3.6. Gu Dexin, *1996.8.26*, 1996. Photograph, 24.8×20.1 inches. © Gu Dexin. Courtesy of Gu Dexin, Fei Dawei, and Asia Art Archive, Hong Kong.

in rendering a piece of flesh flat. This focus on the work's minorness resists a symbolic or indexical reading. This is strikingly different from how Gu is framed in *Magiciens* as an artist who approaches universalized concerns like "intellectual truth" and "instinct." The curators of the Shenzhen Biennial instead privilege sensation and the mundane over grand narratives.

Liu Ding, Carol Lu, and Su Wei return to these canonical artists, Gu and Huang, in ways that question the relationship between established approaches to curation and the production of history and knowledge. By emphasizing the affective and sensorial, the team reconsiders curation for the way it predominantly relies on logics like import, potential, significance, and the proper. They bring to the fore these logics in order to question what notions we rely upon to produce and curate history. The team's focus on minor aspects is not meant to simply expand our epistemological bases to construct history. Instead, they deploy the minor as method to highlight our dominant reliance on facts and import. In addition, they explore how such major understandings of history render art to be an index of a particular space and world. They ultimately seek, however, to extend history as a way to consider the universal, albeit in its little and minor form.

Little Movements and Affect as Method

In their curatorial projects like *Little Movements* and the Shenzhen Biennial, Liu Ding, Carol Lu, and Su Wei work against the creation of a proper history, whereby art becomes indexical of a world/reality. Rather than rewrite the history of contemporary Chinese art or create a better or more proper one, they focus on the methods and ethics that undergird the larger turn to "historicizing" non-Western art: what we use to construct and remember the past and how we exist within and in relation to it. The curators are unique in that their emphasis on seemingly minor things rethinks the larger project of curation at hand.

The notions of *little* and *movements*, the framework for their first collaboration, clarify these goals and methods. First, *little* does not solely refer to scale (big or small); little demands an attention to localized, personalized practices and internal affects. Lauren Berlant reveals the potential of these minor practices and affects in that they "provide a way to assess the disciplines of normativity in relation to the disorganized and the disorganizing processes of labor, longing, memory, fantasy, grief, acting out, and sheer psychic creativity through which people constantly (consciously, unconsciously, dynamically) renegotiate the terms of reciprocity that contour their historical situation."[45] The curators deploy affect in similar ways that reveal how individuals contend with history, time, and their attending processes of labor, grief, and desire. The minor engages the structural. Affect activates history at the level of experience (how we exist in time); it moves away from discourses surrounding an event which often rely on predefined processes shaped by psychological, sociological, or political-economic frameworks. As such, the curators render unstable past events from legible forms by emphasizing, as Berlant describes it, "being in history as a densely corporeal, experientially felt thing whose demands on survival skills map not the whole world in one moment but a way to think about the history of sensualized epistemologies in the atmosphere of a particular moment now (aesthetically) suspended in time."[46] To translate the littleness or minorness of affect at the level of curation requires a renegotiation of space and senses. The curatorial team returns to canonical works and artists to find the shadows and senses that were once overlooked, ultimately enabling us to better understand experience and the past.

The import of time for affect engages the second notion of *movements*. Movements work against teleology or ideas of proper development for history. A movement, instead, occurs in multiple directions—to the side, backward, forward, standing still, and simply gesturing in place. The curators' use of movements does not correspond to a sense of progress, where one event leads to the next. Movements are also plural, ongoing, and multiple. History is typically experienced and made known through narratives that erase the messiness of ordinary life. Historical accounts often privilege measurable forms of evidence to reconstruct the past, ignoring the precarious and presumably minor processes that shape experience, feelings, and senses; these narratives also ignore details that may seem unimportant.

The curatorial layout for both the Shenzhen Biennial and *Little Movements* help translate these lofty goals. The artist-curators deemphasize the notion of a linear progression for a viewer. Rather than having clearly demarcated entrances and exits, the curators do not provide signage as to where to begin one's experience of their shows. They encourage attendees to meander, linger, be confused, and explore. It is precisely at the level of the senses that the curatorial team reworks our dominant ways of being in space and time. Although the exhibition catalogs for both *Little Movements* and the Shenzhen Biennial are structured thematically, the layouts of both shows are not organized in similar ways. Rather, works are juxtaposed in less direct means—they do not follow the logic of the exhibition's text. Compared to other curatorial approaches, this is certainly less didactic in form. The team plays on the predictability and demands for immediate legibility for curation in order to highlight how it reproduces dominant notions of temporality, experience, and canonization. The curators engage experience ontologically, forcing us to question our norms surrounding experience (particularly, what we might consider a satisfying or productive experience when it comes to a show). Rather than producing an idealized path for the audience, the curators privilege what art historian Irit Rogoff describes as a project of "looking away."[47] Rogoff emphasizes the need to deprivilege an ideal viewer and allow moments of impasse, confusion, and lingering to emerge in experiences with art.

The curatorial goals also translate through the placement of objects. In the Shenzhen Biennial, Wang Luyan's *Walking Man* (1991) is located in the center of a room. This work is within the sight line of Ding Yi's *Appearance of Crosses* series from the mid-1980s (figure 3.7). The relationship between Wang's and Ding's works is not obvious, since they do not overlap in aesthetic style or time. Instead, the curators focus on how these artists related to their respective peers in terms of their own experimentation with formalism. For Wang, his own works and collaborations with the New Measurement Group attempted to function differently from the Political Pop Art that became emblematic of contemporary Chinese art during the '90s. Wang's abstraction of the human body shifts away from the kitsch aesthetic of Political Pop. For Ding, his projects responded to the dominance of critiquing ideological repression during the 1980s. Similar to Wang's relationship to Political Pop, Ding's use of formalism and repetition reacts to the lack of formalism in relation to his own peers as Ding refuses to reaffirm his moment's focus on state censorship.

Although these artists existed at different times within the history of contemporary Chinese art, the curators place these works together in order to show similarities surrounding the use of form to work against dominant aesthetics. The curators emphasize how artists related to their respective historical moments as they work "in the shadows." In addition, rather than comparing Wang's work to the likes of Giacometti or other similar works from a Western canon or explaining the sociopolitical critique of *Walking Man* (which most have done in terms of the man lacking direction or purpose), the curators stress *Walking Man*'s affective contours in terms of its relationship to previous moments in art history.

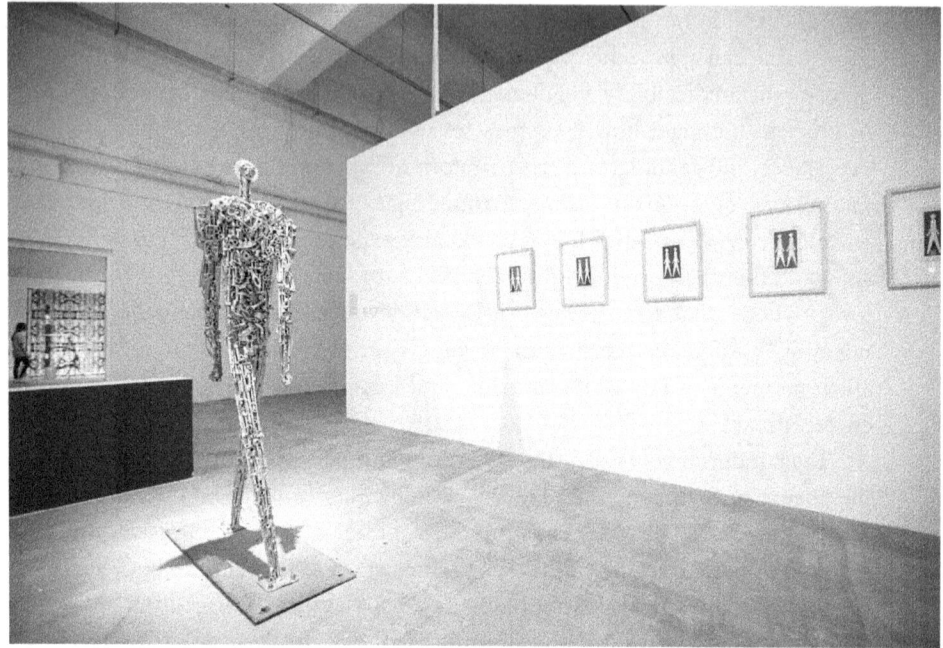

Figure 3.7. Liu Ding, Carol Lu, and Su Wei, view of *Walking Man* and *Appearances of Crosses*, 2012. Seventh Annual Shenzhen Biennale, *Accidental Message: Art Is Not a System, Not a World*. Photograph. Courtesy of the artists.

Ethics and Minoring the Universal

Liu Ding, Carol Lu, and Su Wei rethink history, particularly the epistemological bases that construct it. And they engage history in this way so as to reconsider the universal. For them, the universal is limited in scope and does not operate as a single grand narrative. This approach is admittedly difficult to do, considering the ways curation is often mired in expectations around clarity, significance, and import. And in fact, *Little Movements* has been critiqued for not fulfilling these expectations. Following the creation of the exhibit, Lance Wang in LEAP, one of the main publications on contemporary Chinese art, dismisses the curatorial team's method for not providing a proper or reliable account of the past:

An oral history, even one recounted by a central figure like Wang, is overly simplistic when the goal is to understand the origins and nature of a moment in history. An oral history is not a primary source; the facts asserted therein need the corroboration of other, additional materials. The biggest problem with oral histories is not that the narrator intentionally obscures or alters historical facts, it is that during the process of recounting, the narrator unconsciously selectively forgets. This is the reason why autobiographies include primary sources, because the presence of these documents serves to rectify facts that the narrator forgot.[48]

This review relies upon a proper and "objective" idea of history, reconfirming the dominant expectations around curation to reveal truths and indexes about a space. The critic thus dismisses the minor, which he locates in oral history, as a historical method. However, the curators' goal is to highlight the dominant assumptions around what counts as history. They ask us to rework the register in which we engage curation and produce history. Questioning the ontology and epistemology of history is important for China since a development-based model of time is what entraps China within the proper and as situated "behind" the West. The team disrupts the notion of teleological development that so often enshrines and limits understandings of culture and China. They ultimately seek to expand their work beyond being an index of China so that it comes into conversation with the universal.

The larger ethics surrounding their minor approach to curation revolve around how the non-West defines itself. By doing so, they open up relations to the universal and global. Liu Ding, Carol Lu, and Su Wei have critiqued Chinese artists' fixations on accessing the United States and Europe, high lighting the problematic of defining oneself in relation to the West. The irony in this is that they are quite successful on the global art market. Thus, rather than relying on nativism, fetishizing the particular, or ignoring power differences, they work through the complexities of circulating on the global art market as contemporary Chinese artists and curators: they have access to this market yet are nonetheless rendered within the condition of the major and proper that delimits understandings of the non-West. To grapple with this complex condition, they focus on how they relate to others within this global landscape. Similar to their approach to art as not being about a system or world, they produce relations to others in minor ways. They do not propose a strong relationality with others across the globe. Rather, they minimize their relations and theorize them as fleeting and momentary.

The team's approach has garnered interest from a range of art-world institutions in Europe and the United States. Much of the Western reception of *Little Movements* could be described as simply either (1) reproducing a universalism around art, or (2) legitimating Chinese artists to Western audiences, and therefore dismissed as such. However, the curators hope for another possibility in their relations to the transnational and universal: they desire to be in conversation with others. Akin to the way they limit art's potential, these conversations and relations are not about possibility to radicalize the world or produce a resistant multitude. Within the expanse of the globe, we find a seemingly simple need to find connections. During interviews with the curatorial team, they often stressed the need to simply be together, to be with others. They focus on placing things in relation to one another in order to create weak affective bonds.

The universal tends to operate at a daunting scale, abstracting beyond the concerns of particular groups to create affiliations that span space and time. Stabilized and complete relational connections often form our sense of the universal. However, what happens if these bonds are not presumed stable but perhaps momentary and fleeting? The weakening of these ties renders the universal minor, asking us to reconsider not only the scale of the universal but also how we conceptualize our relations to others. This is not a move to dismiss the universal; rather, the minoring of the universal provides a different ethical encounter for relationality.

Susan Buck-Morss directs us to such a rethinking, as she moves away from "giving multiple, distinct cultures equal value, whereby people are recognized as part of humanity indirectly through the mediation of collective cultural identities."[49] The universal thus

> emerges in the historical event at the point of rupture. It is in the discontinuities of history that people whose culture has been strained to the breaking point give expression to a humanity that goes beyond cultural limits. And it is in our *empathic identification* with this raw, free, and vulnerable state, that we have a chance of understanding what they say. Common humanity exists in spite of culture and its differences. A person's nonidentity with the collective allows for subterranean solidarities that have a chance of appealing to universal, moral sentiment, the source today of enthusiasm and hope.[50]

Buck-Morss deploys the 1791 Haitian Revolution to illustrate this sense of universal history. She does not look for the universal in the particular "Haitian articulation of that event," but rather searches for the universal within "the moment of the slaves' self-awareness that the situation was not humanly tolerable, that it marked the betrayal of civilization and the limits of cultural understanding, the nonrational, and nonrationalizable course of human history that outstrips in its *in*humanity anything that a cultural outlaw could devise."[51] Put differently, the momentary affective tie of vulnerability temporarily produces the universal, whereby different populations come into relation with one another. These connections, however, cannot permanently sustain themselves. Instead, we must scale back the universal and relational so that they expire and dissipate.[52] By doing so, as established in chapter 2, we are compelled to continue searching to be with others, without presuming relations knowable and stable.

The ephemeral nature of such affective bonds forges limited connections that make us feel less alone in this world. However, since these connections merely flicker, we are unable to fully know an other—this is not a loss but a condition that compels us to return. The universal not only emerges from these moments of brief encounter, but also disappears immediately after connecting. Although Liu Ding, Carol Lu, and Su Wei are not necessarily looking back at an established event like the Haitian Revolution, they attempt to capture a sense of this momentary and shared vulnerability in their notion of little movements. This minoring of the universal does not produce a full sense of relationality with an other. The relational moment, rather than bond, is about finding temporary comfort instead of producing political possibility. Their curatorial approach thus scales back and renders minor the universal. *Little Movements* brings together artists and collaborators who operate in this fashion. The curators drew the title from the 1986 Zhuhai symposium at the Painting Institute, where early practitioners of experimental art debated many key concerns. One concern surrounded the relationship between group and individual for artistic production; for one participant, Wang Guangyi, the latter prevailed. The curators take up this focus on the individual beyond a neoliberal narrative. Instead, they curate individual practices that provide a sense of related but distinct forms of vulnerability; the curators bring together these singular projects so as to momentarily produce the universal.

Both Yan Xing and Liu Ding, Carol Lu, and Su Wei direct us to the limits of the proper and major for approaching China. Disciplinary histories around the universal and particular often maintain the logics of the proper and major. However, these artists collectively provide minor methods to hesitate across disciplines and to question dominant approaches to curating, displaying, and depicting the non-West. Yan Xing deploys the anti-Oedipal, affect, and becoming to expand our methodological approaches to the particular as they relate to individual and national bodies. Meanwhile, the curatorial team's minor methods rethink dominant approaches to curation, encouraging us to reconsider history and the universal in their major forms.

4

Minor Agencies

REFORMULATING DEMYSTIFICATION
AND PERFORMATIVITY THROUGH
THE WORKS OF ZHANG HUAN,
HE CHENGYAO, AND CAO FEI

The subject and agency, along with understandings of history and the nation, shape how we understand China through the proper. In particular, Chinese artists are typically understood as herculean, conscious subjects resisting the authoritarian state. But these are overdetermined renderings of how political change occurs. In this chapter, I turn to theorizations of subjects and their agency to reconsider the ways Chinese artists have been understood as these resisting subjects. In doing so, my goal is to rethink agency and resistance in ways that take stock of what undergirds these overdetermined renderings of how political change operates beyond a formulaic model defined by demystification and performativity. The aesthetic is deployed to buttress this narrative. Art or culture is presumed properly political when it enables a linear relationship across art object, repressed subject, conscious demystified awareness, and performed resistance. In other words, the aesthetic finds value when a subject understands one's abuses by capital, which then leads to revolt. This formula for political change often requires didactic, legible aesthetic objects to be in the service of political ends or results in aesthetic readings that obscure the minor complexities of an artwork. However, what happens when we open up this linear relationship by expanding not only what counts as political art, but also how subjects learn and perform what it means to be political?

This chapter works through the forces that maintain narratives around non-Western subjects and their resistance as performed critique. This relation between action and resistance, however, does not solely arise within liberal models of social change. It also has much to do with Marxist-inflected notions around the way the proletariat is imagined to become aware of their exploitation by capitalism. In other words, both liberal and Marxist models of political change rely upon an equation, whereby an individual's awareness of exploitation manifests into performed action. The notion of performativity takes on a strong force that establishes norms around agency and resistance. I take stock of performativity and how we might be able to render minor what I call elsewhere our strong performative impulses.[1] How we conceptualize consciousness through notions of demystification and performativity is central to debates around agency, action, and change. I analyze different modes of cognition, *meditation* and *fabulation*, to rethink normative Marxist and liberal frameworks.

In this chapter, in order to track these different modes of cognition and performed action, I turn to Zhang Huan, He Chengyao, and Cao Fei, three artists whose works circulate on the global art market and are often curated to demonstrate herculean ideas about Chinese subjects. However, before engaging these artists, to help provide background on their work in relation to notions of sovereign subjects, this chapter first examines the entwinement of demystification and performance to produce the dominant paradigm for agency and political change. I also look at the way these artists reformulate the cognitive norms that undergird political legibility, a crucial issue for understanding how agency, action, and change come together. In particular, I analyze how, through meditation, Zhang Huan's iconic *12m²* provides different modes of being in time that move beyond intention and action (figure 4.1). Rather than performing endurance art that enacts a masculinist notion of challenge, Zhang Huan lingers in time, helping render supple the notion of endurance. Meditation in He Chengyao's *99 Needles* additionally offers a sense of being that rethinks the framework of trauma for Chinese women (figure 4.2). Her performance confronts human rights discourse that relies upon legible modes of trauma that transfix non-Western women as colonial objects requiring Western intervention. For Zhang and He, the haptic sensations produced through Buddhist practices of meditation reframe endurance and resistance to contend with less determined modes of consciousness. Lastly, fabulation in Cao Fei's *Cosplay* photo series rethinks the presumption that the performance of agency must always translate into direct action in order to be considered properly political (figure 4.3). Fabulation directs

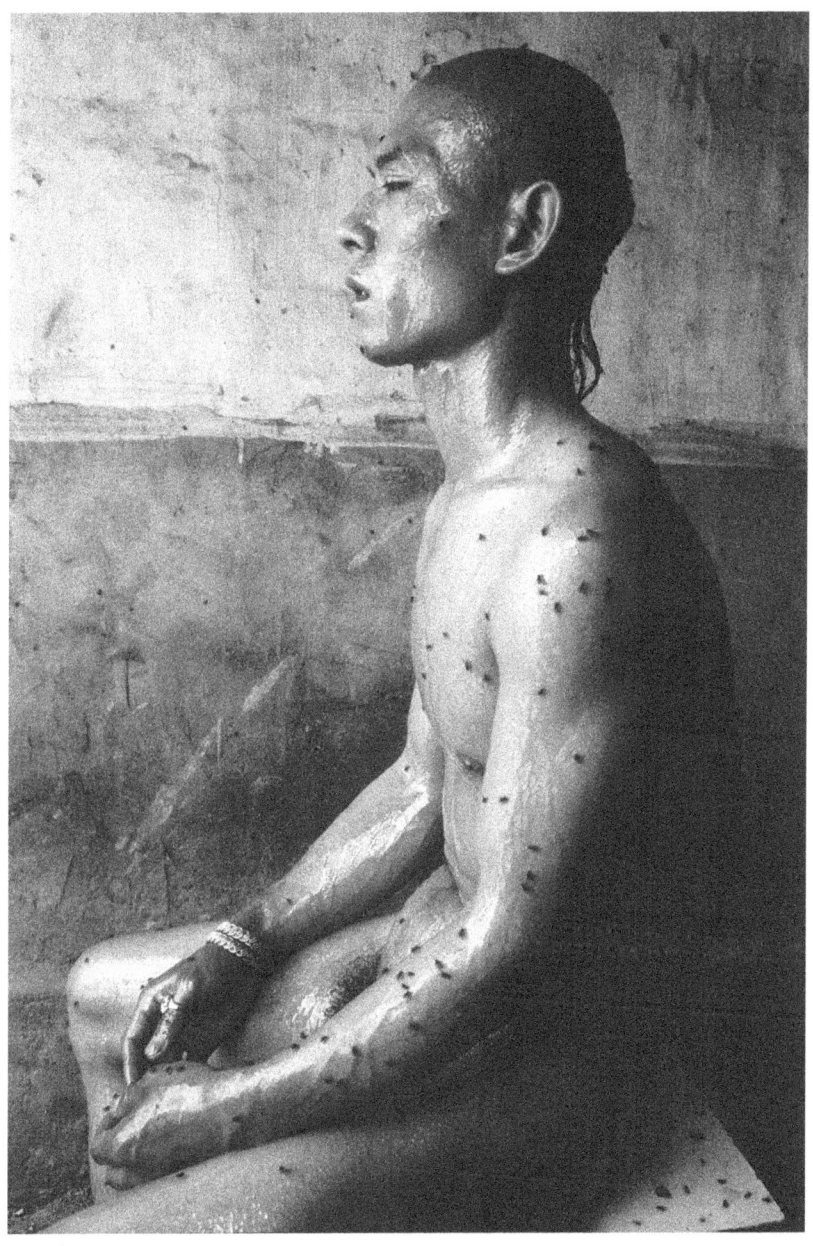

Figure 4.1. Zhang Huan. *12m²*, 1994. Performance, Zhang Huan Studio, Beijing, China. Courtesy of the artist.

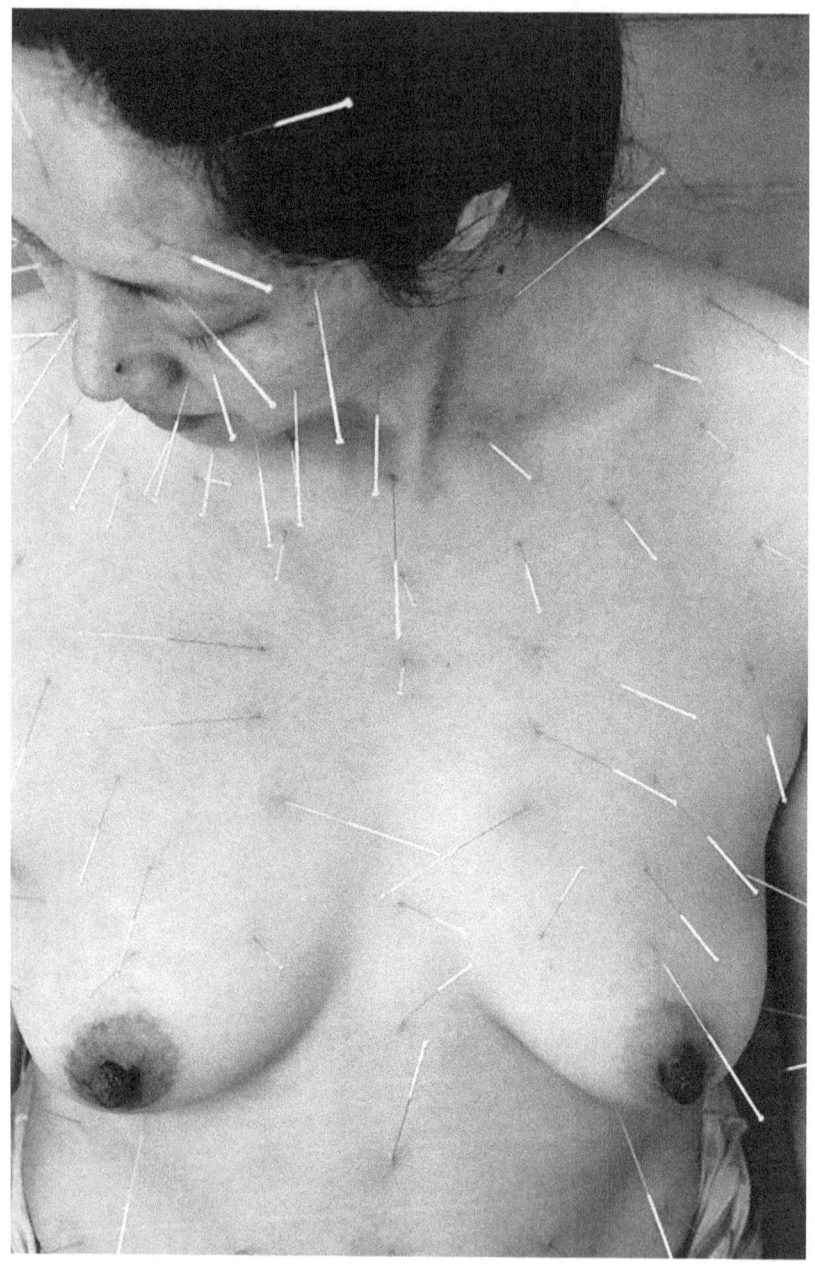

Figure 4.2. He Chengyao, *99 Needles*, 2002. This photo of He Chengyao's performance is discussed in this chapter to illustrate the import of meditation to rethink demystification and performance.

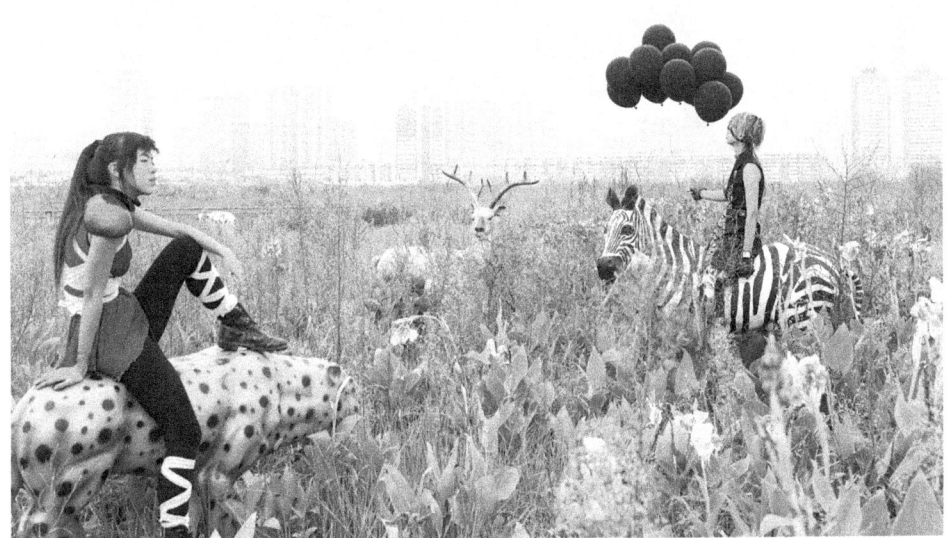

Figure 4.3. Cao Fei, *A Mirage*, 2004.
Inkjet print on paper, 75 × 100 cm.
Courtesy of the artist and Vitamin
Creative Space.

us to an etiolated notion of performativity that provides space for the fact that we are not always on, activated, or ready to critique. Both meditation and fabulation enable hesitation, as we refrain from prescribing predictable narratives of resistance to produce value for the aesthetic. These artists collectively reframe how the political occurs at the level of subjective awareness and performed action, ultimately recalibrating our conceptualization of the political toward the minor.

Demystification, Alienation Effects, and Performativity

Within academic and journalistic accounts of the United States' decline in relation to China's "rise," China is often depicted as possessing economic and industrial strength due to its hyperproductivity while lacking one key component "unique" to the West: ingenuity. Although China is understood as lacking creativity, it simultaneously possesses a work ethic that enables the hyperexecution of action. *New York Times* columnist Thomas Friedman echoes this essentializing logic: "Even the Chinese will tell you that they've been good at making the next new thing, and copying the next new thing, but not imagining the next new thing."[2] He explains how the Chinese tech industry stresses the need to develop creative capital among its workers, positing the imagination as at once the source of the West's current sense of superiority and its future anxiety in relation to China. Within the shift from Fordist to post-Fordist economies, the imagination and consciousness become the dominant modes by which the privileged forms of immaterial labor arise, supposedly blurring the line between play and labor.[3] Immateriality relies upon the imagination to produce, in positivistic ways, new ideas that benefit the entrepreneurial spirit of post-Fordism. In other words, the imagination is rendered as having conscious thoughts that can be logically rationalized, scientifically verified, and productively performed.[4] This trope circulates in areas like education,[5] business,[6] and discourses of the body. Thus, expanding the theoretical possibilities of imagination and consciousness beyond dominant notions of agency illuminates these limited economic, cultural, and aesthetic discourses. To be more explicit, my aim in augmenting theorizations of agency and consciousness is not to replace past models by arguing that the Chinese imagine like the West or that the Chinese imagine in specifically Chinese ways. Rather, through destabilized forms of consciousness, I direct us toward the presumed and normalized ways of thinking, behaving, and performing that often predetermine how non-Western otherness is discursively geared toward the major and proper.

Let us begin with *12m²* by Zhang Huan. Born in 1965, he is often cited as one of the main performance artists in China, as he was central to the development of the burgeoning art scene in Beijing's East Village during the 1990s. *12m²* has become emblematic of this early moment in his career. In photos of the performance taken by noted photographer and collaborator Rong Rong, with eyes closed, Zhang Huan situates himself in a moment of stasis as he exists within multiple states.[7] During the peak heat of a summer's afternoon, he sits naked on top of a public toilet in the less developed outskirts of Beijing. The size of the toilet area is precisely twelve square meters. With Zhang's head seemingly finding balance on top of his slightly curved spine, the weight of his torso gravitates downward on top of his lower body that rests on a toilet seat. The counterbalance of his upward-sensing spine against the weightedness of his sitting produces a temporary stasis. This momentary and precarious balance and state of being are amplified by Zhang's lack of reaction to the swarm of flies stuck onto and around his honey and fish sauce–smeared body. The sonic and tactile vibrations from the congregating flies produce multiple sensations for the artist to sit through. The horde of flies makes the viewer aware of not only the intense stench of shit that permeates the seemingly serene moment that Zhang inhabits, but also the tickling of his skin. In additional archival photos of the event, one sees used bits of toilet paper left on the floor, providing a deeper sense of the haptic, along with the summer heat and the smell of urine and feces. The photograph captures a breathing stasis in medias res from a forty-minute performance.

Discourses on Zhang Huan often frame him as possessing a political agenda or program that demystifies and reveals the problems with China's rapid "rise," with his endurance art presumably critiquing the rural and urban divides in the shifting neoliberalizing space of China.[8] The artist is conceptualized as an aware subject who is fully conscious of the problems that surround him, resulting in a performed resistance by which he endures pain and discomfort. From such a framing, he performs resistance through endurance. In other words, Zhang turns into a subject of demystification: he becomes conscious of problems, actively resists, and ultimately demystifies through performance the problems of the state to Chinese and international publics. Within this framework that patterns most narrations of non-Western art, consciousness is conceptualized as the driving force that enables awareness and a subsequent performed critique. The stakes in destabilizing consciousness are to rework investments in such a holistic, intentional subject. Demystification elides the sense of internal meditation, practice, and momentary confusion within Zhang's performance. As the dominant scholarly paradigm, demystification often reproduces and privileges a Chinese subject that operates in linear and purposeful ways, ultimately leading to performed action.

Zhang and other Chinese artists are situated within the norm of stable consciousness, as they are theorized as performing this dominant critical mode. Paul Ricoeur locates demystification's relation to consciousness within the works of Sigmund Freud, Friedrich Nietzsche, and Karl Marx.[9] Ricoeur reflects that "the *Genealogy of Morals* in Nietzsche's sense, the theory of ideologies in the Marxist sense, and the theory of ideals and illusions in Freud's sense represent three convergent procedures of demystification" that counteract the Cartesian reliance upon a stable consciousness.[10] As Ricoeur argues, although all three are invested in mining hidden ideologies, they maintain consciousness as operating with full awareness. Even though these theories critically undo Enlightenment presumptions of a steady consciousness, the paradigm of demystification relies upon consciousness to remain stable or whole in order to produce critique. This consciousness merely redirects its "powers" and potential toward unveiling society's ills and does not complicate the notion of consciousness itself. Rather than examining how ideology functions along with its operating assumptions, consciousness for Marx, Freud, and Nietzsche instead only follows ideology's problems. Within this equation, consciousness remains intact and major while its critical focus varies.

Minor turns have emphasized the need to rework the notion of the subject. Rey Chow directs us to the dominant relation between consciousness and radical politics, where material change "is conceived of as, or analogized with, agency—more precisely, an agency of motion and transformation, an agency aimed at an increasingly *better* (that is, more advanced, more enlightened, and more democratic) world."[11] In this formulation, "materialism/materiality (understood as human activity), change (understood as progress), and agency" are intertwined as forms of action (resistance and activity) that arise from conscious intent.[12] Chow encourages a reconceptualization of "a unified 'being' with a rational 'mind' or 'consciousness.'" This formula connecting consciousness, agency, and performed resistance predetermines how Chinese artists, like Zhang, are interpreted as agents of demystification and as resistant, enduring, and sovereign subjects. As such, it is crucial to reconsider what maintains this formula.

Jane Bennett extends critiques of demystification toward "the vitality of matter," as demystification "reduce[s] *political* agency to *human* agency."[13] Through an emphasis on the mattering of nonhuman objects, Bennett reveals our theoretical assumptions around formulations of human agency. I would extend these insights to highlight how agency is also often presumed to cognitively function in normalized ways. In other words, the lens of disability pushes Bennett's critique to reformulate agency through not only objects, but also human bodies that have often never been afforded agency. Some populations have historically been situated as an object and, hence, denied a sense of will or capacity. In addition to disability, race directs us to the rendering of people as objects. China, as the mysterious Orient, has been racialized as the West's unknowable other. Chinese subjects become objects that require translation for the West, placing them outside of this human economy. As discussed earlier, the ways the Chinese are imagined as lacking post-Fordist ingenuity further exemplify their object status. Thus, demystification requires not only an expansion of the ableist presumptions surrounding consciousness, but also a consideration of the racialized and gendered contours that have repeatedly refused human agency to certain populations.

Demystification and agency also have much to do with notions of performativity. Demystification presumably leads to the enactment or performance of critique. Performance establishes our understanding of social engagement, as performance presumably represents action and the execution of conscious intent and desires. The field of performance studies has developed out of such a model. Although the field arises from diverse approaches and multiple disciplines, ranging from philosophy, linguistics, and anthropology, to music, theater, dance, and art history, the relationship of agency and resistance to performance remains. A thinker central to the dominant formulations of agency and performance within theater and performance studies is Bertolt Brecht. Brecht drew from Marxist and Frankfurt School ideologies to develop his theorizations of aesthetics and politics.[14] Although Brecht himself was a contentious figure within the Frankfurt School, he nonetheless based many of his aesthetic theories in relation to these peers. Of particular import is his notion of *alienation effects* in its role in creating an epic theater. Brecht first developed alienation effects in his 1936 essay "Alienation Effects in Chinese Acting." Moving away from Aristotelian rhetorical models based on empathy and identification with actors, Brecht's alienation effects focus more on an audience's "acceptance or rejection of [an actor's] actions and utterances . . . to take place on a conscious plane, instead of, as hitherto, in the audience's subconscious."[15] Brecht theorizes consciousness as a stable and knowable plane by which an audience becomes aware. The Chinese technique that enables the alienation effects to take hold within this conscious plane is the actor's ability to remove the "fourth wall" separating them from the audience.

To achieve this separation, actors observe themselves and engage with the audience to reveal a sense of removal from their characters. Such an engagement emerges from a lack of passion and a limited affect, qualities that Brecht praises in the Chinese: "These Chinese artist's performance often strikes the Western actor as cold. That does not mean that the Chinese theater rejects all representation of feelings. The performer portrays incidents of utmost passion, but without his delivery becoming heated."[16] The Chinese produce the alienation effect through a restrained sense of affect, "not in form of absence of emotion, but in the forms of emotions which need not correspond to those of the characters portrayed."[17] Brecht finds the Chinese actor's ability to produce a distanced affective relationship to the portrayed character a key tool for the alienation effect, one that can be transferred to other cultures: "It is not entirely easy to realize that the Chinese actor's A-effect is a transportable piece of technique: a conception that can be pried loose from the Chinese theatre."[18] Affect becomes a techne, in that the Chinese production of distanced feeling becomes a tool and means that can be learned, repeated, and reperformed. Alienation effects, as produced through the techne of distanced affect, ultimately enable the audience to become conscious of power. For Brecht, this consciousness must be stabilized in order for such alienation effects to make one and others aware.

The fields of theater, dance, and performance studies, along with those who work on China within these fields, have inherited this avant-garde, Brechtian tradition.[19] In addition, the field upholds performance for its ability to instill and inspire "political effects" through alienation and other mechanisms. Many performance scholars rely on rendering theater, dance, and performance applicable to the political by formulating a sense of unity and community to challenge societal ills. Performance is often understood as the means to gain consciousness, leading into action. Within this equation, Brecht's presumptions around consciousness remain intact. Performance theorists often glorify performance's possibilities due to an overreliance on a dominant notion of consciousness that leads to agency, resistance, and, ultimately, political action.

The presumptions undergirding performance need to be unpacked, since it is often imagined as potential to challenge the static temporality of other forms of art. In relation to other art forms and discourses, performance is cited for the possibilities it provides through the notion of performativity. J. L. Austin theorizes how speech acts are not merely statements but can become performative, hence affecting and activating a social space. Theorists rely upon performativity to show how language and other art forms become more than just words or objects. Through performativity, language and objects become active participants. To develop this notion, Austin privileges felicitous performatives over infelicitous ones in his linguistic accounts in *How to Do Things with Words*. This particular privileging is perpetuated within performance studies, as it theorizes performance in primarily felicitous over infelicitous modes. Later in this chapter, I destabilize this reliance on felicity in relation to the work of Cao Fei.

Although the infelicitous certainly arises within performance studies through analyses of gender constructs and queer shame in the works of Peggy Phelan, Judith Butler, José Muñoz, and Eve Sedgwick, among others, the felicitous is the primary mode of analysis and the privileged site for the field to imagine performance's social possibilities. What remains is a sense of a unified being as operating within consciousness, agency, and performed resistance. Shannon Jackson acknowledges the failure of agency and the complications of this dominant form of consciousness within Judith Butler's notion of performativity and José Muñoz's development of disidentification.[20] Yet, Jackson questions how these theoretical gestures may not "resolv[e] the issues of intentionality. The defamiliarization paradigm still might assume the self-consciousness of a subject who does the displaying, the pointing, and the outlining—that is, the subject who has a 'program.'"[21] Following Jackson's provocation, I complicate these ideas of self-conscious awareness and a unified being that undergird performance studies through meditation and fabulation. This reliance on the felicitous furthers a Marxist-Brechtian project of social change, agency, and demystification through performance. China and expanded notions of consciousness and performance undo the equation surrounding performance's "success" through intentionality, agency, and resistance. As I will discuss in relation to the work of Cao Fei, the notion of sustaining a character within theater studies perpetuates the dominance of the felicitous. While Erving Goffman and others acknowledge the ways people use multiple roles in the everyday, most performance theorists rely on positivistic notions of "action" but have not fully questioned the *intensity* by which these characters enact or present. In other words, we are not always "on."

Zhang Huan and *Melete*: From Endurance Art to Lingering Art

Endurance is a key frame for understanding performance art as a form of political critique, as the artist's body undergoes pain and presumably performs resistance. Endurance has been utilized to describe both Western and non-Western artists. For Chinese performance artists, the label of endurance is consistently deployed as they presumably undergo durational pain to perform a critique of society and show resistance against the state. However, the repeated reliance on narratives of endurance problematically limits theorizations of contemporary Chinese art within overdetermined notions of resistance. It appears that there are few analytic options to discuss non-Western art beyond endurance and resistance, while the discursive possibilities seem to be more expansive in relation to Western artists.[22] This section questions the theoretical knot that binds conscious and demystified critique, agency, and performed endurance, particularly as such notions limit our grasp of Zhang Huan's practices. When the imaginative capacity of the non-Western other is reduced to conscious critique, we are unable to explore alternative forms of imagination or cognition that may not be fully accounted for by demystification. Furthermore, within such accounts of consciousness and resistance, the subject is presumed to embody a normative and holistic sense of being. Drawing from disability theorists Bradley Lewis, Mel Chen, and Jasbir Puar, I renegotiate consciousness and resistance by destabilizing such ableist orientations surrounding cognition.[23] Rather than expanding our categorizations of consciousness, I delve into the possibilities of theorizing from less determined states to rethink normative ideas of proper or improper, better and functional subjects.

Zhang Huan's *12m²* is an iconic work in the archive of contemporary Chinese art that has been situated within this economy of endurance art, as he is fashioned as consciously resisting state practices and social norms.[24] Art historian Wu Hung has described *12m²* as "combin[ing] personal experience with a social critique."[25] Although these interventions and framings have certainly been necessary,[26] their repeated invocation perpetuates an understanding of the Chinese, non-Western other as always situated within the proper. In particular, the dimensions of breath, affect, and other seemingly minor details in their works are eschewed in light of discourses on the Chinese state, tradition, and politics, while such minor dimensions have been more liberally applied to Western artworks.

The minor frames of breath and feeling in the works of Zhang Huan and, in the following section, He Chengyao, provide methodological approaches. By engaging the haptic sensations produced within the practice of meditation, I reframe notions of endurance away from purposeful forms of resistance toward confused and less determined modes of consciousness. I examine what it means to sit with, breathe, and be present in order to minimize the associations of efficacy, opposition, and challenge embedded within endurance. Meditation reframes dominant Marxist formulations of consciousness, critically engaging the possibilities of failure and melancholy in lieu of overt agentic "resistance." Rather than reinforcing a binary between awareness and nonawareness—true consciousness and false consciousness—the concept of meditation offers ways to track different dispositions, modes of apprehension that emphasize relationality, play, and a variety of other pervasive, if minor, affects.

Both Zhang and He Chengyao have explicitly referenced Buddhism in relation to their works.[27] The Buddhist custom of meditation offers a sense of self-practice that tempers understandings of intentionality and critique. Minor yet multiple flicks, bites, reverberations, and penetrations enfold into Zhang's and He's corporeal experiences: the sonic and haptic vibrations from the flies on Zhang's body and the punctures from needles on He's. The stimulation on the skin becomes part of their present moment rather than an external challenge they must endure. They do not intend to display resistance by waiting to end their durational performances. Instead, they linger, sit, and breathe with such haptic sensations in order to cultivate a deeper grasp of being in the present moment. In other words, breath and meditation situate these works as modes of practice that are more about lingering within the moment than performing and enduring from start to finish. A viewer of *12m²* might also feel the familiar tickle of the flies on Zhang's body. However, in his performance, the presence of insects is multiplied to an unbearable degree, along with the fact that Zhang refrains from swatting the flies away. In other words, he does not solely endure these sensations, but rather practices being present with them.

Buddhist texts and the latter works of Michel Foucault offer insights on meditation as an epistemological analytic.[28] Meditation is an alternative mode for the dominant forms of consciousness and imagination that undergird demystification. Before further developing meditation, let me clarify my use of Buddhism in relation to critical theory and critiques of Orientalism. Although we have been trained to historicize non-Western sites, we often resist the idea of difference for fear of being essentialist. For example, my invocation of Buddhism, informed primarily by Asian studies, could be dismissed for re-entrenching cultural distinctions, from an Asian Americanist perspective. However, non-Western sites have differently become. As discussed in the introduction and chapter 3, China has *become* from a distinct history, which does not solely demand particularity but rather requires a re-negotiation of the very terms that structure how we discuss the non-Western other. Dismissing a turn to Eastern practice as "Orientalist" is too easy an answer. As such, I utilize Buddhism to bring to the fore such tensions that arise between Asian and Asian American studies, since these fields are differently invested in ideas like tradition or religion. When placed in relation to gender and racialization, Buddhism teeters at the intersection of ethnic and area studies to produce different practices of reading, theorizing, and relating: one must contend with material differences that have conditioned China and produced a unique vernacular culture, without dismissing such particularities nor maintaining such distinctions as essential or emblematic for all of China. To remark on the metaphysical within Zhang's and He's respective works takes pause from Orientalist and essentialist critiques without attributing Buddhism to all Chinese artists.

In addition, Buddhism does not simply refer to the spiritual practices of these two artists. Buddhism offers an epistemological framework to rethink theoretical categories. Similar to M. Jacqui Alexander, I utilize religious practices not as "cultural retention and survival" but as a means "to get inside of the meaning of the spiritual as epistemological, that is, to pry open the terms, symbols, and organizational codes."[29] In other words, in utilizing meditation as an additional epistemology by which to rethink key minor concepts, I contribute to expanding theorizations around cognition, agency, and the subject. Since secularist critical theory often predetermines the conditions of the non-West, my use of Buddhism as an epistemological category destabilizes the operating presumptions and dominant terms of theory.

Meditation is a mode of imagination that refrains from rapid judgment, where one experiments and lingers outside of the finite temporality that typically structures time-based art. Meditation is not a form of imagination that provides consciousness of power or class alienation; rather, it lingers within the ordinary and the present moment. Although meditation within the Buddhist tradition involves diverse genealogies, most stress how meditation requires "a set of practices or experiments in awareness that are performed with an enormous amount of rigor."[30] Practice emerges from the ways Zhang's and He's bodies are trained through sitting, breathing, and being with corporeal sensations so as to be present. In preparation for $12m^2$, Zhang tested different food products to smear onto his body in order to amplify the attraction of flies to his skin. His practices involved placing himself in the scents of a public toilet in the middle of the summer and sitting with the tactile sensation of hundreds of flies crawling on his body. These itches and the buzzing of flies on his face and in his ears make one aware of sensations beyond the visual. The tactile, olfactory, and auditory locate Zhang in a space of practice and training. His performance does not simply endure through a finite moment of discomfort in order to intentionally perform a critique. His use of breath emphasizes self-cultivation, amplifying one's awareness of a present moment. Within the present tense, one is not fully conscious of problems, critique, and the future. Rather, consciousness becomes less directed when mired in the ordinary and momentary. These practices, as such, are not wholly intentional. Zhang and He engage in these multiple cognitive modes that swim in and out of intentionality; they linger within sensations and feelings in order to practice being present.

Similar concerns around meditation as practice are central to Foucault's turn to the Stoics. He uncovers practices of "meditation and preparation" in Plato's *Alcibiades* which involved "to study, to read, to prepare for misfortune or death."[31] Foucault's last two lectures shift his primary concerns away from defining power or knowledge and are directed to the question of "What are we in our actuality?"[32] He relies on discourses from the eighteenth century and the Stoics, as these two schools were concerned with the formation of the self. Foucault distinguishes technologies of the self from technologies of production (objects), signs (meaning and signification), and power (organizing individuals). Meditation is one such technology of the self, "which permit[s] individuals to effect by their own means or with the help of others a certain number of operations on their own bodies and souls, thoughts, conduct, and way of being, so as to transform themselves in order to attain a certain state of happiness, purity, wisdom, perfection, or immortality."[33] Foucault's use of the term *technology* implicates the realm of practice as such repeated, minute "means" and "operations" cultivate a self, a being.

Foucault's formulation of meditation becomes a different form of consciousness that is not structured around resistance to power and, rather, involves multiplicity and openness. The Latin term for meditation, *melete*, is a technique where one must "imagin[e] the articulation of possible events to test how you would react," and is that which "trains thought."[34] Foucault clarifies that care of the self is "not of the body but of the soul."[35] In order to care for the soul, one "cannot know itself except by looking at itself in a similar element, a mirror. . . . In this divine contemplation, the soul will be able to discover rules to serve as a basis for just behavior and political action."[36] As exemplified by Zhang and He, it is through self-cultivation and breath that meditation tempers dominant modes of knowing away from solely being about conscious intent. Zhang and He respectively invest in a training that does not produce immediate political critique, but rather an ethics and care that is cultivated by being with the present. These acts of meditation ultimately expand the legibility and meaning of being political.

Lingering in Time

In addition to practice, meditation offers an experience with time that shifts from marking a duration to locating oneself in the murky, affective present. By renegotiating understandings of time in this way, experience and consciousness become located as less precise, direct, and purposeful. Through discourses of endurance art, the Chinese are usually framed as experiencing time in finite ways, from the beginning of a performance to its end. Endurance situates artists as resisting pain, where one performs such resistance as a critique of the political problems of which one has become aware. The formula of consciousness of social ills, agency to critique, and then the performance of resistance is embedded in how we frame Zhang Huan as an agent of demystification. Furthermore, this formula informs the dominant logic surrounding endurance art and durational performance. By focusing on self-practice and time within meditation, we complicate the paradigm of demystification and locate different temporal and political dispositions. Through repeated practice, meditation provides a state of being where one becomes "present, so replete with awareness" that traditional notions of time, along with how subjects exist within time, are destabilized.[37] When present, subjects expand their boundaries in relation to past objects and others; in other words, subjects become relational. Within the Taoist Qigong tradition, delineations between the self, nature, and others are complicated as one's body is connected to a larger metaphysical entity or force. Meditation contributes to this metaphysical blurring of subject and object distinctions.

In addition, temporality shifts beyond clock time. Duration becomes not only marked time, but also destabilized time that does not develop teleologically. Zhang exists in such durations that simultaneously border the defined and fluid, along with the material and metaphysical. The physical world continues to mark time. However, as Zhang enters his internal meditation, time cannot be quantified in similar ways. The multiple media capturing Zhang's actions amplify these temporal lapses. Across performance time and photographic time, *12m²* indexes temporal slippages. Zhang directs viewers to linger in the immediate present captured by the photograph, along with his ongoing performed negotiations to deal with the smells and sensations surrounding him. Is the notion of endurance sufficient to capture time as simultaneously marked yet unstable? What does it mean to have a time-based art practice in light of such destabilizations of time?

With a focus on meditation's temporality, the notions of time-based and durational art come to the fore. Through the frameworks of the state and historical trauma, Zhang's performances are envisioned as endurances from start to finish. However, meditation refashions time and practice, forcing us to reconsider endurance and conscious critique for their normative presumptions. In particular, *endurance* and its related terms, *durational* and *time-based*, are often discussed in gender neutral, colorblind, and ableist ways, even though time-based practices possess a normative, white, and masculinist genealogy.[38] Most cite the works of Vito Acconci and David Hall in framing time-based practice. The term purportedly first arose in print in Hall's writings during the early 1970s, as he sought to account for the shift away from object-based art into time-based mediums such as film, video, performance, and sound. Hall emphasizes a shift in our relations to objects, where seemingly ephemeral forms become generative for the formation of time-based as a category. His use of time "encompass[es] any work structured specifically as a durational experience."[39]

The notion of duration that time-based art relies upon implies a finite moment, revealing a normative and linear sense of time structured around a beginning, middle, and end. Teleology frames these performances of demystification from the development of thought (beginning) to performed action (end): one becomes conscious of the negative event, has agency to act, performs endurance or critique, and finally demystifies the situation. This teleological model undergirds our comprehension of not only the durational and time-based, but also endurance as a political act.[40] Similar to time-based art, endurance art has been connected to masculinist and racialized practices.[41] Thus, the whiteness, masculinity, and normative assumptions embedded within endurance inflect how we theorize non-Western subjects in relation to such time-based practices. Although endurance may be an aspect of these works, the label entwines the other into the paradigm of demystification, neglecting other relations to time and consciousness. Endurance is mediated within these norms, perpetuating a narrative of resistance.

The oft-eclipsed dimensions of meditation, self-practice, and time in Zhang's practices question the normative foundations of time-based as a conceptual category. Since meditation changes our understanding of how we experience time as unstable and less determined, the practice of breathing undoes the category of time-based art. However, what term or conception of time might capture this sensibility?

Zhang does not merely endure pain from start to finish in order to produce a critique. Within his acts of self-cultivation, he experiences time as *lingering*, where temporality becomes less determined and not pregnant with symbolic meaning. Zhang Huan shifts away from endurance and notes his own discomfort with the narratives of purposefulness and performativity often attributed to his work. Zhang prefers ordinariness and practice: "The source for my creative inspiration comes from the most inconspicuous aspects of daily life, the matters that are easily neglected. . . . *12m²* was produced in this way. . . . I try my best to experience an extant reality throughout the process of my work. Only when I finish a work can I finally realize what I have achieved and what I have expressed. I loathed the performance element within the work."[42] Zhang hesitates from the notions of endurance and purpose, preferring ideas related to lingering and indeterminacy; he distances himself from the notion of a performative intent and critique. Rather than ascribing political meaning to *12m²*, Zhang lingers in less defined modes.

Lingering brings to light the limits of the category of endurance art. Endurance implies resistance because one must work against a negative force throughout the performance. However, Zhang lingers. Endurance primarily implicates a fixed sense of time, while lingering describes the melancholic feeling and dwelling in space and time. When looking at the etymologies of both words, one sees a convergence of the meanings of *linger* and *endure* as structured around continuation and existence in the fifteenth century. However, before the fifteenth century, these terms had different meanings, where *endure* implies "to undergo or suffer" and "to make hard, harden," while *linger* involved "to resolve, dwell, or prolong."[43] To endure involves a durational period where one either suffers or hardens, while to linger implicates dwelling and staying. Similarly, in Mandarin, the characters for endure (*jing, ting, ren,* and *ai*) refer to a similar notion of suffering and hardening, while the characters for linger (*panhuan* and *yingrao*) connote prolonging. It is within these etymological differences that lingering implicates a melancholic weight and indeterminate existence for duration.

Lingering differentiates how one experiences time, particularly in relation to meditation. Although Henri Bergson has connected duration to enduring, his theorization of duration lies more in what I identify as lingering in its prolonged and ongoing form.[44] Bergson distinguishes time from duration—the former being a scientific measurement, while the latter is "what one feels and lives."[45] He thus emphasizes the constant movement of duration: "The inner life is all that at once, variety of qualities, continuity of progress, unity of direction. It cannot be represented by images."[46] Similar to lingering, duration for Bergson involves a movement that is formless. Zhang's *lingering art* makes duration an object not to prolong but to work through and practice within.

Zhang lingers in the pleasures and difficulties of pain and the social. As Zhang sits within the multiple tactile, olfactory, and auditory sensations of his practiced meditation, he does not suffer or try to prove a point through resistance. Rather, he dwells and engages in these multiple haptic dimensions. At the end of his piece, he walks to a local river to wash off the honey and fish sauce on his skin. Zhang does not end his durational endurance at this moment. As noted above, even after Zhang "finishes" his project, he lingers in order to reflect on his process. For Zhang, meaning and purpose do not precede action. Zhang cultivates a sense of self not to simply question and endure power; instead, he performs a more nuanced notion of lingering in power, pain, and time. Lingering complicates the predominant forms of resistance, endurance, and consciousness that have structured how the Chinese have been understood.

He Chengyao: Trauma, Bios, and Chinese Women

On one hand, masculinist forms of endurance reproduce ideas of a herculean subject for China. On the other, feminized forms of victimhood not only instantiate the agentic subject, but also reinvigorate the trope of "saving brown women from brown men."[47] This next section further investigates the racialized and gendered dimensions of agency, particularly in relation to the frame of trauma and history. I first build upon the framework of meditation to situate He Chengyao's *99 Needles*. I then use meditation and lingering to contend with the predominance of trauma for understanding Chinese women.

As discussed in chapter 1, the Cultural Revolution looms as the historic event that continues to shape different generations of artists. Due to the egregious acts of authoritarian state control, the framework of trauma predominates across discourse on artists and Chinese subjects.[48] Zhang Huan's and He Chengyao's works function within an economy that places photography, China, trauma, and resistance together. The photos of their performances circulate within a larger tradition that includes the iconic image from June 5, 1989—the stopping of tanks in Tiananmen Square by a single person. In *Disability Aesthetics*, Tobin Siebers discusses this image in relation to trauma. In theorizing the increased circulation of the wounded body, Siebers stresses the import of disability in formulating understandings of global media: "Trauma art is at once impersonal and painful—which means it both communicates between cultures and retains an affective power. . . . On the one hand, media images of traumatic and disabled bodies travel so easily . . . because they are floating signifiers of the cultural. On the other hand, these images gain a stunning potency in local contexts because any given culture will readily attach its own communal meanings to them."[49]

99 Needles operates within this economy of images for China. Siebers's framework might initially appear appropriate for theorizing He's photograph, as her work certainly represents a particular Chinese context where one understands the wounded body in *99 Needles* as related to trauma. However, *99 Needles* helps us rethink this relationship, specifically as it pertains to non-Western women. From the horrors inflicted by Japanese troops on comfort women to US imperialist violence enacted upon women in Vietnam, trauma has become the dominant frame for understanding women through-out Asia. Trauma conceptualizes culture, law, and other acts of resistance as the primary means of agency in addressing past harm. However, this frame-work not only relies on spectacular and legible forms of state violence, but also pathologizes victims as unable to let go until adequate redress arrives through self-expression, culture, or legal reparations.

As Mimi Nguyen reveals in relation to US imperialism in Vietnam, trauma "often reproduces a relation of psychic to political dispossession that is ubiquitous and presumptuous."[50] Trauma is thought to "impos[e] itself again and again on [the subject's] consciousness, as nightmare or repeti-tive compulsion."[51] Trauma becomes all-encompassing, as the female victim is imagined as needing adequate redress in order to obtain a sense of clo-sure and to "move on." The subject is imagined as located within a singu-lar historic event and expected to overcome trauma, where the spectacular traumatic event leads to victimization, and only through a process of recu-peration can the normative subject find closure. Chinese women are often situated within this crisis narrative. I thus shift from the frameworks of crisis and trauma in order to examine other dispositions and practices that He's 99 *Needles* offers. In particular, the piece augments trauma by emphasizing acts of *ordinary* violence and the affective weight of melancholy. Through these frames, we avoid pathologizing the victim as unitary to help situate non-Western women within more open forms of being that do not default into dominant, state-defined, human rights frameworks.

Born in 1964 in Chongqing, He Chengyao graduated from the Sichuan Academy of Fine Arts in painting in 1989. Similar to Zhang, her most notable works have included performance art, of which she produced twenty pieces from 2001 to 2006. In *Mother and I* (2001), she took her first set of photo-graphs with her mother. Her mother sits on a chair in front of He Chengyao, with a white cloth covering the mother's stomach and lower body. Both of their chests are exposed, while He stands behind with hands resting on her mother's shoulders. They peer into the camera lens as if they are taking a family portrait. He Chengyao was born at the start of the Cultural Revolu-tion, and, like many during this moment, her father was relocated to a labor camp. He's mother supported the family alone, since her mother and father were not married. Perhaps due to the stresses and demands of being a single mother, her mother fell into depression. Her family believed that the mother had a mental illness since she would periodically bare her chest in public. This led to her family forcing what they understood as treatment, which in-cluded a coerced round of acupuncture where she was horizontally restrained on top of an abandoned door. In response to witnessing this as a child, He utilized performance to ponder the multiple themes of her mother's experiences, including the effects of the revolution and the trope of the hysterical woman. She reperforms her mother's "treatment" in 99 *Needles* by inserting acupuncture needles into her upper torso and head.

Similar to Zhang, He Chengyao enacts self-practice through and on her body. Acupuncture needles feel like pinches on the body's surface; however, the contact of needles on nerves underneath the skin creates another level of sensation. The intensity of contact on both epidermis and nerves amplifies her practice, as she sits through these punctures along her upper torso and lower body. The performance spans the time taken to insert the needles, about twenty minutes. Upon the acupuncturist finishing the insertion of needles, the intense blood circulation, along with a poorly placed needle in her wrist, makes her faint.

Beyond practice, He reperforms her mother's past injury. The act of reperformance does not replicate her mother's pain but rather involves self-practice through meditation. In particular, additional photo documentation of 99 *Needles* focuses on He's willingness to participate. Unlike her mother, He Chengyao is not physically coerced; she is photographed sitting patiently while an acupuncturist inserts needles onto her face. The act of reperformance renegotiates the insertion of needles away from a mimetic coercion toward a self-engaged practice. Since He is not experiencing the exact conditions around her mother's treatment, reperformance recalibrates the personal and historical stakes in the use of needles. These shifts in stakes and material conditions establish a practice that highlights He's attempts and failures while minimizing the impression of a performative critique through risk and endurance.

99 *Needles* responds to gendered disparities; however, solely recuperating her work as resistant to gendered norms and the state ignores the additional and nuanced contours of her political critique. She responds to both gender and disability, as she reenacts the abusive treatment her mother was forced to undergo to "deal" with her perceived mental illness. Similar to Zhang, He Chengyao deploys performance as a form of meditation. She not only reenacts her mother's pain, but also develops a sense of self through reperformance. As such, He Chengyao produces a Foucauldian ethics that does not create direct action but rather a practice and internal contemplation that mediates her sense of being.

Further, He Chengyao's practice destabilizes the line between subject and object and, more importantly, the temporal boundaries that separate

He's present self with her mother's past. The corporeal and temporal borders temporarily loosen to reconstitute He's selfhood. Feminist Buddhist scholar Anne Klein describes this reconstitution of time and self within meditation: "Experience of mind and body as only a seething flow of sensations is a dismembering of the self. But there is also a remembering, a bringing together, in the sense that mind and self are reconstituted for one's experience."[52] He Chengyao engages temporal instability through a feminist critique that unmoors the fiction of a stable subject; her mother's past binds with the present performance.

Amid this renegotiation of the self, however, He Chengyao encourages audience members to linger in the material realities of gendered disparities in China. In addition to performing a feminist analysis around the policing of women and their presumed hysteria, she expands the possibilities of such a critique by diminishing the stability surrounding self and other, subject and object, and past and present. He Chengyao reminds us that the destabilization of the self does not simply reduce the realm of politics to a mere illusion. The reconstruction of the self and the slippages of subject with object also require a consideration of the material world. Klein reveals the productive tension that arises between the instability of the self and the demand for the production of a political or essentialized category: "Some feminists make a case for referring to 'woman' as an essentialized category when this is useful for political purposes, even though they recognize this term as a fiction. In contrast to such strategic essentialism, Buddhist theories and practices envision a subject for whom groundlessness *and* a sense of the constructed nature of self can be simultaneous, so that there is never a necessity to 'choose' strategically between them."[53] As past and current temporalities momentarily collapse in He Chengyao's performance, she reconstructs her sense of self through meditative practice that offers the opportunity to feel, think, and reflect on her mother's past.[54] In the words of Alexander, "the embodiment of the Sacred dislocates clock time, meaning linearity, which is different than living in the past or being bound by tradition. . . . Time becomes a moment . . . experienced in the now, but also a space crammed with moments of wisdom about an event . . . already having inhabited different moments."[55] Notions of time exist beyond duration, from start to finish, as discussed in relation to Zhang Huan. In addition, time becomes malleable, as He's present practice enfolds into her mother's past.

The blurring of subject and object is not an end in itself. This troubling of subject and object is situated in relation to Chinese women and a global landscape. As discussed earlier, the Cultural Revolution looms as the historic event that continues to shape proper narratives about China and its subjects through trauma. Further, in various exhibitions of *99 Needles*, curators describe the work as emblematic of criticisms of the state and oppressive gendered practices. He Chengyao is thus often framed within a feminist mode of recuperation that contends with the traumas of her family history and its imbrication with proper events. *99 Needles* is emblematic of Chinese performance art and its relation to trauma. Hong Kong theorist Eva Kit Wah Man situates He's "performance in its cultural context," where Man cites the Cultural Revolution and "madness and family traumas" as "the main references of her artistic creativity."[56] She frames performance as a form of art therapy, reproducing the idea that one can repair oneself into a holistic subject. The gendered artist's subjectivity is imagined as fully cognizant of past wrongs and seeking closure through performance.

He Chengyao's performance, however, renegotiates how trauma overdetermines discourses on Chinese women. Cathy Caruth and Shoshana Feldman have primarily theorized trauma through the Holocaust.[57] Some have critiqued these formative works as overdetermined for non-Western contexts. In particular, Michael Rothberg has called for a "decolonizing [of] trauma studies," encouraging us to not only expand the sites engaged with trauma, but also rethink the analytic itself.[58] Such critiques have, at this point, become well established in relation to trauma studies. This section's goal is more modest. I focus on China to examine how trauma renders legible the figure of the Third World woman requiring Western human rights intervention. The frame of trauma overdetermines the very understanding of gendered and racialized agency amid the global. Thus, by attending to both the event of the revolution and forms of everyday trauma, we can begin to rethink the place of the Chinese woman as subject within biopolitical regimes. *99 Needles* turns to the global and racial to renegotiate trauma beyond an event-based model toward traces of less spectacular forms of violence. Thus, I examine the place of melancholy and affect to shift away from trauma's pathologization of the non-Western woman as a unitary and legible victim and to direct us toward the lingering and melancholic weight of events in the everyday.

Wang Nanming notes how most Chinese critics dismiss He's use of nudity as gratuitous and sensational; as a result, Wang curated a show of He's oeuvre in order to respond to these gendered devaluations. In Wang's show, He Chengyao's use of nudity is meant to "illustrate . . . intense memory."[59] Wang challenges other critics' responses to He's work by shifting the use of nudity away from sensational meaning toward the ordinary. He Chengyao utilizes the haptic feel of needles on her naked body in order to linger within the ordinary and sensation, not only legible traumatic events. Rather than depicting He's exposed body as a political statement, Wang tempers He's deployment of nudity as emblematic of her quotidian memories and condition. Similar to Zhang, He Chengyao shifts from the purposeful to linger in the indeterminate zone of the everyday. She cycles in and out of lingering, rather than finding closure or repair.

Her meditative practice of inserting the needles into the body trains her sensations, allowing her to linger in an indeterminate and expansive space and time. Time weighs upon her body much like melancholy, as the subject continually returns to linger. Anne Cheng describes melancholy as "the introjection of a lost, never-possible perfection, an inarticulable loss that comes to inform the individual's sense of his or her own subjectivity."[60] The temporal knot and bind of melancholy work against narratives of closure, redress, and resistance. For the Chinese woman then, lingering more aptly captures this sense of being. Lingering and melancholy offer ways to understand how a victim grieves and sits within one's own pain beyond closure.

Akin to lingering, melancholy opens up space to account for trauma's excesses. In particular, melancholy considers the ineffable effects of historic trauma, along with forms of repeated ordinary violences that are normally eschewed in trauma's formula for legibility. Although melancholy cannot seek full repair, it carries a subject through time; melancholy becomes a mechanism for survival, a way to subsist although anxiously. The affect most closely associated with melancholy is anxiety.[61] Anxiety's state of constant unease directs us to melancholia as a condition and state of being within the ordinary, as opposed to an easily identifiable feeling associated with the traumatic event. As such, melancholy more aptly encompasses the lingering and ongoing everydayness of historical injury. Unlike trauma, melancholy helps account for the ineffable anxieties that condition the melancholic subject and for the ordinary orientations that structure life beyond trauma. Sianne Ngai emphasizes that "there is an underlying assumption that an appropriate emotional response to . . . violence exists, and that the burden lies on the racialized subject to produce that appropriate response legibly, unambiguously, and immediately."[62] Such expectations are often fulfilled through discourses of trauma and resistance; however, what would it mean to grapple with trauma's excesses?

He Chengyao augments trauma to understand pain and historical time. Such a destabilization of trauma for China is important for the way trauma predominantly functions in relation to state-defined human rights discourse, along with proper modes of awareness, agency, and performed critique. Melancholy, meditation, and lingering augment trauma and historical pain, accounting for the ordinary, everyday, and minor. This shift is important since the rhetoric of trauma rationalizes Western intervention. Trauma governs: it conceptualizes the figure of the non-Western woman as traumatized to rationalize state intervention and occupation. By accommodating the ordinary, along with more open forms of agency, we attend to trauma's biopolitical functions. He Chengyao's critique and melancholic lingering bring to the fore how notions of legal justice cannot make the racialized and gendered subject whole. These subjects have never existed in completion. She lingers in the sensations of ninety-nine needles because there are no other forms of repair nor redress for her mother. Rather than repeating a discourse of trauma that ossifies China as inhuman and authoritarian, rationalizing Western intervention, He directs us to this condition for the Chinese, non-Western woman.

Cao Fei: Fabulating on Performativity

In addition to meditation, fabulation contends with the limits of demystification as it relates specifically to performativity. In particular, fabulation produces a minor model of how to do things with performance. In *Cosplayers* (2004), Cao Fei presents a video and photo series that explore the world of cosplay. Short for "costume play," cosplay arises from the growing popularity of animation and large-scale gaming cultures. Originating in Japan in the 1990s, the social practice involves groups of primarily young people that congregate and dress like, but do not fully reenact, their favorite manga, anime, and animated characters. These fans meet in public spaces, like convention halls and cultural festivals. Photography is a key medium that captures the trend, as websites not only archive but also distribute the aesthetics of cosplay. Within cosplay's behavioral norms, participants often walk around gatherings in their costumes but interact in pedestrian ways. When one is photographed, however, participants become *animated*. The moment of photographic capture demands normalized behavior, as cosplayers often pose and perform as their costumed characters. However, beyond these moments of photographic capture, cosplayers often return to a disengaged affective state. Most cosplayers walk around convention centers in fabulous gear without performing in character. It is primarily when one is taking a photograph that cosplayers suddenly embody their costumes and characters. Cao Fei captures this detached mode of performance, helping us reconsider how subjects exist beyond a model of intention and direct action.

Cao Fei explores this interplay of multiple performative states from the everyday to the animated. Her project uses cosplay and new media culture to complicate definitions of performance and the subject. In one image from the series, *A Mirage*, two cosplayers wear costumes that do not reference popular animated characters but are generalized references to the culture of animation. The costumes are not indexical of identifiable characters; instead, they are generic. One player wears a short purple dress over black leggings. She wraps white fabric in a crisscross pattern on the lower part of her leggings and around her torso. This player sits on top of a replica of a cheetah that stares across a field at a zebra. Another player rests atop the zebra, dressed in all black while holding a large bunch of black balloons. He stares off into the hazy smog-encompassed city of Guangzhou, which serves as the background for the photo. The players peer off in opposite directions and appear not to pose in the customary ways of cosplay. They linger in their thoughts, as they are perched atop animals and amid a luscious green field littered with orange flowers and a gilded plastic antelope. Cao Fei photographs a moment of disengagement that is normally part of the repertoire of the everyday. In other words, the apparatus of the camera captures the fact that we are not always on or engaged, which is not how traditional cosplay imagery normally functions. It is within this disconnect between moments of everyday and animated behavior that Cao complicates traditional notions of performance. She shifts performance away from forms of coherence, felicitousness, and awareness.

Born in 1978, Cao Fei is a part of a generation of Chinese artists whose works have attained much international acclaim. Her pieces have been exhibited in New York, Shanghai, Venice, Hong Kong, Taipei, London, and the Netherlands, among other places. Growing up under the economic reforms of Deng Xiaoping in the 1980s, Cao came of age during an era of rapid change in mainland China. Much continues to be written on Deng's program of "socialism with Chinese characteristics," which I will not discuss here in relation to Cao Fei. However, it is important to note that this historical period provided access to travel and popular culture that was not as easily accessible to earlier generations. During this era of shifting power, Cao's location in the southern city of Guangzhou enabled travel to Hong Kong with her family. There, she gained exposure to a globalized pop culture, including MTV during the late 1980s and 1990s.[63]

Drawing from these biographical details, most scholars frame Cao Fei as an artist who consciously critiques the rural-urban divides in the rapidly shifting neoliberalizing space of China.[64] Cao Fei is often discussed as possessing a political agenda or program that reveals the problems with China's rapid "rise" during the late twentieth century. Chinese artists are situated within these overdetermined formations of agency, as they are framed as intentional subjects who are fully conscious of the problems that surround them and, hence, perform accordingly. *Cosplayers* is usually understood in terms of critiquing, depicting, and performing the social realities of China. Most have stressed the way Cao mediates the shifting demands of urbanization, globalization, and modernization for China's youth. Maya Kovskaya places Cao Fei within China's political landscape: "Cao Fei emphasizes the problem of shifting and constraining social roles that have been brought to the forefront by China's attempts at 'modernization.' Perhaps now, more than ever, people need to tap into the power of their imagination."[65] Although Kovskaya gestures to imagination, she situates it as a major possibility that allows one to performatively "do something" with intention and awareness. Kovskaya's use of imagination is framed within the arithmetic of consciousness, agency, and performed action. These frames reveal the tendency to read Cao Fei's work as exposing the realities and paradoxes of modernity and urban development—displacement, effects of digital economies, and globalization at large. Agency becomes limited to forms of resistance to the state, as the artist possesses the type of consciousness and intent that translates into informed, demystified, and performed critique. Although Cao Fei certainly engages the themes discussed above, I trace other conceptualizations of agency in her work so as to reconsider the strong performative impulse within accounts of agency and across academic fields.

Art and culture in China come to be discussed through a direct correlation, or mediation, between conscious intent and performed action. However, in interviews I conducted with Cao Fei, she often offered a less direct relationship between intent and action. She acknowledged how her work is understood and read as political in relation to China; however, she stressed the ambiguities of her political critique within her work. Rather than attributing these sentiments to an overly simplified and romanticized discourse surrounding artistic intent, I took this as a way to reconsider our own definitions of the political and action. More importantly, a discursive and movement analysis of *Cosplayers* complicates the notion of consciousness, as the affective qualities of cuteness, lightheartedness, and levity present a less determined correlation between awareness and performed critique. In other words, Cao fabulates and imagines other ways of behaving beyond the linear relationship between agency, intent, and performance. Drawing on and departing from the work of Henri Bergson, Saidiya Hartman, Baruch Spinoza, Gilles Deleuze, Tavia Nyong'o, and Rey Chow, I engage fabulation as a mode of imagination that enables an open-ended, nondidactic exploration of existing, being, and becoming. Fabulation provides a sense of purposelessness that does not signify a certain political discourse nor easily ascribe to narratives of resistance against the state.[66] Similar to meditation and lingering, fabulation further undoes the presumed relationship of the subject to agency and performed action.

Fabulation complicates how we do things with performativity. The *Cosplayers* series consist of photos and an eight-minute film made in 2004 and 2005. The work follows six youth in Guangzhou who "costume play," dressing in anime costumes as they traverse the city in real time while fighting, moving, and dreaming in an urban landscape. Through the act of cosplay, the youth do not fully embody nor completely reenact their characters. Instead, they vacillate between different states of engagement. When one experiences the photos as a series, one has a sense that all of the characters traverse multiple affective states. They range from being "in character" as they fully engage in a fight sequence (*Deep Breathing*; figure 4.4) to being semi-disengaged as they traverse city streets or sit idly in apartments or fields (*A Mirage*; figure 4.3). For example, in *Deep Breathing* the cosplayers' corporeal positions straddle the ground; they are crouched in defensive postures. Cao Fei captures the moment before the fight. *A Mirage* involves these same cosplayers but they peer into the hazy blue sky and fields. They seem to levitate amid the animals and balloons of Cao's curated scene. Their gestures, a bent wrist and relaxed shoulders, and the levity provided by the open sky and bundle of floating balloons inspire lightness. When juxtaposed against one another, *Deep Breathing* and *A Mirage* span multiple states. Further, as mentioned earlier, their costumes reference the practice of cosplay without indexing a specific character. The frayed edges of the purple skirt and the bumpy folds of white tape additionally create the sense of nonspecificity. Their costumes amplify a playful sense toward the generic. Cosplay often involves legible modes of referentiality to specific icons and characters. Through the generic costumes and varied states of dis/engagement, Cao expands our understandings of performance.

Cao Fei does not offer immediately legible characters with consistent emotions and actions. She reveals multiple states of engagement. Anthropologist Teri Silvio describes these multiple states as *acts of alterity* that

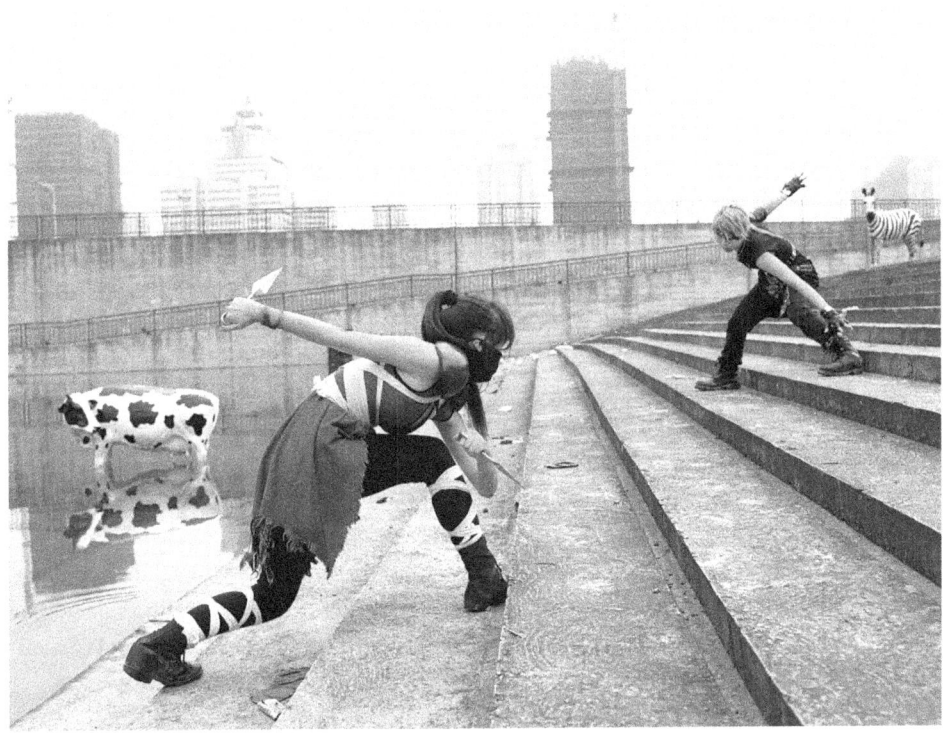

Figure 4.4. Cao Fei, *Deep Breathing*, 2004. Inkjet print on paper, 75 × 100 cm. Courtesy of the artist and Vitamin Creative Space.

cannot become actions of self-identity—actions that do not necessarily portray an internal self or intentional, purposeful desire.[67] These acts of alterity do not always align with an "authentic" self. Silvio understands cosplay as one of these acts of alterity and uses it to complicate performance and performativity. Cosplay as a social phenomenon does not require sustaining a character; there are moments of infelicitous action that traverse the space between character and self. Silvio offers an additional concept that helps us recalibrate notions of performance and performativity to direct us to these multiple states: *animation*. Silvio defines animation as a means of "projection of qualities perceived as human—life, power, agency, will, personality, and so on—outside of the self, and into the sensory environment, through acts of creation, perception and interaction . . . [which] requir[e] a medium."[68] This rich definition of animation emphasizes the projection of the self onto various objects.

Projection's imbrication with performance allows us to better understand the phenomena of cosplay and animation, where embodiment and projection intersect. In particular, there are a myriad of objects in the *Cosplayers* series. The reappearance of plastic replicas of animals, like zebras and cheetahs, renders palpable the production of "acts of alterity." Cao Fei consistently complicates the lines we produce across fake and real, with her use of the camera that captures moments well beyond the usual grammar of cosplay practices. Further, the use of fake animals brings to the fore the concepts of surface and artifice. The artist explores how animation practices, when comingled with performance, muddle the presumptions surrounding a subject's real and authentic behavior. She then explores and displaces this discourse through the amplification of artifice, as exemplified by the plastic animals that litter her photos.

This interplay of animation, performance, and absurdity can be further tracked in her series *East Wind*, which photographs a life-size replica of the children's book character Thomas the Tank Engine traversing the landscape of rural China (figure 4.5). This animated television program and popular book anthropomorphises a train. Cao Fei fabulates and builds upon popular animation and new media practices in order to direct us to different ways of being in the contemporary. Through the imbrication of animation and performance, fabulation and its affective contours become an important means to understand contemporary Chinese art. Fabulation is a mode of imagination that emphasizes nondidactic and nonnormative ways of thinking, feeling, and being, where performance and action are rendered incomplete and indeterminate.

Rather than bemoaning the false for the lack of truth, Cao Fei relishes in these moments of indeterminate behavior that destabilize the line across performed action and inaction. For Cao Fei, fabulatory imagination arises out of the affective resonances of the cute and lighthearted that continually appear in her body of work. The lighthearted is an affect that involves a relationality that seems inconsequential or without purpose. In "Is Art Lighthearted?," Adorno associates lighthearted art with Kant's notion of *purposelessness* in which it is "not [art's] content but its *demeanor, the abstract fact that it is art at all*, that . . . opens out over the reality to whose violence it bears witness at the same time."[69] This purposelessness provides the means by which to rethink the political, which I discuss below.

Although *demeanor* possesses the current connotation of behavior, its original meaning from fifteenth-century England involves a sense of self-management or conduct. In the full series of *Cosplayers*, one can track the

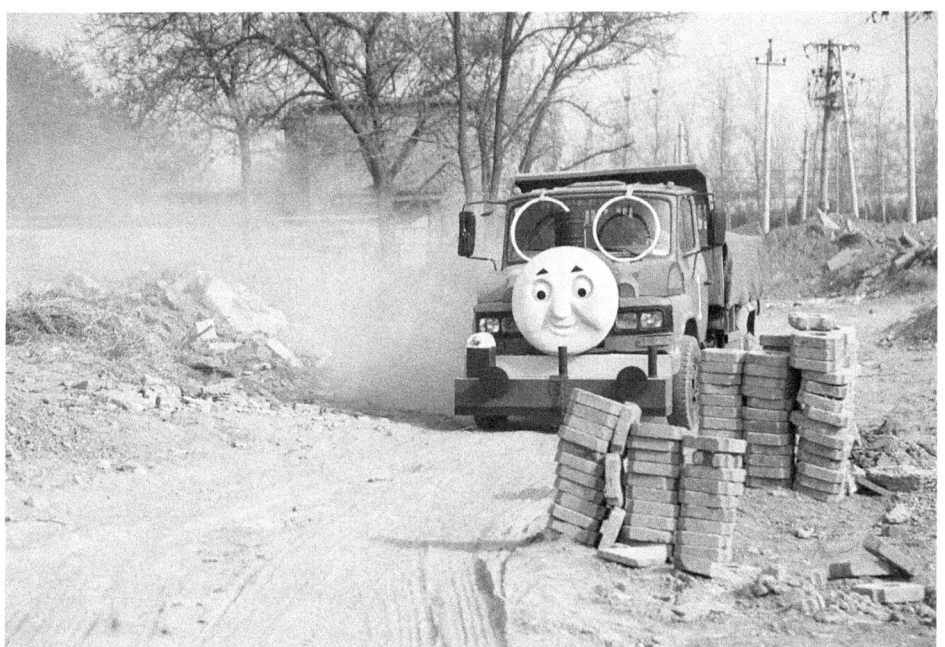

Figure 4.5. Cao Fei, *East Wind*, 2011. Single-channel video, color, with sound, 11 minutes, 11 seconds. Courtesy of the artist and Vitamin Creative Space.

lighthearted in relation to self-management. The elaborate costumes of the cosplayers are juxtaposed against the daily wear of drab khakis and dingy t-shirts of those around them. In *A Ming at Home*, the cosplayer in *A Mirage* and *Deep Breathing* is taken out of the fight and placed next to presumably her father. The affective relationship between the two is one of disconnect; he sits with his house sandals, reading the paper, while his daughter texts away on her cellphone in relaxed repose (figure 4.6). Their disconnected relationality is amplified by the everydayness of the scene, where the usual apartment fixtures (white walls, old posters, tile floors, old bottles, and tea kettle) litter the photo. In addition, in *Diversionist*, the public does not notice the large scythe being swung on the city streets (figure 4.7). The intense corporeal engagement of pounding across the sidewalk evokes a flamboyant flâneur. However, the intense movement of the flâneur with weapon in hand is ignored with equal levels of disregard. The scythe in bare daylight disappears in the small symphony of umbrellas and disengaged residents.

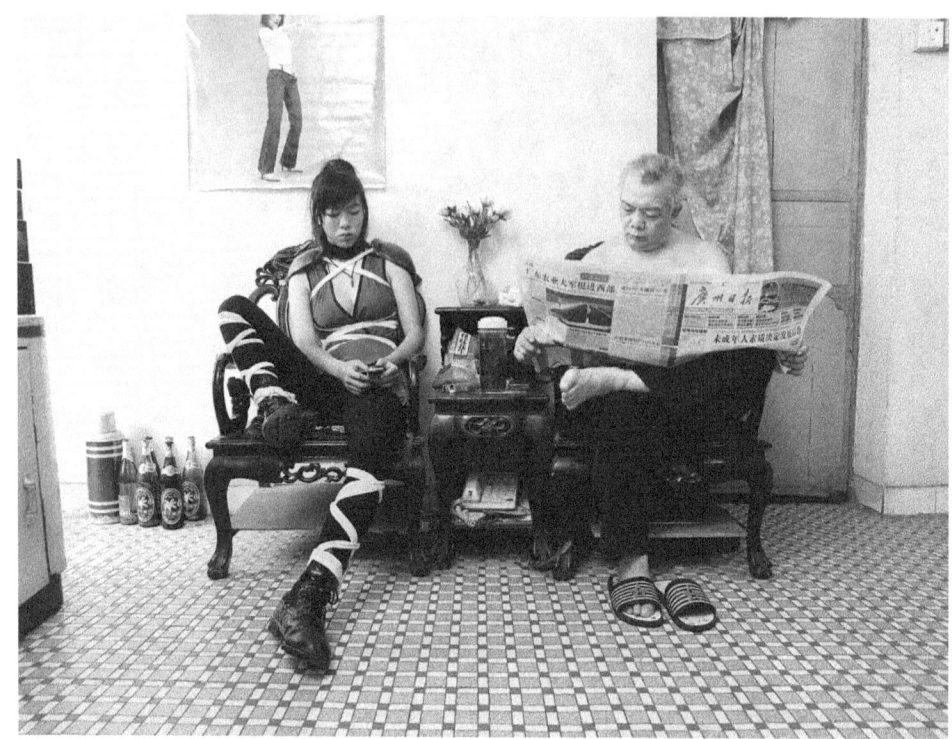

Figure 4.6. Cao Fei, *A Ming at Home*, 2004. Inkjet print on paper, 75×100 cm. Courtesy of the artist and Vitamin Creative Space.

Both Cao's cosplayers and those surrounding them ignore their immediate environments and each other. Cao's photos capture little tension between cosplayers and those who are not. The affective force of levity and humor arises from this juxtaposition in costumes and corporeal positions.

In addition, the demeanor of Cao's work operates within the framework of cuteness. Ngai critiques the privileging of aesthetic categories like the beautiful over the "cute . . . whimsical . . . or wacky."[70] It is within these oft-ignored, minor aesthetic categories that Ngai reveals the capacity to "conceive the powerlessness of both poetic forms and the social formations built around their production in the arena of political action as the source of an unsuspected power in the domain of political imagination: a fantasy about the very capacity to fantasize."[71] In a related series, *Cos-Cosplayers*, Cao amplifies this capacity and desire for fantasy. She removes the youth from city landscapes and presents them in full "cuteness," from head to toe. Formally,

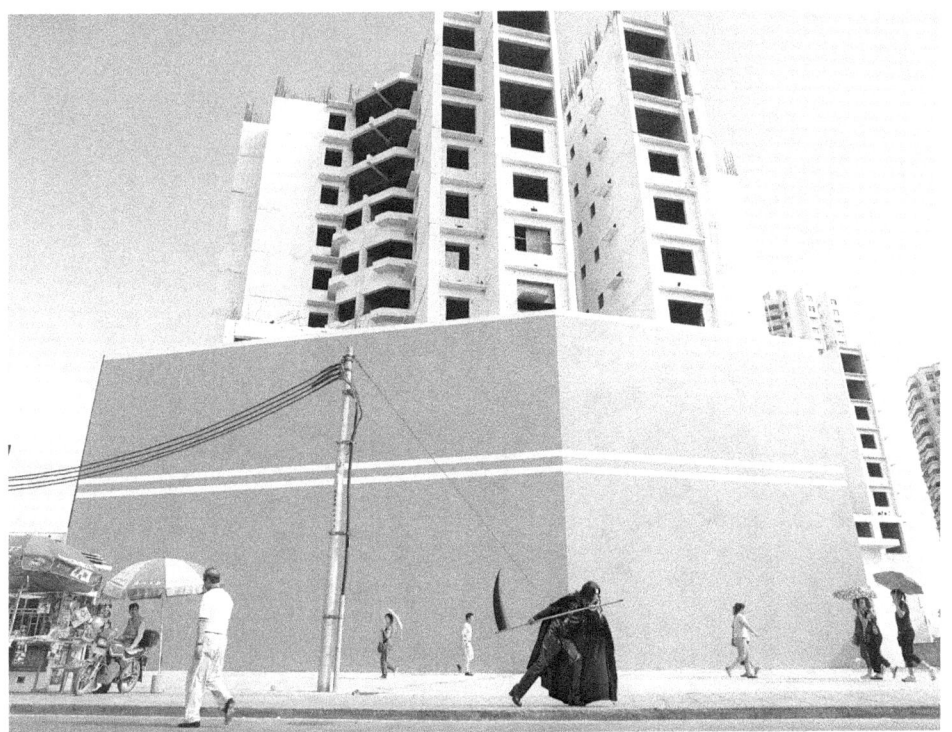

Figure 4.7. Cao Fei, *Diversionist*, 2004.
Inkjet print on paper, 75×100 cm.
Courtesy of the artist and Vitamin
Creative Space.

she constructs her photos to remove the background. The stark white background drastically foregrounds the vibrant costumes of her cosplayers (figure 4.8). They reference and juxtapose seemingly opposing characteristics: Hello Kitty's head sits on top of a yellow animal jumpsuit, while Darth Vader's head is placed on top of a frilly lacey dress. The affective dimensions of cuteness and whimsy emerge through her use of popular culture and animated characters. Cuteness, in this series, fails to provide a single narrative or commentary.

Within a framework of speech act theory, Cao does not present felicitous performative acts; she offers humorous and cute yet infelicitous and failed moments. In other words, the multiple affects that surround her work move beyond the idea of performing and maintaining a single character. Through the lighthearted and cute, Cao highlights the many dimensions and intensi-

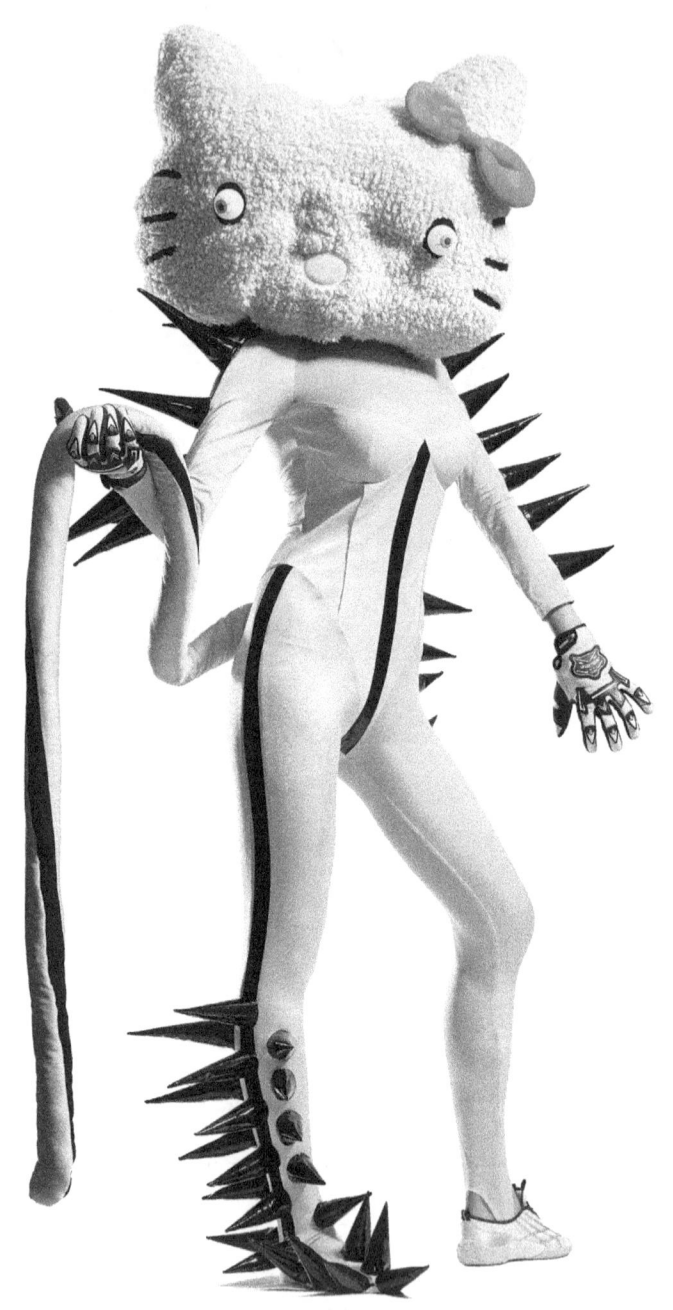

Figure 4.8. Cao Fei, *Cos-Cosplayers: Desert Cat*, 2005. Inkjet print on paper, 170×110 cm. Courtesy of the artist and Vitamin Creative Space.

ties located within a single body. The multiple photographs present a range within performance from being "in character" to failing, playing, fantasizing, and disengaging. Cao Fei captures many moments of being in and out of character, which becomes *the* normative mode of existence. In this regard, animation, in conjunction with performance, helps develop a discourse on infelicitous acts that shifts performance studies' privileging and investment in the felicitous—its strong performative impulse. Cao's work as a speech act of alterity explores fabulation for how we might do different things with performance and contemporary Chinese art.

Fabulation and meditation bring to the fore the presumptions surrounding normative understandings of performed political change and its entwinement with individual agency. These different cognitive modes highlight how notions of a sovereign subject undergird the major and proper. However, to do so, they operate in ways that appear to be without purpose, direction, or ends. In order to grasp what meditation and fabulation offer, we must renegotiate in minor ways how the political is defined. Walter Benjamin's notion of *pure means* is a starting point to make more precise the political stakes in these approaches.[72] Benjamin delineates between means and ends in order to illustrate the difference between the methods and aims of political action. In a state of pure ends, any means necessary are used to obtain a goal. Meanwhile, pure means luxuriate in less direct approaches due to the fact that the ends are wholly fabulous, extravagant, impossible, and materially failed. Fabulation and meditation each produce a pure means that reimagines the ends of the political beyond the predefined, major equation of demystified awareness, performed action, and change.

5

Tout-Monde and the Minor

THE CINEMATIC AND THEATRICAL CHINESE WOMAN IN ISAAC JULIEN'S *TEN THOUSAND WAVES*

The birth of the racial subject—and therefore of
Blackness—is linked to the history of capitalism.
—Achille Mbembe, *The Critique of Black Reason*

After the long competition between capitalism
and socialism, the formation of the three-world
structure, and the end of the cold war, the
few remaining socialist nations have been, to
different degrees, drawn into the magnetic field
of global capitalism.
—Kuan-Hsing Chen, *Asia as Method*

Sometimes, by taking up the problems of the
Other, it is possible to find oneself. . . .The tale of
errantry is the tale of Relation.
—Édouard Glissant, *Poetics of Relation*

How are we to hold onto the minor in light of the grandeur of the world, capitalism, and a long durée of time? After all, the spatial and temporal dimensions of the world are, put simply, overwhelming. Nonetheless, capitalism aims to make our world appear smooth, shiny, and efficient, as one world devoid of histories of racialized violence, genocide, and extraction. In addition, Marxism often seeks to accelerate capital to a point of unifying the world under the banner of revolution. Throughout this book, I have developed the minor as method, rather than the minor as representation, to focus on social structuration as the means to contend with the minor within totality; or the minor amid the massive scale of our world. Such an analysis emerges from a re-thinking of—and interactions across—history, the state, subjects, and their agency. Social structuration indexes the production of our world and its re-bounds and shifts from modernity to postmodernity, capital to late capital, liberalism to late liberalism, and material to immaterial labor. In order to engage these ebbs and changes, throughout the preceding chapters I have deployed Marxist-inflected approaches for both analyses of states, and also minor forms. Some precursors to the minor as method include, for example, the Frankfurt tradition of the *Denkbilder* (the thought image), and Deleuzo-Guattarian notions of the *fold* and *monad* which have used glimpses, flashes, and single objects to produce a sense of the world in its totality. In brief, both the Denkbilder and monad are methods that use minor forms like images and momentary flickers to enable a larger critique, producing philosophy outside of the traditional modes of thought, speech, and prose. The Denkbilder and monad collapse multiple histories and ideas into a single, minor object. In this book, I have drawn from these approaches in order to move away from thinking of art or culture as a singular ethnographic index for China. Art, in this sense—and playing off the title of the Shenzhen Biennial discussed in chapter 3—may not be a system or a world. Instead, art may be about all systems and all worlds. In other words, when art moves away from being solely an object and an ethnographic aperture for a single space like China, it begins to open up understandings of the total world at large, its social structuration.

This chapter examines how we obtain the social structuration of the world from the minor. The minor geographic space, subject, and even method are not solely illustrative of their respective place, being, or approach. China therefore helps us contend with immaterial labor, late capital, late liberalism, and postmodernity. However, in order to trace a full sense of all worlds, we must encounter not only China, but also the ontological conditions that enable these shifts from modernity, capital, liberalism, and material labor that China has been identified as engendering. This is a purposefully impossible task in which the attempt to do so is necessary and the ultimate point. In order to demonstrate additional key issues in any understanding of the minor in late liberalism—particularly in the context of the global art market—this chapter turns to the work of the British artist Isaac Julien, an artist producing outside of China. Julien's larger oeuvre is particularly important for pointing to the ways Blackness offers an ontological anchor for China in order to produce a total sense of the world and its changes, as many have argued, including those in the epigraphs at the beginning of this chapter.[1] But in addition to race, Julien's work also engages totality and several other notable frameworks that provide a valuable lens for grappling with issues that directly contribute to larger concerns of minor China and late liberalism, specifically mediation and the tout-monde, modernism, capital, racial and gendered objecthood, and the senses. Julien's film installation *Ten Thousand Waves*, for example, deploys and reimagines the Marxist tradition around the minor form to engage totality. The work is a multimedial object, presented on numerous screens inside a single gallery, that confronts issues surrounding China and race. Although an art star like many in this book, Julien is certainly a different artist from the others in my archive for minor China. Julien grew up in London, as a child of immigrants from the Caribbean island of Saint Lucia. He was initially known for his work in queer film but has since transitioned into multimedia practice.

Julien's *Ten Thousand Waves* does not produce a sense of a single, unified world with his take on China nor does it simply show relations across Blackness and Asianness. Instead, Julien approaches China with and through his long engagement with theorizations of Blackness in order to remark upon changes in capital and labor. However, my point in turning to Julien's work is not to dissipate the notion of Chinese to include anyone who discusses China. After all, race is not simply about anyone concerned with a specific location or culture; race is imbricated within logics that dictate history, guide the biopolitical control of populations, and have material ramifications for bodies legible within devalued phenotypes, genotypes, and national and religious origins. Instead, I examine Julien's work because it provides a useful lens for expanding the minor method, the minoring of China, and a Marxist genealogy of minor forms. Julien's art offers a particularly direct engagement with these multiple valences of the minor in ways that contend with the social structuration of the world. The material differences across forced enslavement and indentured labor, alongside distinct forms of objecthood from Black flesh to yellow woman, articulate a fuller sense of social structuration.[2] As such, pace Glissant, Julien ethically takes on the concerns of the other to offer a sense of the totality of the world in its divisions and fractures that are central to projects surrounding relationality and racialization. As a result, his work illuminates how the minor as method can be deployed for understanding minor and major Chinas, and the importance of the minor more generally. His creative output destabilizes who speaks for difference and what sense of the world this provides.[3] He draws from a genealogy of art practice that reconfigures expectations surrounding identity and production. In particular, Julien operates alongside artists like the Vietnamese director and theorist Trinh Minh-ha. Her *Reassemblage* (1982) reimagined the imbrication of ethnography and documentary in West Africa and astutely redefined the ways we engage beyond critiques of appropriation and exotification.

Among Julien's recent large-scale works, *Ten Thousand Waves* is particularly notable for its use of the minor. *Ten Thousand Waves* takes its viewers through three eras of Chinese history: the Ming Dynasty, 1930s Shanghai, and contemporary China. Julien weaves together narratives that he imagines for each historical moment. These narratives are based loosely around the lives of Chinese women. The earliest era references the role of the goddess Mazu, a character from the Tale of Yishan Island. Played by famed Hong Kong actress Maggie Cheung, Mazu protects the sea-laboring workers of Fujian Province; this mythologization around protectionism has expanded well beyond this province and the Pacific Rim (figure 5.1). The second era that the work studies—colonial Shanghai—focuses on the life of early Chinese celebrity Ruan Lingyu acting in the role of a sex worker in the 1934 film *The Goddess*. Zhao Tao, a muse for filmmaker Jia Zhangke, plays the central role of both sex worker and celebrity actress (figure 5.2). The last moment of contemporary Shanghai is shot at the Pudong Hyatt Hotel, where the same actress, Zhao Tao, exists within the changing landscape of contemporary China (figure 5.3). The narratives for each of these characters are not mediated linearly, since each story is displayed across nine screens. These screens are draped across an art gallery or atrium, depending on the site, and face different directions.

Julien deploys the minor form to contend with questions related to changes in capital and modernity. The narratives for the three eras are displayed across nine screens, with the total run time for all videos at just under an hour. Different parts of the three stories are interspersed across the screens, as a continuous narrative is thwarted by the formal construction of the work. Additionally, flashes of multiple historical moments fracture the development of the piece. In particular, there are images of the main event that inspired this project: the 2004 tragedy at Morecambe Bay in the United Kingdom, which involved twenty-three Chinese migrant workers who were

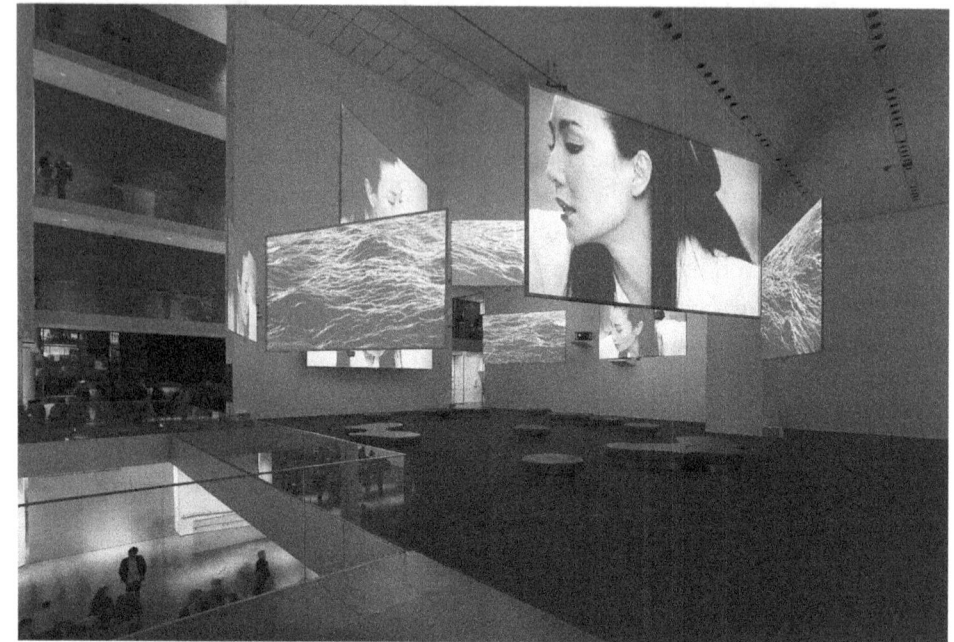

Figure 5.1. Isaac Julien, *Ten Thousand Waves*, 2013. Installation view, Museum of Modern Art, New York. Courtesy of the artist, Art Resource, and Victoria Miro, London/Venice.

employed as cockle pickers. On the evening of February 25, these workers were caught in a storm during high tide. The failed rescue mission was televised across Britain. There are close-ups of crashing ocean waves and images of the rescue team discovering the bodies, along with photos of the workers. Helicopter views from the rescue attempt flash in and out, along with the audio of emergency phone calls. In addition, calligraphy of the characters for *ten*, *thousand*, and *waves* are drawn by Gong Fagen across panes of glass (figure 5.4). There are also scenes of a goddess being floated across a green screen by workers and rendered ethereal by the winds from an industrial-sized fan (figure 5.7). The soundscape by Jah Wobble and the Chinese Dub Orchestra, along with Maria Delver, amplify the sonic experience of the work. The sound designer Mukul Patel and editor Adam Finch produce an environment that is both immersive at some points and alienating at others. Julien uses these multiple medial practices to explore our senses as they relate to late capital and postmodernity.

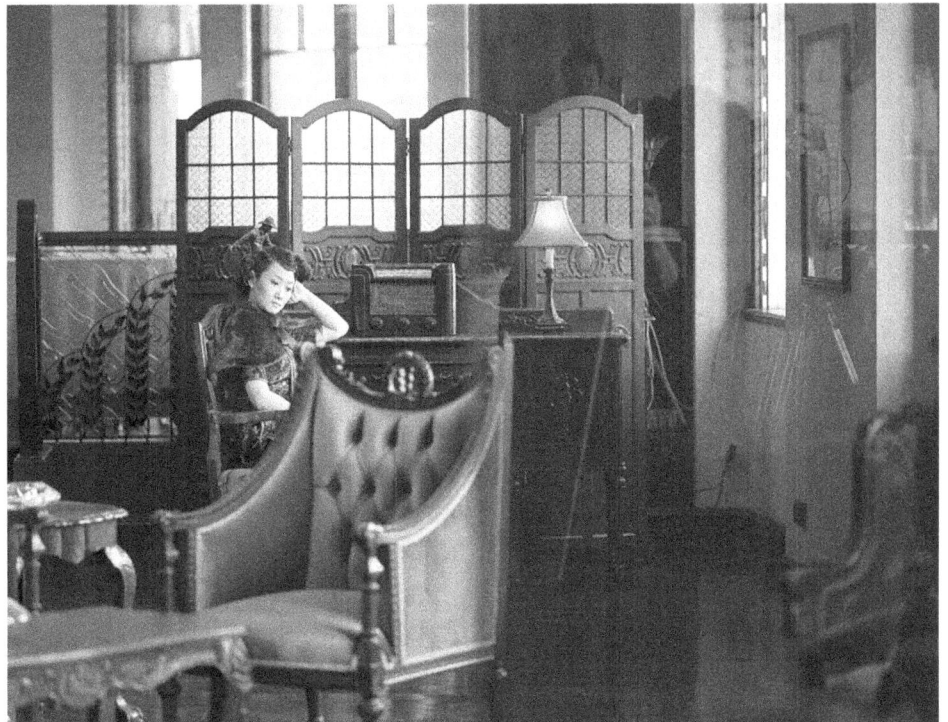

Figure 5.2. Isaac Julien, Glass House (*Ten Thousand Waves*), 2010. Endura Ultra photograph, 70.87×94.49 inches (180×240 cm), MP 81. Courtesy of the artist and Victoria Miro, London/Venice.

This chapter focuses on how Julien uses changes in media to track our contemporary condition. In particular, Julien's *Ten Thousand Waves* shifts the Frankfurt School tradition of the Denkbilder from the flash of a single image to the single art object that involves multiple screens displaying images of centuries of Chinese history. In addition, the installation contends with modernity, theater, and cinema as they come to be entangled with the figure of the Chinese woman so as to rethink minor objecthood. These medial and aesthetic shifts occur in relation to capital and the production of the world. In other words, Julien's approach to minor China provides a total sense of all worlds, what Édouard Glissant calls the *tout-monde*. In brief, the tout-monde questions totality's universalizing tendencies that gloss over negativity and difference, as discussed in relation to the structural affect of racial anger in chapter 2. To do so, Glissant offers the tout-monde to focus on

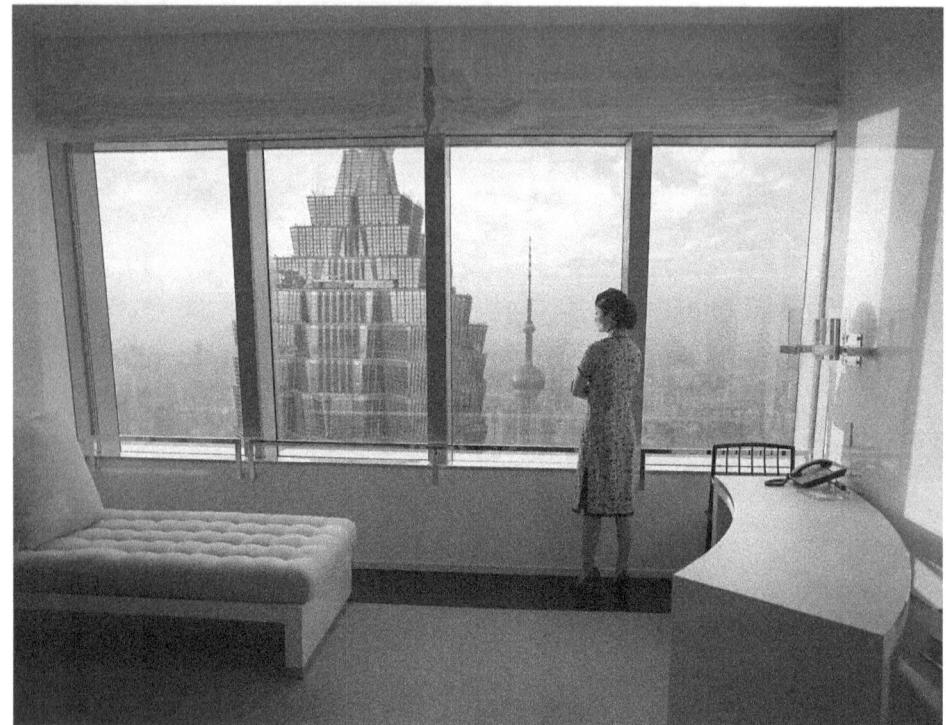

Figure 5.3. Isaac Julien, Hotel (*Ten Thousand Waves*), 2010. Endura Ultra photograph, 70.87×94.49 inches (180×240 cm), MP 91. Courtesy of the artist and Victoria Miro, London/Venice.

the fractures produced by looking at all worlds. He challenges us to embark on the impossible task of tracing all worlds so as to inspire modes of relationality that privilege dissensus over consensus, hesitation over certainty and continuity. Ultimately, I trace these medial changes in relation to Chinese women in order to better understand how Julien updates the Marxist tradition around minor forms through an account of racialized and gendered objecthood, fragmentation, and relationality. In brief, the Chinese woman as both a theatrical surrogate and cinematic icon offers an ethic for the tout-monde that minorly and simply attempts building relations amid the grandeur and intensity of modernity's tragic conditions.[4] This ethic informs a minor method that toggles across difference and repetition; expiration and return; and subjecthood and objecthood.

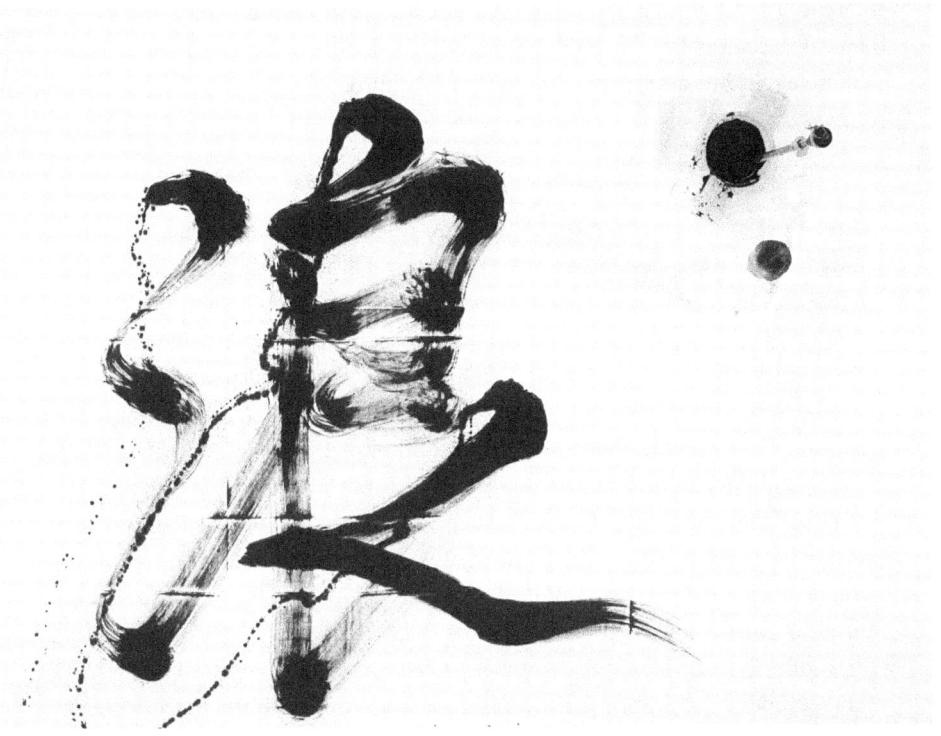

Figure 5.4. Isaac Julien, Waves (*Ten Thousand Waves*), 2010. Endura Ultra photograph, 180×239.8×7.5 cm. Courtesy of the artist and Victoria Miro, London/Venice.

This chapter is focused less on producing a proper analysis of Marxist totality than on a sense of the tout-monde.[5] The many theoretical (and generally poststructuralist) figures who inform this book share a "common denominator," as Martin Jay succinctly referred to it—an "unremitting hostility towards totality."[6] An implicit tension arises when considering proper forms of Marxist critique when situated within and against those like Glissant, Deleuze, and Guattari who are more interested in fragmentation, difference, and exceptions. Ultimately, such a tension resonates with the notion of the force of law that has animated this book, with the force's demand for legible critique. I thus renegotiate the Frankfurt School tradition around the Denkbilder and Marxist tradition around totality. I engage the Denkbilder to further clarify the minor as method; I also focus on how Julien rethinks totality in ways that amplify the stakes of social structuration and questions around relationality. Through this approach, I suture and amplify the productive tensions across these oft-separated approaches.

Minor Forms for the *Tout-Monde*

The social structuration of the world can be traced through what Marxists have historically called *totality*. The Frankfurt School advanced an approach using minor forms to obtain a glimpse of this total understanding of the world. Julien assembles a related but different sense of the world that reworks these traditions by centralizing racialization's imbrication with modernity. In *Ten Thousand Waves*, Julien envisions the goddess Mazu as the angel of history. This reference hails Marxist and Frankfurt genealogies that deploy the Denkbilder to understand totality and history's relationship to comprehending the whole. In "On the Concept of History," Walter Benjamin uses this angel to construct a philosophy of history that frames totality through an understanding of violence rather than progress.[7] The angel is a single image used to illustrate a larger philosophical issue. Benjamin had a melancholic relationship to a Marxist teleology of proletarian revolution, along with liberal democratic commitments to development. For Benjamin, both political movements construct historical narratives that obscure the devastation that emerges from the aftermaths of their respective actions under the banner of "progress."[8] This prevents a true understanding of totality for the historian and intellectual. Benjamin's angel of history highlights the devastation inherent in both Marxist and liberal approaches to the world.

Julien reconfigures not only Benjamin's approach to the minor, but also Marxist relations to totality. Considering the saturation of images today, Julien queries the limits of single images for understanding the world. His refiguring of Frankfurt School and Marxist approaches emerges from a long-standing relationship to these traditions. Growing up in working-class London as a child of immigrants, Julien's life has been shaped by tensions across immigrant experiences and those involving avant-garde art practices and education. The artist is not only informed by Marxism through engagements with cultural studies, but also draws deeply from global Marxist and Black diasporic discourses. Julien's training as an artist has a long relationship to radical education and politics that toggle across racialization and universalization. Beyond training at Central Saint Martins School of Art, he was involved in communal education and art practices at Kingsley Hall, a historic center in the East End of London known for political activism. Further, he was part of the publicly funded Sankofa Film and Video Collective that notably shifted the landscape of Black Arts in the UK and globally. The collective's work operated in relation to contemporary discourses around postcolonial theory and cultural studies. *Ten Thousand Waves* can be situated within this intersection of experimental aesthetics, minoritarian commitments, cultural theory, and leftist politics. Julien's concerns are informed by Marxist thought and Black diasporic discourse that draw from Caribbean theorists like Sylvia Wynter, Frantz Fanon, Stuart Hall, and Glissant. Julien develops these related and unique Marxist traditions in ways that grapple with racialization and changes in aesthetic mediation.

First, Julien considers the Denkbilder and its reliance on a single image alongside today's changes in media. The Frankfurt tradition of the Denkbilder, or "thought image," involves a small form or object "hovering between philosophical critique and aesthetic production."[9] The flicker or snippet becomes "neither programmatic treatises nor objective manifestations of a historical spirit."[10] The Denkbilder manifests into a single image or form while possessing an expansive critique. Benjamin's Denkbilder of the angel of history is blown away from both an immediate catastrophe and the long detritus of accumulated historical destruction. Based on Paul Klee's painting *Angelus Novus*, the angel is described in terms of motion, direction, and gesture. Benjamin's choreographic description captures both a sense of the angel's corporeal movement and his affective state:

> [Klee's painting] shows an angel who seems about to move away from something he stares at. His eyes are wide, his mouth is open, his wings are spread. This is how the angel of history must look. His face is turned toward the past. Where a chain of events appears before us, he sees one single catastrophe, which keeps piling wreckage upon wreckage and hurls it at his feet. The angel would like to stay, awaken the dead, and make whole what has been smashed. But a storm is blowing from Paradise and has got caught in his wings; it is so strong that the angel can no longer close them. This storm drives him irresistibly into the future to which his back is turned, while the pile of debris before him grows towards the sky. What we call progress is *this* storm.[11]

The wind known as progress is what pushes the melancholic angel away from the aftermath of history. The angel's face is sad, as he is torn away from the wreckage of the past, only to see the ruins of history arising from what liberals and Marxists deem progress. Corporeally, the angel's body is in flight and is directed toward history's debris and remnants. From this vantage point, the angel obtains a full, holistic view of the carnage of history as a long reoccurrence of destruction. As such, the angel shifts us away from conceptualizing history as a set of events and toward understanding history as a condition. Unable to close his wings from the storm's wind, the angel hurls his body into the future even though he desires to go back in time. Beyond the contours of the body, Benjamin's description delves into the angel's gestures and expressions, his wide eyes and open mouth. These expressions connote surprise, disgust, and negativity. Benjamin relies on the single image of the angel of history to produce "the crystal of the total event."[12]

Julien reconfigures this tradition. The artist develops the minor form of the angel of history, as she directs us across multiple seascapes, wreckages from the past, and the historical expanse encompassing Black enslavement, Chinese indentured labor, Marxism, and capital. By casting Klee's angel of history with Maggie Cheung, Julien draws from the Denkbilder to think through the role of film and other media in the production of multiple images (figure 5.5). Julien considers what happens to the minor form when thought about in series and repetition. Cheung plays the mythical figure of Mazu, as this character becomes the one who not only looks back but also is able to fly through different moments in history. Julien's angel of history is errant and traverses space and time. Her face appears to be in pain from witnessing historical devastation and the future to come. Mazu is less in shock than Benjamin's angel. She responds to the pleas and prayers of those victimized by capitalism's abuses—those lost in the wreckage at Morecambe Bay. Unlike Benjamin's angel, Mazu is a figure that responds through concern. And rather than being catapulted by the wind's direction, Mazu floats atop the world across space and time. Her errant flight is not fully dictated by the wind of progress.

Julien's angel of history intermingles the Denkbilder with another tradition around minor forms. Gilles Deleuze describes the monad as pleats and folds of time that crystallize into an object: "As an individual unit each monad includes the *whole series*: hence it conveys the entire world, but does not express it without expressing more clearly a small region of the world, a 'subdivision,' a borough of the city, a finite sequence."[13] Deleuze develops the monad also in relation to the work of Paul Klee. By taking Klee's relationship to lines and form, Deleuze extends Klee's aesthetics to the production of the monad as that which represents a region or part of the larger whole. The monad crystallizes into a sense of the world and includes multiple historical moments into a single form. The fold of time helps us trace a larger

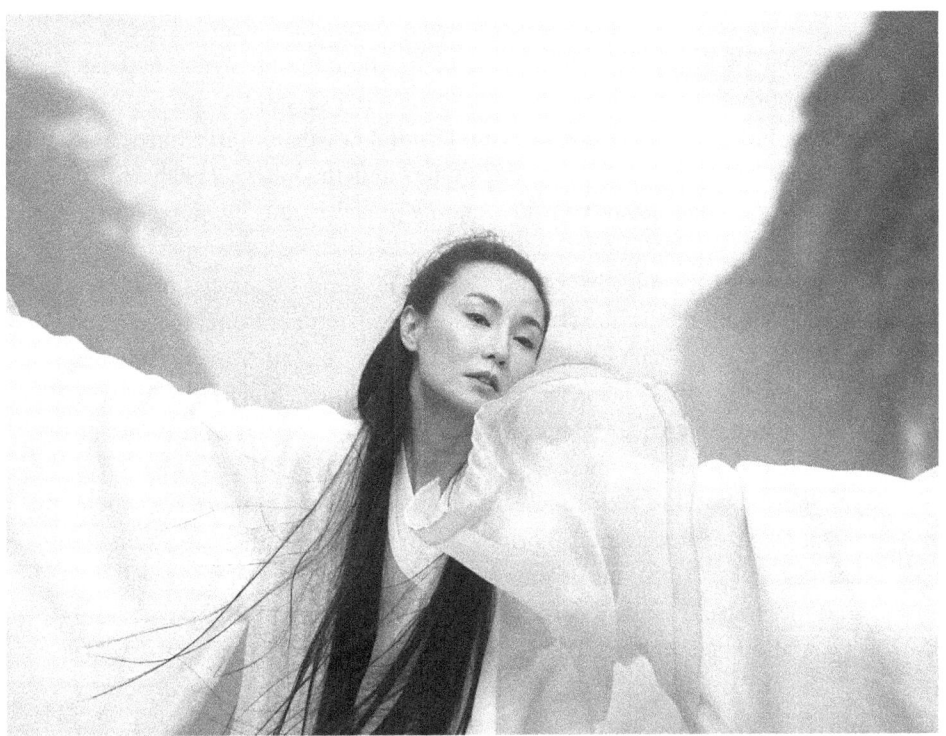

Figure 5.5. Isaac Julien, Maiden of Silence (*Ten Thousand Waves*), 2011. Endura Ultra photograph, 70.87×94.49 inches (180×240 cm). Courtesy of the artist and Victoria Miro, London/Venice.

sequence or series of images, an aesthetic shift that Julien highlights through not only the angel but also the city and sea.

In particular, Julien examines the city of Shanghai in series. As his film vacillates across narratives and historical moments, we witness different temporalities for the cityscape of Shanghai from the 1930s to the contemporary. By shifting from archival and newly produced images of Shanghai street life and rail cars during the early twentieth century, Julien offers a sense as to how citizens navigated public space. Julien then focuses on contemporary Shanghai with its freeways and masses of cars. As Paris grounds Benjamin's ideas, Shanghai serves a similar function for Julien. Neither Julien nor Benjamin were born in the cities central to their respective projects, and both grapple with the shifting roles these sites play in relation to capitalism and historicity.

In addition, the seascape functions as a monad that indexes a series of sites whereby racial capitalism accumulates. Building off Arjun Appadurai's notion of *scapes*, Sean Metzger develops the seascape as an aesthetic strategy and theoretical analytic to understand circulations of Chineseness and labor.[14] For Metzger, the seascape offers a methodological analytic that reframes dominant narratives surrounding globalization. By moving away from purely economic understandings around land mass, seascapes expand the purview of the affective resonances of the world—seascapes become a monad. Put differently, the seascape offers a way to understand racial capital in series, affording a sense of all worlds. However, rather than rendering equivalent all forms of labor that have traveled the seas, Julien highlights the fractures and differences that arise in the monad of the seascape. Although his monad focuses on China, it ultimately offers a relational critique that highlights variations across seascapes as they relate to distinct systems of capital. The seascape as monad brings together not only Julien's focus on the long history of China, but also the history of racial capitalism that was and continues to be dependent on Black enslavement, indigenous genocide, and immigration in its entanglement with race, property, and labor.

The sea is a central focus for the poetry that informed *Ten Thousand Waves*. Wang Ping's poems bring to the fore the names and bodies lost at sea—a recuperative gesture that is near impossible for Black and indigenous subjects. Most of these poems are named after the dead laborers; the last poem is a plea to the goddess Mazu, the protector of the sea. Wang Ping, along with Julien, focuses on the role of Chinese labor on the global seascape. However, the seascape as a monad resists buttressing a racial liberalist logic. When considered in series, the seascape comes to resonate differently depending on the racial capitalist system of enslavement or indentured labor. The differences across Black enslavement and Asian indentured servitude allow us to track the shifts in racial capital of the tout-monde that have created fractures across communities. Although some attempt to trace a continuity from slavery to indentured labor by focusing on the ways the same ships facilitated both forms of labor,[15] this theorization implies a relationality premised on continuity and flow rather than the fractures that arise throughout the history of capital. Studies of global migration over the last forty years have been heavily influenced by Hugh Tinker's 1974 argument that the indentured labor system was a new system of slavery.[16] However, Asian indentured labor exists quite differently from Black enslavement. The Chinese laborers' bodies at Morecambe Bay and in Julien's work take on a relation of difference and repetition in the racial order of capital.

Ian Baucom illuminates this difference across these two forms of labor. He focuses on the *Zong* massacre, the 1781 killing of 130 African slaves on the British ship. He reminds us that the "*Zong* trials constitute an event in the history of capital *not* because they treat slaves as commodities but because they treat slaves as commodities that have become the subject of insurance . . . the general equivalents of finance capital."[17] As an insured commodity, the Black body is distinct from contracted labor power. This fact does not limit the abuses enacted upon Chinese indentured labor or the twenty-three cockle pickers, but it is offered, rather, to track the differential relations across racial capitalism that have enabled the circulation and distribution of bodies. The Chinese have existed under a different financial structure: that of a theoretically 'voluntary' low-wage labor. Baucom emphasizes how the insurance of Black laboring bodies reformulates their use value, creating a difference in the worlds of racial capital that arise from slavery and indentured labor. The monad of the seascape illuminates these differences when racial capital is seen in series. Julien thus helps us trace such differences in *Ten Thousand Waves*, as he intensely focuses on the experiences of these Chinese laborers so as to refute continuity with Black enslavement. The Chinese do not simply follow *in the wake*, to use Christina Sharpe's astute phrase, of slavery's aftermath; instead, we must understand the differences across these populations as they have disparate relations to social life and death.[18] By wrestling with these distinct conditions, we provide ontological anchors that formulate the tout-monde—a sense of all worlds built on fractures and fragments rather than on a smooth totality or holism. Put differently, the monad offers a minor method that tracks this expansive and fractured relational critique through an attention to a single object like Julien's seascape.

Second, Julien uses the minor forms of the Denkbilder and monad to grapple not only with totality, but also the tout-monde. Rather than solely attempting to give a fuller picture of totality through the inclusion of China, Julien furthers the Denkbilder's aims by emphasizing fragments and the impossibility of fully depicting totality. In particular, Julien produces what Glissant calls a tout-monde, an "all-world" rather than one world. Capitalism and Marxist revolution envision a single world. For capitalism, the world appears seamless and interconnected, forgetting history and racialized extraction as the means for producing the first world. Meanwhile, for Marxist revolution, the world progresses toward unity through the proletariat, similarly forgetting that to seize the means of production from the first world is premised upon the continual extraction of resources from the third. Both ideas of the world gloss over racial difference, with the racial as something that progress presumably diminishes.

However, Glissant's tout-monde centralizes the racial while furthering Benjamin's project of attending to the violences of history. Glissant confronts how accounts of racial worlds foreclose a complete or total framing of space and time. The function of the tout-monde rethinks Marxism by fragmenting our sense of the world through an account of every and all worlds—an impossible task that requires an ethics and practice of continual attempts rather than full completion. The project of the tout-monde resists the impulse for clarity and the depiction of a single world. Similar to cosmopolitanism, the tout-monde is a relational account of the world; however, unlike the former, the tout-monde builds this relationality less on what might be unifying and more on fractures and difference.[19] By accounting for all possible worlds, we move beyond the self to produce relations that attend to asymmetries.

Although *tout* as an adjective and noun in French means "all" or "whole," *tout* also means "every" (as an adjective) and "everything" (as a noun). The connotation of "every" for *tout-monde* forms an idea of the world that does not become a singular universal space. Instead, the tout-monde forces us to contend with every world, to inquire about those other worlds forgotten and those to come. This distinction between "whole" and "every" for *tout* is critical because it demonstrates Glissant's commitment to moving away from a universal, complete, and singular idea of the world. Jaime Hanneken describes this differentiation in Glissant's work as "ways of describing a totality in flux that nonetheless refuses the generalization of a universal view . . . and moves toward a sense of the Whole as it obtains in endless particularities. Insofar as Glissant considers these concepts to be views wrought from the experience of modernity—the suffering caused by conquest, colonization, the territorialization of the earth and its people, and other projects of 'root' thinking—their primary goal is, in fact, to discredit and replace universality."[20] The tout-monde questions totality's universalizing tendencies, as the tout-monde does not view the racial as solely exceptions and particularities but rather as the very means to grasp the tout-monde. Glissant fragments and displaces the universal from a congealed form to an aspiration. Akin to the curators discussed in chapter 3, Glissant renders minor the universal.

Fractures are the basis for understanding this idea of totality. The tout-monde does not fulfill multicultural desires. Rather, the tout-monde highlights radical, violent difference in order to offer errant connections that enable one to relate to others—to expand beyond the self. Instead of offering an image of the world through unity and cohesion, however, Julien's tout-monde confronts racialization and its fractures. After all, Glissant reminds us that the tout-monde "which is totalizing, is not (for us) total."[21] The tout-monde fragments totality by contending with the ruptures across different forms of racialization and by avoiding a smooth sense of a single total world. In this vein, the tout-monde generates an ethics that constantly accounts for one another rather than presuming relations stable and known. Put differently, the tout-monde cannot promote a racial liberalism, as the tout-monde requires that we grapple with the histories that have uniquely shaped and distinguish racial groups from one another.

As the angel of history, Maggie Cheung illustrates how an account of all worlds cultivates relationality. She traverses the temporal and spatial folds of the monad. She performs an errantry across not only space but also history. Unlike Benjamin's, Julien's angel flies both horizontally and vertically—she traverses the screen in diagonals, and flies with and against the wind. Her rhizomatic and errant pathways direct us to the spread of space and time beyond a single space or subject. In addition, unlike the winds of heaven that project Benjamin's angel, fans and workers' bodies propel Julien's angel through the monad. Under Julien's direction, Mazu, as the angel of history, performs an errantry that arises from and is explicitly reliant upon labor.

Glissant uses errantry to bring together all worlds in ways that produce relation: "Because the thought of errantry is also the thought of what is relative, the thing relayed as well as the thing related."[22] The tout-monde furthers Glissant's larger project around relationality, as established in *Poetics of Relation*. Relations are built through the fractures and differences across populations—by not asking the lumpen, so forths, and racialized to cast aside difference for the sake of Marxist revolution. I emphasize fractures since Glissant begins his text on relationality with visceral accounts of the violent and inhumane practices that occurred on slave ships traversing the Atlantic Ocean.[23] Methodologically, errant relations arise when situated within and in relation to histories of Black subjection and enslavement. The theorist highlights how errantry, when articulated through all worlds produced across multiple forms of racialization, enables a political project of relationality. Such a project thus seeks "to know the totality of the world yet already know[ing] he will never accomplish this—and knows that is precisely where the threatened beauty of the world resides."[24] In this vein, errantry "conceives of totality but willingly renounces any claims to sum it up or to possess it."[25] The tout-monde and relationality arise from an account of Blackness and its centrality to the production of all other worlds. Furthermore, errantry is a practice and method, not a finite act, that drives the impossible yet necessary attempt to account for all worlds, the tout-monde.

Julien invokes Glissant's tout-monde to privilege racialization over universality; fractures over unity and cohesion; and errantry over rootedness. The tout-monde arises from historic forms of Black subjection to help us think through the conditions of late capital that entwine many other forms of racialized and gendered labor. Most importantly, the tout-monde is not simply meant to unite us into one world. All disconnects and difficult affects, like racial anger as discussed in chapter 2, across communities cannot be glossed over by a racially liberal notion of a singular world (what might be called "a small world after all"). *Ten Thousand Waves* crosses temporal and geographic locations in order to produce a rhizome, allowing us to track the power differentials that create the horizontal expanse and vertigo of the world and time. Julien extends Glissant's work by focusing on Chinese laborers as a way to bring into violent relation other forms of racial subjugation, particularly with Black subjection. Rather than equating China and Blackness, Julien encourages us think through their differences in order to produce a relationality rooted in historic forms of dispossession, whereby "interrelations principally procee[d] through *fractures* and *ruptures*."[26] Julien entangles temporality and subjects in ways that work across spaces and histories; media assist in this process.

Mediation, Capital, and the Senses

Julien's installation is notably less singular in form in comparison to Benjamin's Denkbilder that relies on a single image to produce his angel of history. Julien plays with the minor form and expands it from a single image to a single art object. Art objects, however, have undergone radical transformation due to technological advances, changes in medial specificity, and renewed (although still needing significant updates to) academic approaches to intermedial art. Julien plays with these shifts in media (and discourse) to index and track transformations in capital and our sense of all worlds. In particular, the tout-monde requires an alteration of the senses, as both media and capitalism have expanded in form. The historian and philosopher who earlier grasped totality through the angel of history must now develop a larger apparatus and sensory capacity to contend with late capital.

For Benjamin, the angel is meant to illustrate the limits surrounding how we historicize and how we obtain totality. Julien highlights how we need to develop new sensory approaches in order to further work toward Benjamin's goals. Mazu serves less of a pedagogical function in comparison to Benjamin's angel. Julien uses the single object to bring our focus to the spectator in ways that demonstrate late capital's conditioning. The viewer is overwhelmed and oversaturated within the single space of the gallery. His use of multiple media produces a phenomenological onslaught, an effect Metzger identifies as "ebbing" which involves "repeatedly turning one's body and adjusting one's orientation to view the circle of screens."[27] The spectator's ebbing emphasizes the multiple viewpoints needed to grapple with capital, along with the spectator's and art object's own entwinement with capital itself. As Fredric Jameson has established, the shift toward late and multinational capital is entangled with postmodernist aesthetics and logics, demanding that we renegotiate our senses and modes of critique.[28] Julien contends with Jameson's claims by using the minor form to illuminate, not per se answer, this demand. Due to changes in capital and their relation to the senses, the artist focuses on the minor form and aesthetics to direct us to the conditions surrounding the spectator. Media and capital require more from a viewer, expanding our perspective away from the singular vantage point of the historian or philosopher.

Julien delves into the senses that are necessary to approach the minor form in ways that index the tout-monde, while acknowledging the simultaneous necessity yet impossibility of this task. When discussing *Ten Thousand Waves*, the artist focuses on the impossibility of picturing reality: "What does something look like when it can't be pictured—when invisibility is silent, so to speak?"[29] This condition informs Julien's errant relation to space, time, and others. If capital and all worlds are so abstract that they melt into air, Julien asks us to shift our methods from answering this quagmire to analyzing what must change in order to contend with this condition. His aesthetics and approach, however, do not focus on every possible population or space (he does not reproduce multiple issues of *National Geographic*, so to speak). Instead, he delves deeply into a singular minor object/subject (in this case, China as a monad) in order to produce errant relations, an approach that has informed his earlier works. Take for example his film *Frantz Fanon: Black Skin, White Mask* (1998), as it provides not only a biopic about this historic figure, but also a way to analyze larger concerns surrounding global decolonial movements.

Ten Thousand Waves furthers this method, as Julien skews away from solely depicting the tragedy at Morecambe Bay. Although the event shapes his interests, he uses it to think through the relationship between senses and late capital, along with all worlds. During his initial research period into the

Chinese workers at Morecambe Bay immediately after the event, Julien first developed *Western Union: Small Boats* (2007) to focus on stories around migration. Shot in Sicily and displayed across three screens, *Western Union* documented processes of globalization around the journey of African migrants. His earlier experimentation with multiple screens and his concerns related to relationality and seascapes were then further explored in *Ten Thousand Waves*. This format of multiple screens and narratives has come to inform subsequent works: *Playtime* (2014), *Stones against Diamonds* (2015), and *Lessons of the Hour* (2019). Julien deploys this format, as facilitated by changes in media, to assist in a larger political project of relationality and the tout-monde. In other words, Julien's *Ten Thousand Waves* furthers the method of minor China by enhancing the Marxist tradition around minor forms. Akin to Yan Xing, as discussed in chapter 3, Julien produces a multimedial work that uses mediation and form to renegotiate our overdetermined understandings of history, nation-state, and subject. And similar to Cao Fei, as discussed in chapter 4, Julien fabulates so as to not simply display resistance to capital but rather reimagine the political project at hand. Ultimately, Julien's *Ten Thousand Waves* turns to China in order to account for it beyond a singular index of a geographic space; the artist pushes us outside of major constructs of China through his development of the monad so as to reimagine the larger world.

To pivot from the singular to the relational in *Ten Thousand Waves*, Julien first engages the particulars of China and then deploys media and mediation to enable errantry. The use of nine screens is not simply the amplification of media, however, whereby more mediation presumably means a better idea of space and reality. Rather, his use of mediation questions how information, affects, and connections across difference are negotiated. Julien's shift from one to nine screens indicates a move away from the documentarian observation of a single camera toward an overwhelming abundance of parts and fragments. Through the latter mode of mediation, the other comes to be understood outside of ethnographic, objective clarity. Julien's art is indeed not an index to a proper, single world. This disjointed and fragmented sense of time and space emerges through the anchor or monad of China to ultimately expand across the vastness of the Pacific and Atlantic seascapes.

It is of no surprise then that many theorists who write about Julien have focused on medial relations across his work. Elizabeth Freeman examines Julien's formulation of queer time and desire through cinema in *The Attendant*.[30] José Muñoz similarly engages medial relations to query Julien's production of a complex mode of subject negotiation, disidentification.[31]

Further, Jennifer A. Gonzalez shows how an analysis of Julien's interplay with film and other media informs how the artist engages the political outside of prescribed modes of ethnic realism or multicultural ethnography.[32] A focus on mediation thus helps us consider Julien's interplay of media as producing the fragments for the tout-monde. *Ten Thousand Waves* displays a monadic and errant sense of space and time; there is only a glimmer of the world which moves away from the demand often placed on minoritarian artists to fully expose and transparently show the total operations and realities of their lived, singular experiences as minor subjects.

Julien instead alludes to many aesthetic approaches and worlds. For example, he draws from avant-garde cinema through the likes of not only Jean-Luc Godard but also contemporary Chinese film, specifically Fifth and Sixth Generation directors and more recent experimental directors like Jia Zhangke. Julien engages poetry, through his collaboration with Wang Ping. Julien's collaborator, noted Chinese visual artist Yang Fudong, plays a role in the film as well. The work also relies and builds upon histories surrounding sculpture and installation. Further, Julien develops his long-standing experimentation with sound, choreography, and dance.[33] *Ten Thousand Waves* was included in the Serpentine Gallery's show *Move: Choreographing You*, which focused on the intersection of dance and visual art. In other words, Julien engages multiple media. Through the nine-screen work that capaciously plays with sound, writing, performance, movement, installation, and film, the relationship across media becomes a central concern that highlights for viewers the need to expand their sensory apparatuses. Through sensorial adaptation, we come to better grapple with late capital and the tout-monde.

For Julien, this relationship across media is not linear. Speech and text do not have a direct mediation across one another. Julien does not offer subtitles in the installation for all parts spoken in Mandarin. Further, only certain installations of *Ten Thousand Waves* had translated printouts of Wang Ping's poems that are read throughout the piece. Since this work circulates globally and often outside of a Sinophone context, speech and writing are not presumed stable. Julien develops mediation to highlight how meaning exceeds translation. In particular, the sonic assists in providing meaning for non-Mandarin speakers who might rely on the affective tension in a speaker's breathing or the crashing of waves on the coast of Morecambe Bay to better understand the work. Through Julien's use of multiple media and the multiplication of senses, *Ten Thousand Waves* demands different vocabularies and sensory approaches that extend well beyond the visual and linguistic.

Julien calls this aesthetic method an elliptical one, where the juxtaposition of images allows meaning to emerge through the absent and unstated: "Slowly the multiple screens have become our gateway into a more complete and more immersive kind of environment. . . . The multiple-screen, cross-lateral technique is good for this—much better than editing on a single screen could be. On a single screen, the narrative will always take over. This is why I prefer a more *elliptical method*, where, in juxtaposing images against each other, a more poetic third meaning is allowed to emerge."[34] Julien articulates his desire to move beyond a single screen and to play with technological advances so as to offer spectators distinct ways to engage the world. By doing so, Julien's experiments with media enable other narratives about the world to arise that move beyond ethnographic realism and truth. The interplay of movement and sound with visuality facilitates gaps in meaning for the tout-monde to emerge.

For him, this change in format toward multiple screens "allows a certain choreography that emphasizes movement and flexibility in narrative progression."[35] Julien asks the viewer to not simply map the reality of a single world. Instead, he pushes a viewer to question what constructs our sense of space and time. Julien is not willing to let go of realism, however. He uses multiple screens and narratives to bring to the fore the intensity of material life. For example, following shots of the rescue mission of the Chinese laborers in Morecambe Bay, the repetition of the crash of waves is disrupted by the performance of a calligrapher. Images of green screens and lush forests come to be interspersed with documentary and news footage. Aerial shots of the rescue mission transition into the angel of history's view from above the landscape of Fujian Province. This juxtaposition of realism with the fantastic does not equate the two. Instead, Julien's fictional elements bring to the fore and amplify the intensity of violent events. We have become anesthetized by the repeated onslaught of violent images in the news and daily life, similar to the 2004 broadcast throughout the UK of the failed rescue mission of the Chinese cockle pickers. Although viewers might initially have been moved by this news, it eventually became replaced by another horrific headline. The constant cycle of news requires that we forget an event and move onto another. Julien, however, lingers in the 2004 event not to display its "reality" for those Chinese workers but to use it as a Denkbilder for today. And his play with multiple media facilitates how we might linger within that moment in order to begin to understand its relationship to all other moments, all other worlds. Julien plays with realism, mediation, and narrative progression to disrupt the rhythm of today's oversaturation in media. This errant and elliptical method offers the spectator different perceptual and sensorial apparatuses for receiving images in late capital.

Although the effect of *Ten Thousand Waves* on a spectator might be overwhelming, it is done so in order to provide approaches and tools for the viewer. Julien's larger reason for his use of an elliptical method is to enable what he calls "parallel montage."[36] He does not provide an ideal place for an audience member to experience the piece. He asks the spectator to take in the magnitude of the work and to pause the desire to make immediate sense of the works' critique or artistic goals. Instead, he invites a viewer to linger in the moments of incompleteness and to take note of these aesthetic demands. As a result, a spectator can bring into relief other parallel or similar moments in other worlds to see it all in series, as a monad. The monads of the seascape and the city of Shanghai, as discussed above, provide such opportunities for a viewer. In this vein, Julien furthers Benjamin's approach to historical materialism, a methodological concern surrounding how to track the production of worlds and capital. As Benjamin articulates, "Must the Marxist understanding of history necessarily be acquired at the expense of the perceptibility of history?"[37] Benjamin uses "montage into history," which he does "to assemble *large-scale constructions* out of the *smallest and most precisely cut components*. Indeed, to discover in the analysis of the small individual moment the crystal of the total event."[38] By doing so, both Julien and Benjamin "needn't say anything. Merely show."[39] This approach offers minor things, like fragments and details, so as to produce a minor effect, to simply show. Through the minor method of montage, we bring together other worlds as a means to sense the tout-monde. This method permits an errant approach to all worlds, rather than a holistic picture or map of one.

Mediation and the *Tout-Monde*: The Chinese Woman between Cinema and Theater

Like the other artists discussed in the preceding chapters, Julien's focus on the minor points to important ways that the minor can be conceived and understood, and thus utilized for understanding the condition of major China. One of the key ways Julien does this is through his enabling of errant relations and a sense of the tout-monde, specifically through a focus on media. In addition and most crucially, however, Julien furthers the projects of errantry and the tout-monde through an attention to a specific minor subject within a national space: the Chinese woman. In particular, Julien engages this racialized and gendered object through media and mediation by tracking this figure across cinema and theater. He does so in order to query what the Chinese woman across cinema and theater offers as an ethic and approach for the tout-monde: rather than being recognized as subject, her objecthood allows her to produce relations amid other expansive and difficult forms of objecthood. This woman becomes the anchor and monad from which to ultimately extend out into all worlds.

In Julien's acclaimed film *Looking for Langston* (1989), he focused on the reuse of the Black male body throughout time.[40] He shifts in *Ten Thousand Waves* to another object of history that indexes what Anne Cheng calls *ornamentalism*. Cheng sketches out "a theory of being" that focuses on the "yellow woman" who "survives as someone too aestheticized to suffer injury but so aestheticized that she invites injury."[41] In the rendering ornament and object of this figure, we shift away from major forms of sovereign agency toward a rethinking of the modern subject, since "Asiatic femininity in the Western racial imagination does not need to pass through the biological or natural in order to acquire its most palpable, fully sensorial, supple, and vibrant presence."[42] Julien furthers Cheng's intervention by deploying this figure to reconsider the condition of objecthood as it manifests across cinema and theater. For theater, the Chinese play a central role for Brecht and his theorizations of the alienation effect, as discussed in chapter 4. Brecht admires the Chinese for being ideal surrogates, as they embody roles through training that propitiously repeat and perform a distanced, cold affect. And for cinema, the Chinese female icon has a long history from the likes of Anna May Wong and Ruan Lingyu to Maggie Cheung, Gong Li, Zhang Ziyi, Joan Chen, and Michelle Yeoh. The recognizability of these Chinese female film stars' names highlights how these women function through iconicity. Julien analyzes the Chinese woman as simultaneously both cinematic icon *and* theatrical surrogate.

The dynamic produced, when situating the theatrical Chinese woman and the cinematic Chinese woman together, renegotiates the subject and relationality. Julien plays across these dual figures to harken Marxist genealogies around Brecht and Benjamin that help us further grasp the tout-monde through the yellow woman. However, rather than create a teleology that advances and separates cinema from performance, Julien analyzes the constant mediation across theatrical surrogate and cinematic icon that the Chinese woman engenders. And rather than solely ascribing this mediation to a single subject, Julien engages these minor figures as they exist across media to illustrate a larger condition of being. The almost schizophrenic vacillation across these two related yet distinct forms of object repetition indicate a critical ethics and mode of existence for the tout-monde.

Cheng's ideas provide the groundwork for how the figure of the Chinese woman as ornament offers insight into shifting discourses on minor objecthood. She focuses on an earlier cinematic Chinese woman, Anna May Wong. Cheng's reading of Wong highlights the aesthetic effects that render her an object in the film *Piccadilly* (1929). Wong plays in the film and embodies in real life the celebrity whose shimmering costumes produce "fascination [which] enables contact with objectness."[43] Cheng notes how "Wong's celluloid body enthralls through corporeal absence."[44] And she demonstrates how even Benjamin himself understood Wong through ornamentation and objecthood.[45]

Cheng's analytic illuminates how Julien develops minor China through the objecthood of the Chinese woman. Although some Chinese women are able to achieve celebrity status or iconicity, they nonetheless must still contend with objecthood, forcing us to produce modes of agency beyond sovereignty and to renegotiate the project of entrance into modern, liberal personhood. Cinematic iconicity is generally considered as having achieved true singularity and recognition; however, when iconicity is understood alongside race, gender, and theatrical surrogacy, a rethinking of subject, object, modernity, and personhood for relationality arises. Theatrical surrogacy illuminates this inevitable condition of objecthood for iconicity, while iconicity provides the optimistic drive to simply try and *merely show* amid the tragic realities of sheer object repetition. Even if one remains as object and surrogate, iconicity nonetheless compels us to exist and endeavor, even if ephemeral, fleeting, and impossible. This becomes an ethic for the tout-monde.

Julien investigates how these multiple mediated roles for the Chinese woman bring to the fore a condition that surrounds all worlds. For Julien, figures like the yellow woman and the enslaved flesh of Black womanhood produce errant relations across the tout-monde. However, Julien resists the allure of universal narratives by delving into the fragments and difficulties that work beyond totalization. These figures' statuses as objects, in other words, do not demand humanization but rather enable a method. In particular, the ruptures between the theatrical and cinematic reproductions of the Chinese woman offer an approach for questions surrounding difference and repetition, expiration and return, and representation or iconicity and surrogation. In other words, this method, which arises from an ethic, is the infinite attempt to achieve the impossible amid modernity's tragic realities, vacillating across two extreme poles that does not defeat us but rather momentarily compels us to be with others, in relation.

The medial distinctions that the Chinese woman indexes highlight differences across forms of representation from recognizable (cinematic) icon to replaceable (theatrical) surrogate. This line between recognition and replaceability places the (liberal idea of the) representation of the subject on hold due to the impossibility of proper or full representation. Instead, we shift toward finding what exists in objecthood that makes the subject/object both unique yet "all look the same." Similar to Ai Weiwei then, as discussed in chapter 2, Julien hesitates from simply humanizing the Chinese subject and instead considers what it means to operate as a being (plural) singular plural. And by doing so, he encourages us to enact a search for the lumpen and so forths who are always missing, discovering moments of recognition that eventually expire. In other words, we can more explicitly consider the minor as method toward the question of relationality which has undergirded this book.

The recognition of and relationality with others are momentary and flicker, compelling us to search again for connection. We must always return amid the errant search for relationality within the tout-monde. Relationality thus is not a finite or fully achievable goal; rather, relationality is an infinite process amid the impossible, requiring a method that allows for continual attempts and returns. Put differently, relationality perpetually expires, compelling us to try again.[46] In order to enact Glissant's project of the tout-monde, we must work within and across specific binaries: the filmic icon with the theatrical surrogate; minor subjects for both their repetition and singularity; and the expectation of expiration (or letting go) of one's own self-interest in order to produce relationality, while simultaneously destabilizing relationality itself so that it forces one to return in ways that always consider what in our relations is missing. The Chinese woman across media illustrates this minor method.

Theatrical Surrogate, Cinematic Icon, and the Impossible

In *Ten Thousand Waves*, Maggie Cheung as the angel of history floats through and across worlds rather than being propelled in a single direction by the winds of progress. Unlike Benjamin's angel of history, Mazu is able to stop and glare at these different moments in time—a use of historical pasts that is not merely in the name of progress nor regress. She flies errantly. As she crosses space, however, Julien reveals the source of the winds that enable her to travel through divergent moments in history. The wind of progress does not blow in a single direction toward futurity, as Benjamin articulates. Rather, the winds that propel and guide Cheung as Mazu emerge from an apparatus of fans, green screens, supporters carrying pulleys, harnesses, and a stunt double. Throughout *Ten Thousand Waves*, Julien depicts the large-scale production apparatus that created the filmed scenes. A stunt double for Cheung is held in a harness and system of pulleys, as she is blown by a fan, carried across by laborers, and filmed against a green screen (figures 5.6 and 5.7). Julien's cinematic images denaturalize progress into an apparatus. It is not the hand of God that propels us forward; it is rather the system, apparatus, and laborers, particularly the Chinese hands that fuel the rapidity of late capitalism, that hoist the angel of history away from fully reckoning with the detritus of capital.

Julien exposes the apparatus for flight in order to render the angel of history strange, a technique learned from Brecht's alienation effect. This effect aims to demystify the operations of capital by understanding the labor and extraction necessary to maintain production, in this case the products being the cinematic image and art. Julien furthers this Marxist and Frankfurt School tradition by focusing on the corporeal labor relied upon to develop Brecht's theories: the Chinese. In particular, Mei Lan Fang, the Chinese opera actor known for his female lead roles, shaped Brecht's theories. The Chinese body in theater provides the basis from which to develop the alienation effect, whereby, as discussed in chapter 4, a cold affect becomes a techne for other performance traditions. It is precisely the reproducibility or repetition of the alienation effect that allows Brecht's aesthetic and political project to flourish. He uses the Chinese as a *surrogate* to direct us to such a method. According to Jameson, Brecht's exposure methodologically allows us "to evaluate seemingly artificial or secondary 'experiences' generated prosthetically."[47] As such, Julien enacts this approach with his fans and Chinese hands. Progress shifts from being a wind from the unknown heavens to an entire apparatus of pulleys, wires, body doubles, and fans. The Chinese workers control these objects and the larger apparatus. The winds of progress are not a disembodied force majeure, counter to Benjamin's image. The performed cold femme aesthetic of Chinese opera becomes one anchor for Julien to engage the Chinese woman: as repeated and replaceable theatrical surrogate. However, through the interplay of media, specifically theater and film, Julien delimits Brecht's overall project. Julien contends with the modes of hesitation that are necessary so as to track the temporal and spatial slippages of the tout-monde. These fractures throughout *Ten Thousand Waves* require that

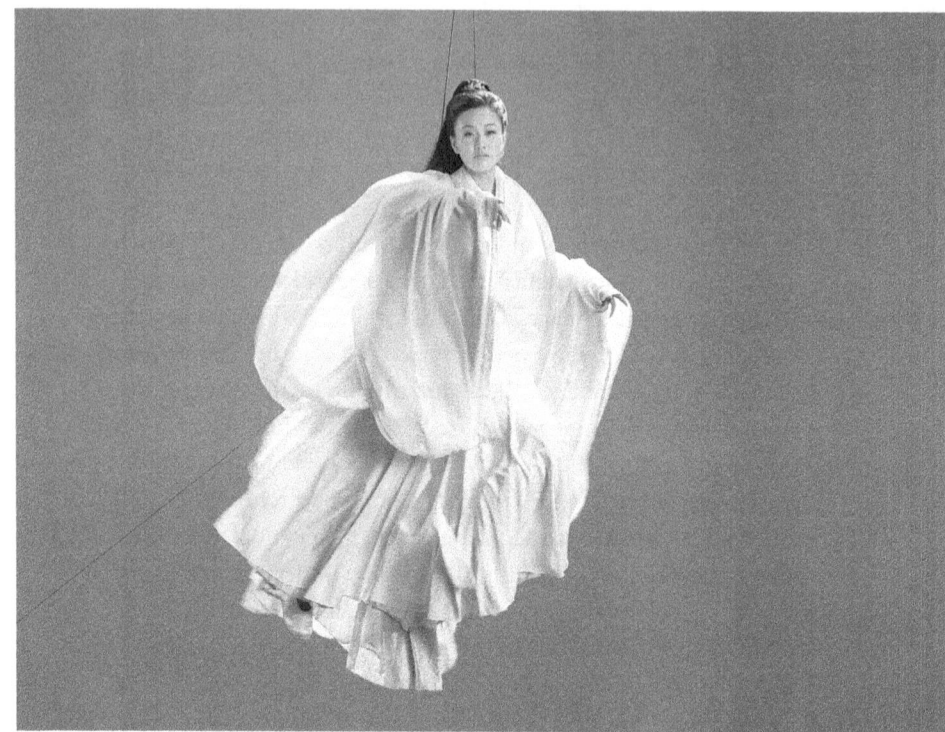

Figure 5.6. Isaac Julien, Green Screen Goddess (*Ten Thousand Waves*), 2010. Endura Ultra photograph, 70.87×94.49 inches (180×240 cm), MP 82. Courtesy of the artist and Victoria Miro, London/Venice.

we move out of a mode of direct critique. In other words, the tout-monde cannot arise from an immediately legible critique involving demystification and performed resistance; instead, we must curb the presumed thrust and direct force of Brecht's aesthetics, its alienating effects.

Julien nonetheless draws from Brecht's approach and a performance-based genealogy and situates them with the role the Chinese woman plays in cinema. The Chinese woman in cinema has a range of functions that vary across national cinemas from early 1900s Shanghai, Hong Kong, Fifth and Sixth Generation Beijing, and Taiwan. Within these variations, Julien notes the uneven ways repetition sits with iconicity or singularity. Specific Chinese women in cinema have certainly embodied complex and individualized roles. However, they are perpetually situated within objecthood, ornamentation,

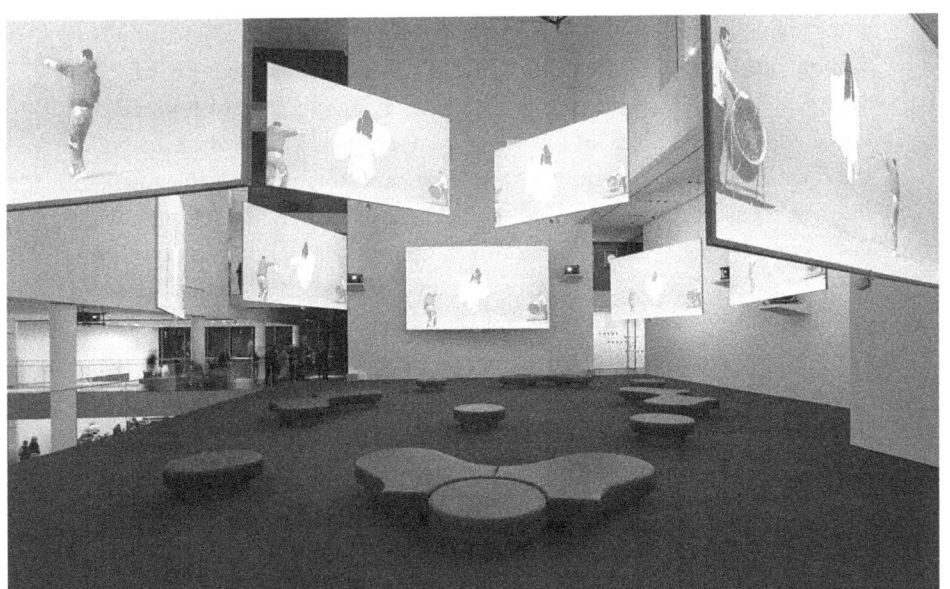

Figure 5.7. Isaac Julien, *Ten Thousand Waves*, 2013. Installation view, Museum of Modern Art, New York. Courtesy of the artist; Art Resource; and Victoria Miro, London/Venice.

and repetition even as icons, as Cheng establishes. Such a condition expands our understanding of subjects beyond sovereignty. The juxtaposition of these two unique roles across different media (surrogation for theater and iconicity for cinema) produces varied notions of the subject/object that preclude them from proper subjecthood and liberal recognition. As such, these objects of history remain as objects, but they differ in their relations to repetition. Julien toggles across this line in order to linger in objecthood without simply dismissing the condition, thus formulating an ethic for the tout-monde.

In particular, how roles are cast in cinema as opposed to theater provides an aperture into these variations across cinematic and theatrical roles. Films can be thought about as singular objects. Although they can be distributed and remakes might be produced, films nonetheless are each imagined as a single moment, especially in their casting of actresses in their iconic roles. Put differently, cinematic roles are generally understood through iconicity, celebrity, and singularity. Theater, however, is often theorized for its repetition and restaging. Even when a film is remade and recast, this becomes another singular production that can be distributed. Meanwhile, there is nothing spectacular about the restaging of a play. Restagings and reperformances are expected in the medium of theater or performance. Unlike the cinematic, the theatrical relies on a recurrence, return, and fracturing of the singular. Further, roles for the theater (and performance, generally) might initially be envisioned for a single person; however, the restaging of performance provides space for a role to be inhabited anew. Because of this difference, the making of icons is more palpable for film than theater. And thus, theatrical roles involve surrogacy. For performance theorists, surrogation involves the recasting of past roles. This is often expanded to understand death beyond individuals toward social death and the ways it demands racialized populations to engage in surrogation.[48]

Julien directs us to the differing relations surrogation and iconicity have to repetition and difference for objects of history. The condition brought about by these two unique forms of objecthood provides avenues to rethink individual singularity and sheer repetition compulsion. We can neither give up due to objecthood nor simply work hard toward entering an idealized liberal personhood; this system is set up to exhaust us or have us live in denial. Instead, through the Chinese woman as both surrogate and icon, Julien gestures toward an ethic that does not slip into a simplistic nihilism or liberal optimism.

In particular, Julien deploys Maggie Cheung to illustrate this ethic through these differences across media. Cheung is an icon of film; however, her replaceability by a body double in the scenes of the green screen highlights slippages across filmic and theatrical roles. The Chinese woman vacillates across these distinct relations to singularity and repetition. Furthermore, in *Ten Thousand Waves*, both Zhao Tao and Cheung embody their iconicity as renowned film actresses. Zhao Tao has come to be a staple in the arthouse films of Jia Zhangke. Her roles in Jia's *The World* (2004), *Still Life* (2006), and *Mountains May Depart* (2015) have garnered her international acclaim. Meanwhile, Cheung first caught public attention playing Jackie Chan's girlfriend in *Police Story* (1985). She was further catapulted into fame as a starlet of arthouse films through the work of Wong Kar-wai. Her leading roles in *In the Mood for Love* (2000) and *2046* (2004) cemented her singular status as a film icon. Further, Cheung's relationship to Hong Kong and England, along with her fluency in multiple Asian and Western European languages, indicates a global iconicity that cannot be easily subsumed under repetition compulsion. However, Julien's critical choice to fully display

Cheung's stunt double (and thereby not amplifying Cheung's singular status) illuminates the need to query notions of iconicity alongside repetition and replaceability.

Julien depicts the Chinese woman in ways that minimize her sovereign status and singularity in order to examine how she exists alongside ornamentation, objecthood, and surrogation. Even as a cinematic icon, the Chinese woman must contend with objecthood. Julien grapples with this dilemma, as he highlights the film star's status while also revealing her function as laborer or worker. For example, in the section depicting modern Shanghai in *Ten Thousand Waves*, Zhao Tao reperforms the role of her predecessor, Ruan Lingyu, in the 1934 film *The Goddess*. This film originally established the career of the celebrity Ruan Lingyu, as she became one of the most prominent women to come out of the 1930s Shanghai film scene. In other words, as an icon, Zhao Tao reperforms the role of another icon. Zhao Tao, in *Ten Thousand Waves*, repeats and labors within the space of celebrity, reformulating her filmic status in ways that appear more akin to that of a theatrical one. Furthermore, Maggie Cheung also played Ruan Lingyu in Stanley Kwan's 1991 biopic, *Actress* or *Center Stage*.[49] Cheung won the Best Actress Award at the Berlin Film Festival for this role.

These multiple icons playing an icon teeter across cinema and theater; they labor within both iconicity and surrogation. In other words, Julien highlights the inability to achieve absolute iconicity (proper recognition and liberal subjecthood), while also exploring forms of repetition that cannot be fully subsumed under theatrical surrogation or object repetition compulsion. In particular, the artist carves out space to reconsider utter repetition by using iconicity as the drive to simply try, attempt, and endeavor, even as objects of history. When Zhao Tao and Maggie Cheung as icons themselves play the icon Ruan Lingyu, Julien emphasizes how the Chinese woman brings to the fore the necessity *and* the impossibility of fully existing anew amid surrogacy. Regardless, they still try, albeit minorly. Through these figures, Julien thus illuminates a limited ethic and a restricted commitment that help produce relationality and the tout-monde.

Julien ultimately ruptures a simplistic binary that might separate cinematic from theatrical roles. The body of the stage performer enfolds multiple moments into one, conjuring the emotions of those who have performed before and including them into her living labor. However, this form of surrogation or repetition is then placed alongside the cinematic, thereby highlighting what singularity provides for objecthood. The body of the cinematic icon shimmers in her singularity, rendering it almost impossible to replicate her.

And yet, the Chinese woman as cinematic icon remains a repeated object *but with difference*. This difference amid repetition signals a compulsion that momentarily and minorly interrupts the cyclical nature of surrogacy and objecthood. Although this could be understood as demonstrating a form of agency within performativity, I take it instead as indicative of an ethical commitment for the project of relationality. To be clear, I do so in order to shift this analysis away from studying the social possibility embedded in individual action, like the achievements of Maggie Cheung or Zhao Tao, toward exploring an expansive condition of repetition that affects minor subjects.

Rather than privileging the theater (à la Brecht) or critiquing film (à la Benjamin), Julien operates across media to contend with the ways the Chinese woman illustrates this important ethic and method for the tout-monde. By moving across iconicity and surrogacy, the subject becomes difference and repetition, a fractured being. In turn, this fracturing affords connections with others—relationality. However, these relations are ephemeral. By approaching others as both surrogate and icon, we generate errant relations that cannot sustain themselves; these errant connections dissipate upon the moment of relation. The minor as method attends to this condition beyond futility. Instead, this method requires an ethic, whereby we return to one another over and over; do not presume our relations stable; and continually attend to the differences and fractures that make it difficult to be together. In sum, relationality is an infinite practice and method rather than a finite achievement.

Ultimately, such an approach facilitates a relationality that embraces the *impossible, impractical,* and *illiberal.* The simultaneous impossibility and necessity of errantry produce an ethical commitment for the tout-monde. This ethic requires that we constantly return to relationality and errantry since, according to Glissant, we "will never accomplish this—and know that is precisely where the threatened beauty of the world resides."[50] More specifically, unlike the repeated objecthood inherent in surrogacy, the objecthood of iconicity involves a minor difference that signals an attempt, a drive, and a pulse. This slight compulsion indexes this ethic; it provides space for the surrogate-icon to search for temporary bonds with others that operate beyond full recognition, repair, and contiguity. Rather than giving into nihilism (fatigue from absolute objecthood) or liberal optimism (working hard enough to enter and be recognized as singular and within modern personhood), this minor compulsion induces us to infinitely attempt the impossible of subsistence and maintenance amidst the grand tragedy known as modernity.

Through the monad of seascapes and the Denkbilder of the angel of history, Julien produces a relationality anchored across two poles that indicate changes in capital, modernity, aesthetic practices, and laboring bodies. Chineseness and Blackness become the central spaces and monads for Julien to produce a sense of all worlds. They arise through their own unique histories, and we witness their contrasts when we understand seascapes and minor objecthood in series. These two worlds come to be situated not for their similarities or continuities throughout history, but rather their differences and fractures. As such, Julien furthers the Marxist genealogy surrounding the minor, as developed throughout this book. The artist provides a critical anchor from which to produce the tout-monde and amplifies the methodological insights of minor China. Following Julien, we thus enhance how social structuration arises through the minor itself, without falling back on the major and liberalist logics that transfix our ideas about the world and the other. The vastness and continuity of the oceanic become the space that brings China and Blackness together and in relation. However, rather than the ocean unifying the two, we might instead focus, as Julien does, on where water meets land, objects, and bodies: the crashing of waves. It is through the repetition of the crash that the major form quietly shifts and comes to be fragmented, rendered minor, and dispersed back again into the oceanic and tout-monde.

For Those Minor in and to China

PROTESTS IN HONG KONG AND SAMSON YOUNG IN VENICE

I write this afterword during the summer of 2019, as I watch multiple months of protest against China's intensified presence in Hong Kong. The protests initially arose as a response against the Hong Kong government's capitulation to Beijing's request for extradition. These protests have since sought to highlight a range of issues: rising housing costs due to an influx of money from China, election practices, police brutality, sovereignty from the Chinese Communist Party, and state censorship. Although this book is meant to think about the long durée of history, I turn to this immediate moment to contend with the idea that China is in fact major. Whenever I would present material from this book, especially to audiences working primarily within Asian studies, one common retort would be: "But China is major, why make it minor?"

What is implied by those arguing that China is in fact major is an investment in possibility. It is an investment in response, protest, and dissent to change the immediate material conditions of the day. These concerns inform how we approach Taiwan's sovereignty, the ongoing silencing and encampment of Uighurs in Xinjiang, the oppression in Tibet, gender and sexual discrimination, and the complicated histories surrounding colonialism for Hong Kong. In this vein, Hong Kong's 2019 protests illustrate the hope for and investment in possibility; and, under liberal logics, this idea of possibility often demonstrates a desire to hear the voice of the people (those minor within and to China) and for them to be represented. I find myself following these events out of a sense of hope, but it is less so as a form of liberal optimism. Within a short span of time, the 2014 Umbrella Movement in Hong Kong, 2014 Sunflower Student Movement in Taiwan, 2018 Yellow Vest Movement in Paris, and the Red for Public Education strikes in the United States starting in 2018 provide an immediate history that informs Hong Kong's 2019 actions. These collective moments renew a sense of possibility that many have dismissed following the 1960s. However, I struggle with ways to express these sentiments beyond the legible discourse of liberal free speech and rights. My hope arises from a commitment to socialism and is fueled by critiques of US empire and its deep entwinement with capitalist modernity. Yet, the language to express this hope is often eclipsed and consumed by liberalism, whereby the US becomes the tacit benchmark for the idea of political progress. But in fact, the US rampantly practices and supports censorship, anti-Blackness, authoritarianism, genocide, misogyny, femicide, violence against populations across the globe, state-sponsored torture, territorial occupation, settler colonialism, capitalist extraction, environmental abuse, and corporate greed, among many other violations the US accuses other nations of enacting.

Even as the events in Hong Kong unfold, I am struck by the discursive and theoretical limits by which to understand forms of critique against major China that do not default into liberalist sentiments. Liberalism informs not only Western media's descriptions of the protests in Hong Kong, but also the activism itself. I find that others seeking to launch a critique of a non-Western state are often delimited by liberalism, whereby a critique of dictatorship, authoritarianism, or suppression is often only legible as demands for individual rights and freedom. This ultimately obscures the historic and ongoing roles of capitalism and Western imperialism in producing the very conditions that affect the lives of those in the non-West. Thus, I end this book by focusing on how the method of the minor brings to the fore the ways liberalism normatively informs and limits the notion of critique.

Although this book has primarily focused on China and artists who are Han Chinese, minor China offers methods for other populations existing in relation to the nation-state. Those minor to and within China experience major China in immediate ways. Even though this book has focused on China in the global and in relation to the West, the nation-state still exists as an imperial force. Thus, how do we begin to discuss this without defaulting into Western democracy and liberalism as the norms that define speech, challenge, and rights? How might a global Marxist legacy help us hold China accountable, rather than relying on capitalist modernity as the model for how the state functions with regard to the individual? I have developed minor China in order to bring to the fore the impulse to render a nation major so as to enter into the league of those belonging to capitalist modernity. Rather than having more nations enter into proper development, I have argued that the goals should be to reorder how we imagine the world, redress histories surrounding racialization and capitalist extraction, and revolutionize and redistribute in ways commensurate to the above. This is a long-term project that extends well beyond the immediate geopolitical moment.

Beyond these issues noted above, which have already been discussed throughout this book, there are additional contributions for minor China, particularly when we expand the focus to those minor in and to China. In particular, the method brings to the fore how liberalism predetermines critiques of the non-West. What might happen if we sought to free the notion of speech from the limits of free speech? Is there a Marxist theory of speech? Although some have examined the ways Marx discusses speech and the press within political theory, I consider the aesthetic as providing critical, minor approaches to these questions.[1]

I ask the above because I am one of those minor to China. My parents are from Taiwan, and I have always been taught that China is major. My parents did not arrive to Taiwan with the Kuomintang (KMT) that became the ruling class after their loss to the Communist Party. My parents' families were among those silenced during the White Terror, whose lands, languages, and already limited resources were stripped with the rise of another colonial power following Japan's colonization. Due to this history, my parents have incessantly focused on how major China is, in its historic articulation through the KMT and also its contemporary presence through the Chinese Communist Party. I hail this personal history because while finishing this book, my father passed away. And while watching the protests in Hong Kong, I have also been parsing through what I have inherited from my father. He was quite active in the Taiwan independence movement, and after fleeing political persecution in Taiwan from the KMT, he came to the United States.

Thus, why would I seek to render China minor when my own familial history and the contemporary moment have continually emphasized China's majorness? I do so in order to better understand how liberalism and capitalist modernity limit the very language and ideas for how we imagine and enact social and political change. Throughout my childhood, I witnessed the deep overlaps surrounding the Christian church and Taiwan's independence movement, as my father was an ordained Presbyterian pastor. His Taiwanese congregation was deeply aligned with the independence movement, and as

I grew up, I learned about the larger global network that sutured these two entities. This overlap was additionally buttressed and informed by a model of liberalism, whereby free speech and rights became the lexicon for voicing Taiwan independence. As a result, I was trained to think of China as major, whereby a critique that was anti–mainland China came to be perpetually conflated with anticommunism or anti-Marxism. Of course, I take ownership of my own conceptual limits, as I now would like to believe that I have done enough personal, therapeutic, and theoretical work to reconsider the ideological trainings enacted by my family and education that have primarily occurred in the United States. This history helps me ground the larger theoretical stakes of minor China as they relate to Marxism.

Beyond my own personal history, these dynamics have come to be mirrored through the populations that are minor to China. They have often increased their identification with the local: Hong Kongers and Taiwanese have asserted more and more their difference from mainland Chinese, particularly following the opening of borders and increased tourism across these regions. These modes of identification come to parallel the logic inherent in the nation's "one China, two systems" policy, whereby one can be part of China but also have its own separate identity (those spaces minor to yet also part of major China). This policy, of course, is now at the crux of the ongoing protests, as China is forced to reckon with this stated ideal and to grapple with if or when autocracy becomes authoritarianism. Regardless, some forms of these local identities for Hong Kong and Taiwan are rooted in xenophobia that perpetuates the racist notion of the Chinese as less civilized than their other counterparts. These types of logics are constantly infused with a sense of advanced racialized development, particularly through a presumed proximity to capitalist modernity.

It seems quite difficult then to articulate a critique of China without defaulting into racialist discourse, alongside liberalism as the tacit ideal. This is a condition that shapes many who are critical of, yet work from, what M. Jacqui Alexander astutely calls the "seat of empire."[2] It is hard for me to pronounce a critique of China without it taking on an anti-Marxist bent that seemingly emerges from liberalism. To be clear, I am as critical of US empire and capitalism as I am of China's relationship to late capital and its oppression of those within and outside of China. However, I find it near impossible to express these simultaneous forms of critique due to the epistemological foundations surrounding critique itself. One can further trace these limits in the media coverage of the Hong Kong activists. In watching the coverage of the protests from the vantage of the US, I have been struck by the ways this movement is only legible through major China and the frameworks of resistance and liberal free speech. Notably, the bipartisan support within the US of the protestors, during an era of rampant partisanship in Congress, further illustrates the limited narratives in which the 2019 protests register. There seems to be little discourse available by which to imagine speech beyond the bounds of free speech. Socialist legacies could provide such models, although at this point less developed. Further, the specters of Stalinism and communism often thwart the ability to imagine a Marxist sensibility surrounding speech.

Thus, I've privileged the aesthetic throughout this book due to the fact that it opens up space beyond political and theoretical discourses that often limit how we imagine what politics and theory are or can be. This is not to privilege the aesthetic as the answer or place of otherwiseness; rather, the aesthetic is both part of the problem of critique and a necessary component to rethink these apparatuses. The aesthetic, when understood in relation to Hong Kong and Taiwan's precarious relationships to China, offers a method to render China minor even though it appears to be quite major. The remainder of this afterword thus grapples with these concerns through the aesthetic in order to rethink this condition surrounding critique, liberalism, and speech. In this vein, minor China is a method for not only China in the Western imaginary but also China throughout the Asia-Pacific region.

At the 2017 Venice Biennale, we arrive at two sets of seascapes. One takes us to the canals and shores of Venice. The other takes us beyond the immediate environs of this global art mecca to the docks of Hong Kong. Samson Young's *Songs for Disaster Relief* premiered at the fifty-seventh edition of the biennale as part of Hong Kong's Pavilion. The multimedia work involves a ludic primary-colored set of ramps (figure A.1), an installation exploring dystopic landscapes, a silenced choir murmuring a version of "We Are the World," and a video of the artist on a sampan in Hong Kong's bay singing "Bridge over Troubled Water" in Cantonese numbers. In this work, Young confronts not only transnational dynamics around charity and first world giving, but also regional dynamics as they relate to China, Hong Kong, and other places minor within—and in relation to—China. From the global centers of the art market to the oceanic expanse of the Atlantic that have appeared throughout this book, I return us to the waters and borders within Asia. By doing so, we contend with a critical question for the minor as method. I discuss Young's

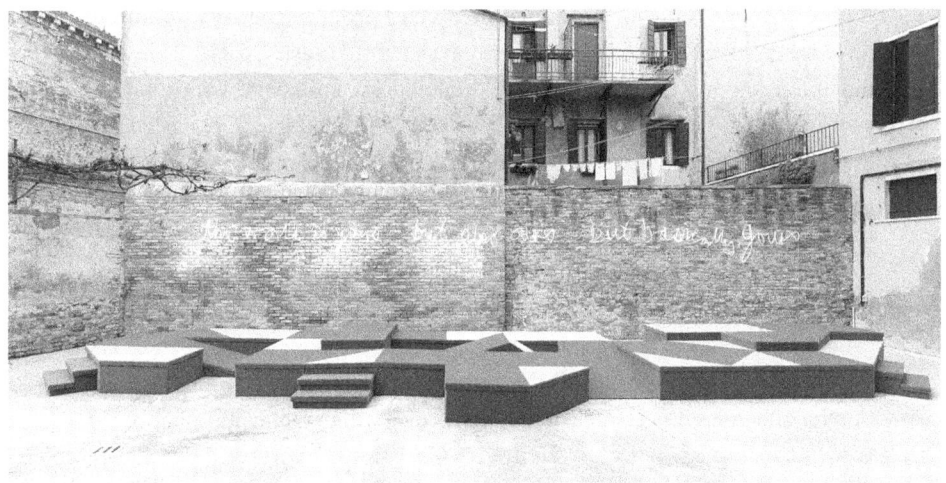

Figure A.1. Samson Young, *Risers*,
2017. Photo by Simon Vogel, Cologne.
Courtesy of the artist.

Songs for Disaster Relief because of the way it helps us think about what we do with the fact that China is major. Its impact on social, political, economic, and environmental fronts reverberates across the region. Despite this reality, minor China provides insights for those minor in and to China as it relates to difference, dissent, and critique.

Throughout this book, I have focused on the fractures across populations in order to contribute to the broader humanistic turn toward relationality. Liberalism glosses over these historical and structural minoritarian differences by delimiting the minor to be primarily about individual subjects and wielding civility as an apparatus for censure. Meanwhile, Marxism has a difficult history with regard to communist practices that silenced critique from within in order to advance revolutionary change. Either civility or authoritarianism muffles dissent. The tendency for both frameworks is to privilege collectivity and holism so as to render minor and minimize difference and dissent. Difference and dissent, however, are necessary to produce political visions that exceed contemporary discourse and the force of law that accompany both liberalism and Marxism.

Young's set of works at Venice takes charity songs as its starting point. These songs arise from national and transnational fundraising drives; they are meant to address, not necessarily redress, disaster. In theory, they function by bringing attention and resources to issues; yet, what often remains uninterrogated is the way nations themselves produce the very conditions for disaster to arise. Even in the event of a natural disaster, catastrophe does not solely happen as an act of God. The relations across and within nation-states bring to the fore the lack of resources and inadequate infrastructure that plague a region and its populations. Young grapples with the kitsch appeal of these charity songs that are meant to bring attention to crisis, while highlighting the limits surrounding neoliberalized forms of charity. One of the songs he uses, "We Are the World," demonstrates this dynamic. Following the urging of activist Harry Belafonte, Quincy Jones and Michael Jackson produced the single in 1985, which was sung by Jackson, Lionel Richie, Tina Turner, Paul Simon, Bruce Springsteen, and Cyndi Lauper, among many others. This song was created after the success of the organization Band Aid's 1984 recording of "Do They Know It's Christmas?" Further, "We Are the World" was remade in 2010, as a way to raise funds for those devastated by earthquakes in Haiti.

Although funds were raised and attention was brought to famine across parts of Africa and a natural disaster in Haiti, these benevolent actions ring hollow. The first world itself is at fault for creating famine and faulty infrastructure due to histories surrounding slavery, debtor nation structures, resource extraction, indigenous genocide, and capital.[3] Disasters occur due to structural issues, rather than being a test on and testament to the character of a people or an individual nation's resources. Young contends with his ambivalence toward these performed modes of solidarity due to such structural realities. For Young's 2017 rendition, he invited the Hong Kong Federation of Trade Unions (FTU) Choir to murmur the lyrics of "We Are the World." While the choir sings the lyrics with raspy voices, Young subdues the musical swells and crescendos of the tune in order to remove the intended emotional reaction as a charity song. He limits the normative affective function of these songs and highlights the expectation of cathecting one's desires and hopes through the genre. In addition, Young negotiates the restraints and possibilities of solidarity with China itself. The FTU is a pro-Beijing and prolabor entity, and Young asked them to participate in the project in order to "put differences aside" and produce a form of solidarity with those he disagrees with. These songs thus bring to the fore the transnational dynamics undergirding charity, along with the fact that China exists as a major force within not only the world but also the region.

To further illustrate this, Young draws from another rich history surrounding the song "Bridge over Troubled Water." In 1991, this single was re-performed in Cantonese by popstars to raise public support for the Eastern

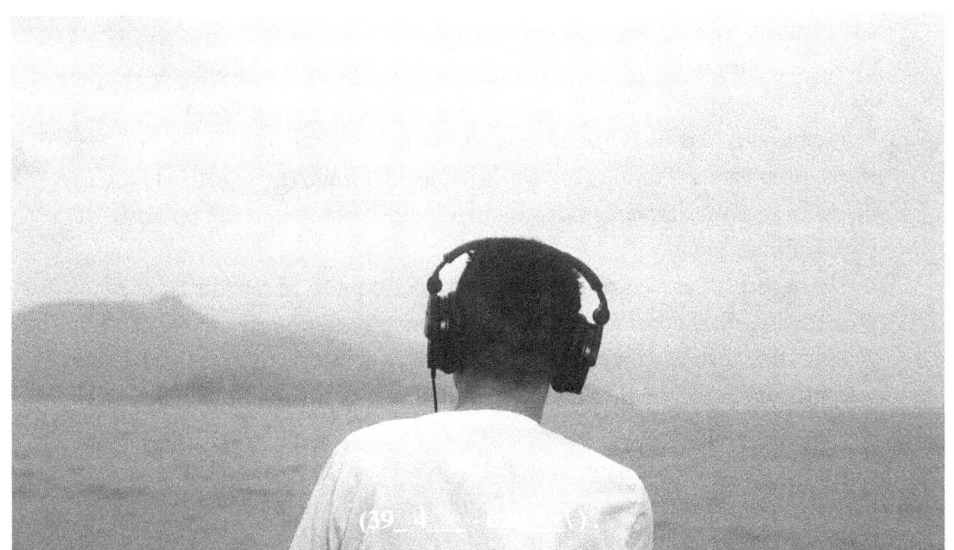

Figure A.2. Samson Young, *Lullaby (World Music)*, 2017. Screenshot image. Courtesy of the artist.

China flood relief. Hong Kong's version of Simon and Garfunkel's original hit was performed as a way to similarly "put differences aside" with China, as a show of solidarity with the nation-state before Hong Kong's 1997 colonial handover from Great Britain. Young's 2017 version is melancholic, as he sits in a sampan floating on the seas overlooking the maritime border that separates China from Hong Kong. In the video, we only see his back, in a white t-shirt wearing headphones (figure A.2). Young sings in Cantonese, but rather than reperform the lyrics, he chants numbers that refer to the steady increase in funds raised during the 1991 performance. Young's voice and his shift from lyrics to numbers have a similar effect of delimiting the emotional expectations of the charity song. Rather than feeling moved to give, we linger in the oceanic. The artist highlights how for a space like Hong Kong, these charity songs require navigating China's dominance in the region. Thus, although Young's work confronts the ecological and global, the artist additionally considers those minor to and in China.

Young provides insights to expand minor China in ways that further consider dissent, forms of critique, and those minor to and in the nation-state. Born in Hong Kong in 1979, Young received his undergraduate training in music, philosophy, and gender studies and graduate work in music composition. Although at first known as a composer and sound artist, he has built a reputation in visual and intermedial arts. Young has become a regular on the global art market, having shown at the Venice Biennale, Museum of Contemporary Art in Taipei, *documenta*, and Art Basel Hong Kong, among many other venues. Young's aesthetics deploy the sonic and affective to highlight the limits of liberalist norms surrounding speech and the presence of major China.

In particular, at Venice, Young hails socialist pasts, as a quote from Mao greets visitors to the Hong Kong Pavilion. In neon blue, the phrase "The world is yours, but also ours, but basically yours" is emblazoned along the brick wall that encompasses the set of risers (figure A.1). The phrase is attributed to Chairman Mao from a 1956 speech to Chinese students studying abroad in Moscow. During the same year as this speech, Mao initiated the Hundred Flowers Campaign to encourage forms of political speech. Although intellectuals and citizens were emboldened to critique the state, this eventually led to heavy efforts a year later in 1957 to silence dissent. Young's use of this phrase emblematizes the limits surrounding how speech can be articulated. It also provides an opening for different genealogies surrounding speech, although the specters surrounding authoritarian censorship and Stalinism reemerge.

Since this quote is placed above the risers, however, we are provided a variety of pathways from which to engage or disengage this history. The multiple pathways mirror the constant negotiation between belonging and not belonging to the collective and these Marxist legacies. In addition, Mao's quote emphasizes a separation between the second and third person. Although the second-person *you* is generally imagined within the *we*, Mao's phrasing articulates a notion of difference that forces us to wonder what separates *you* from *us*. This differentiation highlights a contemporary condition, whereby those who are minor to and in China, like those from Hong Kong and Taiwan, are simultaneously Chinese but not ("yours, but also ours, but basically yours"). Young demonstrates how Mao almost foresees the "one China, two systems" policy, which presumes that a nation is separate (*yours* and *two systems*) but still part of one China (*ours*). Similar to Ai Weiwei who relies on Chinese socialism as an additional political genealogy by which to formulate his critiques, as discussed in chapter 2, Young draws from the complex histories of Maoism to consider what it means to have a world that is yours and ours but basically yours—an ambivalence surrounding governance and speech. Taiwan and Hong Kong, for example, are currently grappling with this condition of governance, whereby notions of speech are being reimagined and negotiated. Through the flicker of the neon light and the foreboding tone of the phrase, Young produces Maoism and past social-ist ideals as affects that float throughout his works at Venice. Rather than dismiss Maoism and Marxism, Young lingers in their complexities. These ambiguous relations to this leftist genealogy are emblematic of his form of critique. In this way, Young enacts the minor as method to offer affective pathways that do not dictate but direct us to the problematic surrounding speech, critique, and the legacies of socialism.

Across from the small video installation of Young's rendition of "Bridge over Troubled Water" is perhaps a rejoinder to Mao. In neon, the artist has emblazoned "Why have you forsaken me?" on one of the walls across the canal (Figure A.3). This phrase assesses the failures of past socialist ideals but also considers Hong Kong's previous colonizer, the United Kingdom. Rather than claiming a colonial nostalgia, however, Young refuses a sim-plistic critique that dismisses Maoism through default liberalism. More spe-cifically, unlike his minor, indirect, and complicated negotiations of Maoism and Marxism, Young performs a candid examination of (neo)liberalism and capital. In particular, Young explicitly names Reaganism and neoliberalism as forces that inform the trend of charity songs and humanitarianism. He calls out Western capital as the driver for boom and bust in his media instal-lation at Venice. For example, his videos pay homage to an imagined figure, Boomtown Gundane, who turned out to be a fictional South African pro-ducer for a satirical song that responded "Yes We Do" to "Do They Know It's Christmas?" Throughout the installation, the artist offers context around neoliberalism and Reaganism to directly critique and consider the illogics of liberalism alongside the audacity of Western charity.

Young thus develops dual modes of critique. The explicit names the dominance of liberalism, while the implicit or indirect operates through the affective, thereby emphasizing less determined ways in which to engage the legacies of Marxism, Maoism, and socialism. Young, in other words, plays with two forms of mediation, linear and indirect. Rather than dictate what is to be done, he highlights the limits of discourse, with liberalism as the tacit benchmark. Young's direct and linear engagement with Reaganism operates through a different political register in comparison to the fuzzy and ambigu-ous modality of leftist "speech" and aesthetics. For example, the ramps offer multiple pathways by which to engage and reimagine Mao's provocations. Further, Young does not directly name the specter of Marx or Mao, as the latter's ideas seem to float throughout the installation. Young imagines speech and action beyond liberalism but hesitantly so, ultimately providing a model by which to rethink critique itself.

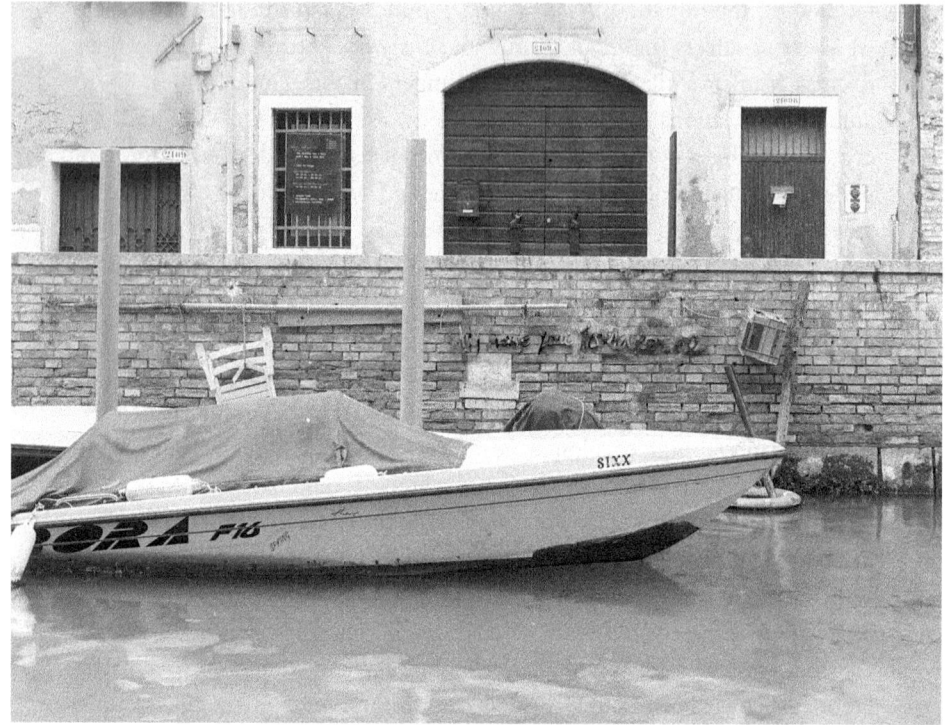

Figure A.3. Samson Young, view of "Why Have You Forsaken Me?" in neon (*Lullaby* (*World Music*)), 2017. Photo by Simon Vogel, Cologne. Courtesy of the artist.

The sonic similarly directs us to other formulations surrounding speech and dissent. *We Are the World, as Performed by the* HK *Federation of Trade Unions Choir (Muted Situation #21)* is part of Young's *Muted Situation* series. In this series of works, the artist plays with expectations surrounding sound. Young dims or minimizes dominant notions of sound to focus on the minor, less noticed forms of performed action and sound. For example, in *Muted Situation #2: Muted Lion Dance*, he removes the percussion that accompanies lion dancing in order to bring attention to the movement and sounds of feet and costumes (figure A.4). For the artist, what he calls muting is not silencing but rather reprioritizing what is noticed. He renders minor the main event so as to bring to the fore our dominant senses and perceptions. He holds back the emotionally driven drums or voices so as to foreground other phenomenological registers. Thus, when "We Are the World" is played without

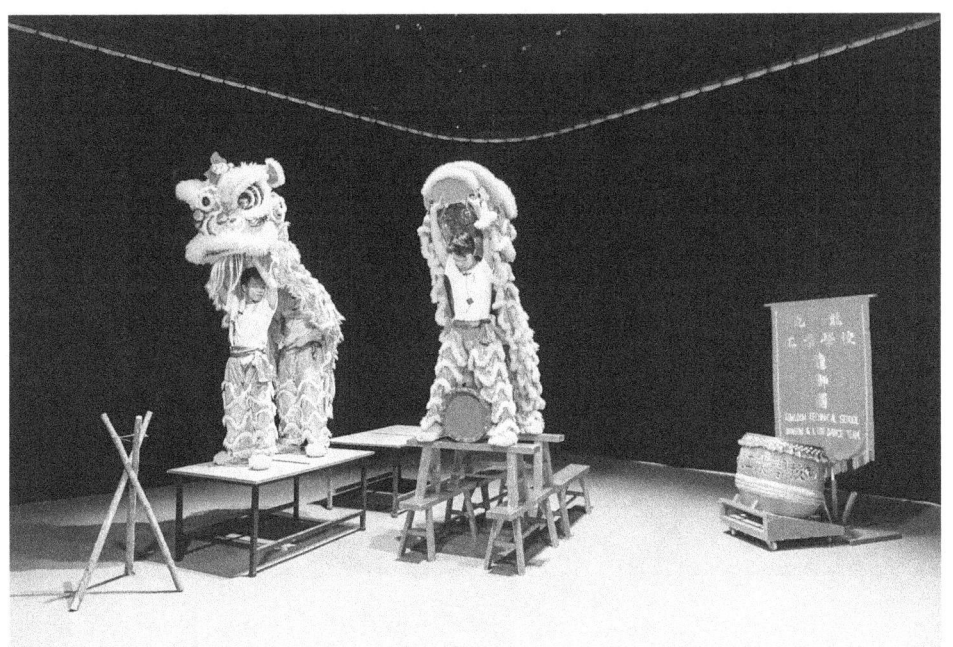

Figure A.4. Samson Young, *Muted Situation #2: Muted Lion Dance*, 2014. Photo by Dennis Man Wing Leung. Courtesy of the artist.

the predictable emotional musical swells or the virtuosic voices, we then focus on the performance of the singers, their expressions, and the murmur of their voices (figure A.5).

These effects reconsider speech and clarity. This is not parody, however. The parodic intimates a humorous exaggeration, as Boomtown Gundane's retort to "Do They Know It's Christmas?" demonstrates. Rather, Young shifts the spectator's focus toward the minor by enacting a mode that is often not deployed in contemporary art: sincerity. Young sincerely aims to grapple with the political realities of the day, considering that Hong Kong is minor to and minor in China. In addition, he immediately experiences this condition. From China's viewpoint, Hong Kong is theoretically "yours, but also ours, but basically yours." With its handover from British colonialism to China in 1997, Hong Kong exists under the "one China, two systems" policy. In practice, Cantonese and English are primarily spoken, and there are vestiges of British law and policy that inform the space. The 2019 protests highlight the difficulties of this policy and the complex negotiation that must happen

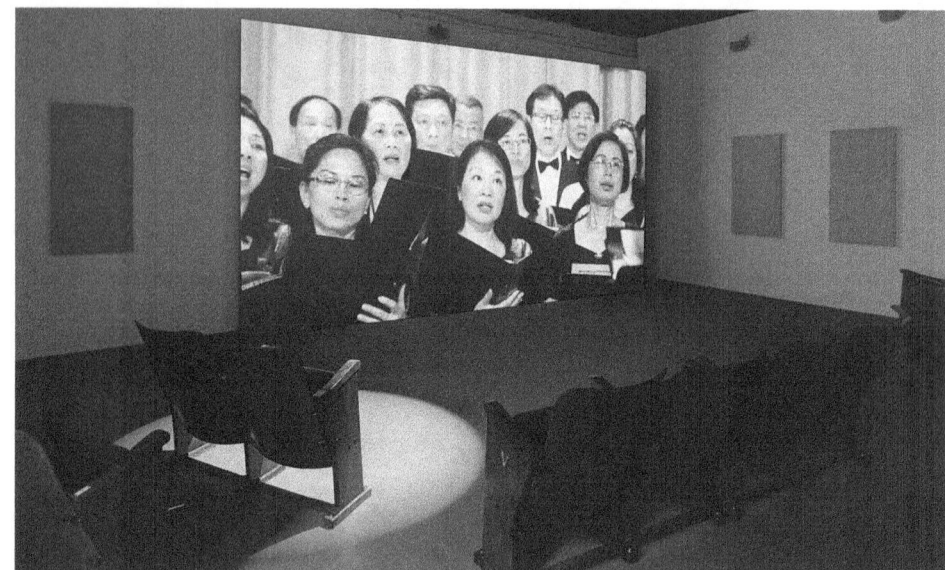

Figure A.5. Samson Young, *We Are the World, as Performed by the HK Federation of Trade Unions Choir (Muted Situation #21)*, 2017. Video and multi-channel sound installation. Photo by Simon Vogel, Cologne. Courtesy of the artist.

when one is minor in and to China. Those minor in and to China anxiously await how China will navigate forms of speech, difference, and dissent—a moment in which to perhaps obtain a glimmer of leftist speech or fear when autocratic rule turns into authoritarian censorship and violence.[4]

Young teeters within this space. He enlisted the FTU Choir for this project since they are a pro-Beijing entity. Young does not parody the troop nor the charity song through his minor method and aesthetic of minimizing dominant sounds. Instead, he sincerely approached the FTU to collaborate in this project. He does so in order to grapple with the reality of China's presence for Hong Kong. He deploys sincerity to bring to the fore the difficult mediation inherent in navigating these dynamics; in other words, sincerity, as a frame, helps us avoid discussing this work as pure resistance. And by reworking and refocusing notions of speech and sound, he highlights the limits of liberal ideals. Young is not simply voicing critique of China through liberal sentiments. Rather, the ambiguity inherent in his affective approach to Maoism and China signals a move away from the liberal demands for clarity, free speech, and direct critique. He privileges indirect mediation when it comes to his aesthetics with regard to the political.

Young's sense of sincerity, along with his mode of political and aesthetic critique, carries over into other works in *Songs for Disaster Relief*. As discussed earlier, the artist presents *Lullaby (World Music)*, where he sits atop a sampan on the Hong Kong bay (figure A.2). He overlooks the oceanic border that separates Hong Kong from China. From this precarious vantage point, he performs another act of sonic sincerity. The song comprises of him humming Cantonese numbers to another charity song. His sonic sincerity registers as melancholic, as he lingers within the complex relations Hong Kong has with China. He peers into the vastness of the sea at this maritime limit point. This border is not something to mock nor discredit; the border sincerely matters. This material and oceanic line resonates with his aesthetics, along with the hopes that animate the 2019 protesters. The dominance of liberalism precludes how these subjects might assert these intricate feelings, emotions, and a sense of what might be possible. Normative forms of speech and direct critiques of major China cannot fully encapsulate what they seek to express, redress, and address.

Young's objects do not provide per se a view of his own personal experience with China. Rather, he directs us to the structural and atmospheric that dictate how to render legible his own life, that of the protestors, and those who experience being minor in and to China. Young highlights the norms surrounding speech and sound that privilege clarity, meaning, and critique. He presents these explicit and legible forms of dissent (a direct mediation across aesthetics and politics) to target and name neoliberalism. However, when it comes to Mao, Young turns to affect, indirect mediation, and a minimization of sound. The artist thus inquires if other forms of speech exist beyond the models of free speech and direct critique we have inherited. Perhaps socialism provides a glimmer into these unexamined genealogies. Even amid China's majorness, Young renders the nation minor to explore such possibilities. Throughout *Songs for Disaster Relief*, China becomes a variety of minor sounds and objects: a hum, a murmur, a flickering neon light, and a raspy voice that echoes socialist pasts and perhaps futures. These residues condition those who are minor in and to China. Rather than prescribing a solution or explicitly critiquing this condition, Young hesitates and takes note as to what shapes the nation, along with speech, action, and being—a minor act that suffices for today considering how overwhelming things are at the border.

NOTES

Introduction

1 The name of the show in Chinese can be more literally translated to *Uncooperative Attitude*.

2 Hou Hanru, "Entropy, Chinese Artists, Western Art Institutions," 61.

3 L. Liu, *Translingual Practice*, xv.

4 Henri Neuendorf, "Ai Weiwei Claims the Chinese Authorities Made Him Famous," Artnet.com, July 18, 2016, https://news.artnet.com/art-world/ai-weiwei-authorities -china-562586.

5 Throughout this book, I privilege the term *non-Western* because it explicitly names the central category that is invisibilized yet structures how we understand culture: the West. My use of the term *non-West* seeks to avoid creating neologisms or reversing the direction from South to North or periphery to center. Further, the more commonly used term *global art* reinforces the centrality of Western dominance by not naming the presumption that the West is considered center while the rest is simply placed under the catchall phrase *global*. I use *non-Western* to compel us to reexamine what undergirds its use.

6 Berghuis, *Performance Art in China*; M. Cheng, *Beijing Xingwei*; Heinrich, *Chinese Surplus*; Pollack, *The Wild, Wild East*; Welland, *Experimental Beijing*.

7 M. Cheng, *Beijing Xingwei*, 428.

8 Jonathan Jones, "Who's the Vandal?," *Guardian*, February 18, 2014.

9 Akin to Theodor Adorno, Ai additionally deploys boredom to critique bourgeois, liberal sensibilities through a Marxist critique. Adorno, *Minima Moralia*, 175–76.

10 P. Liu, *Queer Marxism in Two Chinas*, 168.

11 This book thus follows critics, such as Sylvia Wynter, Hortense Spillers, Alexander Weheliye, and Denise Ferreira da Silva, who have centralized the import of how Black bodies have been subjugated and rendered inhuman to produce the universalized categories of Man and human. Their collective project asserts that one cannot theorize the human without contending with race, not as a form of subject exclusion but rather as a malleable object for the production of universal frameworks. I focus on the minor as method and social structuration to assist in such a project that refuses to maintain subjects as knowable and static since this obscures the fact that they have been and are malleable to power, control, and discourse. However, I examine the ways the Asiatic form enhances a minor method to not only centralize race for theorizations of the human, but also mark the need to attend to the differences surrounding Asian racialization for this discourse.

12 My turn to sense can be differentiated from what Jacques Rancière calls the *distribution of the sensible*, which undergirds his theorizations of aesthetics and

politics. Rancière, *Politics of Aesthetics*. In this introduction and chapter 1, I turn to mediation to reconsider Rancière's formulation of aesthetics and politics as a dominant frame. In particular, I hesitate from arguing for the aesthetic's significance or its agency. As I unpack in chapter 1, the aesthetic is another minor subject that needs to be understood methodologically—the approach I develop throughout this book. I move away from Rancière's formulation that uses the aesthetic, art, or culture to be the vehicle that increases representation and, hence, our sensibilities surrounding what or whom we value, the demos' common sense. I take this to be modeled within liberal logics. Thus, unlike Rancière with his reliance on the sensible, I develop in chapter 1 the notion of sense from those objects and things that are often dismissed within the realm of dominant sensibility. I focus on the physical senses and sensations over common sense and the sensible.

13 See Kwon, *Enchantments*; and Wynter, "Re-enchantment of Humanism."

14 Lowe, "History Hesitant," 98.

15 Chow, *Protestant Ethnic*; Silva, *Toward a Global Idea of Race*; and A. Smith, "Queer Theory and Native Studies."

16 For thorough accounts of representation, aesthetics, and race, see Chuh, *The Difference Aesthetics Makes*; and Lloyd, *Under Representation*.

17 Snorton and Yapp, *Saturation*, 2.

18 Vukovich, *Illiberal China*, 10.

19 For a development of the illiberal in relation to humanism, see Chuh, *The Difference Aesthetics Makes*.

20 The trope of "sick man of Asia" shaped how China was understood during the nineteenth and twentieth centuries as a nation taken advantage of by colonial powers like Japan and Great Britain, among other sites. From the end of the twentieth century into today, China is now understood as central to the world. For discussions on China as behind, see Eng, Ruskola, and Shen, "Introduction: China and the Human"; Hayot, *The Hypothetical Mandarin*; and Heinrich, *Afterlife of Images*.

21 Karl, *Magic of Concepts*, 25.

22 Karl, *Magic of Concepts*, 26.

23 Akin to Sylvia Wynter, I use the practice of *deciphering* to obtain this goal. Further, I rely on the aesthetic as the means to decipher. As Wynter puts it, "the disciplinary practice of criticism itself, not what is said or the approach taken, that functions to 'save' the premise of our present cultural Imaginary" (Wynter, "Rethinking Aesthetics," 264). Wynter locates a trap for minoritarian theorists when analyzing aesthetic objects, whereby ethno-specific and particularizing analytics around transnational subjects are taken as indexical to reality without offering a sense of what structures or upholds the legibility of these subjects and their objects. Wynter reminds theorists of the transnational to not make work about the subject but rather about the world that upholds those subjects' positions—how we value (Wynter, "Rethinking Aesthetics," 271). This minor practice of what Wynter calls deciphering brings to the fore the rules of the game rather than merely playing the game itself—to understand the need for tracking the operations and assumptions

of discourse around how exactly we produce value, rather than responding to immediate demands under the force of law. I explain my use of the force of law later
in this introduction.

24 See Chuh, *Imagine Otherwise*; and Love, "Small Change."
25 Hardt and Negri, *Empire*.
26 Derrida, "Force of Law."
27 Derrida, "Force of Law," 26.
28 Chow, *Woman and Chinese Modernity*, xiii.
29 Chakrabarty, *Provincializing Europe*, 5.
30 Wang Hui, *Politics of Imagining Asia*, 57–58.
31 Kamien, *Music*, 46.
32 Thank you to Matthew Morrison for discussing with me the role of the minor
within musicology.
33 Hegel, *Lectures on the Philosophy of World History*.
34 D. Lowe, *Function of "China" in Marx, Lenin, and Mao*.
35 Vukovich, "China in Theory," 156.
36 Lisa Lowe and Richard Wolin have historicized this French interest in Maoism in
relation to shifting relations to Orientalism (L. Lowe, *Critical Terrains*; and Wolin,
Wind from the East).
37 Vukovich, "China in Theory," 163.
38 Amy Kaplan has emphasized how the transnational turn "has been crucial in
decentering the tenacious model of the nation as the basic unit of knowledge production" to contend with American exceptionalism and empire (Kaplan, "Violent
Belongings," 11).
39 Ella Shohat calls for a relational feminism that moves beyond limited and insular
understandings of subjects from particular spaces. Her work, alongside others
who established the fields of women of color and transnational feminisms, is an
important call for such moves to rethink stabilized formulations of minor subjects
(Shohat, *Taboo Memories, Diasporic Voices*).
40 Allen Chun calls for destabilizing theorizations of China as knowable by moving
beyond the nation's "boundedness" to see how "discourses of culture are really
attempts by the state to grasp . . . the nature of its own modernity" (Chun, "Fuck
Chineseness," 119).
41 Within queer studies and queer of color critique, and specifically as these fields
manifest in relation to Asian American studies, the "subjectless" frame has been
privileged (Eng, Halberstam, and Muñoz, "What's Queer about Queer Studies
Now?").
42 Kandice Chuh offers subjectlessness as a way to contend with the category of
Asian American by hesitating on presuming what is legible within this identity
category. Subjectlessness operates as a method by "foregrounding the discursive
constructedness of subjectivity" in order to avoid falling into the trap of the force
of law that limits who and what a subject is and how they are made legible (Chuh,
Imagine Otherwise, 9). A helpful early theorization of this work comes from David
Lloyd who deploys Deleuze and Guattari's notion of minor literature to argue for

"the disintegration of the individual subject of the bourgeois state, questioning the principles of originality and autonomy that underwrite that conception of the subject" (Lloyd, *Nationalism and Minor Literature*, 24–25).

43 Deleuze, "Control and Becoming," 170.

44 Within ethnic studies, Deleuzo-Guattarian thought has certainly appeared but has less of a presence within the larger field. For helpful examples, see M. Chen, *Animacies*; Puar, *Right to Maim*; Saldanha, *Psychedelic White*; and Saldanha and Adams, *Deleuze and Race*. Within Asian American studies, Metzger considers Deleuze through the work of Olivia Khoo (Metzger, "At the Vanishing Point"). Later, in this introduction, I discuss Black feminist theory as it relates to Francophone metaphysical thought (of which Deleuze and Guattari are certainly a part).

45 Appadurai, "Mediants, Materiality, Normativity," 222.

46 Shaobo Xie offers an overview of the emergence of European postmodern theory in China following the Cultural Revolution. Xie notes the popularity of Foucault, Barthes, Derrida, Lacan, Schopenhauer, and Bakhtin in China (Xie, "Translation and Transformation").

47 I develop this further in chapter 3. In addition, Weihong Bao traces Bergson's influence on philosophical and art discourses (W. Bao, *Fiery Cinema*). Some exciting work around Deleuze and Guattari and affect has developed in China studies. See Schroeder, "On Cowboys and Aliens."

48 After all, in *A Thousand Plateaus*, Deleuze and Guattari describe becoming-animal in ways that do not ignore (nor do they fully contend with) histories around the animalization of racialized groups. Becoming-animal requires sets of relations, whereby "a becoming lacks a subject distinct from itself." Becoming is an analytic that allows us to focus on institutional and historical power: becoming-animal "express[es] minoritarian groups, or groups that are oppressed, prohibited, in revolt, or always on the fringe of recognized institutions." To become China is thus meant to trace how China has become known in its proper and economized form, a process of becoming for China that is not the same as any other becoming (Deleuze and Guattari, *Thousand Plateaus*, 238, 247).

49 Kornbluh, *Order of Forms*, 3.

50 Although many have focused on the notion of mediation, I draw from a genealogy informed by Fredric Jameson. He uses mediation to suture "the formal analysis of a work of art and its social ground" in order to follow a tradition of "dialectical philosophy and Marxism itself [that] have formulated their vocation to break out of the specialized compartments of the (bourgeois) disciplines and to make connections among the seemingly disparate phenomena of social life generally" (Jameson, *Political Unconscious*, 39–40). From within media studies, mediation has a long genealogy that similarly develops across a Marxist analytic. Unlike Marshall McLuhan's famous theory of mediation that offered how the medium is the message, Friedrich Kittler's notion of mediation takes into deeper consideration how information becomes embodied in the medium. Stuart Hall further complicates McLuhan's work by contending with mediation as a process that is always conditioned by structures of power, what Hall calls *encoding* and *decoding*. Both

Kittler and Hall provide approaches to mediation as a complex process that takes mediation and reception outside of a linear relation from superstructure to the subject (Kittler, *Gramophone, Film, Typewriter*; and Hall, "Encoding/Decoding").

Following both Jameson and these theorists from media studies, Alexander Galloway reminds us that mediation has many models, for which he lays out three primary ones: 1) the transference of messages, 2) direct immediacy, and 3) swarms and networks. See Galloway, "Love of the Middle." Galloway's first two models of mediation highlight direct and immediate transfers of information across space. However, his less direct model provides a way to grapple with works that do not fully operate through the linguistic nor as immediately legible as political or even aesthetic. This third model of swarms and networks offers a form of mediation that expands our understanding of aesthetics, politics, and their relation. This less direct relationship between two entities involves not only the transference of information, but also the creation of new data and possibilities. As such, Galloway helps us renegotiate dominant aesthetics and politics discourse. Rancière's notion of the distribution of the sensible has become standard for discussing contemporary art. Sensibility engages Galloway's first model of mediation through the transference of a message. Within this linear mode of mediation, power structures what makes sense and thus shapes how individuals receive and process the world around them. The connection between aesthetics and politics is conceptualized as being mediated through what is considered communal or distributed sensibility. The second model presumes a one-to-one parity where aesthetics and politics overlap in direct ways, where art becomes the core of politics. The issue with this model, however, is that it often limits the forms of aesthetics that are legible as political. A networked and scattered understanding of mediation for aesthetics and politics expands the categories themselves, along with their relation. In chapter 1, I more explicitly develop these ideas as they relate to liberalism and socialism.

51 P. Liu, *Queer Marxism in Two Chinas*; L. Liu, *Translingual Practice*; Savci, "Translation as Queer Methodology"; Shih, *Visuality and Identity*.

52 Metzger, "Seascape."

53 M. Cheng, *Beijing Xingwei*.

54 M. Cheng, *Beijing Xingwei*, 94.

55 See Keeling, "I = Another"; and Musser, "Anti-Oedipus, Kinship."

56 Campt, *Listening to Images*; Snorton, *Black on Both Sides*; Musser, *Sensational Flesh*; Spillers, "Mama's Baby, Papa's Maybe"; Bradley, "Introduction: Other Sensualities"; and Marks, *Skin of the Film*.

57 In this vein, I work similarly to Ari Heinrich who deploys Black feminist theory and Black studies as they relate to China in the global (Heinrich, *Chinese Surplus*).

58 As Grace Hong reminds us, figures like Gloria Anzaldúa and Audre Lorde were concerned with rethinking the Cartesian limits of the subject by imagining subjects as fractured and relational well before our more recent minor turns (Hong, *Death beyond Disavowal*). Hong's work is a critical reminder as we further historicize the epistemological bases of our ongoing minor turns.

59 Deleuze, *Difference and Repetition*, 165.

60 Thoburn, *Deleuze, Marx and Politics*.

61 Cohen, "Punks, Bulldaggers, and Welfare Queens," 438.

62 See Sandoval, *Methodology of the Oppressed*; and L. T. Smith, *Decolonizing Methodologies*. In addition, queer method has developed as a discourse. See Brim and Ghaziani, "Introduction: Queer Methods." Further, many have focused on surface reading and surfeit details to articulate approaches to objects that move beyond a consideration of the solidified subject. I attend to these discussions not to resolve them but rather to highlight an underlying question of *how*, precisely, we focus on surface (Best and Marcus, "Surface Reading"; A. Cheng, *Second Skin*; Love, "Close but Not Deep").

63 Erin Manning has theorized the minor gesture to work against method, whereby method, according to Manning, limits thought and experimentation. For her, method precludes the possibility of expanding what we consider to be materialist. After all, she is justifiably critical of masculinist and Cartesian inflections that situate method as a set of reliable rules, which renders certain things over others as minor or irrelevant. Although I agree with Manning's critique of masculinist tendencies with turns to method, I rely on hesitation as a guiding methodological approach to resist overdetermining how we order things (Manning, *Minor Gesture*, 31–32).

64 More recently, Gayatri Gopinath and Laura Harris have provided unruly and exciting methodological approaches for transnational analysis. They both offer methodological insights that reframe how we engage the global (Gopinath, *Unruly Visions*; L. Harris, *Experiments in Exile*).

Beyond the contemporary, these concerns have a longer history surrounding method and materiality, particularly in relation to poststructuralism. Some of the earliest engagements with poststructuralism demanded that minor subjects not be simply enfolded into its analytics. Abdul R. JanMohamed and David Lloyd's 1987 special issue of *Cultural Critique* on "Minority Discourse" began to work through such limits around poststructuralist methods. The authors discuss a reviewer for their special issue that argued for the need to contend with individual racial groups rather than placing them together and in relation to one another. Lloyd and JanMohamed, however, sought to contend with the import of relationality and the insights provided by multiple minoritarian groups. They did so by connecting poststructuralism to a relational project (JanMohamed and Lloyd, *Nature and Context of Minority Discourse*). This mediation of poststructuralism pushed minoritarian studies beyond the logic of inclusion by analyzing what maintains minoritization. This brief return to poststructuralism is meant to place our contemporary concerns alongside earlier mediations of method.

In addition, Hortense Spillers reminds us that method and formalism are not deracinated analytics. Rather, such analytics require and are made better by a "critic's whole consciousness," and a "specific concentration," a minoritarian ends (Spillers, *Black, White, and in Color*, 85).

65 K. Chen, *Asia as Method*, 212.

66 K. Chen, *Asia as Method*, 212.

67 Within literary studies, new formalism has been contending with such concerns. See Felski, *Limits of Critique*; Kornbluh, *Order of Forms*; and Levine, *Forms*. Beyond literary theory, a special journal issue on queer form deeply informs my concerns (Amin, Musser, and Pérez, "Queer Form").

Chapter 1. We're Going to Party Like It's 1989

1 Stein, *Geographical History of America*, 64.
2 Adam, *Dark Side of the Boom*; Horowitz, *Art of the Deal*; Schnayerson, *Boom*; Don Thompson, *$12 Million Stuffed Shark*.
3 Findlay, *Value of Art*; Thornton, *Seven Days in the Art World*.
4 Hito Steyerl's *Duty Free Art* helpfully situates the art market to global capital.
5 I offer historical background on contemporary Chinese art to revise it in both this chapter and chapter 3. In chapter 3, I discuss how curators Liu Ding, Carol Yinghua Lu, and Su Wei differently approach and revise this history. Curation is a critical mechanism by which to understand how the proper and China intersect; these curators use the minorness of affect to curate the history of Chinese art beyond the notions of import, value, and teleology.
6 In addition to the historicization of the culture wars, the art historical accounts of the global art market place art production in relation to capitalism. Isabelle Graw and Titia Hulst offer a broad overview of the global art market. See Grew, *High Price*; and Hulst, *History of the Western Art Market*. Further, it is the larger ethnographic and sociological turns toward the art world that have provided a trenchant grounding on the context of neoliberalism and financialization that informs the global art market. Nestor Canclini and Matti Bunzl direct us toward the corporatized logics of museums and the art world. The shifts in financialization highlight the growth of the art market for which China plays a crucial role in these multiple sectors. See Bunzl, *In Search of a Lost Avant-Garde*; and Canclini, *Art beyond Itself*. Further, for Marxist analyses of such shifts, see Stallabrass, *Art Incorporated*; Paul Werner, *Museum, Inc.: Inside the Global Art World*; and Wu, *Privatising Culture*.
7 This chapter follows Michael Dutton who offers a helpful method by deploying affect to understand an event like the Cultural Revolution (Dutton, "Cultural Revolution as Method").
8 Some have debated over the historicization of the category of contemporary art from marking years like 1945, 1960, and 1989. See T. Smith, *What Is Contemporary Art?*
9 Weheliye, *Habeas Viscus*, 31. I return to a discussion of minor subjects as ontological absolutes in chapter 3, as the concept relates to work by Yan Xing and notions of diaspora.
10 Scott Reyburn, "The Biggest-Selling Artist at Auction Is a Name You May Not Know," *New York Times*, June 2, 2017, https://www.nytimes.com/2017/06/02/arts/china-art-auction-zhang-daqian.html.
11 One of my anonymous reviewers was helpful in directing me to the overlap between the art market and film industry. And although this book does not focus on the film industry or journalism, I mark these parallels to better understand the

overlap of the art market with other aesthetic practices and industries. Chinese film studies has an established discourse. For some key texts that inform my approach, see W. Bao, *Fiery Cinema*; Chow, *Primitive Passions*; Dai, *Cinema and Desire*; Ma, *Melancholy Drift*; McGrath, *Postsocialist Modernity*.

12 Karl, *Magic of Concepts*, 25.

13 Ferguson, *Reorder of Things*; and Povinelli, *Economies of Abandonment*.

14 Ferguson, *Reorder of Things*, 192.

15 Rancière, *Short Voyages to the Land of the People*, 2. The original version was published in French in 1990.

16 The Frankfurt School is a clear precursor to aesthetics and politics discourse; however, I focus this chapter on Rancière since his theories animate many contemporary debates. Further, Maoism and the Cultural Revolution are important events that inform Rancière's famous break from Althusser.

17 In this chapter, I conflate culture, art, and aesthetics for purposes of this argument surrounding the proper. In my teaching, I emphasize the need to conceptualize each of these terms differently, and I certainly find value in understanding and tracing the unique genealogies surrounding each idea. However, I place culture, art, and aesthetics under a similar rubric here so as to produce my argument around the proper and emphasize how although each might differ in definition, they are often discussed as having agency to contribute to and shape the political. I could theorize the aesthetic as distinct from proper and dominant formulations of culture. However, such a move merely replicates the enshrinement of the aesthetic. I thus use these terms together in order to show a larger, late liberal trend that continually depicts culture, art, and aesthetics as possibility and significant for the political. This is further theorized at the end of this chapter, particularly as it relates to Rancière's oft-cited discourse on aesthetics and politics.

18 Chiu and Zheng, *Art and China's Revolution*; P. Clark, *Chinese Cultural Revolution*.

19 Gao Minglu, *Total Modernity*; Wu Hung, *Exhibiting Experimental Art in China*.

20 See J. Clark, *Chinese Art at the End of the Millennium*; Debevoise, *Between State and Market*; and Gladston, *"Avant-Garde" Art Groups in China*.

21 Of note, recent books shift away from major narratives surrounding contemporary Chinese art, opening up space to consider the works in relation to a larger project surrounding theory. See Heinrich, *Chinese Surplus*; Welland, *Experimental Beijing*; and Wong, *Van Gogh on Demand*.

22 Most collections begin with a history of China after the Cultural Revolution and then open up into discussions over globalization and circulation. See Chiu and Genocchio, *Contemporary Art in Asia*; Gao Minglu, *Total Modernity*; and Wu Hung, *Contemporary Chinese Art*.

23 Hou Hanru, "Entropy, Chinese Artists," 61.

24 Hou Hanru, "Entropy, Chinese Artists," 61.

25 Holland Carter, "The Brave New Face of Art from the East," *New York Times*, September 29, 1996.

26 Desai, *Asian Art in the Twenty-First Century*.

27 Gao Minglu, *Total Modernity*, 6.

28 *Magiciens de la Terre* also had its share of controversy. Most notably, there was a special issue of *Third Text* following the exhibit that heavily critiqued the show. More recently, in 2014, the Asian Art Archive in New York held an event which revisited the construction and controversy surrounding the show, particularly in relation to Chinese artists.

29 Wang Youshen, Wang Guangyi, Xu Bing, Fang Lijun, Li Xianting, Feng Mengbo, Wu Shanzhuan, Geng Jianyi, and Liao Wen were initially a part of Venice.

30 For a thorough overview of many of these shows, see Erickson, "Reception in the West."

31 Ferguson, *Reorder of Things*, 24. See also Ahmed, *On Being Included*.

32 J. Harris, *Global Contemporary Art World*; Horowitz, *Art of the Deal*; and Zarobell, *Art and the Global Economy*.

33 Povinelli, *Economies of Abandonment*, 26.

34 Harootunian, "Postcoloniality's Unconscious."

35 Chuh and Shimakawa, *Orientations*.

36 Arondekar and Patel, "Introduction: Area Impossible."

37 Ferguson, *Reorder of Things*, 36–37.

38 Shohat, *Taboo Memories, Diasporic Voices*, 2.

39 Jean-Hubert Martin, *Magiciens de la Terre*, 8. Translation mine: "Pourtant, de l'idée d'une enquête sur la création dans le monde aujourd'hui, on pouvait imaginer de n'exposer que des auteurs non occidentaux, sachant que l'existence de l'art dans nos centres ne fait pas de doute. C'était persister à mettre des créateurs dans un ghetto, dans une catégorie ethnographique de survivance archaïque issue des expositions coloniales, alors qu'il importe d'affirmer leur existence dans le présent."

40 Martin, *Magiciens de la Terre*, 8–9. Translation mine: "Tous ces object, d'ici ou d'ailleurs, ont en commun d'avoir une aura. . . . C'est par le mot de 'magie' que l'on qualifie communément l'influence vive et inexplicable qu'exerce l'art."

41 Onians, "World Art Studies."

42 Povinelli, *Economies of Abandonment*, 26.

43 Hunter, *Culture Wars*, 42. See also A. Hartman, *War for the Soul of America*; and Rodgers, *Age of Fracture*.

44 Osborne, *Anywhere or Not at All*, 8.

45 For an overview of China's relation to arts and politics, particularly around figures like Lu Xun to Mao Zedong, see Liu Kang, *Aesthetics and Marxism*.

46 Rancière's framing of the sensible has become so central that *Artforum* dedicated an entire issue in 2007 to his work. It is important to historicize Rancière's work as it relates to the Frankfurt School, since someone like Adorno is a key interlocutor to discourses on aesthetics and politics. I do not delve into the Frankfurt School in this book; however, I find this an important area in which to more expansively consider how discourse on aesthetics and politics has shifted.

47 Rancière, *Politics of Aesthetics*, 40.

48 Rancière, *Politics of Aesthetics*, 13.

49 Erickson, "Rent Collection Copyright Breached Overseas," 55.

50 Adrian Searle, "Dearth in Venice: The Gory Chinese Influx Makes a Refreshing Change," *Guardian*, June 15, 1999; Carol Vogel, "At the Venice Biennale, Art Is Turning into an Interactive Sport," *New York Times*, June 14, 1999.

51 Cai Guo-Qiang, "Wenhau zhijan de yaobai," 6.

52 "Boris Groys and Cai Guo-Qiang: A Conversation from a Studio Visit," *e-flux*, February 9, 2017, https://conversations.e-flux.com/t/boris-groys-and-cai-guo -qiang-a-conversation-from-a-studio-visit/7625.

53 This chapter has been gesturing toward the need to return to earlier discourses surrounding causality and Marxism. These earlier debates could be revisited through a deeper attunement to the global and racial so as to further what I have offered here.

54 Dutton, "Fragments of the Political," 134.

Chapter 2. All Look Same

1 Lorde, "Uses of Anger," 124.

2 Laruelle, *General Theory of Victims*, 3.

3 Mill, "On Liberty," 8.

4 Jed Perl, "Ai Weiwei: Wonderful Dissident, Terrible Artist," *New Republic*, February 1, 2013; Roberta Smith, "A Provocateur's Medium: Outrage," *New York Times*, April 17, 2014.

5 Mark Stevens, "Is Ai Weiwei China's Most Dangerous Man?," *Smithsonian Magazine*, September 2012, accessed April 21, 2014, http://www.smithsonianmag.com /arts-culture/is-ai-weiwei-chinas-most-dangerous-man-17989316/?no-ist.

6 In stating this, I do not seek to perform an act of racial liberalism that obscures the uneven ways in which different races experience dehumanization. Being understood as "all look same" does not equally manifest or translate for racialized subjects, since anti-Asian sentiments are not the same as anti-Blackness, for instance. Further, my use of the notion of racial anger certainly has ramifications when understood particularly in relation to Black women. I unpack this dynamic later in this chapter and return to racial liberalism in chapter 5.

7 Buergel, "Leitmotifs."

8 Buergel, "Leitmotifs."

9 Buergel, "Leitmotifs."

10 Press release from *documenta* 12, 2007, https://www.documenta12.de/fileadmin /Ivekovic_11.7/070711_PMAIvekovic_form_en.pdf (last accessed June 30, 2020).

11 Hayward Gallery, "Art of Change."

12 Ai Weiwei, "China's Art World Does Not Exist," *Guardian*, September 10, 2012, http://www.theguardian.com/artanddesign/2012/sep/10/ai-weiwei-china-art -world.

13 Ai Weiwei, "China's Art World Does Not Exist."

14 Ai Weiwei, "China's Art World Does Not Exist."

15 Sorace, "China's Last Communist," 401.

16 P. Liu, *Queer Marxism in Two Chinas*, 7, emphasis added.

17 P. Liu, *Queer Marxism in Two Chinas*, 168.

18 The use of this identity-based term, *tongzhi*—which is a disidentification and redeployment of its use, as the history surrounding the US identity of queer inhabits—also represents a reclaiming of a socialist word to advance a teleological narrative of development away from socialism toward neoliberalism, as Lisa Rofel has trenchantly established. Media theorist Hongwei Bao theorizes the queer comrade as a figure that mediates not only neoliberalism but also socialist legacies. See H. Bao, "Queer Comrades"; and Rofel, *Desiring China*.

19 Lowe, "Metaphors of Globalization and Dilemmas of Excess," 28, emphasis added.

20 Lowe, "Metaphors of Globalization and Dilemmas of Excess," 38.

21 M. Cheng, *In Other Los Angeleses*, 5.

22 M. Cheng, *Beijing Xingwei*, 72.

23 Nancy, *Being Singular Plural*, 62.

24 Nancy, *Being Singular Plural*, xiii.

25 For a productive use of intersubjectivity, see Cartwright, *Moral Spectatorship*. In addition, Maurice Merleau-Ponty's notion of intersubjectivity was crucial for his political philosophy as it critiqued liberalism and explored Marxism (Merleau-Ponty, *Adventures of the Dialectic*). For critiques of the notion of community, see Joseph, *Against the Romance of Community*; and Young and Allen, *Justice and the Politics of Difference*.

26 Nancy, *Inoperative Community*.

27 The film does not provide the farmer's name.

28 Hardt and Negri, *Multitude*.

29 Laruelle, *General Theory of Victims*.

30 Esposito, *Third Person*.

31 Marx and Engels, "Manifesto of the Communist Party," 482.

32 Hardt and Negri, *Multitude*, xv.

33 And for a rethinking of the commons with regard to Hardt and Negri, see theorizations of the undercommons (Harney and Moten, *Undercommons*).

34 Hardt and Negri, *Multitude*, 373n2.

35 Hardt and Negri, *Multitude*, 101; emphasis added.

36 Lorde, "Master's Tools," 111.

37 Racial anger resembles *ressentiment* insofar as they are both negative affects. However, unlike ressentiment, racial anger emerges from long spans of structural violence that make it difficult to fully locate the immediate source of violence. In this way, racial anger operates differently from Wendy Brown's notion of wounded attachments and identity politics as ressentiment. There is no fully defined target for racial anger, which means that it lingers due to the fact that it arises from repeated forms of historical dispossession across long arcs of space and time. Brown, *States of Injury*. For additional approaches to racial anger, see Kim, *On Anger*; and Deborah Thompson, "Exoneration of Black Rage."

38 D. Scott, *Conscripts of Modernity: the Tragedy of Colonial Enlightenment*.

39 S. Hartman, *Scenes of Subjection*, 77.

40 Byrd, "Loving Unbecoming," 211.

41 Yoneyama, *Cold War Ruins*, 11; Derrida, *On Cosmopolitanism and Forgiveness*, 42.

42 Lorde, "Uses of Anger," 131.

43 Alexander, Pedagogies of Crossing, 16.

44 Thoburn, *Deleuze, Marx and Politics*, 48.

45 Thoburn, *Deleuze, Marx and Politics*, 49; emphasis added.

Chapter 3. Minoring the Universal

A portion of the chapter was previously published as "Beyond Minor Subjects: Anti-Oedipus, Affect, and Becoming in Yan Xing's *Kill the TV Set*," *Verge: Studies in Global Asias* 5, no. 1 (2019): 153–81.

1 Eng, Ruskola, and Shen, "Introduction: China and the Human," 5.

2 The debates surrounding the universal and particular have manifested in a variety of ways and throughout many disciplines. In addition, each nation certainly has its respective mediations across universality and particularity: China's historical status as the West's dialectical other resonates differently than Taiwan's relationship to Japanese colonization.

3 See Chakrabarty, *Provincializing Europe*, 5; and Wang Hui, *Politics of Imagining Asia*, 57–58.

4 In this book and chapter, I focus more on Deleuze and Guattari as they relate to field formations pertaining to area, ethnic, and queer studies. These figures, however, play different roles for specific media. Deleuze's books on cinema are central to film studies. However, these figures are less central to a field like performance and dance studies (with the exception of the work of André Lepecki) and occupy varied relations within art history. I highlight these medium-specific approaches with regard to these figures because I do not fully engage this in this chapter.

5 Wang Hui, *Politics of Imagining Asia*, 57.

6 Within the art market, the most discussed Chinese artists have been heterosexual cis-men. In addition to Yan, artists like Fen Ma and Han Bing have dealt with constructions of the effeminate Asian body.

7 Edward Sanderson, "Fantastic Five," *ArtSlant*, September 25, 2011, http://www.artslant.com/cn/articles/show/28128.

8 Deleuze and Guattari, *Anti-Oedipus*.

9 Jasbir Puar's *Terrorist Assemblages* has been critical for situating Deleuze and Guattari within ethnic studies, area studies, and transnational feminisms. Assemblages are the key analytic she draws from *A Thousand Plateaus* to understand bodies and nation-states in unstable forms. I have deployed another concept and text from Deleuze and Guattari to examine the possibilities of the molecular and fuzziness, along with the negotiation of the transnational and affective. *A Thousand Plateaus* (1980) came after *Anti-Oedipus* (1972), remedying some of the binaries produced within *Anti-Oedipus*. However, I rely on the anti-Oedipal to offer another possibility beyond the frame of assemblage, as *Anti-Oedipus* focuses on the influence of global manifestations of colonial power in accounting for the transnational.

10 Freud's schema involves the formation of a "normative" self. For Freud, a son's development involves the desire for the mother and patricide. I do not ignore Freud's

misogyny. As Wendy Brown and David Eng have revealed, his theories must be tempered to produce critical insights. In addition, the Oedipal complex, particularly within the French academy, became a dominant framing against which Deleuze and Guattari were attempting to work.

11 Deleuze and Guattari, *Kafka*, 10.

12 Deleuze and Guattari, *Kafka*, 10.

13 Deleuze and Guattari, *Anti-Oedipus*, 169.

14 Program and poster for Nam June Paik's *Opera Sextronique* (1967) in the Peter Wenzel Collection, Germany.

15 Schneider, *Performing Remains*, 148.

16 Deleuze and Guattari, *A Thousand Plateaus*, 469–70.

17 Deleuze and Guattari, *Anti-Oedipus*, 54.

18 Chun, "Fuck Chineseness."

19 Schneider, *Performing Remains*, 180.

20 Deleuze and Guattari "brin[g] into play processes of temporalization, fragmented formations, and detached parts, with a surplus of value code, and where the whole is itself produced alongside the parts, as a part apart or, as Butler would say, 'in another department' that fits the whole over the other parts." Deleuze and Guattari, *Anti-Oedipus*, 286–87.

21 Deleuze and Guattari, *Anti-Oedipus*, 352.

22 Deleuze and Guattari, *Thousand Plateaus*, 469.

23 Berlant, *Cruel Optimism*.

24 For a discussion of my concept of becoming China, see the introduction.

25 On queer diaspora, see Eng, *Feeling of Kinship*; and Gopinath, *Impossible Desires*. On minor transnationalism, see Shih and Lionnet, *Minor Transnationalism*.

26 Shih and Lionnet use minor transnationalism to replace particularist tendencies: "The postnational assumes that nations have discreet boundaries in order to go beyond them, but our conception of minor transnationalism takes as its point of departure Edouard Glissant's theories of relation" (Shih and Lionnet, *Minor Transnationalism*, 8).

27 Deleuze and Guattari situate the notion of becoming to becoming animal. Although the links between animalization and racialization, particularly in relation to the Chinese imagined as dogeaters, exist, becoming China does not occlude such an exploration but understands how China becomes in relation to such racist images. Rather than discarding the notion of becoming due to its neglect of the relationships between animalization and racialization, I push the theoretical exploration of becoming to enhance its methodological possibilities.

28 Asian aesthetics are often connected to slowness. For example, Butoh and Noh are Japanese performance practices that have come to represent a pan-Asian aesthetics of long duration. Further, Asian film directors have come to be known for producing a slow aesthetic (S. Lim, *Tsai Ming-Liang*).

29 See the introduction for a discussion of these fields.

30 Weheliye, *Habeas Viscus*, 31.

31 Weheliye, *Habeas Viscus*; emphasis added.

32 Weheliye, *Habeas Viscus*; emphasis added.

33 This is larger project that Sylvia Wynter and others have articulated. It is a trenchant one that relies on a centralized focus on racialization, specifically Blackness, as it relates to the production of our modern world (Wynter, "Unsettling the Coloniality of Being/Power/Truth/Freedom"). See also Z. Jackson, *Becoming Human*.

34 Wallerstein, *Modern World-System*.

35 Black studies' reliance on diaspora has its own unique history, which I do not fully account for in this chapter. See chapter 5.

36 Dirlik, *Culture and History in Postrevolutionary China*.

37 Dirlik, *Culture and History in Postrevolutionary China*, 14.

38 Chakrabarty, *Provincializing Europe*.

39 Liu Ding, Carol Yinghua Lu, and Su Wei, *7th Shenzhen Sculpture Biennial*, 277.

40 Martin, *Magiciens de la Terre*, 145. Translation mine: "Pour lui, l'activité artistique est un moyen radical pour libérer la sensualité et l'instinct. C'est aussi un manière d'approcher la vérité intellectuelle."

41 Jean-Hubert, *Magiciens de la Terre*, 12–13. Translation mine: "Est-ce que le decor fait le mur?"

42 Liu Ding, Carol Yinghua Lu, and Su Wei, *7th Shenzhen Sculpture Biennial*, 67.

43 Liu Ding, Carol Yinghua Lu, and Su Wei, *7th Shenzhen Sculpture Biennial*, 67.

44 Liu Ding, Carol Yinghua Lu, and Su Wei, *7th Shenzhen Sculpture Biennial*, 67.

45 Berlant, *Cruel Optimism*, 53.

46 Berlant, *Cruel Optimism*, 64.

47 Rogoff, "Looking Away."

48 Lance Wang, "Wang Guangyi's 'Little Movements'?—On the Origins and Nature of the Zhuhai Symposium," LEAP, February 7, 2012, http://leapleapleap .com/2012/02/wang-guangyi%E2%80%99s-%E2%80%9Clittle-movements -%E2%80%9D%E2%80%94-on-the-origins-and-nature-of-th-e-zhuhai -symposium/.

49 Buck-Morss, *Hegel, Haiti, and Universal History*, 133.

50 Buck-Morss, *Hegel, Haiti, and Universal History*, 133.

51 Buck-Morss, *Hegel, Haiti, and Universal History*, 133–34.

52 I develop the notion of expiration for relationality in an essay on media, women of color, and the 1990s [Yapp, "Feeling Down(town Julie Brown)"].

Chapter 4. Minor Agencies

A portion of the chapter was previously published as "Chinese Lingering, Meditation's Practice: Reframing Endurance Art," *Women and Performance* 24, nos. 2–3 (2015): 1–18.

1 I develop this concept further in relation to the artist Julie Tolentino (Yapp, "To Punk, Yield, and Flail").

2 Thomas Friedman, "From Gunpowder to the Next Big Bang," *New York Times*, November 4, 2005.

3 Bogost, "Gamification Is Bullshit"; Galloway, *Gaming*, 12; Jagoda, "Gamification and Other Forms of Play."

4   The role of gendered relations is important within this nexus of post-Fordism, affect, and the imagination. See Weeks, *Problem with Work*.

5   The popular press has focused on the increased matriculation of Chinese students to US universities. See Emily Eakin, "Writing as a Block for Asians," *New York Times*, May 3, 2003; Friedman, "From Gunpowder to the Next Big Bang"; and Yang Jiadai, "Chinese Schools 'Kill Imagination,'" trans. Luisetta Mudie, *Radio Free Asia*, August 18, 2009.

6   Discourses surrounding China and creative capital have arisen ("China, in Search of Imagination," *New York Times*, November 26, 2006; Richard Florida, Charlotta Melander, and Haifeng Qian, "Creative China? The University, Human Capital, and the Creative Class in Chinese Regional Development," Martin Prosperity Institute website, 2008, last accessed April 30, 2013, http://martinprosperity.org/media/creative_china_october_2008.pdf).

7   Joan Kee helpfully expands understandings of *12m²* through intellectual property. She, in turn, complicates how this piece has come to be documented and highlights the tensions around authorship with regard to Rong Rong's photography and Zhang Huan's performance (Kee, "Property of Contemporary Chinese Art").

8   See Berghuis, *Performance Art in China*; and Wu Hung, *Transience*, 107.

9   In classic Marxist terms, the imagination is one's agency to gain consciousness of class alienation. In the first preface of *A Contribution to the Critique of Political Economy*, Marx famously states, "It is not the consciousness of men that determines their being, but, on the contrary, their social being that determines their consciousness" (Marx, *Contribution to the Critique of Political Economy*, 9). In Marx's formulation, one's consciousness is formulated by one's social situation. In other words, Marx relates the conscious mind to one's being, where one obtains class consciousness through one's alienation and experience. Thus, consciousness becomes the vehicle to become aware of class dynamics.

10 Ricoeur, *Freud and Philosophy*, 34.

11 Chow, "Elusive Material," 223.

12 Chow, "Elusive Material," 224.

13 Bennett, *Vibrant Matter*, xv.

14 Frankfurt School scholars utilized ideology as a method, where they juxtaposed ideological assumptions with material realities. Herbert Marcuse understands the imagination and mind as consciousness: "Art cannot change the world, but it can contribute to changing the consciousness and drives of the men and women who could change the world" (Marcuse, *Aesthetic Dimension*, 5). Marcuse places art at the center of demystification, not in its ability to create material change but to make one conscious and aware of power. Thus, art's potential exists in the sphere of consciousness. This consciousness is the key for demystification in that consciousness drives and directs action/agency: "The need for radical change must be rooted in the subjectivity of individuals themselves, in their intelligence and their passions, their drives and their goals" (3–4).

15 Brecht, "Alienation Effects in Chinese Acting," 95.

16 Brecht, "Alienation Effects in Chinese Acting," 93.

17 Brecht, "Alienation Effects in Chinese Acting," 94.

18 Brecht, "Alienation Effects in Chinese Acting," 95.

19 Haiping Yan and Rey Chow have provided helpful ways to complicate Brecht's relationship to China. Of note is Rey Chow's approach to Brecht. Although I do not fully engage her ideas in this chapter, Chow points to the predominance of Brecht's theoretical and aesthetic approach to theory today. See Chow, *Entanglements*; and Yang, "Theatricality in Classical Chinese Drama." Chinese theater studies scholars Claire Conceison and Rossella Ferrari draw from a Brechtian genealogy for their work on Chinese theater. Both theorists attribute the "avant-garde" goals of the Chinese directors they theorize to a Brechtian aesthetic system. These authors' projects do not question Brecht's theoretical and aesthetic assumptions surrounding the formula of demystification translating into performed action (Conceison, *Significant Other*; Ferrari, *Pop Goes the Avant Garde*).

20 For details on Butler's theory of performativity and Muñoz's notion of disidentification, see Butler, *Bodies That Matter*; S. Jackson, *Professing Performance*, 185–92; and Muñoz, *Disidentifications*.

21 S. Jackson, *Professing Performance*, 191.

22 Although Western art has certainly been placed within paradigms of resistance, I argue, similar to Rasheed Araeen, that Western artists are generally afforded more space to be included in discourses beyond resistance, such as form, affect, and modernism. Araeen, the founder of the art journal *Third Text*, acknowledges the differences in the availability of discursive frameworks due to the fact that the "agencies of white and non-white artists have been historically formulated and formed differently and oppositely by the dominant culture" (Araeen, "New Beginning," 19).

23 M. Chen, *Animacies*; M. Chen, "Brain Fog"; Lewis, "Mad Fight"; Puar, "Prognosis Time."

24 See Berghuis, *Performance Art in China*; Gao Minglu, *Total Modernity*; Alexa Oleson, "Art/Architecture; Making Art of Masochism and Tests of Endurance," *New York Times*, November 11, 2001; and Wu Hung, *Transience*, 107.

25 Wu Hung, *Transience*, 107.

26 During the emergence of discourses about contemporary Chinese art, Chinese scholars emphasized context in order to counteract previously overuniversalized discourses about the emerging art practices in China following the Cultural Revolution. See the introduction for a full overview of this dynamic as it relates to the force of law.

27 Zhang Huan has increasingly referenced Buddhism in his later works during the early twenty-first century, such as *Dharma Circle* (2004) and *Berlin Buddha* (2007). To discuss *12m²* (1994) in relation to Buddhism is not meant to show how Buddhism has been a concern for Zhang Huan since early in his career. Similarly, He Chengyao has referenced Buddhism in some of her latter works and in addition to her performance practice, although she has not spoken explicitly about it with regard to *99 Needles*.

28 Eve Sedgwick also explores the possibilities of meditation in relation to critical theory. Although this chapter will not discuss Sedgwick's insights, they have shaped and informed this analysis. See Sedgwick, *Weather in Proust*.

29 Alexander, *Pedagogies of Crossing*, 293.

30 Wilber, "Foreword," xi.

31 Foucault, *Technologies of the Self*, 27.

32 Foucault, *Technologies of the Self*, 145.

33 Foucault, *Technologies of the Self*, 18.

34 Foucault, *Technologies of the Self*, 36, 37.

35 Foucault, *Technologies of the Self*, 25.

36 Foucault, *Technologies of the Self*, 25.

37 Roshi, "Zazen Meditation in Japanese Rinzai Zen," 12. In addition, queer and performance studies' theorizations around time resonate with Buddhist understandings of temporality, as these distinct fields inform my overall analysis (Freeman, *Time Binds*; Halberstam, *In a Queer Time and Place*; Nyong'o, *Amalgamation Waltz*; Schneider, *Performing Remains*).

38 Although feminist performance artists have gained critical attention, they were critiquing and reacting against masculinist norms. See Schneider, *Explicit Body in Performance*.

39 Heatwole, "Media of Now," 14.

40 Although endurance art typically connotes a sense of resisting and working through extreme bodily pain, I relate endurance to durational and time-based art as all three rely upon a similar sense of teleology. Durational and time-based art may not necessarily require pain; however, the temporal models in which they exist are similar to endurance.

41 See Anderson, *So Much Wasted*; and Schneider, *Explicit Body in Performance*.

42 Huan, "12 Square Meters," 214.

43 *Oxford English Dictionary*, s.v. "endure," accessed June 18, 2014, https://www.lexico.com/definition/endure; *Oxford English Dictionary*, s.v. "linger," accessed June 18, 2014, https://www.lexico.com/en/definition/linger.

44 Bergson, *Creative Mind*, 191.

45 Bergson, *Creative Mind*, 12.

46 Bergson, *Creative Mind*, 194.

47 Spivak, "Can the Subaltern Speak?," 93.

48 Berry, *History of Pain*; Kleinman and Kleinman, "How Bodies Remember"; Plankers, "Psychic Impact and Outcome"; Tonglin Lu, "Fantasy and Ideology in a Chinese Film."

49 Siebers, *Disability Aesthetics*, 115.

50 M. Nguyen, *Gift of Freedom*, 60.

51 M. Nguyen, *Gift of Freedom*, 57.

52 Klein, *Meeting the Great Bliss Queen*, 67.

53 Klein, *Meeting the Great Bliss Queen*, 68–69.

54 *Meditation* can be differentiated from the adjective *meditative*, as the former implies a mode of being while the latter implicates a state. Meditation as a mode

is what allows lingering to occur; meditative action can occur in either the acts of lingering or enduring. I utilize the adjective *meditative* here to refer to meditation practices.

55 Alexander, *Pedagogies of Crossing*, 309.

56 Man, "Expression Extreme," 175, 177.

57 Caruth, *Unclaimed Experience*; Felman, *Juridical Unconscious*.

58 Rothberg, "Decolonizing Trauma Studies."

59 Nanming Wang, "Curator's Statement for *Pain in Soul: Performance Art and Video: Works by He Chengyao*," Shanghai Zendai Museum of Modern Art, 2007, accessed June 20, 2020, http://www.aaa.org.hk/WorldEvents/Details/8726. Wang also discusses He's work in a recent anthology: Wang, "Art in Its Regional Political Context."

60 A. Cheng, *Melancholy of Race*, xi.

61 Ngai, *Ugly Feelings*, 187.

62 Ngai, *Ugly Feelings*, 188.

63 Cao Fei, interviewed by Oyama Hitomi, "A Bridge between Art and Pop Culture: That What I Want to Be," *ARTiT*, 2009, accessed May 6, 2016, http://art-it.asia/u/admin_interviews/ynp3HLEuY6UWvhZtz4XI/.

64 Kovskaya, "Heroes of the Mundane."

65 Kovskaya, "Heroes of the Mundane," 85.

66 Rey Chow uses the notion in *Sentimental Fabulations*, a series of essays about contemporary Chinese film. She primarily relies on Nietzsche's notion of fables as world making and Deleuze's use of fabulation as part of minority literature where fabulation is the "constitution of a people. . . . A people, in a way, is what's missing." Deleuze builds this concept from Bergson's use of fabulation while also attempting to give "political meaning" to Bergson's work (Deleuze, *Negotiations*, 124–25, 174). See also S. Hartman, "Venus in Two Acts"; and Nyong'o, *Afro-Fabulations*.

67 Hastings and Manning, "Introduction: Acts of Alterity." Teri Silvio references and uses this idea of alterity in Silvio, "Animation."

68 Silvio, "Animation," 427.

69 Adorno, *Notes to Literature*, 248; emphasis mine.

70 Ngai, "Cuteness of the Avant-Garde," 812.

71 Ngai, "Cuteness of the Avant-Garde," 838.

72 Benjamin, "Critique of Violence."

Chapter 5. *Tout-Monde* and the Minor

Epigraphs: Mbembe, *Critique of Black Reason*, 179; K. Chen, *Asia as Method*, 70; Glissant, *Poetics of Relation*, 18.

1 See also Silva, *Toward a Global Idea of Race*. By invoking Blackness, I grapple more broadly with the ways indentured and migrant labor and transatlantic slavery emerge with and through the production of Latinidad and whiteness, as they are imbricated with indigenous genocide and settler colonialism. Of course, China played a role in these earlier forms of the world. However, China's contemporary import, alongside considerations of Blackness, illuminates a sense of the larger

world and its production through both early and late capital and modernity and beyond. Further, the monad (which I discuss later in this chapter) offers a method that highlights how a smaller part can illuminate larger issues when understood in series. Thus, the focus on China, I hope, does not foreclose the need to contend more broadly with racialization across multiple populations, histories, and spaces.

2   For a more thorough understanding of flesh, see Musser, *Sensational Flesh*; Spillers, "Mama's Baby, Papa's Maybe"; and Weheliye, *Habeas Viscus*. I use Anne Cheng's term *yellow woman*. She inquires how this figure produces important insights into racialized, gendered, and sexualized objecthood, specifically as this figure relates to theories of flesh (A. Cheng, *Ornamentalism*).

3   As such, this chapter does not assess if Julien is Orientalist or not. For such an engagement, see Yingjin Zhang, "Ways of Seeing China."

4   I further develop some of my insights from chapter 2 here. As I do in chapter 2, I draw from David Scott for my use of tragedy in relation to modernity (D. Scott, *Conscripts of Modernity*).

5   In invoking the notions of world and totality, I am informed by but do not directly engage the thriving discourse on world literature and the production of globality. I find that both Julien's art and Glissant's tout-monde require that I focus less on the production of the concept of the world and more on clarifying what fragments and fractures provide for our sense of the world. For a general understanding of the concept of world literature, see Allan, *In the Shadows of World Literature*; Apter, *Against World Literature*; Cheah, *What Is a World?*; Hayot, *On Literary Worlds*; and Mufti, *Forget English!*

6   Jay, *Marxism and Totality*, 515.

7   Benjamin, "On the Concept of History."

8   For liberal democrats, Enlightenment narratives of modernization inform the notion of progress. For Marxists, proletarian revolution pushes forward the teleological formation of history that leads to the replacement of capitalism, particularly in light of the shifts from socialism to fascism that were occurring during Benjamin's time. These liberal and vulgar Marxist narratives of progress overlap because they both obscure the disasters that have emerged in their respective wakes. Benjamin thus has a melancholic relationship to political movements, particularly Marxism, due to the fact that progress leads to devastation—and, in his case, to the rise of fascism. For a more thorough engagement with this, see Löwy, *Fire Alarm*.

9   Richter, *Thought Images*, 2.

10 Richter, *Thought Images*, 2.

11 Benjamin, "On the Concept of History," 392; emphasis in original.

12 Benjamin, *Arcades Project*, 461.

13 Deleuze, *Fold*, 25; emphasis mine.

14 Metzger, "Seascape."

15 Cho, "Asian Canadian Futures."

16 Tinker, *New System of Slavery*.

17 Baucom, *Specters of the Atlantic*, 139.

18 Sharpe, *In the Wake*.

19 Cosmopolitanism describes a view of the world in which certain class distinctions inform one's circulation in the world. Circulation across multiple cities becomes a key component of an elite global class. The concept has, of course, been rethought to account for questions around class and migration patterns produced by warfare and labor demands. As such, Julien could be understood within this frame. However, I understand Julien as operating in ways similar to Jacques Derrida's theorizations on cosmopolitanism. Derrida shifts away from a reliance on the city and nation-form as providing the means for relief from mass circulation due to refugee crises. He locates the violence inherent in spaces of refuge. Julien operates similarly to Derrida's work in that he points us to the limits of cosmopolitanism due to the fact that the framework often privileges the urban city as the means of possibility, when, in reality, these sites are areas of violence for many seeking refuge (Derrida, *On Cosmopolitanism and Forgiveness*). For those who additionally contend with the classed formations of cosmopolitanism, see Bhabha, "Unsatisfied"; Cheah, *Inhuman Conditions*; Manalansan, *Global Divas*; and Sassen, *Global City*.

20 Hanneken, *Imagining the Postcolonial*, 81.

21 Glissant, *Traité du tout-monde*, 22. Translation mine: "Le Tout-Monde, qui est totalisant, n'est pas (pour nous) total."

22 Glissant, *Poetics of Relation*, 18.

23 Glissant, *Poetics of Relation*, 5–7.

24 Glissant, *Poetics of Relation*, 20.

25 Glissant, *Poetics of Relation*, 21.

26 Glissant, *Traité du tout-monde*, 24. Translation mine: "Les interrelations procèdent principalement par fractures et ruptures."

27 Metzger, "Isaac Julien's *Ten Thousand Waves*," 289.

28 Jameson, *Postmodernism*.

29 Julien, *Riot*, 216.

30 Freeman, *Time Binds*.

31 Muñoz, *Disidentifications*, xx.

32 Gonzalez, "Sea Dreams."

33 Julien, *Riot*, 175.

34 Julien, *Riot*, 144; emphasis mine.

35 Julien, "Long Road."

36 Julien, *Riot*, 193.

37 Benjamin, *Arcades Project*, 461.

38 Benjamin, *Arcades Project*, 461; emphasis mine.

39 Benjamin, *Arcades Project*, 461.

40 One of my anonymous reviewers brilliantly highlighted this distinction for me. I greatly appreciate this insight and have built upon this.

41 A. Cheng, *Ornamentalism*, 18, x.

42 A. Cheng, *Ornamentalism*, 13.

43 A. Cheng, *Ornamentalism*, 70.

44 A. Cheng, *Ornamentalism*, 73.

45 Cheng notes how Benjamin, in a 1928 interview with Wong, talks about her as a "moon," "porcelain bowl," and other objects (A. Cheng, *Ornamentalism*, 63).

46 I began an exploration of this idea in chapter 3, but I develop this larger idea in a separate essay. See Yapp, "Feeling Down(town Julie Brown)."

47 Jameson, *Brecht and Method*, 116.

48 Roach, *Cities of the Dead*. For a brilliant revision of this dominant line of performance theory, see S. Hartman, *Scenes of Subjection*.

49 Thank you to one of my readers who pointed out this critical detail regarding Maggie Cheung.

50 Glissant, *Poetics of Relation*, 20.

Afterword. For Those Minor in and to China

1 There have been helpful approaches to producing a robust theory of Marxist speech through the notion of collective voice. Some have focused on the use of the people's microphone during Occupy protests around 2011. Due to bans on microphones and audio amplification in public spaces, crowds would repeat and amplify what was said using collective voices (King, *Virtual Memory*; Richard Kim, "We Are All Human Microphones Now," *Nation Blogs*, October 3, 2011, https://www .thenation.com/article/we-are-all-human-microphones-now/). In addition, others provide insights that consider the social and economic impacts of speech that move away from individual rights, alongside histories of oppression and speech. See Dunayevskaya, *Marxism and Freedom*; Samuel Farber, "A Socialist Approach to Free Speech," *Jacobin*, February 27, 2017, https://jacobinmag.com/2017/02/garton -ash-free-speech-milo-yiannopoulos; and Luxemburg, *Russian Revolution*.

2 Alexander, *Pedagogies of Crossing*, 16.

3 Fanon, *Wretched of the Earth*; James, *Black Jacobins*; Saldaña-Portillo, *Revolutionary Imagination in the Americas*; Robinson, *Black Marxism*; Rodney, *How Europe Underdeveloped Africa*; Williams, *Capitalism and Slavery*; Wynter, "Unsettling the Coloniality of Being/Power/Truth/Freedom."

4 It is important to note that autocracy does not necessarily involve authoritarianism. The two need be separated from one another for intellectual and political clarity. Autocracy, similar to democracy, is a form of governance. We have seen how both autocracy *and* democracy can delve into authoritarianism. The year 2020 offers a glimpse into how US democracy veers in this direction. In other words, authoritarianism is not unique to autocracy; thus, autocratic governance is a critical yet untapped resource to theorize different models of speech and dissent beyond liberalism.

BIBLIOGRAPHY

Adam, Georgina. *Dark Side of the Boom*. London: Lund Humphries, 2017.

Adorno, Theodor. *Minima Moralia: Reflections from Damaged Life*. Translated by E. F. N. Jephcott. New York: Verso Books, 2006.

Adorno, Theodor. *Notes to Literature*. New York: Columbia University Press, 1992.

Ahmed, Sara. *On Being Included*. Durham, NC: Duke University Press, 2012.

Ai Weiwei. *Fairytale: Documentary*. JRP|Ringier, 2011.

Alexander, M. Jacqui. *Pedagogies of Crossing: Meditations on Feminism, Sexual Politics, Memory, and the Sacred*. Durham, NC: Duke University Press, 2006.

Allan, Michael. *In the Shadows of World Literature*. Princeton, NJ: Princeton University Press, 2016.

Allen, Jafari. "Black/Queer/Diaspora at the Current Conjuncture." *GLQ* 18, no. 2–3 (2012): 211–48.

Amin, Kadji, Amber Jamilla Musser, and Roy Pérez. "Queer Form: Aesthetics, Race, and the Violences of the Social." *ASAP* 2, no. 7 (2017): 227–39.

Anderson, Patrick. *So Much Wasted: Hunger, Performance, and the Morbidity of Resistance*. Durham, NC: Duke University Press, 2010.

Appadurai, Arjun. "Mediants, Materiality, Normativity." *Public Culture* 27, no. 2 (2015): 221–37.

Apter, Emily. *Against World Literature*. London: Verso Books, 2013.

Araeen, Rasheed. "A New Beginning: Beyond Postcolonial Cultural Theory and Identity Politics." *Third Text* 14, no. 50 (2000): 3–20.

Arondekar, Anjali, and Geeta Patel. "Introduction: Area Impossible." *GLQ* 22, no. 2 (2016): 151–71.

Arrighi, Giovanni. *Adam Smith in Beijing: Lineages of the 21st Century*. New York: Verso Books, 2009.

Austin, J. L. *How to Do Things with Words*. Cambridge, MA: Harvard University Press, 1975.

Bao, Hongwei. "Queer Comrades: Transnational Popular Culture, Queer Sociality, and Socialist Legacy." *English Language Note* 49, no. 1 (2007): 131–37.

Bao, Weihong. *Fiery Cinema: The Emergence of an Affective Medium in China, 1915–45*. Minneapolis: University of Minnesota Press, 2015.

Baucom, Ian. *Specters of the Atlantic: Finance Capital, Slavery, and the Philosophy of History*. Durham, NC: Duke University Press, 2005.

Benjamin, Walter. *The Arcades Project*. Translated by Howard Eiland and Kevin McLaughlin. Cambridge, MA: Harvard University Press, 2002.

Benjamin, Walter. "Critique of Violence." In *Walter Benjamin: Selected Writings, Vol. 1: 1913–1926*, edited by Marcus Bullock and Michael W. Jennings, 236–52. Cambridge, MA: Harvard University Press, 1996.

Benjamin, Walter. "On the Concept of History." In *Walter Benjamin: Selected Writings, Vol. 4: 1938–1940*, edited by Howard Eiland and Michael W. Jennings, 389–400. Cambridge, MA: Harvard University Press, 2006.

Benjamin, Walter. *The Work of Art in the Age of Its Technological Reproducibility, and Other Writings on Media*. Edited by Michael Jennings, Brigid Doherty, and Thomas Levin. Cambridge, MA: Belknap Press, 2008.

Bennett, Jane. *Vibrant Matter: A Political Ecology of Things*. Durham, NC: Duke University Press, 2010.

Berghuis, Thomas. *Performance Art in China*. Hong Kong: Timezone 8, 2007.

Bergson, Henri. *The Creative Mind: An Introduction to Metaphysics*. Mineola, NY: Dover Publications, 2010.

Berlant, Lauren. *Cruel Optimism*. Durham, NC: Duke University Press, 2011.

Berry, Michael. *A History of Pain: Trauma in Modern Chinese Literature and Film*. New York: Columbia University Press, 2008.

Best, Stephen, and Sharon Marcus. "Surface Reading." *Representations* 108, no. 1 (2009): 1–21.

Bhabha, Homi. "Unsatisfied: Notes on Vernacular Cosmopolitanism." In *Text and Nation*, edited by Laura Garcia-Moreno and Peter Pfeiffer, 191–207. London: Camden House, 1996.

Bogost, Ian. "Gamification Is Bullshit." *The Atlantic*, August 9, 2011. http://www.theatlantic.com/technology/archive/2011/08/gamification-is-bullshit/243338/.

Bradley, Rizvana. "Introduction: Other Sensualities." *Women and Performance* 24, no. 2–3 (2014): 129–33.

Brecht, Bertolt. "Alienation Effects in Chinese Acting." In *Brecht on Theatre: The Development of an Aesthetic*, translated by John Willett, 91–99. London: Hill and Wang, 1964.

Brim, Matthew, and Amin Ghaziani. "Introduction: Queer Methods." *WSQ* 44, no. 3–4 (2016): 14–27.

Brown, Wendy. *States of Injury: Power and Freedom in Late Modernity*. Princeton, NJ: Princeton University Press, 1995.

Bryant, Levi, Nick Srnicek, Graham Harman, eds. *The Speculative Turn: Continental Materialism and Realism*. Melbourne, Australia: re.press, 2011.

Buck-Morss, Susan. *Hegel, Haiti, and Universal History*. Pittsburgh: University of Pittsburgh Press, 2009.

Buergel, Roger. "Leitmotifs." *documenta 12*, 2007. Last accessed June 20, 2020. http://www.documenta12.de/index.php?id=leitmotive&L=1.

Bunzl, Matti. *In Search of a Lost Avant-Garde: An Anthropologist Investigates the Contemporary Art Museum*. Chicago: University of Chicago Press, 2014.

Bush, Christopher. *Ideographic Modernism: China, Writing, Media*. Oxford: Oxford University Press, 2012.

Butler, Judith. *Bodies That Matter: On the Discursive Limits of Sex*. New York: Routledge, 1993.

Byrd, Jodi. "Loving Unbecoming: The Queer Politics of the Transitive Native." In *Critically Sovereign*, edited by Joanne Barker, 207–28. Durham, NC: Duke University Press, 2017.

Byrd, Jodi. *The Transit of Empire: Indigenous Critiques of Colonialism*. Minneapolis: University of Minnesota Press, 2011.

Cai Guo-Qiang. "Wenhau zhijan de yaobai: Cao Guo-Qiang fantanlu [Vacillations in Culture: Cao Guo-Qiang Interview]." *Diaosu* [Sculpture], no. 1 (2000): 6–10.

Campt, Tina. *Listening to Images*. Durham, NC: Duke University Press, 2017.

Canclini, Néstor. *Art beyond Itself: Anthropology for a Society without a Story Line*. Durham, NC: Duke University Press, 2014.

Cartwright, Lisa. *Moral Spectatorship: Technologies of Voice and Affect in Postwar Representations of the Child*. Durham, NC: Duke University Press, 2008.

Caruth, Cathy. *Unclaimed Experience: Trauma, Narrative and History*. Baltimore: Johns Hopkins University Press, 1996.

Chakrabarty, Dipesh. *Provincializing Europe: Postcolonial Thought and Historical Difference*. Princeton, NJ: Princeton University Press, 2007.

Cheah, Pheng. *Inhuman Conditions: On Cosmopolitanism and Human Rights*. Cambridge, MA: Harvard University Press, 2007.

Cheah, Pheng. *What Is a World?: On Postcolonial Literature as World Literature*. Durham, NC: Duke University Press, 2016.

Chen, Kuan-Hsing. *Asia as Method: Toward Deimperialization*. Durham, NC: Duke University Press, 2010.

Chen, Mel. *Animacies: Biopolitics, Racial Mattering, and Queer Affect*. Durham, NC: Duke University Press, 2012.

Chen, Mel. "Brain Fog: The Race for Cripistemology." *Journal for Literary and Cultural Disability Studies* 8, no. 2 (2014): 171–84.

Cheng, Anne Anlin. *The Melancholy of Race: Psychoanalysis, Assimilation, and Hidden Grief*. Oxford: Oxford University Press, 2001.

Cheng, Anne Anlin. *Ornamentalism*. Oxford: Oxford University Press, 2019.

Cheng, Anne Anlin. *Second Skin: Josephine Baker and the Modern Surface*. Oxford: Oxford University Press, 2011.

Cheng, Meiling. *Beijing Xingwei: Contemporary Chinese Time-Based Art*. Chicago: University of Chicago Press, 2014.

Cheng, Meiling. *In Other Los Angeleses: Multicentric Performance Art*. Berkeley: University of California Press, 2002.

Chiu, Melissa. *Contemporary Asian Art*. London: Thames and Hudson, 2010.

Chiu, Melissa, and Benjamin Genocchio. *Contemporary Art in Asia: A Critical Reader*. Cambridge, MA: MIT Press, 2011.

Chiu, Melissa, and Zheng Shengtian. *Art and China's Revolution*. New Haven, CT: Yale University Press, 2008.

Cho, Lily. "Asian Canadian Futures: Indenture Routes and Diasporic Passages." *Canadian Literature* 199 (2008): 181–201.

Chow, Rey. "The Elusive Material, What the Dog Doesn't Understand." In *New Materialisms: Ontology, Agency, and Politics*, edited by Diana Coole and Samantha Frost, 221–33. Durham, NC: Duke University Press, 2010.

Chow, Rey. *Entanglements, or Transmedial Thinking about Critique*. Durham, NC: Duke University Press, 2012.

Chow, Rey. *Primitive Passions*. New York: Columbia University Press, 1995.

Chow, Rey. *The Protestant Ethnic and the Spirit of Capitalism*. New York: Columbia University Press, 2002.

Chow, Rey. *Sentimental Fabulations*. New York: Columbia University Press, 2007.

Chow, Rey. *Woman and Chinese Modernity: The Politics of Reading between West and East*. Minneapolis: University of Minnesota Press, 1991.

Chuh, Kandice. *The Difference Aesthetics Makes: On the Humanities "After Man."* Durham, NC: Duke University Press, 2019.

Chuh, Kandice. *Imagine Otherwise: On Asian Americanist Critique*. Durham, NC: Duke University Press, 2003.

Chuh, Kandice, and Karen Shimakawa, eds. *Orientations: Mapping Studies in the Asian Diaspora*. Durham, NC: Duke University Press, 2001.

Chun, Allen. "Fuck Chineseness: On the Ambiguities of Ethnicity as Culture as Identity." *boundary 2* 3, no. 2 (1996): 111–38.

Clark, John. *Chinese Art at the End of the Millennium*. Hong Kong: New Art Media, 2000.

Clark, Paul. *The Chinese Cultural Revolution*. Cambridge: Cambridge University Press, 2008.

Clough, Patricia. "In the Aporia of Ontology and Epistemology: Toward a Politics of Measure." *s&F Online* 10, no. 3 (2012): 1–3. http://sfonline.barnard.edu/feminist-media-theory/in-the-aporia-of-ontology-and-epistemology-toward-a-politics-of-measure/.

Cohen, Cathy J. "Punks, Bulldaggers, and Welfare Queens: The Radical Potential of Queer Politics?" *GLQ* 3, no. 4 (1997): 437–65.

Conceison, Claire. *Significant Other: Staging the American in China*. Honolulu: University of Hawaii Press, 2004.

Coole, Diana, and Samantha Frost. *New Materialisms: Ontology, Agency, and Politics*. Durham, NC: Duke University Press, 2010.

Crenshaw, Kimberlé, Neil Gotanda, Gary Peller, and Kendall Thomas. *Critical Race Theory: The Key Writings That Formed the Movement*. New York: New Press, 1996.

Dai Jinhua. *Cinema and Desire*. London: Verso Books, 2002.

Davis, Richard L. *Wind against the Mountain: The Crisis of Politics and Culture in Thirteenth-Century China*. Cambridge, MA: Harvard University Press, 1996.

Debevoise, Jane. *Between State and Market*. London: Brill, 2014.

Deleuze, Gilles. "Control and Becoming." In *Negotiations 1972–1990*, 169–76. New York: Columbia University Press, 1997.

Deleuze, Gilles. *Difference and Repetition*. Translated by Paul Patton. New York: Columbia University Press, 1994.

Deleuze, Gilles. *The Fold*. Translated by Tom Conley. Minneapolis: University of Minnesota Press, 1992.

Deleuze, Gilles. *The Logic of Sense*. Translated by Charles Stivale. New York: Columbia University Press, 1990.

Deleuze, Gilles, and Félix Guattari. *Anti-Oedipus: Capitalism and Schizophrenia*. Translated by Brian Massumi. Minneapolis: University of Minnesota Press, 1983.

Deleuze, Gilles, and Félix Guattari. *Kafka: Towards a Minor Literature*. Translated by Dana Polan. Minneapolis: University of Minnesota Press, 1986.

Deleuze, Gilles, and Félix Guattari. *A Thousand Plateaus: Capitalism and Schizophrenia*. Translated by Brian Massumi. Minneapolis: University of Minnesota Press, 1987.

Deleuze, Gilles, and Félix Guattari. *What Is Philosophy?* Translated by Graham Burchell. New York: Columbia University Press, 1996.

Derrida, Jacques. "Force of Law: The Mystical Foundation of Authority." In *Deconstruction and the Possibility of Justice*, edited by Drucilla Cornell, Michel Rosenfeld, and David Carlson, 3–68. New York: Routledge, 1992.

Derrida, Jacques. *On Cosmopolitanism and Forgiveness*. Hackensack, NJ: Routledge, 2001.

Desai, Vishakha N. *Asian Art History in the Twenty-First Century*. Williamstown, MA: Clark Art Institute, 2008.

Dirlik, Arif. *Complicities: The People's Republic of China and Global Capitalism*. Boulder, CO: Paradigm Press, 2017.

Dirlik, Arif. *Culture and History in Postrevolutionary China*. Hong Kong: Chinese University of Hong Kong Press, 2012.

Dirlik, Arif. *Global Modernity: Modernity in the Age of Global Capitalism*. Boulder, CO: Paradigm Press, 2001.

Doane, Mary Ann. *The Emergence of Cinematic Time: Modernity, Contingency, the Archive*. Cambridge, MA: Harvard University Press, 2002.

Dunayevskaya, Raya. *Marxism and Freedom*. Amherst, NY: Humanity Books, 2000.

Dutton, Michael. "Cultural Revolution as Method." *China Quarterly* (2016): 718–33.

Dutton, Michael. "Fragments of the Political, or How We Dispose of Wonder." *Social Text* 30, no. 1 (2012): 109–41.

Eng, David L. *The Feeling of Kinship: Queer Liberalism and the Racialization of Intimacy*. Durham, NC: Duke University Press, 2010.

Eng, David, Judith [Jack] Halberstam, and José Muñoz. "What's Queer about Queer Studies Now?" *Social Text* 23, nos. 3–4 (2005): 1–17.

Eng, David, Teemu Ruskola, and Shuang Shen. "Introduction: China and the Human." *Social Text* 29, no. 4 (2012): 1–27.

Erickson, Britta. "The Reception in the West of Experimental Mainland Chinese Art of the 1990s." In *Reinterpretation: A Decade of Experimental Chinese Art*, edited by Wu Hung, 105–12. Guangzhou: Guangdong Museum of Art, 2002.

Erickson, Britta. "The Rent Collection Copyright Breached Overseas: Sichuan Fine Arts Institute Sues Venice Biennale." In *Chinese Art at the Crossroads*, edited by Wu Hung, 52–55. Hong Kong: New Art Media, 2001.

Esposito, Roberto. *The Third Person*. Cambridge: Polity Press, 2012.

Fanon, Frantz. *The Wretched of the Earth*. New York: Grove Press, 1963.

Felman, Shoshana. *The Juridical Unconscious: Trials and Traumas in the Twentieth Century*. Cambridge, MA: Harvard University Press, 2002.

Felski, Rita. *The Limits of Critique*. Chicago: University of Chicago Press, 2015.

Ferguson, Roderick. *The Reorder of Things: The University and Its Pedagogies of Minority Difference*. Minneapolis: University of Minnesota Press, 2012.

Ferrari, Rossella. *Pop Goes the Avant-Garde: Experimental Theater in Contemporary China*. Chicago: University of Chicago Press, 2013.

Findlay, Michael. *The Value of Art*. Munich: Prestal Verlag, 2014.

Foucault, Michel. *The Hermeneutics of the Subject: Lectures at the Collège de France 1981–1982*. New York: Picador, 2005.

Foucault, Michel. *Technologies of the Self: A Seminar with Michel Foucault*. Amherst: University of Massachusetts Press, 1988.

Freeman, Elizabeth. *Time Binds: Queer Temporalities, Queer Histories*. Durham, NC: Duke University Press, 2010.

Galloway, Alexander R. "The Cybernetic Hypothesis." *differences* 25, no. 1 (2014): 107–31.

Galloway, Alexander R. *Gaming: Essays on Algorithmic Culture*. Minneapolis: University of Minnesota Press, 2006.

Galloway, Alexander R. "Love of the Middle." In *Excommunication: Three Inquiries in Media and Mediation*, edited by Alexander Galloway, Eugene Thacker, and McKenzie Wark, 25–76. Chicago: University of Chicago Press, 2013.

Gao Minglu. *Inside Out: New Chinese Art*. Berkeley: University of California Press, 1998.

Gao Minglu. *Total Modernity and the Avant-Garde in Twentieth-Century Chinese Art*. Cambridge, MA: MIT Press, 2011.

Gladston, Paul. *"Avant-Garde" Art Groups in China, 1979–1989*. Bristol, UK: Intellect, 2013.

Glissant, Édouard. *Poetics of Relation*. Translated by Betsy Wing. Ann Arbor: University of Michigan Press, 1997.

Glissant, Édouard. *Traité du tout-monde*. Paris: Gallimard, 1997.

Gonzalez, Jennifer. "Sea Dreams: Isaac Julien's Western Union: Small Boats." In *The Migrant's Time: Rethinking Art History and Diaspora*, edited by Saloni Mathur, 115–29. New Haven, CT: Yale University Press, 2011.

Gopinath, Gayatri. *Impossible Desires: Queer Diasporas and South Asian Public Cultures*. Durham, NC: Duke University Press, 2005.

Gopinath, Gayatri. *Unruly Visions: The Aesthetic Practices of Queer Diaspora*. Durham, NC: Duke University Press, 2018.

Grew, Isabelle. *High Price: Art between the Market and Celebrity Culture*. Berlin: Sternberg Press, 2009.

Halberstam, Judith [Jack]. *In a Queer Time and Place: Transgender Bodies, Subcultural Lives*. New York: New York University Press, 2005.

Hall, Stuart. "Encoding/Decoding." In *Culture, Media, Language*, edited by Stuart Hall, Dorothy Hobson, Andrew Love, and Paul Willis, 128–38. London: Hutchinson, 1980.

Hall, Stuart. "The West and the Rest." In *Modernity*, edited by Stuart Hall, David Held, Don Hubert, and Kenneth Thompson, 184–227. Oxford: Blackwell, 1996.

Hanneken, Jaime. *Imagining the Postcolonial: Discipline, Poetics, Practice in Latin American and Francophone Discourse*. Albany: State University of New York Press, 2016.

Hardt, Michael, and Antonio Negri. *Empire*. Cambridge, MA: Harvard University Press, 2001.

Hardt, Michael, and Antonio Negri. *Multitude: War and Democracy in the Age of Empire*. New York: Penguin Books, 2005.

Harney, Stefano, and Fred Moten. *The Undercommons: Fugitive Planning and Black Study*. Brooklyn: Autonomedia, 2013.

Harootunian, Harry D. "Postcoloniality's Unconscious/Area Studies' Desire." In *Learning Places: The Afterlives of Area Studies*, edited by Masao Miyoshi and H. D. Harootunian, 150–74. Durham, NC: Duke University Press, 2002.

Harris, Jonathan. *The Global Contemporary Art World*. Hoboken, NJ: Wiley-Blackwell, 2017.

Harris, Laura. *Experiments in Exile: C. L. R. James, Hélio Oiticica, and the Aesthetic Sociality of Blackness*. New York: Fordham University Press, 2018.

Hartman, Andrew. *A War for the Soul of America*. Chicago: University of Chicago Press, 2015.

Hartman, Saidiya. *Scenes of Subjection: Terror, Slavery, and Self-Making in Nineteenth-Century America*. Oxford: Oxford University Press, 1997.

Hartman, Saidiya. "Venus in Two Acts." *Small Axe* 26, no. 2 (2008): 1–14.

Hastings, Adi, and Paul Manning. "Introduction: Acts of Alterity." *Language and Communication* 24, no. 4 (2004): 291–311.

Hayot, Eric. *The Hypothetical Mandarin: Sympathy, Modernity, and Chinese Pain*. Oxford: Oxford University Press, 2009.

Hayot, Eric. *On Literary Worlds*. Oxford: Oxford University Press, 2012.

Hayward Gallery. "Art of Change: New Directions from China." Southbank Centre, 2012. Accessed April 21, 2014. http://china.southbankcentre.co.uk/exhibition/.

Heatwole, Joanne. "Media of Now: Interview with David Hall." *Afterimage* 36, no. 1 (2008): 14–17.

Hegel, G. W. F. *Lectures on the Philosophy of World History*. Cambridge: Cambridge University Press, 1975.

Heinrich, Ari. *The Afterlife of Images: Translating the Pathological Body between China and the West*. Durham, NC: Duke University Press, 2008.

Heinrich, Ari. *Chinese Surplus: Biopolitical Aesthetics and the Medically Commodified Body*. Durham, NC: Duke University Press, 2018.

Hong, Grace. *Death beyond Disavowal: The Impossible Politics of Difference*. Minneapolis: University of Minnesota Press, 2015.

Horowitz, Noah. *Art of the Deal*. Princeton, NJ: Princeton University Press, 2014.

Hou Hanru. "Entropy, Chinese Artists, Western Art Institutions." In *On the Mid-Ground: Selected Texts*, edited by Yu Hsiao-Wei, 54–63. Hong Kong: Timezone 8, 1994.

Hulst, Titia. *A History of the Western Art Market: A Sourcebook of Writings on Artists, Dealers, and Markets*. Berkeley: University of California Press, 2017.

Hunter, James. *Culture Wars: The Struggle to Define America*. New York: Basic Books, 1991.

Jackson, Shannon. *Professing Performance: Theatre in the Academy from Philology to Performativity*. New York: Cambridge University Press, 2004.

Jackson, Shannon. *Social Works: Performing Art, Supporting Publics*. New York: Routledge, 2011.

Jackson, Zakiyyah Iman. *Becoming Human: Matter and Meaning in an Antiblack World*. New York: New York University Press, 2020.

Jagoda, Patrick. "Gamification and Other Forms of Play." *boundary 2* 40, no. 2 (2013): 113–44.

James, C. L. R. *The Black Jacobins*. New York: Vintage Books, 1963.

Jameson, Fredric. *Brecht and Method*. London: Verso Books, 1998.

Jameson, Fredric. *The Political Unconscious*. Ithaca, NY: Cornell University Press, 1982.

Jameson, Fredric. *Postmodernism, or, The Cultural Logic of Late Capitalism*. Durham, NC: Duke University Press, 1990.

JanMohamed, Abdul, and David Lloyd, eds. *The Nature and Context of Minority Discourse*. Oxford: Oxford University Press, 1991.

Jay, Martin. *Marxism and Totality*. Berkeley: University of California Press, 1984.

Jones, Andrew F. *Developmental Fairy Tales: Evolutionary Thinking and Modern Chinese Culture*. Cambridge, MA: Harvard University Press, 2011.

Joseph, Miranda. *Against the Romance of Community*. Minneapolis: University of Minnesota Press, 2002.

Julien, Isaac. "The Long Road: Isaac Julien in Conversation with B. Ruby Rich." *Art Journal* 61, no. 2 (2002): 51–67.

Julien, Isaac. *Riot*. New York: Museum of Modern Art, 2014.

Kamien, Roger. *Music: An Appreciation*. Boston: McGraw Hill, 2007.

Kaplan, Amy. "Violent Belongings and the Question of Empire Today: Presidential Address to the American Studies Association—Hartford, Connecticut, October 17, 2003." *American Quarterly* 56, no. 4 (2004): 1–18.

Karl, Rebecca. *The Magic of Concepts: History and the Economic in Twentieth-Century China*. Durham, NC: Duke University Press, 2017.

Kee, Joan. "The Property of Contemporary Chinese Art." *Law and Humanities* 12, no. 2 (2018): 251–77.

Keeling, Kara. "I = Another: Digital Identity Politics." In *Strange Affinities*, edited by Grace Hong and Roderick Ferguson, 53–75. Durham, NC: Duke University Press, 2011.

Kim, Sue. *On Anger: Race, Cognition, Narrative*. Austin: University of Texas Press, 2013.

King, Homay. *Virtual Memory: Time-Based Art and the Dream of Digitality*. Durham, NC: Duke University Press, 2015.

Kittler, Friedrich. *Gramophone, Film, Typewriter*. Stanford, CA: Stanford University Press, 1999.

Klein, Anne Carolyn. *Meeting the Great Bliss Queen: Buddhists, Feminists, and the Art of the Self*. Ithaca, NY: Snow Lion, 2008.

Kleinman, Arthur, and Joan Kleinman. "How Bodies Remember: Social Memory and Bodily Experience of Criticism, Resistance, and Delegitimation Following China's Cultural Revolution." *New Literary History* 25, no. 3 (1994): 707–23.

Klima, Alan. *The Funeral Casino: Meditation, Massacre, and Exchange with the Dead in Thailand*. Princeton, NJ: Princeton University Press, 2002.

Kornbluh, Anna. *The Order of Forms*. Chicago: University of Chicago Press, 2019.

Kovskaya, Maya. "Heroes of the Mundane: The Syncretic Imagination of Cao Fei." *Yishu* (2007): 82–85.

Kwan, SanSan. *Kinesthetic City: Dance and Movement in Chinese Urban Spaces*. Oxford: Oxford University Press, 2013.

Kwon, Marci. *Enchantments: The Art of Joseph Cornell*. Princeton, NJ: Princeton University Press, 2021.

Laruelle, François. *General Theory of Victims*. Cambridge: Polity Press, 2015.

Levine, Caroline. *Forms: Whole, Rhythm, Hierarchy, Network*. Princeton, NJ: Princeton University Press, 2017.

Lewis, Bradley. "A Mad Fight: Psychiatry and Disability Activism." In *The Disability Studies Reader*, edited by Lennard Davis, 339–54. New York: Routledge, 2013.

Lim, Song Hwee. *Tsai Ming-Liang and a Cinema of Slowness*. Honolulu: University of Hawaii Press, 2014.

Liu, Lydia. *Translingual Practice: Literature, National Culture, and Translated Modernity—China, 1900–1937*. Stanford, CA: Stanford University Press, 1995.

Liu, Petrus. *Queer Marxism in Two Chinas*. Durham, NC: Duke University Press, 2015.

Liu, Petrus. "Why Does Queer Theory Need China?" *positions* 18, no. 2 (2010): 291–320.

Liu Ding, Carol Yinghua Lu, and Su Wei. *The 7th Shenzhen Sculpture Biennale*. Shenzhen: OCT Contemporary Art Terminal, 2012.

Liu Kang. *Aesthetics and Marxism: Chinese Aesthetic Marxists and Their Western Contemporaries*. Durham, NC: Duke University Press, 2000.

Lloyd, David. *Nationalism and Minor Literature: James Clarence Mangan and the Emergence of Irish Cultural Nationalism*. Berkeley: University of California Press, 1987.

Lloyd, David. *Under Representation: The Racial Regime of Aesthetics*. New York: Fordham University Press, 2019.

Lorde, Audre. "The Master's Tools Will Never Dismantle the Master's House." In *Sister Outsider: Essays and Speeches*, 100–103. Berkeley: Crossing Press, 2007.

Lorde, Audre. "The Uses of Anger." In *Sister Outsider: Essays and Speeches*, 115–25. Berkeley: Crossing Press, 2007.

Lorde, Audre. *Zami: A New Spelling of My Name—A Biomythography*. New York: Crossing Press, 1982.

Love, Heather. "Close but Not Deep." *New Literary History* 41, no. 2 (2010): 371–91.

Love, Heather. *Feeling Backward: Loss and the Politics of Queer History*. Cambridge, MA: Harvard University Press, 2009.

Love, Heather. "Small Change: Realism, Immanence, and the Politics of the Micro." *Modern Language Quarterly* 77, no. 3 (2016): 419–45.

Lowe, Donald. *The Function of "China" in Marx, Lenin, and Mao*. Berkeley: University of California Press, 1966.

Lowe, Lisa. *Critical Terrains: French and British Orientalisms*. Ithaca, NY: Cornell University Press, 1991.

Lowe, Lisa. "History Hesitant." *Social Text* 33, no. 4 (2015): 85–107.

Lowe, Lisa. *Intimacies of Four Continents*. Durham, NC: Duke University Press, 2014.

Lowe, Lisa. "Metaphors of Globalization and Dilemmas of Excess." In *Saturation: Race, Art, and the Circulation of Value*, edited by C. Riley Snorton and Hentyle Yapp, 25–54. Cambridge, MA: MIT Press, 2020.

Löwy, Michael. *Fire Alarm: Reading Walter Benjamin's "On the Concept of History."* Translated by Chris Turner. London: Verso Books, 2016.

Luxemburg, Rosa. *The Russian Revolution*. Ann Arbor: University of Michigan, 1961.

Lye, Colleen. *America's Asia: Racial Form and American Literature*. Princeton, NJ: Princeton University Press, 2004.

Ma, Jean. *Melancholy Drift*. Hong Kong: Hong Kong University Press, 2010.

Man, Eva Kit Wah. "Expression Extreme and History Trauma in Women Body Art in China: The Case of He Chengyao." In *Subversive Strategies in Contemporary Chinese Art*, edited by Mary Bittner Wiseman and Liu Yuedi, 171–90. Leiden: Brill, 2011.

Manalansan, Martin. *Global Divas: Filipino Gay Men in the Diaspora*. Durham, NC: Duke University Press, 2003.

Manning, Erin. *The Minor Gesture*. Durham, NC: Duke University Press, 2016.

Marcuse, Herbert. *The Aesthetic Dimension: Toward a Critique of Marxist Aesthetics*. Boston: Beacon Press, 1979.

Marks, Laura. *The Skin of the Film: Intercultural Cinema, Embodiment, and the Senses*. Durham, NC: Duke University Press, 2000.

Martin, Jean-Hubert. *Magiciens de la Terre*. Paris: Centre Georges Pompidou, 1989.

Marx, Karl. *A Contribution to the Critique of Political Economy*. Wolcott, CT: Scholar's Choice, 2015.

Marx, Karl, and Friedrich Engels. "Manifesto of the Communist Party." In *The Marx-Engels Reader*, edited by Robert Tucker, 469–500. New York: W. W. Norton, 1978.

Massumi, Brian. *Parables for the Virtual: Movement, Affect, Sensation*. Durham, NC: Duke University Press, 2002.

Mbembe, Achille. *The Critique of Black Reason*. Durham, NC: Duke University Press, 2017.

McGrath, Jason. *Postsocialist Modernity*. Stanford, CA: Stanford University Press, 2008.

Merleau-Ponty, Maurice. *Adventures of the Dialectic*. Translated by Joseph Bien. Evanston, IL: Northwestern University Press, 1973.

Metzger, Sean. "At the Vanishing Point: Theater and Asian/American Critique." *American Quarterly* 63, no. 2 (2011): 277–300.

Metzger, Sean. "Isaac Julien's Ten Thousand Waves: Screening Human Traffic and the Logic of Ebbing." In *The Routledge Handbook of New Media in Asia*, edited by Larissa Hjorth and Olivia Khoo, 285–95. London: Routledge, 2015.

Metzger, Sean. "Seascape: The Chinese Atlantic." In *Framing the Global*, edited by Hilary Kahn and Saskia Sassen, 128–38. Bloomington: Indiana University Press, 2014.

Mill, John Stuart. "On Liberty." In *On Liberty and Other Essays*, 5–130. Oxford: Oxford University Press, 1998.

Miyoshi, Masao, and Harry Harootunian. 2002. *Learning Places: The Afterlives of Area Studies*. Durham, NC: Duke University Press, 2002.

Mufti, Aamir. *Forget English!: Orientalism and World Literature*. Cambridge, MA: Harvard University Press, 2016.

Muñoz, José Esteban. *Disidentifications: Queers of Color and the Performance of Politics*. Minneapolis: University of Minnesota Press, 1999.

Muñoz, José Esteban. "'Gimme Gimme This . . . Gimme Gimme That': Annihilation and Innovation in the Punk Rock Commons." *Social Text* 31, no. 3 (2013): 95–110.

Musser, Amber. "Anti-Oedipus, Kinship, and the Subject of Affect: Reading Fanon with Deleuze and Guattari." *Social Text* 30, no. 3 (2012): 77–95.

Musser, Amber. *Sensational Flesh: Race, Power, and Masochism*. New York: New York University Press, 2014.

Nancy, Jean-Luc. *Being Singular Plural*. Translated by Anne O'Byrne. Stanford, CA: Stanford University Press, 2000.

Nancy, Jean-Luc. *The Inoperative Community*. Edited by Peter Connor. Minneapolis: University of Minnesota Press, 1991.

Ngai, Sianne. "The Cuteness of the Avant-Garde." *Critical Inquiry* 31, no. 5 (2005): 811–47.

Ngai, Sianne. *Our Aesthetic Categories: Zany, Cute, Interesting*. Cambridge, MA: Harvard University Press, 2012.

Ngai, Sianne. *Ugly Feelings*. Cambridge, MA: Harvard University Press, 2007.

Nguyen, Mimi Thi. *The Gift of Freedom: War, Debt, and Other Refugee Passages*. Durham, NC: Duke University Press, 2012.

Nguyen, Mimi Thi. "Minor Threats." *Radical History Review* 122 (2015): 11–24.

Nietzsche, Friedrich. *On the Genealogy of Morality*. Translated by W. Kaufman and R. J. Hollingdale. New York: Vintage, 1969.

Nyong'o, Tavia. *Afro-Fabulations: The Queer Drama of Black Life*. New York: New York University Press, 2018.

Nyong'o, Tavia. *The Amalgamation Waltz: Race, Performance, and the Ruses of Memory*. Minneapolis: University of Minnesota Press, 2009.

Onians, John. "World Art Studies and the Need for a New Natural History of Art." *Art Bulletin* 78, no. 2 (1996): 206–9.

Osborne, Peter. *Anywhere or Not at All*. London: Verso Books, 2013.

Pollack, Barbara. *The Wild, Wild East: An American Art Critic's Adventures in China*. Hong Kong: Blue Kingfisher, 2010.

Povinelli, Elizabeth. *Economies of Abandonment: Social Belonging and Endurance in Late Liberalism*. Durham, NC: Duke University Press, 2011.

Puar, Jasbir K. "Prognosis Time: Towards a Geopolitics of Affect, Debility, and Capacity." *Women and Performance* 19, no. 2 (2009): 161–72.

Puar, Jasbir K. *The Right to Maim: Debility, Capacity, Disability*. Durham, NC: Duke University Press, 2017.

Puar, Jasbir K. *Terrorist Assemblages: Homonationalism in Queer Times*. Durham, NC: Duke University Press, 2007.

Rancière, Jacques. *The Politics of Aesthetics: The Distribution of the Sensible*. Translated by Gabriel Rockhill. New York: Continuum, 2004.

Rancière, Jacques. *Short Voyages to the Land of the People*. Translated by James Swenson. Stanford, CA: Stanford University Press, 2003.

Richter, Gerhard. *Thought Images: Frankfurt School Writers' Reflections from Damaged Life*. Stanford, CA: Stanford University Press, 2007.

Ricoeur, Paul. *Freud and Philosophy: An Essay on Interpretation*. Translated by Denis Savage. New Haven, CT: Yale University Press, 1977.

Roach, Joseph. *Cities of the Dead*. New York: Columbia University Press, 1996.

Robinson, Cedric. *Black Marxism*. Chapel Hill: University of North Carolina Press, 2000.

Rodgers, Daniel. *Age of Fracture*. Cambridge, MA: Harvard University Press, 2003.

Rodney, Walter. *How Europe Underdeveloped Africa*. London: Verso Books, 2018.

Rodowick, D. N. *Afterimages of Gilles Deleuze's Film Philosophy*. Minneapolis: University of Minnesota Press, 2010.

Rofel, Lisa. *Desiring China: Experiments in Neoliberalism, Sexuality, and Public Culture*. Durham, NC: Duke University Press, 2007.

Rogoff, Irit. "Looking Away: Participations in Visual Culture." In *After Criticism: New Responses to Art and Performance*, edited by Gavin Butt, 117–34. London: Blackwell, 2005.

Roshi, Shodo Harada. "Zazen Meditation in Japanese Rinzai Zen." In *Zen Training*, 10–15. Boston: Tuttle, 2002.

Rothberg, Michael. "Decolonizing Trauma Studies: A Response." *Studies in the Novel* 40, nos. 1–2 (2008): 224–34.

Sakai, Naoki. "Positions and Positionalities: After Two Decades." *positions* 20, no. 1 (2012): 67–94.

Saldaña-Portillo, María Josefina. *The Revolutionary Imagination in the Americas and the Age of Development*. Durham, NC: Duke University Press, 2003.

Saldanha, Arun. *Psychedelic White: Goa Trance and the Viscosity of Race*. Minneapolis: University of Minnesota Press, 2007.

Saldanha, Arun, and Jason Adams, eds. *Deleuze and Race*. Edinburgh: Edinburgh University Press, 2012.

Sandoval, Chela. *Methodology of the Oppressed*. Minneapolis: University of Minnesota Press, 2000.

Sassen, Saskia. *The Global City*. Princeton, NJ: Princeton University Press, 2001.

Savci, Evren. "Translation as Queer Methodology." In *Other, Please Specify: Queer Methods in Sociology*, edited Compton D'Lane, Tey Meadow, and Kristen Schilt, 249–61. Berkeley: University of California Press, 2018.

Schnayerson, Michael. *Boom: Mad Money, Mega Dealers, and the Rise of Contemporary Art*. New York: Public Affairs, 2019.

Schneider, Rebecca. *The Explicit Body in Performance*. New York: Routledge, 1997.

Schneider, Rebecca. *Performing Remains: Art and War in Times of Theatrical Reenactment*. New York: Routledge, 2011.

Scott, David. *Conscripts of Modernity: The Tragedy of Colonial Enlightenment*. Durham, NC: Duke University Press, 2004.

Schroeder, William. "On Cowboys and Aliens." GLQ 18, no. 4 (2012): 425–52.

Sedgwick, Eve Kosofsky. *Touching Feeling: Affect, Pedagogy, Performativity*. Durham, NC: Duke University Press, 2003.

Sedgwick, Eve Kosofsky. *The Weather in Proust*. Durham, NC: Duke University Press, 2011.

Sharpe, Christina. *In the Wake: On Blackness and Being*. Durham, NC: Duke University Press, 2016.

Shih, Shu-mei. "Is the Post in Post-Socialism the Same Post in Post-Humanism." *Social Text* 30, no. 1 (2012): 27–50.

Shih, Shu-mei. *Visuality and Identity: Sinophone Articulations across the Pacific*. Berkeley: University of California Press, 2007.

Shih, Shu-mei. "World Studies and Relational Comparison." PMLA 130, no. 2 (2015): 430–38.

Shih, Shu-mei, and Francoise Lionnet. *Minor Transnationalism*. Durham, NC: Duke University Press, 2005.

Shohat, Ella. *Taboo Memories, Diasporic Voices*. Durham, NC: Duke University Press, 2006.

Siebers, Tobin. *Disability Aesthetics*. Ann Arbor: University of Michigan Press, 2010.

Silva, Denise Ferreira da. *Toward a Global Idea of Race*. Minneapolis: University of Minnesota Press, 2007.

Silvio, Teri. "Animation: The New Performance?" *Journal of Linguistic Anthropology* 20, no. 2 (2010): 422–38.

Smith, Andrea. "Queer Theory and Native Studies: The Heteronormativity of Settler Colonialism." GLQ 16, no. 1–2 (2010): 42–68.

Smith, Terry. *What Is Contemporary Art?* Chicago: University of Chicago Press, 2009.

Smith, Tuhiwai Linda. *Decolonizing Methodologies: Research and Indigenous Peoples*. London: Zed Books, 2012.

Snorton, C. Riley. *Black on Both Sides: A Racial History of Trans Identity*. Minneapolis: University of Minnesota Press, 2017.

Snorton, C. Riley, and Hentyle Yapp, eds. *Saturation: Race, Art, and the Circulation of Value*. Cambridge, MA: MIT Press, 2020.

Sorace, Christian. "China's Last Communist: Ai Weiwei." *Critical Inquiry* 40, no. 2 (2014): 396–419.

Spillers, Hortense. *Black, White, and in Color: Essays on American Literature and Culture*. Chicago: University of Chicago Press, 2003.

Spillers, Hortense. "Mama's Baby, Papa's Maybe: An American Grammar Book." *Diacritics* 17, no. 2 (1987): 64–81.

Spivak, Gayatri. "Can the Subaltern Speak?" In *Colonial Discourse and Post-colonial Theory*, edited by Patrick Williams and Laura Chrisman, 66–111. Hampstead, UK: Harvester, 1993.

Stallabrass, Julian. *Art Incorporated*. Oxford: Oxford University Press, 2004.

Stein, Gertrude. *Geographical History of America*. Baltimore: Johns Hopkins University Press, 1995.

Steyerl, Hito. *Duty Free Art: Art in the Age of Planetary Civil War*. London: Verso Books, 2017.

Thoburn, Nicholas. *Deleuze, Marx and Politics*. New York: Routledge, 2003.

Thompson, Deborah. "An Exoneration of Black Rage." *South Atlantic Quarterly* 116, no. 3 (2017): 457–81.

Thompson, Don. *The $12 Million Stuffed Shark*. New York: St. Martin's Griffin, 2010.

Thornton, Sarah. *Seven Days in the Art World*. New York: W. W. Norton, 2009.

Thrift, Nigel. *Non-Representational Theory: Space, Politics, Affect*. New York: Routledge, 2007.

Tinker, Hugh. *A New System of Slavery: The Export of Indian Labour Overseas, 1830–1920*. Oxford: Oxford University Press, 1974.

Tonglin Lu. "Fantasy and Ideology in a Chinese Film: A Zizekian Reading of the Cultural Revolution." *positions* 12, no. 2 (2004): 539–64.

Tsu, Jing. *Sound and Script in Chinese Diaspora*. Cambridge, MA: Harvard University Press, 2011.

Vukovich, Daniel. "China in Theory: The Orientalist Production of Knowledge in the Global Economy." *Cultural Critique* 76 (2010): 48–172.

Vukovich, Daniel. *Illiberal China*. New York: Palgrave Macmillan, 2019.

Wallerstein, Immanuel. *The Modern World-System*. Vol. 1. Berkeley: University of California Press, 2011.

Wang, Nanming. "Art in Its Regional Political Context: Exhibition and Criticism." In *A New Thoughtfulness in Contemporary China*, edited by Jorg Huber and Zhao Chuan, 131–42. London: Transaction, 2011.

Wang Hui. *The Politics of Imagining Asia*. Edited by Theodore Huters. Cambridge, MA: Harvard University Press, 2011.

Weeks, Kathi. *The Problem with Work: Feminism, Marxism, Antiwork Politics, and Postwork Imaginaries*. Durham, NC: Duke University Press, 2011.

Weheliye, Alexander. *Habeas Viscus: Racializing Assemblages, Biopolitics, and Black Feminist Theories of the Human*. Durham, NC: Duke University Press, 2014.

Welland, Sasha Su-Ling. *Experimental Beijing: Gender and Globalization in Chinese Contemporary Art*. Durham, NC: Duke University Press, 2018.

Werner, Paul. *Museum, Inc.: Inside the Global Art World*. Chicago: Prickly Paradigm Press, 2006.

Wilber, Ken. "Foreword." In *The Experience of Meditation: Experts Introduce the Major Traditions*, edited by Jonathan Shear, 1–3. St. Paul, MN: Paragon House, 2006.

Wilderson, Frank. *Red, White, and Black: Cinema and the Structure of U.S. Antagonisms*. Durham, NC: Duke University Press, 2010.

Williams, Eric. *Capitalism and Slavery*. Chapel Hill: University of North Carolina Press, 1994.

Wolin, Richard. *The Wind from the East: French Intellectuals, the Cultural Revolution, and the Legacy of the 1960s*. Princeton, NJ: Princeton University Press, 2012.

Woloch, Alex. *The One vs. the Many: Minor Characters and the Space of the Protagonist in the Novel*. Princeton, NJ: Princeton University Press, 2003.

Wong, Winnie Won Yin. *Van Gogh on Demand: China and the Readymade*. Chicago: University of Chicago Press, 2014.

Wu, Chin-tao. *Privatising Culture*. London; Verso Books, 2003.

Wu Hung. *Contemporary Chinese Art*. London: Thames and Hudson, 2014.

Wu Hung. *Exhibiting Experimental Art in China*. Chicago: Smart Museum, University of Chicago, 2000.

Wu Hung. *Transience: Chinese Experimental Art at the End of the Twentieth Century*. Chicago: University of Chicago Press, 2005.

Wu Hung and Peggy Wang, eds. *Contemporary Chinese Art: Primary Documents*. Durham, NC: Duke University Press, 2010.

Wynter, Sylvia. "The Re-enchantment of Humanism: An Interview with Sylvia Wynter." Interview by David Scott. *small axe* 8 (2000): 118–207.

Wynter, Sylvia. "Rethinking Aesthetics: Notes to a Deciphering Practice." *Ex-Iles: Essays on Caribbean Cinema*, edited by Mbye B. Cham, 237–78. Trenton, NJ: Africa World Press, 1992.

Wynter, Sylvia. "Unsettling the Coloniality of Being/Power/Truth/Freedom: Towards the Human, After Man, Its Overrepresentation—An Argument." *CR: The New Centennial Review* 3, no. 3 (2003): 257–337.

Xie, Shaobo. "Translation and Transformation: Theory in China, China in Theory." *International Social Sciences Journal* 1, no. 1 (2014): 2–11.

Yang, Haiping. "Theatricality in Classical Chinese Drama." In *Theatricality*, edited by Tracy Davis and Thomas Postlewait, 65–89. Cambridge: Cambridge University Press, 2003.

Yapp, Hentyle. "Beyond Minor Subjects: Anti-Oedipus, Affect, and Becoming in Yan Xing's *Kill the TV Set*." *Verge: Studies in Global Asias* 5, no. 1(2019): 153–81.

Yapp, Hentyle. "Chinese Lingering, Meditation's Practice: Reframing Endurance Art." *Women and Performance* 24, nos. 2–3 (2015): 1–18.

Yapp, Hentyle. "Feeling Down(town Julie Brown): Sensing Up and Expiring Relationality." *Journal of Visual Culture* 17, no. 1 (2018): 3–21.

Yapp, Hentyle. "To Punk, Yield, and Flail: Julien Tolentino's Insincerities and the Strong Performative Impulse." *GLQ* 24, no. 1 (2018): 113–38.

Yingjin Zhang. "Ways of Seeing China through Isaac Julien's *Ten Thousand Waves*: Evocative Translocality, Fantastic Orientalism, Nameless Labor." *Prism: Theory and Modern Chinese Literature* 16, no. 1 (2019): 174–96.

Yoneyama, Lisa. *Cold War Ruins: Transpacific Critique of American Justice and Japanese War Crimes.* Durham, NC: Duke University Press, 2016.

Young, Iris Marion, and Danielle S. Allen, eds. *Justice and the Politics of Difference.* Princeton, NJ: Princeton University Press, 2011.

Zarobell, John. *Art and the Global Economy.* Berkeley: University of California Press, 2017.

Zhang Huan. "12 Square Meters (12 Pingfang Mi)." In *Contemporary Chinese Art: Primary Documents*, edited by Hung Wu and Peggy Wang, 214–15. Durham, NC: Duke University Press, 2010.

INDEX

aura: and inclusion, 58, 60–61. See also *Magiciens de la Terre* (exhibit)

Austin, J. L.: on speech acts, 150

autocracy: vs. authoritarianism, 243n4

Band Aid: "Do They Know It's Christmas?," 214, 217, 219

Bao, Hongwei: on the queer comrade, 233n18

Bao Dong, 47. See also *On/Off* (exhibit)

Baucom, Ian: on the insurance of Black laboring bodies, 189

becoming, 22–23, 36, 109–10, 121–26, 140, 226n48, 235n27; of China, 122–26, 153; and history, 22; and knowability, 22; and the relational, 124; and temporality, 22

behavior: vs. performance, 28–29

being singular plural, 87–93; being (plural) singular plural, 91–93, 200. *See also* Ai Weiwei: "all look same"; Nancy, Jean-Luc

Benjamin, Walter, 58, 198, 206; on history, 184–87, 190–93, 197, 200–201; pure means, 175; on Wong, 199, 243n45. *See also* aura; history

Bennett, Jane: on demystification and agency, 148–49

Bergson, Henri, 30, 168; and Deleuze and Guattari, 22–23; on time vs. duration, 158

Berlant, Lauren: on being in history, 133–34

biennials, 24, 60. *See also* Havana Biennial; São Paulo Biennial; Shenzhen Biennial; Venice Biennale

Blackness, 191; anti-, 36, 95, 98, 209, 232n6, 240n1; the Black body, 198, 223n11; and capitalism, 176; and China, 178, 192, 207

body, the: and *12m²* (Zhang), 147, 152–54; and *99 Needles* (He), 152–54, 160–65; and affect, 35; Black, 198, 223n11; of cinematic icons, 199, 205; and "ebb-ing," 193; and *Fairytale* (Ai), 72, 75, 87; and imagination, 146; and *Kill (the) TV-Set* (Yan), 105, 109, 115, 117, 120–23, 140; and knowability, 118; and politics, 29; and temporality, 5; and *Walking Man* (Wang), 135–36. *See also* *12m²* (Zhang); *99 Needles* (He); *Fairytale* (Ai); *Kill (the) TV-Set* (Yan); nudity

boredom: of Adorno, 223n9; of Ai Weiwei, 4–5, 223n9

Bradley, Rizvana, 31

Brecht, Bertolt: on alienation effects and the Chinese actor, 149–50, 198, 201–2, 206, 238n19

"Bridge over Troubled Water" (Simon and Garfunkel), 212, 214–15, 217. *See also* Young, Samson: *Songs for Disaster Relief*

Brown, Trisha, 79

Buck-Morss, Susan: on the universal, 138–39

Buddhism, 152–54, 238n27. *See also* *12m²* (Zhang); *99 Needles* (He); meditation

Buergel, Roger: and *documenta 12*, 78–79

Butler, Judith, 150–51

Byrd, Jodi: on racial liberalism, 98

Cage, John, 26, 116–18; *26'1.1499"*, 107–8, 112–13, 116, 118. *See also* Moorman, Charlotte; Paik, Nam June

Cai Guo-Qiang, 10; *Venice's Rent Collection Courtyard*, 34, 39, 41, 65–69

Caminero, Maximo: and Ai Weiwei, 3–4

Campt, Tina: on listening to images, 31

Cao Fei, 10, 16, 24, 35, 150–51, 194; *Cosplayers* series, 172–74; *Cosplay* series, 142, 145, 165–75; *East Wind* series, 170–71

Caruth, Cathy, 163

censorship: aesthetic, 1–2, 71; and photography, 1

Chakrabarty, Dipesh, 21: on the provincialization of concepts, 125; on universals, 17

Jameson, Fredric, 193; on Brecht's alienation effect, 201; on mediation, 226n50

JanMohamed, Abdul R.: on the import of relationality, 228n64

Jay, Martin: on questioning totality, 183

Jiang Qing: on Wang's *Rent Collection Courtyard*. *See also* Mao Zedong; Wang Guangyi: *Rent Collection Courtyard*

Jia Zhangke, 179, 195, 204

joy: of conga lines and landscapes, 93; and pain (and art), 78

Julien, Isaac, 10; *The Attendant*, 194; elliptical method of, 195–97; *Frantz Fanon: Black Skin, White Mask*, 193; *Lessons of the Hour*, 194; *Looking for Langston*, 198; *Playtime*, 194; *Stones against Diamonds*, 194; *Ten Thousand Waves*, 35–36, 178–207; *Western Union: Small Boats*, 194

Kafka, Franz: "Letter to the Father," 113–14

Kaplan, Amy: on the transnational turn, 225n38

Karl, Rebecca: on "economically monotone, global space," 44; on the "new inclusionary impulse," 11–12

Kee, Joan: on Zhang's *12m²*, 237n7

Kill (the) TV-Set (Yan), 26–27, 105–26; and bodies, 105, 109, 115, 117, 120–23, 140. *See also* Cage, John; Moorman, Charlotte; Paik, Nam June; remakes; Yan Xing

kitsch: bonsai cultivation as, 123; and charity songs, 214; and the Cultural Revolution, 47; of Political Pop Art, 135

Kittler, Friedrich: on mediation, 226n50

Klee, Paul: and Benjamin's angel of history, 185; and Deleuze's monad, 186. *See also* Benjamin, Walter: on history; monad

Klein, Anne: on time and self within meditation, 162

knowability, 11–12, 15, 19–20, 40, 48, 60–61, 78, 118–21, 148, 225n40; and becoming, 22; and the body, 118; and the global, 84; and inclusion, 54; incomplete, 23, 139; and the proper, 60

Kornbluh, Anna: on the Rancièrean approach to aesthetics and politics, 24

Kovskaya, Maya: on Cao Fei and imagination, 167

"Kung Fu Fighting" (Douglas), 18

Kusama, Yayoi, 41

Kwan, Stanley: *Center Stage*, 205

labor: labor-saving operation, 20; as performance, 67–69; and play, 146

Laruelle, François: on intellectuals and victims, 70–71

law: force of, 15–16, 20–21, 48, 53, 183, 213; natural(ized), 17–18. *See also* Derrida, Jacques

Lego: and Ai, 86, 94. *See also* Ai Weiwei

Leibniz, Gottfried Wilhelm, 31

Lewis, Bradley, 152

lightheartedness, 167–74. *See also* Coa Fei; cuteness

Li Liao: *Consumption*, 47–49

Lionnet, Francoise. *See* Shih, Shu-mei and Francoise Lionnet

Little Movements (exhibit), 109–11, 127–40. *See also* Liu Ding; Lu, Carol Yinghua; Su Wei

Liu, Lydia: on Chinese artists and resistance discourse, 2. *See also* resistance: artists as "resistors"

Liu, Petrus, 6; on Chinese Marxism, 82

Liu Ding, 10, 34, 105, 103–11, 126–40. See also *Little Movements* (exhibit); Lu, Carol Yinghua; Su Wei

Lloyd, David: on aesthetics, 224n16; on nationalism and the individual subject, 225n42; on relationality, 228n64

201–2; and the Chinese woman, 36; difference and, 182–83, 188, 199, 204–5; and Ding Yi, 135; and emotional response, 196; and iconicity, 199–207; and Isaac Julien, 186; and relationality, 93–95; and speech, 243n1; and theater, 203–4; and trauma, 160–61; and Yan Xing, 126. *See also* Ai Weiwei: "all look same"; remakes

representation, 54–57, 63–64, 208; limits of, 83–84, 200; without Marxism (Snorton/Yapp), 9. *See also* inclusion

resistance, 25; artists as "resistors," 2–6, 14, 16, 24, 26, 34–35, 47, 57, 65–67, 71, 78–80, 103–4, 111–12, 141–42, 147–48, 151, 155–58, 167; and culture, 45

Ricoeur, Paul: on demystification's relation to consciousness, 147

Rofel, Lisa: on the term *tongzhi*, 233n18

Rogoff, Irit: on "looking away," 135

Rong Rong, 146, 237n7. *See also* *12m²* (Zhang)

Rosenthal, Stephanie, 80. See also *Art of Change: New Directions from China* (exhibit)

Rothberg, Michael: on trauma studies, 163

Ruan Lingyu, 179, 198, 205. *See also* iconicity; *Ten Thousand Waves* (Julien)

Ruskola, Teemu: on China vs. Europe, 103

Sandoval, Chela, 32

São Paulo Biennial, 42

Schneider, Rebecca: on (live) performance vs. photography, 118

Scott, David: on tragedy and the modern world, 98, 241n4

sculpture: and performance, 67–69

seascapes, 186, 188–89, 194, 197, 207, 212, 215, 221. *See also* monad

Sedgwick, Eve, 150

sensible, the: distribution of (Rancière), 63–64, 67, 78, 223n12, 226n50. *See also* Rancière, Jacques

Sharpe, Christina, 189

Shen Shuang: on China vs. Europe, 103

Shenzhen Biennial, Seventh (*Accidental Message: Art Is Not a System, Not a World*), 109–10, 126–33, 177. *See also* Liu Ding; Lu, Carol Yinghua; Su Wei

Shibli, Ahlam: as a "political" artist, 79

Shih, Shu-mei, and Francoise Lionnet: on minor transnationalism, 235n26

Shimakawa, Karen: on Asian American studies, 55–56

Shohat, Ella: on "additive operations," 56; on relational feminism, 225n39

Siebers, Tobin: on trauma art, 159

silence: of invisibility, 193; maiden of (in Julien's *Ten Thousand Waves*), 187; muting vs. (for Young), 218; deployed by Yan, 118. See also *Kill (the) TV-Set* (Yan)

Silvio, Teri: on acts of alterity (and cosplay), 168–69. *See also* alterity: acts of

sincerity: deployed by Young, 219–21

slowness, 235n28; deployed by Yan, 118, 122–23. See also *Kill (the) TV-Set* (Yan)

Smith, Linda Tuhiwai, 32

Snorton, C. Riley: on fungibility as a political, sensory, and aesthetic category, 31; on representation without Marxism, 9

Songs for Disaster Relief (Young), 36, 212–21. *See also* Young, Samson

Sorace, Christian, on Ai's politics, 81

spatiality: and curation, 127, 135–36; and the minor subject, 125

speech, 150, 173–75; beyond free speech, 210–12, 216–21; and repetition, 243n1

Spillers, Hortense, 30–31, 223n11, 228n64

Spinoza, Baruch, 31, 168

spite, 96, 98, 100, 102

Stars Art Group, The (The Stars), 48–49

Stein, Gertrude: on forms of china, 37–38

Sun Dongdong, 47. See also *On/Off* (exhibit)

www.ingramcontent.com/pod-product-compliance
Lightning Source LLC
Chambersburg PA
CBHW051210170526
45166CB00005B/1831